Microsoft 365 Administrator MS-102 Exam Guide

Master the Microsoft 365 Identity and Security Platform and confidently pass the MS-102 exam

Aaron Guilmette

BIRMINGHAM—MUMBAI

Microsoft 365 Administrator MS-102 Exam Guide

Author: Aaron Guilmette

Reviewer: Paweł Serwan

Publishing Product Manager: Anindya Sil

Development Editor: Arunkumar Govinda Bhat

Senior Editor: Ketan Giri

Production Editor: Shantanu Zagade

Editorial Board: Vijin Boricha, Megan Carlisle, Ketan Giri, Alex Mazonowicz, Aaron Nash, Abhishek Rane, and Ankita Thakur

Production reference: 1181223

Published by Packt Publishing Ltd.

Grosvenor House

11 St Paul's Square

Birmingham

B3 1RB

ISBN 978-1-83508-396-3

www.packtpub.com

Contributors

About the Author

Aaron Guilmette is a Principal Architect at Planet Technologies, providing architectural guidance as well as taking specifications from customers and giving them to engineers. He primarily focuses on collaborative and automation technologies, including Microsoft Exchange and Teams, Power Automate, and scripting solutions.

He has been involved with technology since 1998, working with customers that span the government, education, and commercial sectors. Aaron has also worked on certification exams, and a dozen other technical books.

Aaron lives in Detroit, Michigan, with his five kids. When he's not busy solving technical problems, writing, or teaching yet another child to drive, he's trying to decide whether to make pizza or tacos.

I'd like to thank my girlfriend, Christine, who always believes me when I say, "This is the last book this year." I'd also like to thank my children because I'd never hear the end of it if I didn't mention them. And of course, my great friend and coauthor, Yura, who has put up with me through four books now.

I'd like to thank my girlfriend, Christine, who graciously tolerates my throngs of adoring fans. Throngs? I meant tens. I'd also like to thank my children because without them, I'd probably be able to retire sooner.

I wish to thank the team at Packt for another great opportunity to help the Microsoft technical community level up quickly by getting this book out the door.

Finally, I want to thank Microsoft for continuing to develop products that empower all of us to do more, even if it doing more includes taking tests.

About the Reviewer

Paweł Serwan is a senior IT architect and IT consultant with 15 years of professional experience in topics related to identity and access management, security, end user computing, and the Microsoft 365 platform. He currently works as a senior principal architect at SoftwareOne, where he provides strategic advisory to customers implementing Microsoft 365 services in their organizations.

Paweł also regularly speaks at conferences and user group meetings, both in person and virtually. Together with his colleagues, he runs a blog (ITContructors.com). He is a local leader of the Microsoft 365 User Group in Poland.

Table of Contents

2

3

4

Implementing and Managing Identity Synchronization with Azure AD   127

5

Implementing and Managing Authentication   167

6

Implementing and Managing Secure Access   209

7

Managing Security Reports and Alerts by
Using the Microsoft 365 Defender Portal   235

8

Implementing and Managing Email and Collaboration Protection by Using Microsoft Defender for Office 365   277

9

Implementing and Managing Endpoint Protection by Using Microsoft Defender for Endpoint — 319

10

Implementing Microsoft Purview Information Protection and Data Lifecycle Management   391

11

Preface

Microsoft 365 is a productivity and collaboration platform designed to help you achieve more with a mix of innovative, intelligent cloud services and intuitive apps. It includes several integrated **Software-as-a-Service (SaaS)** applications, including Exchange Online, SharePoint Online, and Microsoft Teams, as well as security and data governance products.

The Microsoft 365 platform suite is used by millions of users and businesses every day to enhance communications, build relationships, connect communities, and create new experiences.

This book, *Microsoft 365 Administrator Exam MS-102 Guide*, has been designed from the ground up to help you learn how to administer the Microsoft 365 platform effectively.

This book will focus on the following key exam areas:

- Provisioning a Microsoft tenant with domains, users, and groups
- Configuring features like multi-factor authentication and administrative roles
- Deploying Microsoft 365 Defender security products
- Investigating and resolving threats across Microsoft 365 workloads
- Configuring compliance and data governance capabilities

The MS-102 exam tests you on the core tasks to get a Microsoft 365 tenant up and running, including adding domains and configuring identity synchronization with Active Directory. Approximately 25% of the exam focuses on the Microsoft 365 Defender platform, including the Microsoft 365 Defender portal and incident management, Microsoft Defender for Office 365, and Microsoft Defender for Endpoint.

This book will also help you understand the privacy and data governance capabilities of Microsoft 365, including labeling, retention, eDiscovery, and other features of the Microsoft Purview compliance portal.

By the end of this book, you'll not only be equipped to pass the exam but also to confidently administer Entra ID and Microsoft 365 Defender.

Who This Book Is For

Microsoft 365 Administrator: Exam MS-102 Guide is targeted at Microsoft 365 administrators who want to prove their knowledge across Entra ID, Defender, and Microsoft Purview by passing the MS-102 certification exam. The qualified exam candidate should be able to demonstrate foundational knowledge of identity concepts as well as intermediate experience with the Microsoft 365 Defender and Microsoft Purview compliance products. You can learn more about this exam a `https://learn.microsoft.com/en-us/credentials/certifications/exams/ms-102/`.

What This Book Covers

Chapter 1, Implementing and Managing a Microsoft 365 Tenant, begins by explaining the foundational concepts of a Microsoft 365 tenant.

Chapter 2, Managing Users and Groups, expands your knowledge into areas such as creating users, contacts, and groups as well as administering Microsoft 365 licensing.

Chapter 3, Managing Roles in Microsoft 365, explains the concepts around Entra ID roles, privileged identity management, and administrative units.

Chapter 4, Implementing and Managing Identity Synchronization with Azure AD, helps you link on-premises identities to the cloud using both Entra Connect (formerly Azure AD Connect) and Entra Connect cloud sync (formerly Azure AD Connect cloud sync).

Chapter 5, Implementing and Managing Authentication, provides guidance for deploying common authentication features such as multi-factor authentication and self-service password reset.

Chapter 6, Implementing and Managing Secure Access, discusses ID protection as well as planning and implementing Conditional Access policies.

Chapter 7, Managing Security Reports and Alerts by Using the Microsoft 365 Defender Portal, explores managing threats, alerts, and incidents using the Microsoft 365 Defender portal.

Chapter 8, Implementing and Managing Email and Collaboration Protection by Using Microsoft Defender for Office 365, expands Microsoft 365 Defender products to collaboration workloads such as Exchange Online, SharePoint Online, and Teams, and covers features such as Safe Links, Safe Attachments, and managing threats with Explorer. Microsoft Defender for Office 365 also includes a training product to help educate users on responding to phishing attacks.

Chapter 9, Implementing and Managing Endpoint Protection by Using Microsoft Defender for Endpoint, introduces the Microsoft 365 Defender for Endpoint product to protect computer and mobile device endpoints. This chapter also explores the Vulnerability Management dashboard.

Chapter 10, Implementing Microsoft Purview Information Protection and Data Lifecycle Management, explores key features of compliance, governance, and data protection, including sensitive info types, retention concepts, and sensitivity labeling.

Chapter 11, Implementing Microsoft Purview data loss prevention (DLP), provides guidance on configuring and deploying data loss prevention policies to cloud workloads and endpoints.

To Get the Most Out of This Book

The Microsoft 365 platform is best experienced with either a laptop or desktop computer running a modern operating system, such as Windows 10 or later or macOS X 10.12 or later. Additionally, modern browsers such as Microsoft Edge or a current version of Chrome, Safari, or Firefox are necessary for the Office 365 portal user interface to render properly. Older versions of Microsoft Internet Explorer may not work correctly.

A Microsoft 365 tenant will also be required to follow along with some of the configuration examples. You can sign up for a trial tenant (no credit card required) at `https://www.microsoft.com/ en-us/microsoft-365/business/compare-more-office-365-for-business- plans`. Some configuration options will require an Entra ID Premium subscription, which you can obtain as part of a Microsoft 365 trial or by activating an Entra ID Premium trial within the Azure portal (`https://portal.azure.com`) once you have obtained a trial Microsoft 365 tenant.

Some examples may require various tools, such as the SharePoint Online Management Shell (`https://www.microsoft.com/en-us/download/details.aspx?id=35588`), the Microsoft Teams module (`https://www.powershellgallery.com/packages/ MicrosoftTeams/`), or the Office Deployment Tool (`https://www.microsoft.com/ en-us/download/details.aspx?id=49117`).

Download the Color Images

We also provide a PDF file that has color images of the screenshots and diagrams used in this book. You can download it here: `https://packt.link/MS102graphics`.

Conventions Used

There are a number of text conventions used throughout this book.

`Code in text`: Indicates code words in text, database table names, folder names, filenames, file extensions, pathnames, dummy URLs, user input, and Twitter handles. Here is an example of a dummy URL: "When you sign up for a Microsoft 365 subscription, you are prompted to choose a name from Microsoft's `onmicrosoft.com` managed namespace. The name you select will need to be unique across all other Microsoft 365 customers."

Bold: Indicates a new term, an important word, or words that you see onscreen. For instance, words in menus or dialog boxes appear in **bold**. Here is an example: "To export a list of audit log entries, an administrator can open the audited data and click on **Export results**."

Any command-line input or output is written as follows:

```
Get-AzureADUser -Top 10 -Filter "Department eq 'Project Management'" |
Select DisplayName,UserPrincipalName,Department
```

> **Tips or important notes**
> Appear like this.

Get in touch

Feedback from our readers is always welcome.

General feedback: If you have questions about any aspect of this book, email us at *customercare@packt.com* and mention the book title in the subject of your message.

Errata: Although we have taken every care to ensure the accuracy of our content, mistakes do happen. If you have found a mistake in this book, we would be grateful if you would report this to us. Please visit www.packtpub.com/support/errata and fill in the form.

Piracy: If you come across any illegal copies of our works in any form on the internet, we would be grateful if you would provide us with the location address or website name. Please contact us at *copyright@packt.com* with a link to the material.

If you are interested in becoming an author: If there is a topic that you have expertise in and you are interested in either writing or contributing to a book, please visit authors.packtpub.com.

Practice Resources – A Quick Tour

> **IMPORTANT**
>
> Before you start using the free online resources, you'll need to unlock them. Unlocking **takes less than 10 minutes, can be done from any device**, and **needs to be done only once**. Head over to the beginning of *Chapter 7, Managing Security Reports and Alerts by Using the Microsoft 365 Defender Portal* for unlock instructions.

This book will equip you with all the knowledge necessary to clear the exam. As important as learning the key concepts is, your chances of passing the exam are much higher if you apply and practice what you learn in the book. This is where the online practice resources come in. With interactive mock exams, flashcards, and exam tips, you can practice everything you learned in the book on the go. Here's a quick walkthrough of what you get.

A Clean, Simple Cert Practice Experience

You get a clean, simple user interface that works on all modern devices, including your phone and tablet. All the features work on all devices provided you have a working internet connection. From the Dashboard (*Figure 0.1*), you can access all the practice resources that come with this book with just a click. If you want to jump back to the book, you can do that from here as well.

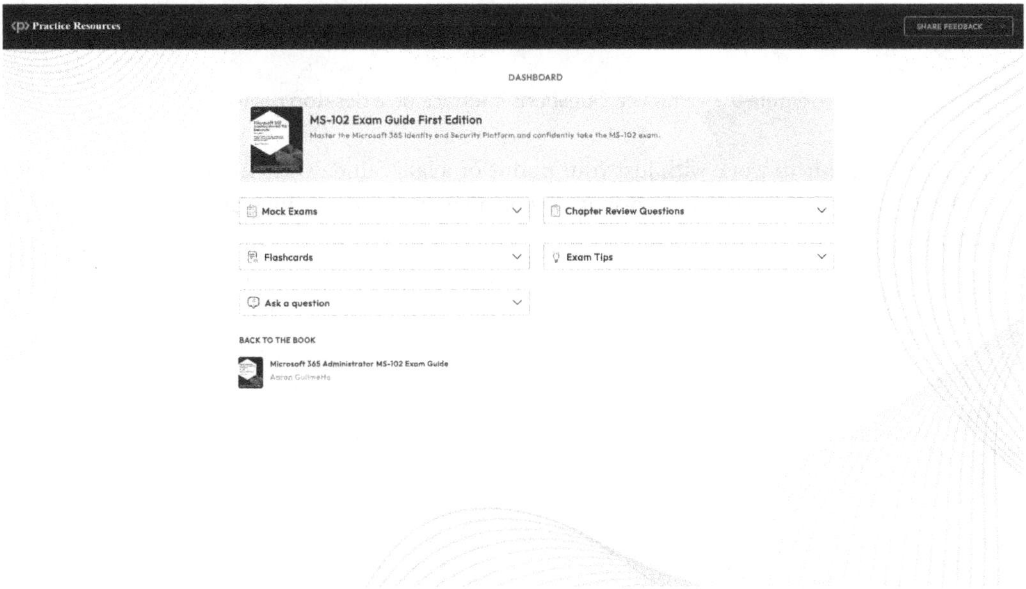

Figure 0.1 – Dashboard interface on a desktop device

Practice Questions

The **Quiz Interface** (*Figure 0.2*) is designed to help you focus on the question without any clutter. You can navigate between multiple questions quickly and skip a question if you don't know the answer. The interface also includes a live timer that auto-submits your quiz if you run out of time. Click **End Quiz** if you want to jump straight to the results page to reveal all the solutions.

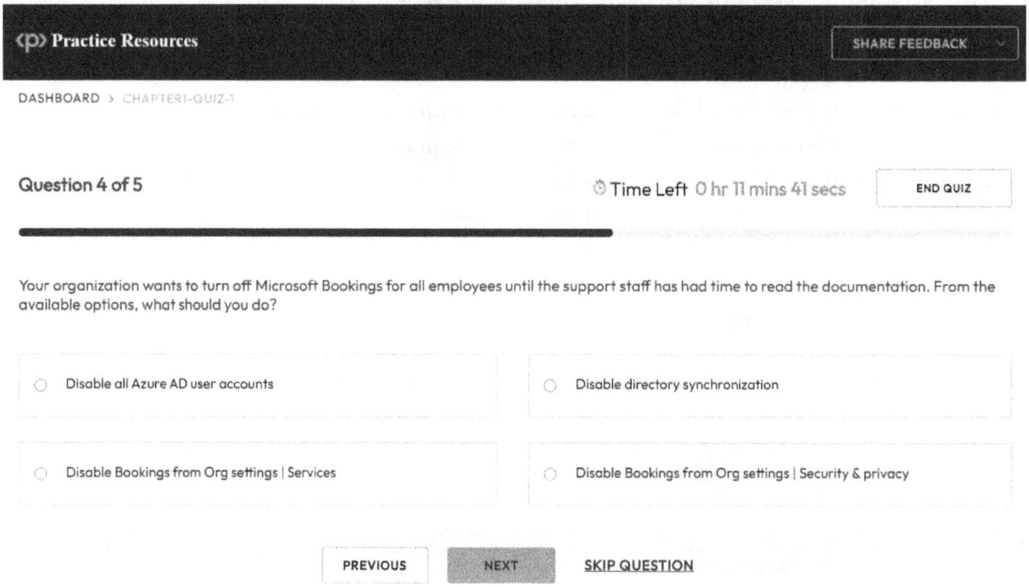

Figure 0.2 – Practice Questions Interface on a desktop device

Be it a long train ride to work with just your phone or a lazy Sunday afternoon on the couch with your tablet, the quiz interface works just as well on all your devices as long as they're connected to the internet.

Figure 0.3 shows a screenshot of how the interface looks on mobile devices:

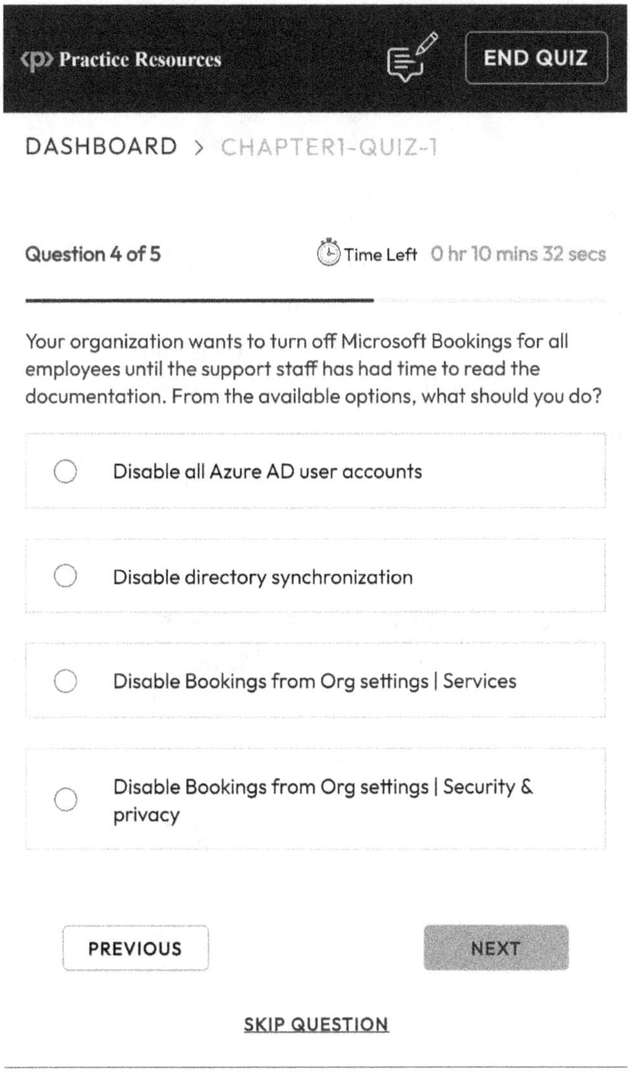

Figure 0.3 – Quiz interface on a mobile device

Flashcards

Flashcards are designed to help you memorize key concepts. Here's how to make the most of them:

1. We've organized all the flashcards into stacks. Think of these like an actual stack of cards in your hand.

2. You start with a full stack of cards.

3. When you open a card, take a few minutes to recall the answer.

4. Click anywhere on the card to reveal the answer (*Figure 0.4*).

5. Flip the card back and forth multiple times and memorize the card completely.

6. Once you feel you've memorized it, click the **Mark as memorized** button on the top-right corner of the card. Move on to the next card by clicking **Next**.

7. Repeat this process as you move to other cards in the stack.

8. You may not be able to memorize all the cards in one go. That's why, when you open the stack the next time, you'll only see the cards you're yet to memorize.

9. Your goal is to get to an empty stack ensuring you've memorized each flashcard in the stack.

Figure 0.4 – Flashcards interface

Exam Tips

Exam Tips (see *Figure 0.5*) are designed to help you get exam-ready. From the start of your preparation journey to your exam day, these tips are organized such that you can review all of them in one go. If an exam tip comes in handy in your preparation, make sure to mark it as helpful so that other readers.

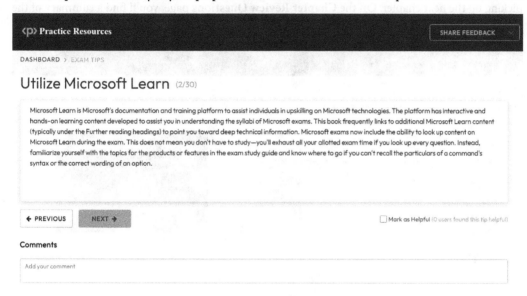

Figure 0.5 – Exam Tips Interface

Chapter Review Questions

You'll find a link to *Chapter Review Questions* at the end of each chapter, just after the *Summary* section. These are designed to help you consolidate your learning from a chapter before moving on to the next one. Each chapter will have a benchmark score, aim to match that score or beat it before picking up the next chapter. On the **Chapter Review Questions** page, you'll find a summary of the chapter for quick reference, as shown in *Figure 0.6*:

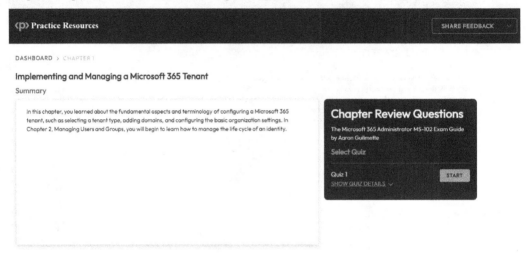

Figure 0.6 – Chapter Review Questions Page

Share Feedback

If you find any issues with the platform, the book, or any of the practice materials, you can click the **Share Feedback** button from any page and reach out to us. If you have any suggestions for improvement, you can share those as well.

Back to the book

To make switching between the book and practice resources easy, we've added a link that takes you back to the book (see *Figure 0.7*). Click it to open your book in Packt's online reader. Your reading position is synced so you can jump right back to where you left off when you last opened the book.

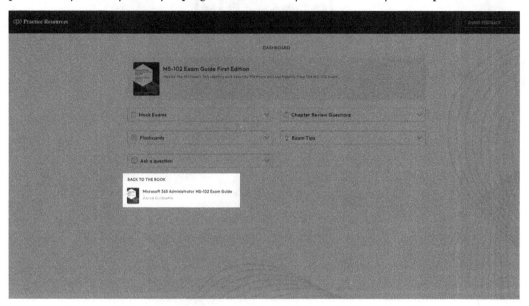

Figure 0.7 – Jump back to the book from the dashboard

> **Note**
> After the publishing of this book, certain elements of the website might change over time and thus may end up looking different from how they are represented in the screenshots.

Share Your Thoughts

Once you've read *Microsoft 365 Administrator MS-102 Exam Guide*, we'd love to hear your thoughts! Scan the QR code below to go straight to the Amazon review page for this book and share your feedback.

https://packt.link/r/183508396X

Your review is important to us and the tech community and will help us make sure we're delivering excellent quality content.

Download a Free PDF Copy of This Book

Thanks for purchasing this book!

Do you like to read on the go but are unable to carry your print books everywhere?

Is your eBook purchase not compatible with the device of your choice?

Don't worry, now with every Packt book you get a DRM-free PDF version of that book at no cost.

Read anywhere, any place, on any device. Search, copy, and paste code from your favorite technical books directly into your application.

The perks don't stop there, you can get exclusive access to discounts, newsletters, and great free content in your inbox daily.

Follow these simple steps to get the benefits:

1. Scan the QR code or visit the link below:

https://packt.link/free-ebook/9781835083963

2. Submit your proof of purchase.
3. That's it! We'll send your free PDF and other benefits to your email directly.

1

Implementing and Managing a Microsoft 365 Tenant

Making the Most out of This Book - Your Certification And Beyond

This book and its accompanying online resources are designed to be a complete preparation tool for your **MS-102 exam**.

The book is written in a way that you can apply everything you've learned here even after your certification. The online practice resources that come with this book (*Figure 1.1*) are designed to improve your test-taking skills. They are loaded with timed mock exams, interactive flashcards, and exam tips, to help you work on your exam readiness from now till your test day.

> **Before You Proceed**
>
> You need to unlock these resources before you start using them. Unlocking **takes less than 10 minutes, can be done from any device**, and **needs to be done only once**. Head over to the start of *Chapter 7, Managing Security Reports and Alerts by Using the Microsoft 365 Defender Portal* in this book for instructions on how to unlock them.

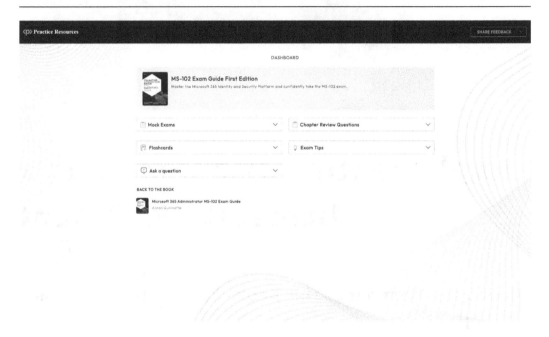

Figure 1.1 – Dashboard Interface Of MS-102 Practice Resources

Here are some tips on how to make the most out of this book so that you can clear your certification and retain your knowledge beyond your exam:

1. Read each section thoroughly.

2. **Make ample notes**: You can use your favorite online note-taking tool or use a physical notebook. The free online resources also give you access to an online version of this book. Click the **BACK TO THE BOOK** link from the **Dashboard** to access the book in Packt Reader. You can highlight specific sections of the book there.

3. **Chapter Review Questions**: At the end of this chapter, you'll find a link to review questions for this chapter. These are designed to test your knowledge of the chapter. Aim to score at least 75% before moving on to the next chapter. You'll find detailed instructions on how to make the most of these questions at the end of this chapter in the *Exam Readiness Drill - Chapter Review Questions* section. That way, you're improving your exam-taking skills after each chapter, rather than doing it at the end.

4. **Flashcards**: After you've gone through the book and scored 75% more in each of the chapter review questions, start reviewing the online flashcards. They will help you memorize key concepts.

5. **Mock Exams**: Solve the mock exams that come with the book till your exam day. If you get some answers wrong, go back to the book and revisit the concepts you're weak in.

6. **Exam Tips**: Review these from time to time to improve your exam readiness even further.

Microsoft 365 Tenant

The **Microsoft 365 tenant** is the security and content boundary for your organization. While deploying a tenant is a simple task of entering contact and payment details, there are many considerations that go into designing and implementing a tenant. These considerations will be used to securely provide access to an organization's data.

In this chapter, you'll explore the core components of planning your Microsoft 365 experience as it pertains to the MS-102 exam. The objectives and skills covered in this chapter include the following:

- Creating a tenant
- Implementing and managing domains
- Configuring organizational settings
- Identifying and responding to service health issues
- Configuring notifications for service health
- Monitoring adoption and usage

By the end of this chapter, you should be able to articulate the core concepts around planning and implementing a Microsoft 365 tenant successfully.

Creating a Tenant

A **tenant**, from a Microsoft 365 perspective, is the top-level structure that identifies your organization. It's a boundary that separates your users and data from those of other organizations that use the Microsoft 365 service. Creating the tenant is the primary prerequisite step to working with Microsoft 365. The first step in creating a tenant is to plan a tenant, followed by provisioning a tenant.

Planning a Tenant

There are a number of early planning stages for creating a Microsoft 365 tenant, but the one you'll carry out first will be deciding which kind of tenant to acquire. Tenants are available for organizations of different sizes as well as different industry verticals. Many of these early planning choices can't be changed later, so you want to make sure you have a thorough understanding of all of the options before hastily clicking through selection screens.

Selecting a Tenant Type

Microsoft has made a variety of packages available, targeting different types of organizations, as shown in *Figure 1.2*:

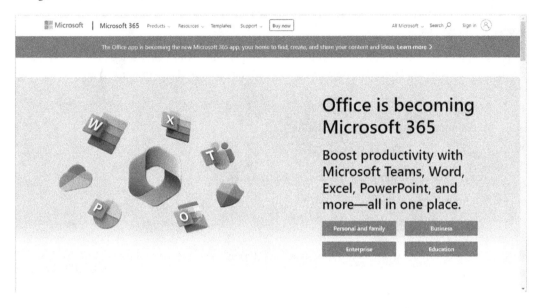

Figure 1.2 – Types of tenants

Table 1.1 below lists the types of tenants available for customers to choose from:

Tenant type	Target customer
Microsoft 365 Personal	Single person or home user
Microsoft 365 Family	Single person, up to 6 users
Microsoft 365 Business	Up to 300 users
Microsoft 365 Enterprise	Unlimited users
Microsoft 365 for US Government	Unlimited users
Microsoft 365 for Education	Unlimited users

Table 1.1 – Tenant types and target customers

For the purposes of the MS-102 exam, you'll focus on the **Microsoft 365 Enterprise** service plans.

> **Tenant Type Deep Dive**
>
> The MS-102 exam focuses on the feature set and product, or service bundles, available in Microsoft 365 Enterprise plans, though the technologies available are largely the same across all plans. Microsoft 365 for US Government is available only for local, state, and federal government customers (and their partners or suppliers) and has a subset of the currently commercially available features, trailing by anywhere from 6 months to 2 years, depending on the certification level of the environment. Microsoft 365 for Education has the same feature set as the commercial enterprise set, with a few added features targeted to educational institutions. Microsoft 365 for Education is only available to schools and universities.

Selecting a Managed Domain

After choosing what type of tenant you'll acquire, one of the next steps you'll be faced with is naming your tenant. When you sign up for a Microsoft 365 subscription, you are prompted to choose a name from Microsoft's `onmicrosoft.com` managed namespace. The name you select will need to be unique across all other Microsoft 365 customers.

> **Tenant Name Considerations**
>
> The tenant name (or managed domain name) cannot be changed after it has been selected. As such, it's important to select one that is appropriate for your organization. The tenant name is visible in a handful of locations, so be sure to select a name that doesn't reveal any privacy information and looks professionally appropriate for the type of organization you're representing.

Provisioning a Tenant

The act of provisioning a tenant is a relatively simple affair, requiring you to fill out a basic contact form and choose a tenant name. Microsoft periodically changes what plans are available for new trial subscriptions. As of the time of writing, Office 365 E3 is available for a trial subscription. Currently, the available public trial subscriptions require the addition of payment information, which will cause a trial to roll over into a fully paid subscription after the trial period ends. See *Figure 1.3*:

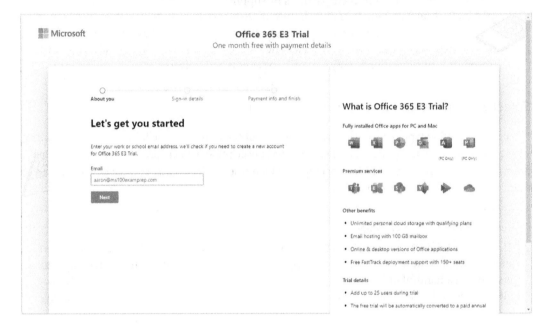

Figure 1.3 – Starting a trial subscription

The signup process may prompt for a phone number to be used during verification (either a text/SMS or call) to help ensure that you're a valid potential customer and not an automated system.

After verifying your status as a human, you'll be prompted to select your managed domain, as shown in *Figure 1.4*:

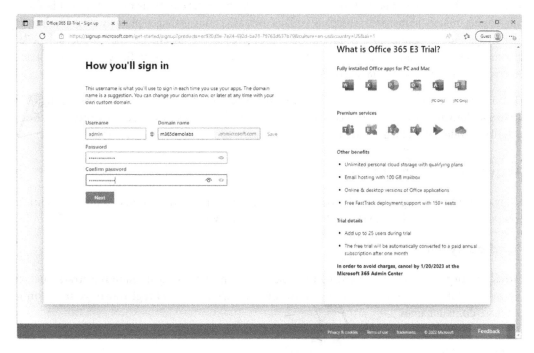

Figure 1.4 – Choosing a managed domain

In the **Domain name** field, you'll be prompted to enter a domain name. If the domain name value you select is already taken, you'll receive an error and be prompted to select a new name.

> **Region Selection**
>
> Microsoft automatically provisions your tenant based on a combination of your source IP address and what type of tenant (enterprise, government, or personal) you're selecting. You need to ensure that you're not using any external VPN services that mask your location. Region selection determines not only where your tenant data is located physically but also, in some cases, what services are available. Once your tenant is provisioned into a region, it can't be changed.

After you've finished, you can enter payment information for a trial subscription. Note the end date of the trial; if you fail to cancel by that time, you'll be automatically billed for the number of licenses you have configured during your trial!

Implementing and Managing Domains

The managed domain is a part of the Microsoft 365 tenant for its entire life cycle. While it is a fully functioning domain namespace (complete with its own Microsoft-managed publicly available domain namespace), most organizations will want to use their organization's domain name—especially when it comes to sending and receiving email or communicating via Microsoft Teams. You cannot add custom DNS records to the managed namespace.

Organizations can use any public domain name with Microsoft 365. Microsoft supports configuring up to 900 domains in a tenant; you can configure both top-level domains (such as `contoso.com`) as well as subdomains (such as `businessunit.contoso.com`) with your Microsoft 365 tenant.

Acquiring a Domain Name

Many organizations begin their Microsoft 365 journey with an existing domain name. In addition, you can purchase new domain names to be associated with your tenant.

Third-party Registrar

Most large organizations have existing relationships with third-party domain registrars, such as Network Solutions or GoDaddy. You can use any ICANN-accredited registrar in your region to purchase domain names.

About ICANN

The **Internet Corporation for Assigned Names and Numbers** (**ICANN**) is a non-profit organization tasked with providing guidance and policy around the internet's unique identifiers (domains). It was chartered in 1998. Prior to 1998, Network Solutions operated the global **Domain Name System** (**DNS**) registry under a subcontract from the United States Defense Information Systems Agency.

You can search a list of domain registrars here:
`https://www.icann.org/en/accredited-registrars`.

Microsoft

In addition to choosing a third-party registrar, organizations may also wish to use Microsoft as the registrar. Depending on your subscription, you may be able to directly purchase domain names from within the Microsoft 365 admin center, as shown in *Figure 1.5*:

Figure 1.5 – Purchasing a domain through the Microsoft 365 admin center

When purchasing a domain through Microsoft, you can select from the following top-level domains:

- `.biz`
- `.com`
- `.info`
- `.me`
- `.mobi`
- `.net`
- `.org`
- `.tv`
- `.co.uk`
- `.org.uk`

Domain purchases will be billed separately from your Microsoft 365 subscription services. When purchasing a domain from Microsoft, you'll have limited ability to manage the DNS records. If you require custom configuration (such as configuring an MX record to point to a non-Microsoft 365 server), you'll want to purchase a domain separately.

Configuring a Domain Name

Configuring a domain for your tenant is a simple procedure and requires access to your organization's public DNS service provider. Many large organizations may host DNS themselves, while other organizations choose to pay service providers (such as the domain registrar) to host the services.

In order to be compatible with Microsoft 365, a DNS service must support configuring the following types of records:

- **Canonical Name (CNAME)**: CNAME records are alias records for a domain, allowing a name to point to another name as a reference. For example, let's say you have a website named www.contoso.com that resolves to an IP address of 1.2.3.4. Later, you want to start building websites for na.contoso.com and eu.contoso.com on the same web server. You might implement a CNAME record for na.contoso.com to point to www.contoso.com.

- **Text (TXT)**: A TXT record is a DNS record used to store unstructured information. **Request for Comments (RFC) 1035** (https://tools.ietf.org/html/rfc1035) specifies that the value must be text strings and gives no specific format for the value data. Over the years, **Sender Policy Framework (SPF)**, **DomainKeys Identified Mail (DKIM)**, and other authentication and verification data have been published as TXT records. In addition to SPF and DKIM, the Microsoft 365 domain addition process requires the administrator to place a certain value in a TXT record to confirm ownership of the domain.

- **Service Locator (SRV)**: An SRV record is used to specify a combination of a host in addition to a port for a particular internet protocol or service.

- **Mail Exchanger (MX)**: The MX record is used to identify which hosts (servers or other devices) are responsible for handling mail for a domain.

In order to use a custom domain (sometimes referred to as a vanity domain) with Microsoft 365, you'll need to add it to your tenant.

To add a custom domain, follow these steps:

1. Navigate to the Microsoft 365 admin center (https://admin.microsoft.com) and log in.

2. Expand **Settings** and select **Domains**.

Figure 1.6 – Domains page of the Microsoft 365 admin center

3. Click **Add domain**.

4. On the **Add domain** page, enter the custom domain name you wish to add to your Microsoft 365 tenant. Select **Use this domain** to continue.

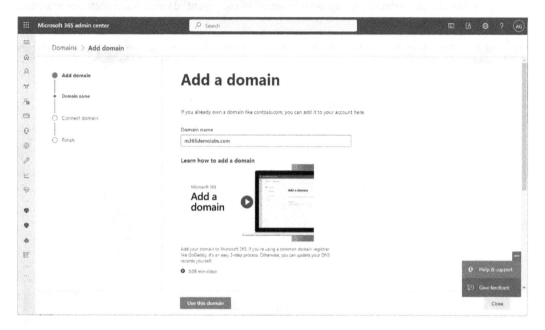

Figure 1.7 – Add domain page

5.   If your domain is registered at a host that supports **Domain Connect**, you can provide your credentials to the Microsoft 365 **Add domain** wizard and click **Verify**. Microsoft will automatically configure the necessary domain records and complete the entire DNS setup for you. You can also select **More options** to see all of the potential verification methods available, as shown in *Figure 1.8*:

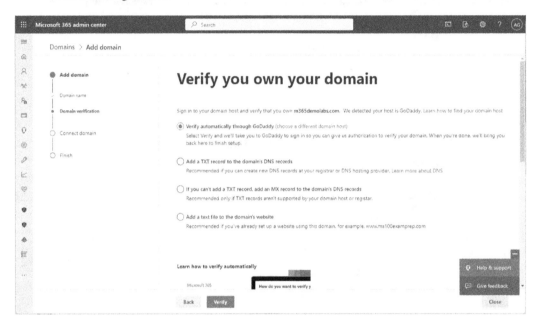

Figure 1.8 – Verify domain ownership

If you choose any of the additional verification options (such as **Add a TXT record to the domain's DNS records**), you'll need to manually add DNS records at your DNS service provider. Microsoft provides the value configuration parameters necessary for you to configure with your own service provider. After entering the values in your service provider's DNS console, you can come back to the wizard and select **Verify**, as shown in *Figure 1.9*:

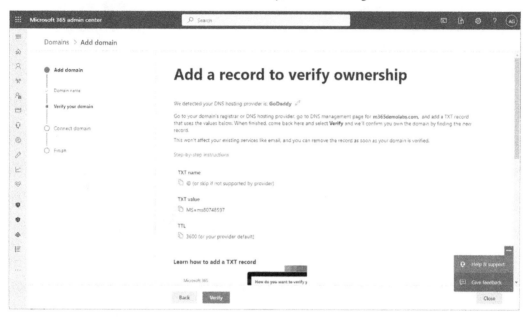

Figure 1.9 – Completing verification records manually

6. If using a registrar that supports Domain Connect, enter the credentials for your registrar. When ready, click **Connect**. See *Figure 1.10*:

Figure 1.10 – Authorizing Domain Connect with GoDaddy to update DNS records

7. Select **Let Microsoft add your DNS records (recommended)** to have the Microsoft 365 wizard update your organization's DNS records at the registrar; however, if you are going to be configuring advanced scenarios such as Exchange Hybrid for mail coexistence and migration or have other complex requirements, you may want to consider managing the DNS records manually or opting out of select services. Click **Continue**.

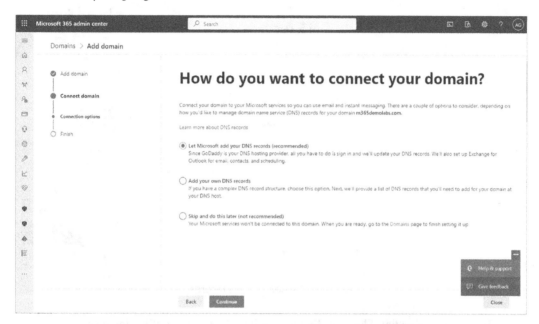

Figure 1.11 – Connecting domain to Microsoft 365

8. Choose whether to allow Microsoft to add DNS records. Expand the **Advanced options** dropdown:

   I.   The first checkbox, **Exchange and Exchange Online Protection**, manages DNS settings for Outlook and email delivery. If you have an existing Exchange Server deployment on-premises (or another mail service solution), you should clear this checkbox before continuing. You'll need to come back to configure DNS settings to establish hybrid connectivity correctly. The default selected option means that Microsoft will make the following updates to your organization's DNS:

      i.   Your organization's MX record will be updated to point to Exchange Online Protection.

      ii. The Exchange Autodiscover record will be updated to point to `autodiscover.outlook.com`.

      iii. Microsoft will update your organization's SPF record with `v=spf1 include:spf.protection.outlook.com -all`.

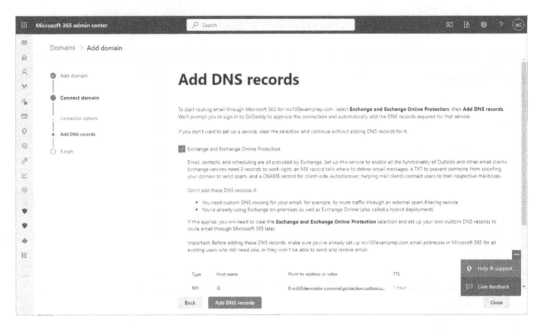

Figure 1.12 – Adding DNS records

II. The second setting, **Skype for Business**, will configure DNS settings for Skype for Business. If you have an existing Skype for Business Online deployment or you're using Skype for Business on-premises, you may need to clear this box until you verify your configuration:

      i. Microsoft will add two SRV records: `_sip._tls.@<domain>` and `_sipfederationtls._tcp@<domain>`.

      ii. Microsoft will also add two CNAMEs for Lync: `sip.<domain>` to point to `sipdir.online.lync.com` and `lyncdiscover.<domain>` to point to `webdir.online.lync.com`.

III. The third checkbox, **Intune and Mobile Device Management for Microsoft 365**, configures applicable DNS settings for device registration. It is recommended to leave this enabled:

    i.   Microsoft will add the following CNAME entries to support mobile device registration and management: `enterpriseenrollment.<domain>` to `enterpriseenrollment.manage.microsoft.com` and `enterpriseregistration.<domain>` to `enterpriseregistration.windows.net`.

9.   Click **Add DNS records**.

10. If prompted, click **Connect** to authorize Microsoft to update your registrar's DNS settings.

11. Click **Done** to exit the wizard or **View all domains** to go back to the **Domains** page if you need to add more domains.

You can continue adding as many domains as you need (up to the tenant maximum of 900 domains).

Adding a Domain Deep Dive

To review alternative steps and more information about the domain addition process, see `https://learn.microsoft.com/en-us/microsoft-365/admin/setup/add-domain`.

Managing DNS Records Manually

If you've opted to manage DNS records manually, you may need to go back to the Microsoft 365 admin center and view the settings. To do this, you can navigate to the **Domains** page, select your domain, and then select **Manage DNS**, as shown in *Figure 1.13*:

Figure 1.13 – Managing DNS settings for a domain

On the **Connect domain** page, click **More options** to expand the options, and then select **Add your own DNS records**. From here, you can view the specific DNS settings necessary per service by record type. You can also download a CSV file or a zone file that can be uploaded to your own DNS server. See *Figure 1.14*:

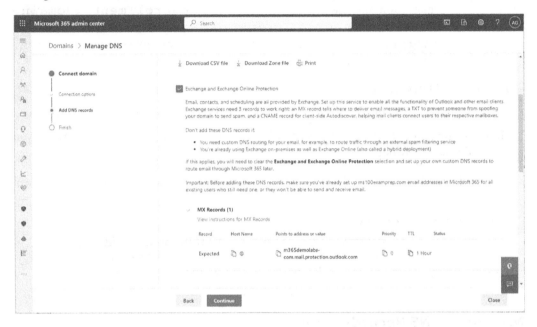

Figure 1.14 – Viewing DNS settings

The CSV output is formatted as columns, while the zone file output is formatted for use with standard DNS services and can be imported or appended to BIND or Microsoft DNS server zone files.

Configuring a Default Domain

After adding a domain, Microsoft 365 automatically sets the first custom domain as the default domain that will be used when creating new users. However, if you have additional domains, you may choose to select a different domain to be used as the default domain when creating objects.

To manage which domain will be set as your primary domain, select the domain from the **Domains** page and then click **Set as default** to update the setting, as shown in *Figure 1.15*:

Figure 1.15 – Setting the default domain

The default domain will be selected automatically when creating cloud-based users and groups, though it can be changed.

Custom Domains and Synchronization

When creating new cloud-based objects, you can select from any of the domains available in your tenant. However, when synchronizing from an on-premises directory, objects will be configured with the same domain configured with the on-premises object. If the corresponding domain hasn't been verified in the tenant, synchronized objects will be set to use the tenant-managed domain.

Next, you'll look at the core organizational settings in a tenant.

Configuring Organizational Settings

Organizational settings, as the name implies, are configuration options that apply to the entire tenant. They are used to enable or disable features at the service or tenant level. In many instances, organizational settings are coarse controls that can be further refined by the configuration settings inside each individual service.

To access the organizational settings, follow these steps:

1. Navigate to the Microsoft 365 admin center (`https://admin.microsoft.com`).
2. In the navigation pane, expand **Settings** and select **Org settings**.

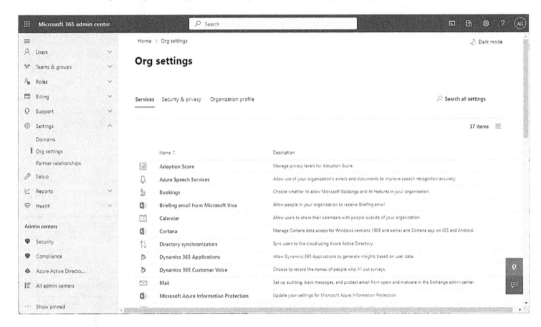

Figure 1.16 – Org settings in the Microsoft 365 admin center

The **Org settings** page has three tabs, as shown in *Figure 1.16*:

- **Services**
- **Security & privacy**
- **Organizational profile**

In the next section, each of these settings will be explained in detail.

Services

The **Services** tab displays settings available for workloads, services, and features available in the Microsoft 365 tenant. *Table 1.2* lists the services that have configurable options in the tenant:

Service	Description
Adoption Score	Manage privacy levels for Adoption Score as well as setting the scope for users to be included or excluded.
Azure Speech Services	Manage whether Azure Speech Services can work using content in your tenant to improve the accuracy of speech services. Disabled by default.
Bookings	Choose whether the Bookings service is available for use in the tenant. If Bookings is enabled, you can also configure specific options, such as whether social sharing options are available or whether Bookings can be used by users outside the organization, as well as restricting the collection of customer data.
Briefing email from Microsoft Viva	Choose whether to allow users to receive the Viva briefing email. By default, the briefing email is enabled. Users can unsubscribe themselves.
Calendar	Choose whether to enable users to share their calendars outside the organization. If sharing is enabled, choose what level of detail is supplied.
Cortana	Choose whether to allow Cortana on devices to connect to data in your Microsoft 365 tenant.
Directory synchronization	Provides a link to download the Azure AD Connect synchronization tool.
Dynamics 365 Applications	Choose whether to allow insights for each user, aggregated insights for other users (non-identifiable), or identifiable insights for other users.
Dynamics 365 Customer Voice	Configure email parameters for collecting survey data from Dynamics 365.

Service	Description
Mail	There are no org-wide settings to manage here; however, there are links to various tools in the Exchange admin center and Microsoft Defender 365 portal for things such as transport rules and anti-malware policies.
Microsoft Azure Information Protection	There are no settings to manage for this feature; it is a link to documentation for configuring Azure Information Protection settings.
Microsoft communication to users	Choose whether to enable Microsoft-generated training and education content delivery to users.
Microsoft Edge product messaging for users	Provides information on configuring the Edge Spotlight experience for end users.
Microsoft Edge site lists	Manage lists of sites and specify which browser experience (Edge or Internet Explorer) users should receive when navigating to those sites.
Microsoft Forms	Manage external sharing settings for Microsoft Forms as well as capturing the names of internal organization users who fill out forms.
Microsoft Graph Data Connect	Choose this to enable Microsoft Graph Data Connect for bulk transfer of data to Azure.
Microsoft Planner	Choose whether Planner users can publish to Outlook or iCal.
Microsoft Search in Bing homepage	Customize the Bing.com search page for organization users.
Microsoft Teams	Choose whether to enable Teams organization-wide. Disabling Teams from this interface will make it unavailable for all users, including users who are already licensed. Also, choose the coarse control for whether guest access is allowed in Teams.
Microsoft To Do	Choose to provide internal users the ability to join and contribute to external task lists and receive push notifications.

Service	Description
Microsoft Viva Insights (formerly MyAnalytics)	Manage which Viva Insights settings users have access to. By default, all options are selected (Viva Insights web experience, Digest email, Insights Outlook add-in and inline suggestions, and Schedule send suggestions).
Microsoft 365 Groups	Configure guest access and ownership settings for Microsoft 365 Groups.
Modern authentication	Provides links to information on configuring modern authentication and viewing basic authentication sign-in reports.
Multi-factor authentication	Provides links to information on configuring and learning about multi-factor authentication.
News	Choose organization and industry settings used to display relevant news information on the Bing home page as well as settings for delivering Microsoft-generated industry news to your organization users.
Office installation options	Choose an update channel for Microsoft 365 apps.
Office on the web	Choose whether to allow users to connect to third-party cloud storage products using Office on the web products.
Office Scripts	Configure Office Scripts settings for Excel on the web.
Reports	Choose how to display users' personally identifiable information in internal reports and whether to make data available to Microsoft 365 usage analytics.
Search & intelligence usage analytics	Choose whether to allow usage analytics data to be filtered by country, occupation, department, or division.
SharePoint	Choose whether to enable external sharing.
Sway	Choose whether to allow sharing of sways outside the organization as well as what content sources are available (Flickr, Pickit, Wikipedia, and YouTube).

Service	Description
User consent to apps	Choose whether users can provide consent to OAuth 2.0 apps that access organization data.
User owned apps and services	Choose whether to allow users to auto-claim licenses as well as start trials and access the Office Store.
Viva Learning	Choose which content provider data sources to use for Viva Learning. By default, LinkedIn Learning, Microsoft Learn, Microsoft 365 Training, and Custom Uploads are enabled. You can also manage the level of diagnostic data sent to Microsoft.
What's new in Office	Choose whether to display messages to users about new features available. This does not change the availability of the feature—only the display of the notification message.
Whiteboard	Choose whether to allow the Whiteboard app to be used. Additionally, manage the amount of diagnostic data collected.

Table 1.2 – Organizational service settings

You should spend time exploring the options for the services in the Microsoft 365 admin center.

Security & Privacy

The **Security & privacy** tab houses settings that govern various security controls for the organization. On this page, you'll find access to the settings listed in *Table 1.3*:

Setting	Description
Bing data collection	Choose whether to allow Bing to collect organization query data.
Idle session timeout	Configure the idle session timeout period for Office web apps.
Password expiration policy	Choose whether to enable password expiration. Password expiration is disabled by default (and the password policy is governed by the on-premises Active Directory if password hash sync has been configured).
Privacy profile	Configure a URL for the organization's privacy policy and the organization's privacy contact. The privacy URL is displayed on the Privacy tab of the Settings & Privacy page in the user account profile and when a sharing request is sent to an external user.
Self-service password reset	Provides a link to the Azure portal to configure self-service password reset.
Sharing	Choose whether to allow users to add guests to the organization.

Table 1.3 – Security & privacy settings

These options can be used to broadly configure security and privacy settings for your organization. As with the settings on the **Services** tab, these are coarse controls. Fine-grained control is available for some of these items inside their respective admin centers.

Organization Profile

Settings on the **Organization profile** tab are largely informational or used to manage certain aspects of the user experience. On this tab, you'll find the settings listed in *Table 1.4*:

Setting	Description
Custom app launcher tiles	Configure additional tiles to show up on the Microsoft 365 app launcher.
Custom themes	Create and apply themes to the Microsoft 365 portal for end users, including mandating the theme as well as specific organization logos and colors.
Data location	View the regional information where your tenants' data is stored.
Help desk information	Choose whether to add custom help desk support information for end users to the Office 365 help pane.
Keyboard shortcuts	View the shortcuts available for use in the Microsoft 365 admin center.
Organization information	Update your organization's name and other contact information.
Release preferences	Choose the release settings for Office 365 features (excluding Microsoft 365 apps). The available options are Standard release for everyone, Targeted release for everyone, and Targeted release for select users. The default setting is Standard release for everyone.
Support integration	Use the settings on this page to configure integration with third-party support tools such as ServiceNow.

Table 1.4 – Organization profile settings

Like the other **Org settings** tabs, the settings on this page will be used infrequently—typically when just setting up your tenant and customizing the experience. As with the other **Organization profile** setting areas, you should spend some time in a test environment navigating the tenant to view these settings and updating them to see their effects.

Identifying and Responding to Service Health Issues

Service health information is available from the Microsoft 365 admin center
(`https://admin.microsoft.com`). Microsoft provides health information for a
variety of services and features, including SaaS services such as Exchange Online and SharePoint
Online, the health of the directory synchronization environment, as well as Windows operating
system feature issues and service health.

You can check the overall service health by navigating to the health dashboard (**Health | Dashboard**),
as shown in *Figure 1.17*:

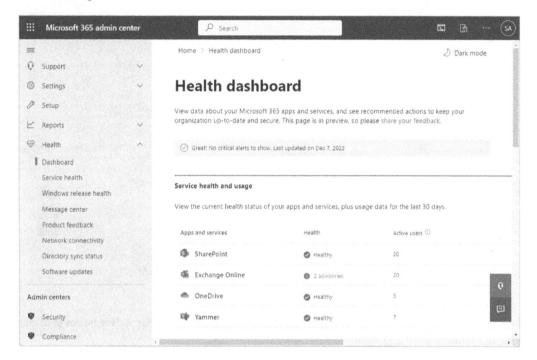

Figure 1.17 – Service health dashboard

The health dashboard contains the current health status of all Microsoft 365 services. Normally, services
will appear as *healthy*, though this status will be updated when a service is experiencing an issue.

The **Service health** page (**Health | Service health** or `https://aka.ms/servicehealth`) will display the most detailed and comprehensive information on any ongoing or resolved issues. See *Figure 1.18*.

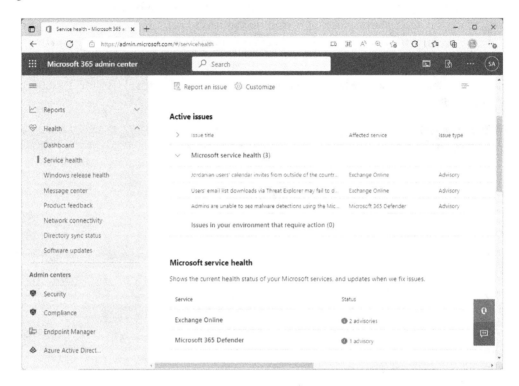

Figure 1.18 – Service health page

If a service has an advisory or incident, you can expand the issue item under **Active issues** to display relevant events, as shown in *Figure 1.19*:

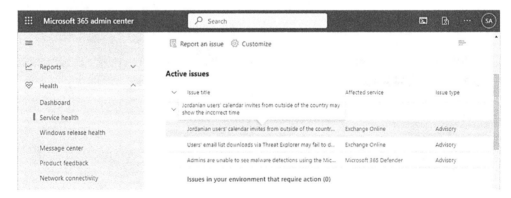

Figure 1.19 – Service health active issues

Selecting an individual item reveals expanded information about the particular issue. See *Figure 1.20* for an example:

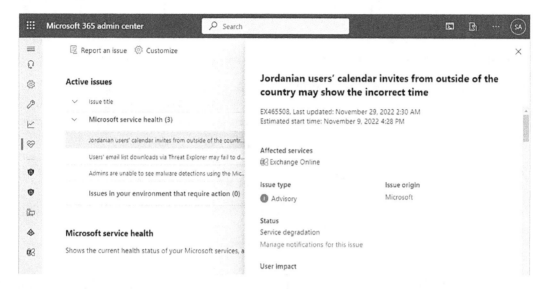

Figure 1.20 – Expanded active issue

Each service incident will display a status. Possible statuses include the following:

- **Normal service**: This status indicates that the service is available and has no current incidents or incidents during the reporting period.

- **Extended recovery**: This status indicates that while steps have been completed to resolve the incident, it may take a period of time for operations to return to normal. During an extended recovery period, some service operations might be deleted or take longer to complete.

- **Investigating**: This status indicates that a potential service incident is being reviewed.

- **Service restored**: This status indicates that an incident was active earlier in the day, but service was restored.

- **Service interruption**: This status indicates the service isn't functioning and that affected users are unable to access the service.

- **Additional information**: This status indicates the presence of information regarding a recent incident from a previous day.

- **Service degradation**: This status indicates the service is slow or is occasionally appearing unresponsive for brief periods.

- **PIR published**: This status indicates that a post-incident report of the service incident has been published.

- **Restoring service**: This status indicates the service incident is being resolved.

As an administrator, it's important to frequently check the service health dashboard to stay informed of alerts or incidents. If a service issue is affecting the Microsoft 365 admin center, you can also try the Office 365 status page (`https://status.office.com`) and the Azure status page (`https://status.azure.com`).

Configuring Notifications for Service Health

In addition to viewing service health information in the Microsoft 365 admin center, you can also configure email-based notifications for services.

To configure email notifications for service health, follow these steps.

1. Navigate to the **Service health** page (`https://aka.ms/servicehealth`) and click **Customize**. See *Figure 1.21*:

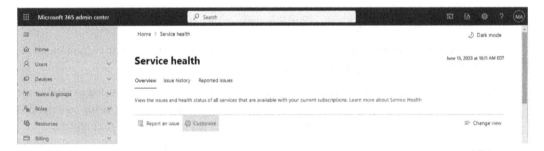

Figure 1.21 – Service health page with Customize highlighted

2. On the **Customize** flyout, select the **Email** tab.

3. Select the **Send me email notifications about service health** checkbox.

4. Enter up to two email addresses to be notified of issues.

5. Scroll the flyout to enable or disable email notifications for issue types and Microsoft 365 services, as shown in *Figure 1.22*.

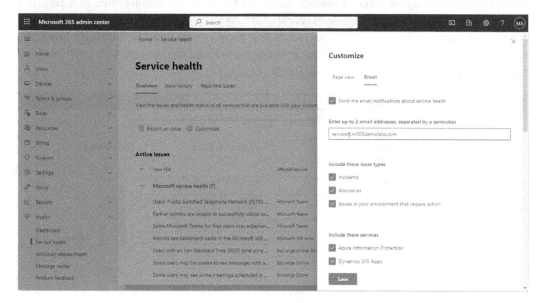

Figure 1.22 – Enabling notifications

6. Click **Save** to update commit changes.

You will be notified of future service issues for the selected services. You can update the selections at any time.

Next, you'll look at tracking Microsoft 365 service adoption across the enterprise.

Monitoring Adoption and Usage

In order for your organization to get the most benefit from a Microsoft 365 investment, it's important that users adopt the services and features. You can monitor end user adoption and consumption metrics through a variety of tools, including **Microsoft 365 usage metrics**, **Viva Insights** (formerly known as **Workplace Analytics**), and the **Adoption Score** (formerly known as the **Productivity Score**).

Microsoft 365 Usage Reports

The **Microsoft 365 usage reports** are available inside the Microsoft 365 admin center. They are broad reports that can be used to get a high-level snapshot of how your organization is using the Microsoft 365 platform. Report data includes statistics such as how many files are stored in SharePoint, how many Exchange mailboxes were active during the reporting period, and engagement with other products such as Viva Engage (formerly Yammer) or Forms.

Figure 1.23 – Microsoft 365 usage reports

Usage reports can be accessed by navigating to the Microsoft 365 admin center (https://admin.microsoft.com), expanding **Reports**, and selecting **Usage**.

Viva Insights

Formerly known as **Workplace Analytics**, Viva Insights provides recommendations about personal and teamwork habits. Viva Insights has four core areas:

- Personal insights
- Teamwork habits
- Organization trends
- Advanced insights

Each of these areas has unique features that are part of the Viva story.

Personal Insights

As the name suggests, personal insights are tailored to an individual. Personal insights are private and are only visible to the individual for whom they are intended. Personal insights are best viewed using the Viva Insights app in Microsoft Teams, as shown in *Figure 1.24*:

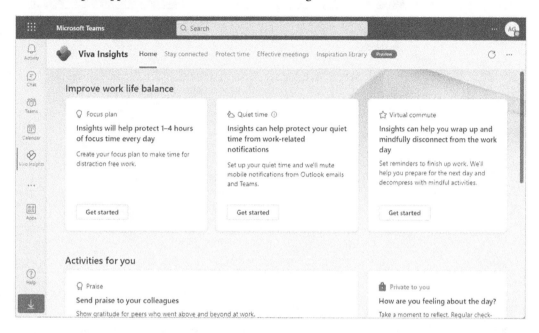

Figure 1.24 – Viva Insights app in Microsoft Teams

The Viva Insights app has functions to allow you to make a focus plan (sometimes referred to as the **protect time** feature), send praise to your colleagues either publicly or privately, and stay connected through AI-based task suggestions and meeting assistance.

The Viva Insights app also features **Headspace** guided meditation and mindfulness exercises as well as prompts to take a break and reflect on your personal feelings. Using the reflection activity card, you can even set daily reminders to check in with yourself. See *Figure 1.25*:

Figure 1.25 – Reflection activity card

Viva Insights also has a daily ramp-up and wind-down micro-app called **Virtual Commute**, which lets users review upcoming meetings and tasks, block focus time, and initiate a variety of mini-break, meditative, and reflective activities. See *Figure 1.26*:

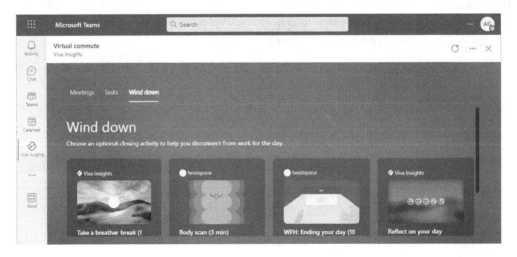

Figure 1.26 – Virtual commute activity card

Together, these insight features can help users manage both their productivity and personal well-being.

Teamwork Habits

Viva Insights **Teamwork habits**, which is part of the premium Viva Insights experience, allows managers to gain additional recommendations for managing people. Teamwork habits helps managers identify regular after-hours work, meeting overload conditions, and lack of dedicated focus time.

Managers can set up teams by manually adding users, or can use the suggested list if the manager property has been populated in Azure Active Directory. See *Figure 1.27*:

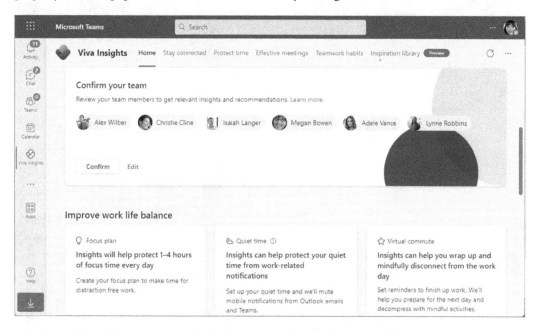

Figure 1.27 – Confirming team members

Three additional core features of Teamwork habits are the following:

- Scheduling recurring 1:1 times with managed employees
- Analyzing quiet hours impact to determine how work habits impact employees outside of their configured working hours
- Configuring shared plans for no-meeting days and shared focus times

Organizations that utilize the Teamwork habits tools can improve their employees' well-being and work-life balance. The Teamwork habits feature requires a premium Microsoft Viva Insights license.

Organization Trends

The **My organization** tab shows organization trends as well as business leader and manager insights to help understand how to effectively manage your teams. Insights include such as identifying work patterns and suggestions for boosting employee engagement. See Figure 1.28:

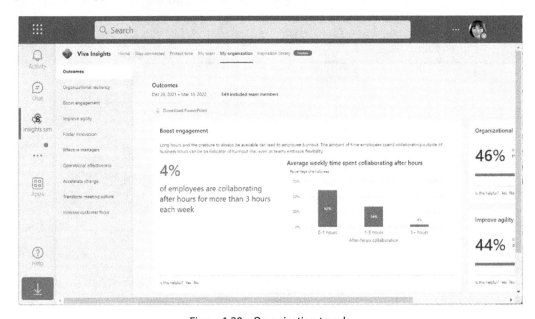

Figure 1.28 – Organization trends

Organization trends data is privacy-oriented, requiring a minimum of 10 people (including the manager) to be in the management chain, either directly or indirectly. In addition, access to Organization trends requires granting access to manager insights through the Viva setup.

Advanced Insights

Microsoft Viva advanced insights is a reporting tool that provides research-based behavioral insights into organizational work patterns, such as hybrid work, work-life balance, and employee well-being.

The advanced insights reporting tools come with a number of built-in templates and analysis tools to really help organizations understand everything from meeting effectiveness to employee performance trends correlated to 1:1 manager meetings. The **Manager coaching** report, which is part of Viva Insights, is shown in *Figure 1.29*:

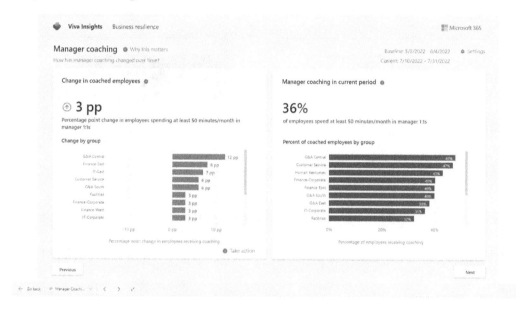

Figure 1.29 – Viva Insights Manager coaching report

With large organizational changes such as hybrid and remote work scenarios, it can be important to understand how those work patterns affect performance, including interesting data points such as how much time is spent during meetings multitasking or how much work is getting done outside normal business hours.

Information about working hours is available in the **Work-life balance and flex work** report (part of the **Hybrid workforce experience** reporting section), shown in *Figure 1.30*:

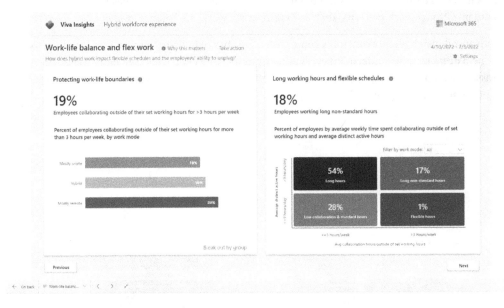

Figure 1.30 – Advanced insights working hour details

The advanced insights Power BI report templates provide an analysis of employee engagement and work patterns. The reports include the following:

- **Business resilience**: Overall business report highlighting performance and employee well-being.

- **Hybrid workforce experience**: This report highlights how different work modes (onsite, hybrid, and remote) affect workers.

- **Manager effectiveness**: Provides insight into patterns exhibited by people managers.

- **Meeting effectiveness**: These reports capture and display information on meeting statistics such as how many meetings happen on short notice or how much multitasking occurs during meetings.

- **Ways of working**: This data helps answer questions such as *are employees receiving enough 1:1 coaching time?* and *who generates the most work by organizing meetings?*

- **Wellbeing – balance and flexibility**: Reporting data used to identify whether employees have enough time to focus on core priorities and can balance that with breaks and time away from work.

- For more information on the advanced insights templates and their reporting capabilities, see `https://learn.microsoft.com/en-us/viva/insights/advanced/analyst/templates/introduction-to-templates`.

Adoption Score

Formerly known as **Productivity Score**, **Adoption Score** is a metric that is used to help measure the success of an organization's use of the Microsoft 365 platform. Before Adoption Score can be used, it must be enabled in the Microsoft 365 admin center under **Reports**, as shown in *Figure 1.31*:

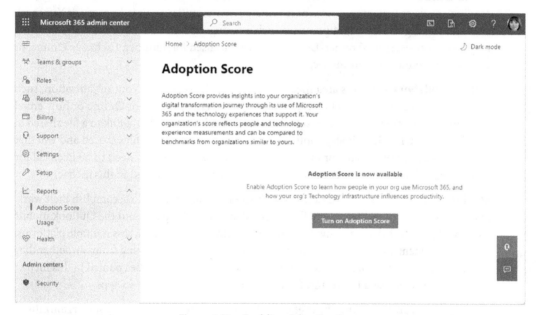

Figure 1.31 – Enabling Adoption Score

Adoption Score provides insights that are broken up into three categories: **people experiences**, **technology experiences**, and **special reports**. When enabling the score, you can select how to calculate insights into people experiences:

- **Include all users**
- **Exclude specific users by group**
- **Don't calculate for any users**

Insights into technology experiences are shown automatically when you enable Adoption Score. If you don't want to collect that data, you can disable **Endpoint analytics scope** in the Intune data collection policy,

If you are performing a staged rollout of services using a pilot program, it may be beneficial to limit the reporting scope to groups of users that are part of the pilot.

People Experiences

The insights into people experiences focus on five categories that show how your users and organization are using the tools in the Microsoft 365 platform. These insight areas are as follows:

- **Communication**: This area measures how people are communicating with each other, such as sending emails or instant messages or posting on communities in Viva Engage (or Yammer). This area highlights important practices such as using @mentions in emails and marking responses as answers in Yammer. Users need to be licensed for Yammer, Exchange Online, or Teams to be counted in this metric.

- **Content collaboration**: This area measures how people use files in your organization, such as creating or sharing files in OneDrive for Business and SharePoint Online or how email attachments are being used (attached files versus a cloud attachment—a link to a file shared in OneDrive or SharePoint). It also captures data about the number of files shared and whether the collaborators are internal or external to the organization. Users need to be licensed for OneDrive for Business, SharePoint, or Exchange Online to be counted in this metric.

- **Mobility**: This measures what devices and interfaces people are using to accomplish their work. For example, a user sending an email from the Outlook desktop app and the Outlook mobile app would be regarded as an individual using the Microsoft 365 apps across multiple platforms. This measurement area also reports on what locations people are working from—whether they are onsite in one of your organization's offices or remotely. In order to be counted in this metric, users need to be licensed for Teams, Exchange Online, or Microsoft 365 apps.

- **Meetings**: This area measures how effectively meetings are used across your organization. Meetings are evaluated against practices such as scheduling meetings at least 24 hours in advance, sharing agendas, and the percentage of invitees that actually show up to the meetings. Other features include measuring interactivity (hand-raising, chat, reactions, or sharing content) during the meeting as well as whether or not attendees are participating via audio or video. Users must be licensed for Microsoft Teams to be included in this metric.

- **Teamwork**: This area is used to measure how people are collaborating in Teams and using shared workspaces (such as teams, channels, Microsoft 365 groups, and SharePoint sites). In order to be counted for this metric, users must be licensed for Exchange Online, SharePoint, or Microsoft Teams.

In addition to users requiring licenses to be assigned, they also need to be active in a service at least once every 28 days to get counted for that service. You can use Adoption Score to review how people are using the Microsoft 365 service and provide coaching on best practices to get the most out of the platform.

Technology Experiences

The technology experiences category focuses on areas relating to the devices that people are using to access Microsoft 365 services:

- **Endpoint analytics**: This area provides insights into the overall performance data of devices that are enrolled in **Intune** or **Configuration Manager** with **tenant attach**. The performance metrics include things such as boot time, how long it takes to sign in and get to a responsive desktop, how much time is spent processing Group Policy, how often applications hang or crash, and the number of active devices that have launched a particular app during the past 14 days. The endpoint analytics reporting has special requirements, such as particular versions of endpoints and being either Azure AD joined or hybrid Azure AD joined, as well as licensed for Intune or Microsoft Endpoint Configuration Manager.

- **Network connectivity**: These metrics provide insights into factors involving network communication between your endpoints and the Microsoft 365 platform. Specific network requirements must be met, such as configuring networks in the Microsoft 365 admin center and enabling location data collection features. For more information on the prerequisites for enabling network connectivity reporting, see `https://learn.microsoft.com/en-us/microsoft-365/enterprise/office-365-network-mac-perf-overview?view=o365-worldwide`.

- **Microsoft 365 Apps**: View insights on how many devices across your organization are up to date with their Microsoft 365 app deployments.

The technology experiences score reports can be helpful in gaining insight into how devices may be affecting the overall adoption and user satisfaction with Microsoft 365 services.

Special Reports

Finally, there is a lightweight version of the **Business Resilience** report (from Viva Insights) that is available to organizations that have at least 100 active Exchange and Viva Insights licenses. This report helps organizational leaders understand how to utilize remote work and maintain a work-life balance, the effectiveness of virtual meetings, and participation in Yammer communities.

Summary

In this chapter, you learned about the fundamental aspects and terminology of configuring a Microsoft 365 tenant, such as selecting a tenant type, adding domains, and configuring the basic organization settings. In *Chapter 2, Managing Users and Groups*, you will begin to learn how to manage the life cycle of an identity.

Exam Readiness Drill - Chapter Review Questions

Benchmark Score: 75%

Apart from a solid understanding of key concepts, being able to think quickly under time pressure is a skill that will help you ace your certification exam. That's why, working on these skills early on in your learning journey is key.

Chapter review questions are designed to improve your test-taking skills progressively with each chapter you learn and review your understanding of key concepts in the chapter at the same time. You'll find these at the end of each chapter.

> **Before You Proceed**
>
> You need to unlock these resources before you start using them. Unlocking **takes less than 10 minutes, can be done from any device**, and **needs to be done only once**. Head over to the start of *Chapter 7, Managing Security Reports and Alerts by Using the Microsoft 365 Defender Portal* in this book for instructions on how to unlock them.

To open the **Chapter Review Questions** for this chapter, click the following link: `https://packt.link/MS102E1_CH01`. Or, you can scan the following QR code:

Figure 1.32 – QR code that opens Chapter Review Questions for logged-in users

Once you login, you'll see a page similar to what is shown in *Figure 1.33*:

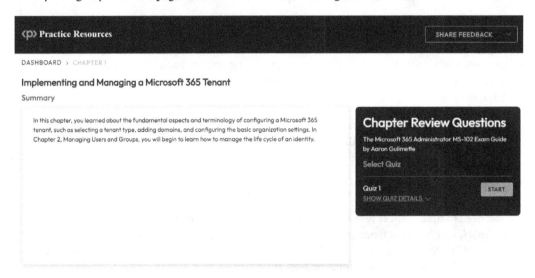

Figure 1.33 – Chapter Review Questions for Chapter 1

Once ready, start the following practice drills, re-attempting the quiz multiple times:

Exam Readiness Drill

For the first 3 attempts, don't worry about the time limit.

ATTEMPT 1

The first time, aim for at least 40%. Look at the answers you got wrong and read the relevant sections in the chapter again to fix your learning gaps.

ATTEMPT 2

The second time, aim for at least 60%. Look at the answers you got wrong and read the relevant sections in the chapter again to fix any remaining learning gaps.

ATTEMPT 3

The third time, aim for at least 75%. Once you score 75% or more, you start working on your timing.

> **Tip**
> You may take more than 3 attempts to reach 75%. That's okay. Just review the relevant sections in the chapter till you get there.

Working On Timing

Target: Your aim is to keep the score the same while trying to answer these questions as quickly as possible. Here's an example of how your next attempts should look like:

Attempt	Score	Time Taken
Attempt 5	77%	21 mins 30 seconds
Attempt 6	78%	18 mins 34 seconds
Attempt 7	76%	14 mins 44 seconds

Table 1.5 – Sample timing practice drills on the online platform

> **Note**
> The time limits shown in the above table are just examples. Set your own time limits with each attempt based on the time limit of the quiz on the website.

With each new attempt, your score should stay **above 75%** while your time taken to complete should decrease. Repeat as many attempts as you want till you feel confident dealing with the time pressure.

2

Managing Users and Groups

As you'll see throughout this book, identity is the foundation of Azure AD (now Microsoft Entra ID). Without it, people wouldn't be able to access services and features, store content, or work with their teams. Azure identity covers a broad range of objects, including cloud-only accounts, synchronized accounts, and external accounts (as well as groups, devices, and contacts).

Each of these types of objects has a purpose and one is generally more suited to a particular business case than another.

In this chapter, you're going to look at the following topics as they relate to the MS-102 exam objectives:

- Creating and managing users
- Creating and managing guest users
- Creating and managing contacts
- Creating and managing groups
- Managing and monitoring Microsoft 365 license allocations
- Performing bulk user management

By the end of this chapter, you should be comfortable articulating the differences between the different kinds of objects and familiar with methods for provisioning and managing them.

Creating and Managing Users

Creating and managing users is central to administrating an information system—whether that system is an application on a small network, an enterprise-scale directory, or a cloud service hosted by a SaaS provider. In any instance, identities are used by people, applications, and devices to authenticate and perform activities.

In the context of Azure AD, there are three core types of identity:

- Cloud-based users

- Synchronized users

- Guest users

When planning out identity scenarios, it's important to understand the benefits, features, drawbacks, and capabilities associated with each type of identity and authentication scheme—including ease of provisioning, integration with existing directory or security products, requirements for on-premises infrastructure, and network availability.

In this section, you'll learn about managing each of these user types.

Creating and Managing Cloud Users

From an Azure AD perspective, **cloud users** are the easiest type of object to understand and manage. When you create an Azure AD or Microsoft 365 tenant, one of the first things you set up is your administrator user identity (in the form of `user@tenant.onmicrosoft.com`). This identity is stored in the Azure AD partition for your Microsoft 365 tenant. The Azure AD cloud users discussed in this context refer to the users whose primary source of identity is in Azure AD.

> **Exam Tip**
>
> Cloud users can be assigned to any domain that is verified in the Microsoft 365 tenant with a single caveat—the domain must be in **managed** mode. If a domain has been federated (such as with AD FS or PingFederate), users can only be assigned that domain when they are provisioned in the on-premises system.

The **initial** domain (or **tenant** domain) will always be a cloud-only domain, since Azure AD will always be the source of authority for it. When you add domains to a tenant, they are initially configured as **managed** domains—that is, Azure AD is used to manage the identity store.

One benefit of configuring cloud-only users is that there is no dependency on any other infrastructure or identity service. For many small organizations, cloud-only identity is the perfect solution because it requires no hardware or software investment other than the Microsoft 365 subscription. Conversely, a drawback of cloud-only users is the lack of integration with on-premises directory solutions and applications.

> **Exam Tip**
>
> As a best practice, Microsoft recommends maintaining at least one cloud-only account in case you lose access to any on-premises environment.

The easiest way to provision cloud users is through the Microsoft 365 admin center (`https://admin.microsoft.com`). To configure a user, expand **Users**, select **Active Users**, and then click **Add a user**. The wizard, shown in *Figure 2.1*, will prompt you to configure an account:

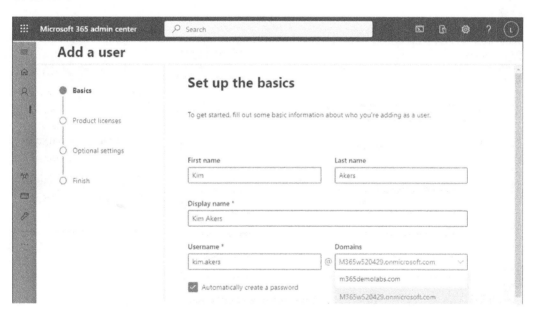

Figure 2.1 – Adding a new cloud user

You can configure the name properties for a user as well as assign them any licenses and a location through the **Add a user** wizard's workflow, as shown in *Figure 2.2*:

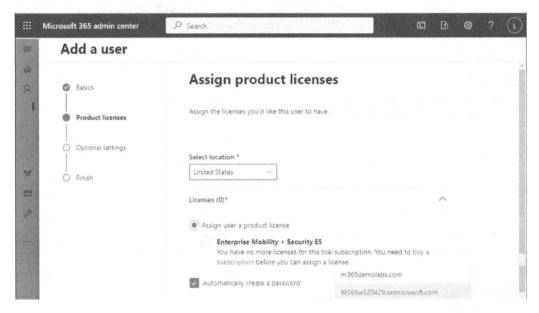

Figure 2.2 – Assign product licenses page

On the **Optional settings** page, you can also configure additional properties such as security roles, job title and department, addresses, and phone numbers, as shown in *Figure 2.3*:

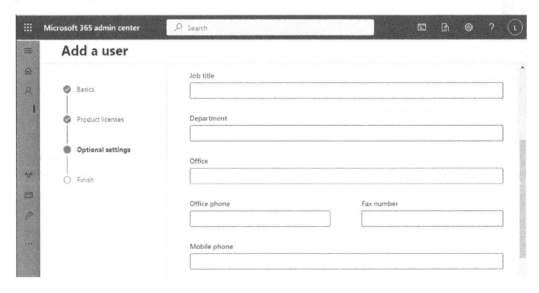

Figure 2.3 – Add a user profile information

You can also add users through the Azure AD portal (`https://aad.portal.azure.com`) or the new Entra ID portal (`https://entra.microsoft.com`). The Azure AD portal is arranged much differently than the Microsoft 365 admin center, due largely to the number of different types of resources and services that can be managed there. There are several differences in managing users and objects between the two interfaces; the Microsoft 365 admin center is a much more menu-driven experience, prompting administrators to configure common options and features inside the provisioning workflow.

> **IMPORTANT – Product Name Update**
>
> Microsoft has recently rebranded Azure Active Directory as Entra ID. MS-102 exam was released in Beta in May 2023. The exam is scheduled to be updated in November 2023. You may see questions that reference either Azure Active Directory or Entra ID—they are synonymous. Administration portals, product SKUs, service plans, and screenshots may reference either terminology or interface experience.

Once you've logged into the Azure AD portal, select **Users** and then select **New user**. The interface, shown in *Figure 2.4*, offers the opportunity to populate similar fields as the one in the admin center:

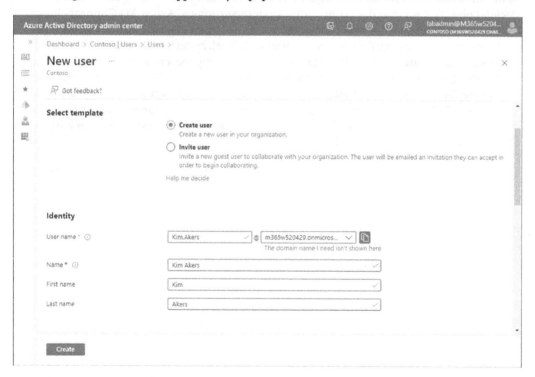

Figure 2.4 – Creating a user through the Azure AD portal

Most organizations that are using Azure from a cloud-only identity perspective will likely provision objects inside the Microsoft 365 admin center.

Creating and Managing Synchronized Users

As you will learn in *Chapter 4, Implementing and Managing Identity Synchronization with Azure AD*, the process of identity synchronization replicates your on-premises identity in Azure AD. Whether you are using Azure AD Connect sync, Azure AD Connect Cloud sync, or a third-party product, the process is largely the same: an on-premises agent or service connects to both Active Directory and Azure Active Directory, reads the objects from Active Directory, and re-creates a corresponding object in Azure AD.

During this provisioning process, the on-premises and cloud objects are linked through a unique, immutable attribute that stays the same throughout the lifecycle of the object.

Exam Tip

Originally, an on-premises object was linked to its corresponding cloud object by converting the on-premise object's `objectGUID` attribute value to a base64 string and stored in the cloud object's `TmmutableID` attribute. Modern versions of Azure AD Connect change this up a little bit and also make use of the `ms-DS-ConsistencyGuid`. The `ms-DS-ConsistencyGuid` attribute in Active Directory is blank by default; after Azure AD Connect is configured to use `ms-DS-ConsistencyGuid` as the source anchor during setup, an object's `objectGUID` value is copied to its corresponding `ms-DS-ConsistencyGuid` attribute. Since a new `objectGUID` is generated every time an object is created, a static value like `ms-DS-ConsistencyGuid` helps organizations maintain the relationship between identities through the Active Directory domain migrations that happen as part of business mergers, acquisitions, and divestitures.

After Azure AD Connect has been deployed, you can create a new synchronized identity by creating a new user in the on-premises Active Directory. See *Figure 2.5*:

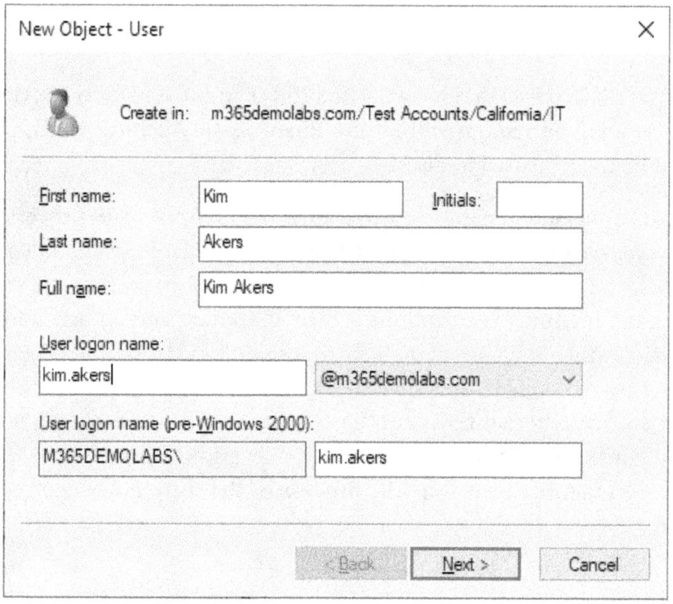

Figure 2.5 – Creating a new user through Active Directory Users and Computers

After synchronization is complete, the new user account is ready to sign into the service. From the Microsoft 365 admin center, it's simple to visually distinguish between cloud and synchronized accounts. *Figure 2.6* shows both a cloud user and a synchronized user:

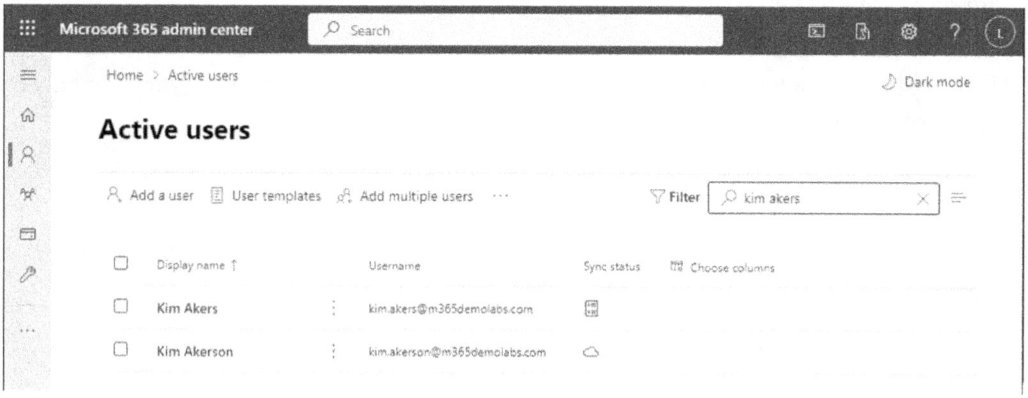

Figure 2.6 – Displaying cloud and synchronized users

In the **Sync status** column, a cloud user is represented by a cloud icon, while the synchronized user is represented by a notebook icon.

Creating and Managing Guest Users

Guest users are special accounts that have limited rights in the Azure AD environment. In most contexts, guest users are synonymous with Azure **Business-to-Business (B2B)** identities, so that's the reference point that will be used to discuss.

Azure B2B guest accounts are generally created through an **invitation** process, such as inviting someone from an external organization to participate in a Microsoft SharePoint site, collaborate on a document in OneDrive, or access files in a Teams channel. When an invitation is sent, an identity object is created in the inviting organization's Azure AD tenant and an invitation email is sent to the external recipient. After the recipient clicks on the link in the invitation email, the recipient is directed to an Azure AD sign-in flow that prompts them to enter credentials corresponding to their own identity source, whether that's another Azure AD or Microsoft 365 tenant, a consumer account (such as Microsoft, Google, or Facebook), or another third-party issuer that uses a SAML/WS-Fed-based identity provider. The process of the recipient accepting the invitation is called **redemption**.

> **More About Guests**
>
> While guests are typically part of an invitation process, with the new Azure AD cross-tenant synchronization feature (currently in preview), you can automate the provisioning of guest objects between trusted tenants like you would with your own directory synchronization. Microsoft recommends this feature only for Azure AD tenants that belong to the same organization. For more information on the new cross-tenant sync feature, see `https://learn.microsoft.com/en-us/azure/active-directory/multi-tenant-organizations/cross-tenant-synchronization-overview`.

While guest users can be viewed and edited in the Microsoft 365 admin center, they can only be provisioned through the Azure AD portal.

Clicking **Add a guest user**, as shown in *Figure 2.7*, in the Microsoft 365 admin center transfers you to the Azure AD portal to complete the invitation process:

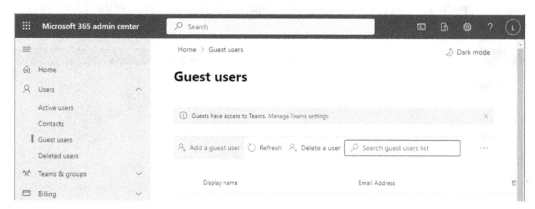

Figure 2.7 – Guest users administration in Microsoft 365 admin center

After either logging into the Azure AD portal or being redirected there from the Microsoft 365 admin portal, you can begin the process of inviting guests. To invite a new guest user from the Azure AD portal, click **New user** and then select **Invite external user**. See *Figure 2.8*:

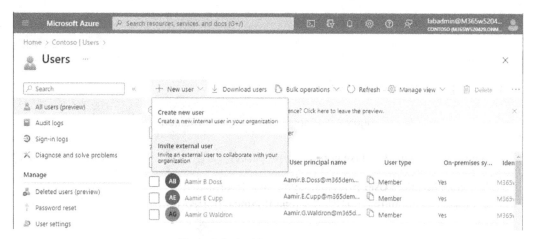

Figure 2.8 – Inviting a new guest user

The user interface elements for inviting a guest user are very similar to those for creating a new cloud user. The main differences are in the selection of the template and, in the case of a guest user, you have the opportunity to supply message content (which will be included as part of the email invitation sent). See *Figure 2.9*:

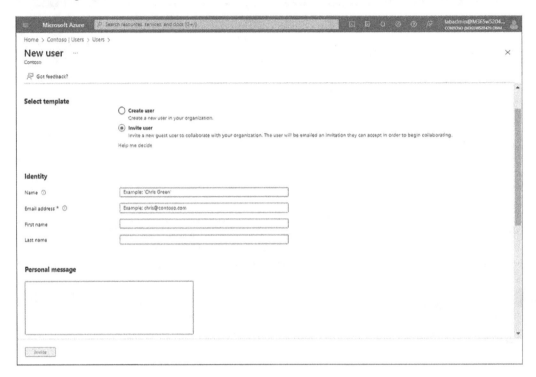

Figure 2.9 – Configuring the guest invitation

Once a guest has been invited, take note of the properties:

- The guest identity's **User principal name** value is formatted as **emailalias_domain.com#EXT#@tenantname.onmicrosoft.com**.

- The user type is set to **Guest**.

- Initially, the **Identities** property is set to **tenant.onmicrosoft.com**

- The invitation state is set to **PendingAcceptance**.

See *Figure 2.10* for reference:

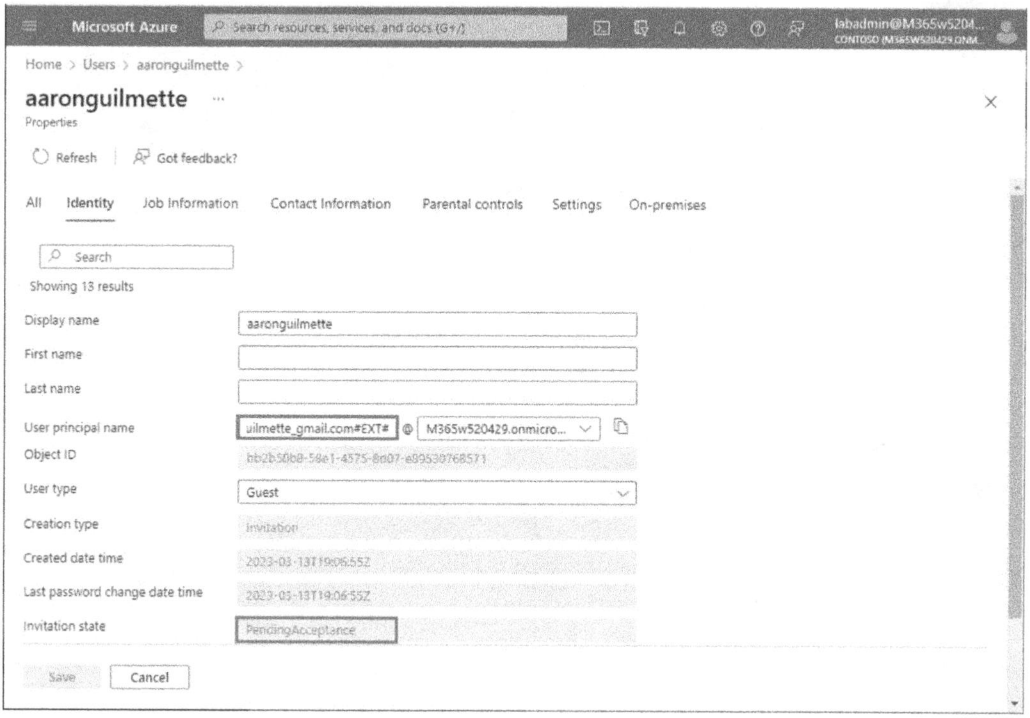

Figure 2.10 – Newly invited guest user

Upon receiving and accepting the invitation, the recipient is prompted to read and accept certain terms and grant permissions:

- Receive profile data including name, email address, and photo
- Collect and log activity including logins, data that has been accessed, and content associated with apps and resources in the inviting tenant
- Use profile and activity data by making it available to other apps inside the organization
- Administer the guest user account

See *Figure 2.11* for reference:

atguilmette@hotmail.com

Permission requested by:

Contoso
M365w520429.onmicrosoft.com

By accepting, you allow this organization to:

∨ Receive your profile data

    Your profile data means your name, email address, and photo

∨ Collect and log your activity

    Your activity data means your access, usage, and content associated with their apps and resources

∨ Use your profile data and activity data

    This data may be used with your access and use of their apps and resources, as well as to create, control, and administer an account according to their policies

You should only accept if you trust Contoso. **Contoso has not provided a link to their privacy statement for you to review.** You can update these permissions at https://myaccount.microsoft.com/organizations Learn More

This resource is not shared by Microsoft.

Figure 2.11 – Invitation redemption consent

After consenting, the invitation state in the Azure portal is updated from **PendingAcceptance** to **Accepted**. Additionally, depending on what identity source the guest user is authenticated against, the **Identities** property could be updated to one of several possible values:

- **External Azure AD**: Azure AD identity from another organization

- **Microsoft Account**: The Microsoft Account (MSA) account ID associated with Hotmail, Outlook.com, Xbox, LiveID, or other Microsoft consumer properties

- **Google.com**: A user identity associated with Google's consumer products (such as Gmail) or a Google Workspace offering

- **Facebook.com**: A user identity authenticated by the Facebook service

- {**issuer URI**}: Another SAML/WS-Fed-based identity provider

Guest users can be assigned licenses, granted access to apps, and delegated administrative roles inside the inviter's tenant.

Creating and Managing Contacts

If you're familiar with using an email application such as Outlook, you're probably familiar with the concept of a **contact**. A contact in Azure AD or Exchange Online is used for the same purpose—to provide a stored entry in the organization's address book that can be used as an email recipient. A contact object can be used to reference any mail-enabled recipient—whether it's an individual's personal email account, an individual at an organization, a distribution or mailing list, or some sort of shared recipient.

Unlike users, contact objects are *not* security principals—that is, they have no login identity or password connected to them. Contact objects, however, can be made members of the distribution lists.

Contact objects can be created in either the Microsoft 365 admin center or the Exchange admin center.

Microsoft 365 Admin Center

The Microsoft 365 admin center provides a streamlined interface for managing contacts, as shown in *Figure 2.12*:

Figure 2.12 – Contacts page in Microsoft 365 admin center

From the Microsoft 365 admin center, you can create individual contacts, import up to 40 contacts in a CSV, and export a list of contacts.

To create an individual contact, click the **Add a contact** button on the **Contacts** page and then fill out the fields shown in *Figure 2.13*:

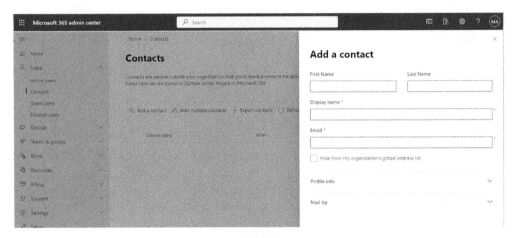

Figure 2.13 – Populating a contact

Required fields are marked with an asterisk (*). You can also fill out additional organization fields such as company, department, and phone numbers under the **Profile info** section. Any value entered into the **Mail tip** section will be displayed in Outlook when composing an email to that contact.

By selecting the **Add multiple contacts** button, you can review the necessary information for uploading a CSV on the **Add multiple contacts** flyout, as shown in *Figure 2.14*:

Figure 2.14 – Add multiple contacts flyout

The Microsoft 365 admin center provides two different templates (one with a sample entry) that have the fields necessary for bulk adding contacts. *Figure 2.15* depicts a sample template:

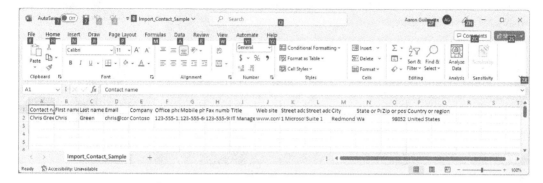

Figure 2.15 – Bulk contact import template

After you've created the CSV, you can upload it in the flyout to create contact objects.

Exchange Admin Center

The **Exchange admin center** also provides an interface for adding contacts. See *Figure 2.16*:

Figure 2.16 – Exchange admin center contact administration

However, the Exchange admin center does not provide a bulk upload or import interface. Adding contacts in the Exchange admin center interface is very similar to the Microsoft 365 admin center experience—select **Add a mail contact** and populate the required fields in the **New Mail Contact** wizard, as shown in *Figure 2.17*:

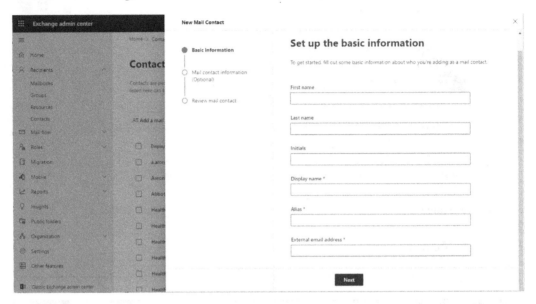

Figure 2.17 – New Mail Contact wizard in Exchange admin center

The Exchange admin center features a few differences from the Microsoft admin center, such as using a wizard instead of a flyout, a few different field names (such as **External email address** instead of **Email address** or **Office Phone** instead of **Work Phone**), and a new required field: **Alias**. When creating a contact through the Microsoft 365 admin center, the user interface generates an alias (also known as a **mail nickname**) automatically, while the Exchange admin center requires you to enter one manually.

Like the Microsoft 365 admin center interface, the Exchange admin center interface allows you to export a list (CSV) of contacts in your organization.

Creating and Managing Groups

Groups are directory objects used to perform operations, grant rights or permissions, or communicate with one or more users collectively. In Azure Active Directory, there are several kinds of groups:

- **Security groups** – This type of group is typically used for granting permissions to resources, either on-premises or in Azure AD.

- **Distribution lists or distribution groups** – These groups are usually used for sending emails to multiple recipients, though they can also sometimes be used to restrict the scope of rules or for filtering purposes in Azure AD, SharePoint Online, and Exchange Online.

- **Microsoft 365 groups** – Formerly called **modern groups** (and sometimes still referred to as **unified groups**), this is an all-purpose group type that can be used as a security group for assigning permissions to resources or a distribution group for handling email. Microsoft 365 groups are special objects that are connected to SharePoint Online sites and form the basis for teams in Microsoft Teams. In addition, each Microsoft 365 group is connected to an Exchange group mailbox, allowing it to store persistent messages (such as email or, in the case of Microsoft Teams, channel conversations). Microsoft 365 groups are only available in Azure AD. There is no on-premises equivalent.

Each of these groups has certain capabilities and benefits. One or more types of groups may be appropriate for a specific task. In Azure Active Directory, security groups can be mail-enabled (or not), while distribution groups and Microsoft 365 groups are always mail-enabled.

In Azure Active Directory, any of the cloud-based groups can be configured to have their membership **assigned** or **dynamic**. With assigned membership, an administrator is responsible for periodically updating group members. Dynamic groups are built by creating an object query that is periodically used to add or remove members. For example, you may choose to create a dynamic group called *Sales* that automatically includes users whose job title or department value is set to *Sales*. Groups in Azure AD can contain users, contacts, devices, and other groups. Groups can be converted between assigned and dynamic membership.

When working with groups, there are several important things to remember:

- An Azure AD tenant can have groups that are synchronized from on-premises environments as well as cloud-only groups.

- Both security and distribution groups can be synchronized from on-premises environments. The exception to this is on-premises dynamic distribution groups. Because they can be based on queries that aren't possible in Azure AD, they are not synchronized. You will have to either recreate the dynamic groups in Azure AD using supported query parameters or modify the on-premises group to be based on assigned membership.

- Microsoft 365 groups, due to their unique construction, cannot be a member of a group nor can they have other groups of any type nested in them.

- Microsoft 365 groups are the only type of object with a cloud source of authority that can be written back on-premises.

You'll next look at configuring and administering groups in Azure AD.

Microsoft 365 Admin Center

For most Azure AD group administration use cases, you'll probably use the Microsoft 365 admin center. To configure groups in the Microsoft 365 admin center, follow these steps:

1. Navigate to the Microsoft 365 admin center (`https://admin.microsoft.com`). Expand **Teams & groups** and then select **Active teams & groups**. See *Figure 2.18*:

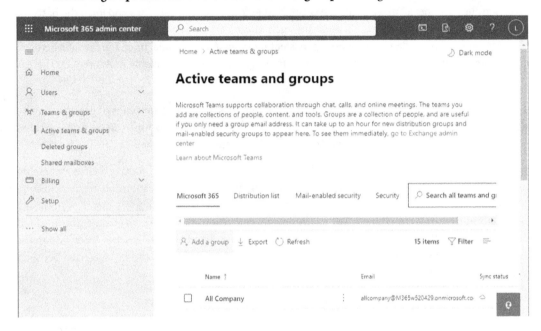

Figure 2.18 – Active teams and groups

2. Click **Add a group**.

3. On the **Group type** page, as shown in *Figure 2.19*, select the type of group you wish to create. Except for **Security** groups, all group types will require essentially the same information (non-mail-enabled security groups do not allow you to add owners or members to the workflow). If you select a **Microsoft 365** group as your group type, you'll also have the option at the end of the wizard to create a Microsoft Teams team from the group.

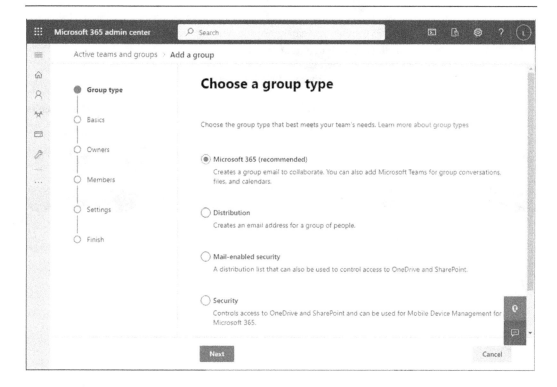

Figure 2.19 – Choose a group type

4. On the **Basics** page, enter a **Name** and an optional **Description** for the group and then click **Next**.

5. On the **Owners** page, click **Assign owners** to assign at least a single owner. Microsoft recommends having at least two owners (in case one leaves the organization or is absent for a period of time). The owner cannot be an external guest. Click **Next** when finished.

6. On the **Members** page, click **Add members** (this is an optional step). Click **Next** to proceed.

7. On the **Settings** page, configure the settings for the group and then click **Next**:

    *   For distribution groups and mail-enabled security groups, this includes an email address.

    *   For Microsoft 365 and security groups, this includes assigning Azure AD roles. The option does not appear for mail-enabled security groups, though it can be added later.

    *   For distribution groups, this includes the ability for users outside the org to email the groups (Microsoft 365 groups must have this setting configured manually in the Exchange properties for the group object afterward).

    *   For Microsoft 365 groups, you can also configure privacy settings (either **Public** or **Private**). Public groups can be browsed and joined by anyone while private groups require an owner to add additional members.

- Also, for Microsoft 365 groups, you can choose to convert the group to a team, though users must have a Teams license assigned to access the group.

8. On the **Finish** page, review the settings and click **Create group**.

After the group has been created, you can modify its settings in either the Microsoft 365 admin center or Azure AD portal, as shown in *Figure 2.20*:

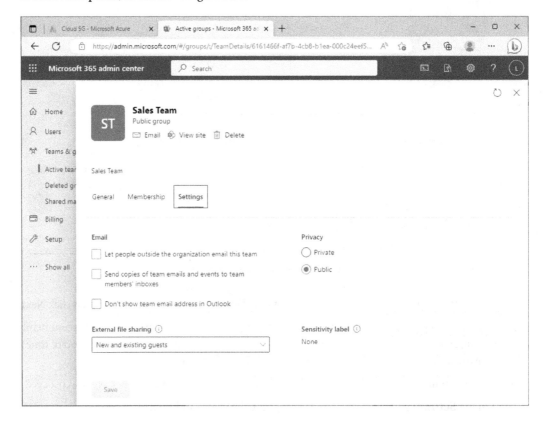

Figure 2.20 – Modifying settings of a Microsoft 365 group

As you can see in *Figure 2.20*, Microsoft 365 groups have some additional properties (such as determining whether to send copies of emails received by the group mailbox to individual team mailboxes or associate with a **sensitivity label**).

Azure AD Portal

The Azure AD portal is the other interface that is used to create and manage groups. As with the user creation options, the Azure AD portal provides a slimmed-down feel without the wizard experience of the Microsoft 365 admin center.

To create and manage groups in the Azure AD portal, follow these steps:

1. Navigate to the Azure AD portal (`https://aad.portal.azure.com`) and select **Groups**.

2. With the default **All groups** navigation item selected, as shown in *Figure 2.21*, click **New group**:

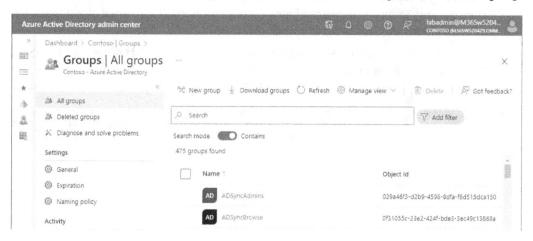

Figure 2.21 – Azure AD all groups

3. On the **New Group** page, as shown in *Figure 2.22*, fill in the **Group type** (**Security** or **Microsoft 365**), **Group Name**, and optionally the **Group description** fields. If you've selected **Microsoft 365** as the group type, you will also be required to enter a value for the **Group email address** field. The security groups created in the Azure portal are not mail-enabled.

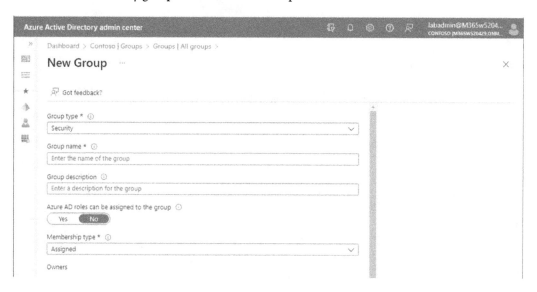

Figure 2.22 – New Group page

4. You can choose whether Azure AD security roles can be assigned to the group. If you select **Yes**, then the group must have assigned membership.

5. Under **Membership type**, you can select **Assigned**, **Dynamic User**, or **Dynamic Device** (if it is a security group). If it is a Microsoft 365 group, you can choose from **Assigned** or **Dynamic User**. Security groups with assigned membership can have all supported object types, but dynamic groups are constrained to a single object type.

6. If you select a group with the **Assigned** membership type, you can add **Owners** and **Members**. If you select a group with either of the dynamic membership types, you must choose the **Add dynamic query** option, as shown in *Figure 2.23*:

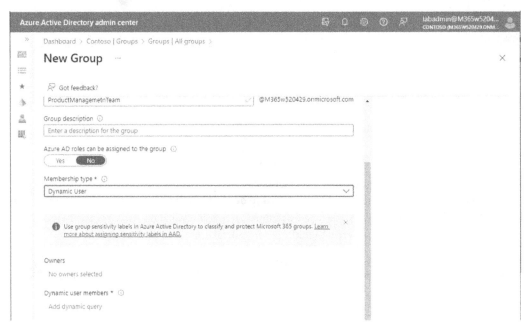

Figure 2.23 – Creating a new dynamic group

7. Click **Add dynamic query** to configure a dynamic query.

8. On the **Configure Rules** tab of the **Dynamic membership rules** page, as shown in *Figure 2.24*, configure an expression that represents the users or devices you want to have included in the group. For example, to create a user membership rule that looks for the `Engineering` value in either the **jobTitle** or **department** user attributes, select the appropriate **Property** option, select **Equals** or **Contains** under **Operator**, and then enter `Engineering` in the **Value** field.

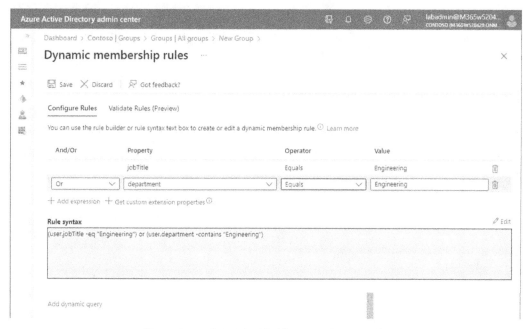

Figure 2.24 – Creating a dynamic membership rule

9. You can view the construction of the rule in the **Rule syntax** output box. If necessary, you can edit the rule free-form to create a more complex rule type.

10. You can select the **Validate Rules (Preview)** tab and add users you think should be in scope or out of scope to verify that the rule is working correctly. Click **Add users** and then select users from the picker. In this example, **Aamir E Cupp** and **Abagael R Rauch** were selected. Aamir's **jobTitle** is *Manager* and his **department** is *Sales*, so the expected result is that he is not included in the group. Abagael's **jobTitle** is *Scientist* but her **Department** is *Engineering*. Based on the way the query is constructed, she is included in the group. See *Figure 2.25*:

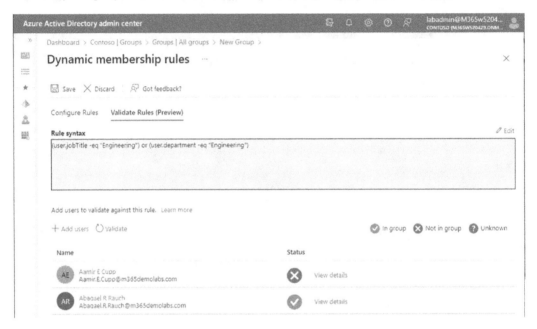

Figure 2.25 – Validating the dynamic membership rule

11. When finished editing the rule, click **Save**.

12. Click **Create** to create the new group.

Using the Azure AD portal, you can also update the membership rules for existing groups or change a group's membership from assigned to dynamic by selecting the group and then editing the details on its **Properties** menu, as shown in *Figure 2.26*:

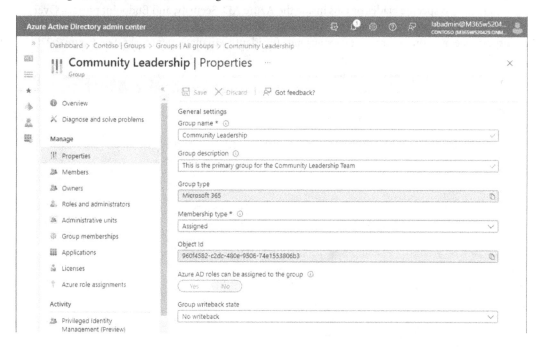

Figure 2.26 – Editing a group

If you change a group's membership from assigned to dynamic, you'll need to create a query. It's important to note, though, that you cannot change a group's type (for example, from security to Microsoft 365) or whether a group is eligible for Azure AD role assignment—those options can only be selected when creating a group.

> **Note**
>
> Microsoft Entra is the new umbrella product that covers Microsoft identity management and governance. Currently, the Microsoft Entra admin center (`https://entra.microsoft.com`) maps to specific blades or tabs inside the Azure AD, Security, and Endpoint portals. Over the next year or two, anticipate that Microsoft will begin emphasizing the Entra admin center experience over the Azure portal experience for identity management tasks. See *Figure 2.27*:
>
>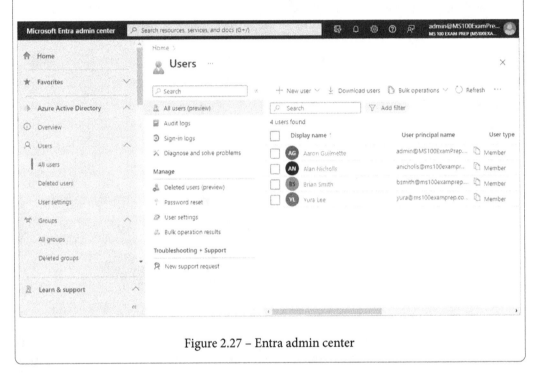
>
> Figure 2.27 – Entra admin center

Next, you'll look at managing Microsoft 365 licenses.

Managing and Monitoring Microsoft 365 License Allocations

If identity is the foundation for security in the Microsoft 365 platform, **licensing** is the entitlement engine that is used to grant identities access to the tools and applications.

Every Microsoft 365 service is tied to a license—whether that's individual product licenses for Exchange Online or SharePoint Online or bundled offerings such as Microsoft 365 G3 that include multiple services.

In Microsoft terminology, there are a number of key terms to be aware of:

- **Licensing plans**: In broad terms, a licensing plan is any purchased licensing item. For example, standalone Exchange Online P2 and Microsoft 365 E3 are both examples of licensing plans.

- **Services**: Also known as **service plans**, these are the individual services that exist inside of a licensing plan. For example, Exchange Online P2 has a single Exchange Online P2 service plan, while Microsoft 365 E3 has an Exchange Online service plan, a Microsoft 365 Apps, service plan, a SharePoint Online service plan, and so on.

- **Licenses**: This is the actual number of individual license plans of a particular type that you have purchased. For example, if you have 5 subscriptions to Exchange Online P2 and 5 subscriptions to Microsoft 365 E3, you have 10 licenses (or 5 each of Exchange Online P2 and Microsoft 365 E3). Licenses are frequently mapped 1:1 with users or service principals, though some users may have more than one license plan associated with them.

- **SkuPartNumber**: When reviewing licensing in PowerShell, the `SkuPartNmber` is the keyword that maps to a licensing plan. For example, Office 365 E3 is represented by the `SkuPartNumber` *ENTERPRISEPACK*.

- **AccountSkuId**: The `AccountSkuId` is the combination of your tenant name (such as Contoso) and the `SkuPartNumber` or licensing plan. For example, the Office 365 E3 licensing plan belonging to the `contoso.onmicrosoft.com` tenant has an `AccountSkuId` of `contoso:ENTERPRISEPACK`.

- **ConsumedUnits**: Consumed units represent the number of items in a licensing plan that you have assigned to users. For example, if you have assigned a Microsoft 365 E3 licensing plan to three users, you have three `ConsumedUnits` of the Microsoft 365 E3 licensing plan. When reviewing licensing from the Azure AD portal, this field is sometimes displayed as **Assigned**.

- **ActiveUnits**: Number of units that you have purchased for a particular licensing plan. When reviewing licensing from the Azure AD portal, this field is sometimes displayed as **Total**.

- **WarningUnits**: Number of units of a particular license plan that you haven't renewed purchasing for. These units will expire after the 30-day grace period. If reviewing licensing in the Azure AD portal, this field is also sometimes displayed as **Expiring soon**.

You can easily view purchased licensing plan details in the Microsoft 365 admin center under **Billing | Licenses**, as shown in *Figure 2.28*:

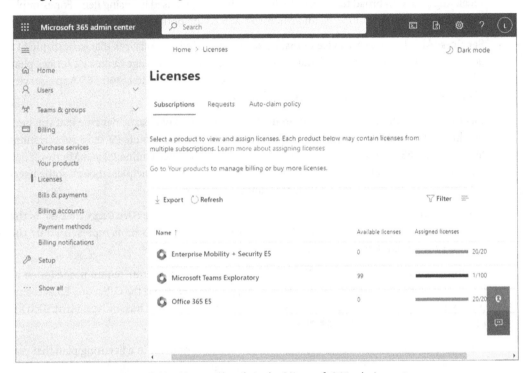

Figure 2.28 – License details in the Microsoft 365 admin center

You can assign licenses in many ways:

- Through the Licenses page in the Microsoft 365 admin center (**Microsoft 365 admin center | Billing | Licenses**)

- On the properties of a user on the **Active users** page in the Microsoft 365 admin center (**Microsoft 365 admin center | Users | Active Users | User properties**)

- To users through the **Licenses** page in the Azure AD portal (**Azure AD portal | Azure Active Directory | Licenses | Licensed users**)

- To users through the **User** properties page in the Azure AD portal (**Azure AD portal | Azure Active Directory | Users | User properties**)

- To groups through group-based licensing (**Azure AD portal | Azure Active Directory | Licenses | Licensed groups**)

- Through PowerShell cmdlets such as `Set-MsolUserLicense`

Each licensing method allows you similar options for assigning license plans to users, including assigning multiple license plans or selectively enabling service plans inside an individual license plan.

For example, in the Microsoft 365 admin center, you can view and modify a user's licenses on the **Licenses and apps** tab of their profile. See *Figure 2.29*:

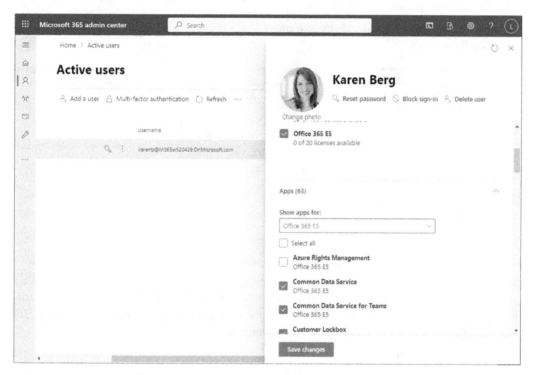

Figure 2.29 – User license management

As you can see in *Figure 2.29*, the user has the **Office 365 E5** licensing plan enabled as well as individual services such as **Common Data Service**, **Common Data Service for Teams**, and **Customer Lockbox**, while the **Azure Rights Management** service plan for this licensing plan is disabled.

> **Note**
>
> In order to assign licenses, a **usage location** is required. The usage location is used to determine what service plans and features are available for a given user. Any user that does not have a usage location set will inherit the location of the Azure AD tenant.

Many organizations may choose to automate some or all of the licensing assignments. Azure AD group-based licensing allows you to specify one or more licenses to be assigned to one or more users or security groups.

To configure group-based licensing, follow these steps:

1. Navigate to the Azure AD portal (`https://portal.azure.com`).

2. Select **Azure Active Directory | Licenses**.

3. Under **Manage**, select **All products**.

4. Select one or more licenses that you want to assign as a unit to a group and then click **Assign**. See *Figure 2.30*:

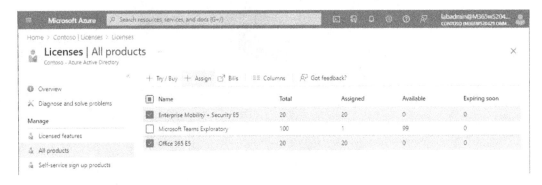

Figure 2.30 – Assign selected licenses to a group

5. On the **Users and groups** tab, click **Add users and groups** and select one or more security groups from the list. You can only select security groups or mail-enabled security groups. The security groups can be cloud-only or synchronized.

6. Click the **Assignment options** tab.

7. Select which services you want to enable for each licensing plan by sliding the toggle to either **Off** or **On**. See *Figure 2.31*:

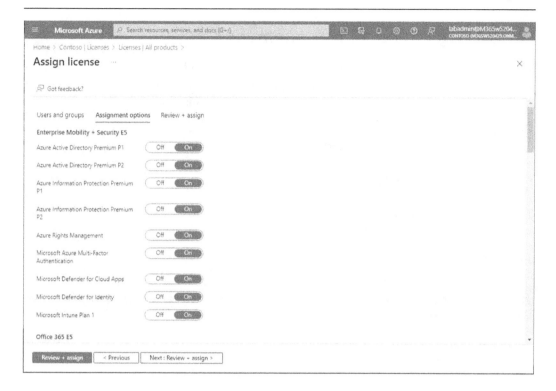

Figure 2.31 – Configuring assignment options

8.   When finished, click **Review + assign**.

9.   Confirm the configuration. When ready, click **Assign**.

Further Reading

For more information on configuring group-based licensing, see `https://learn.microsoft.com/en-us/azure/active-directory/fundamentals/active-directory-licensing-whatis-azure-portal`.

Next, you'll look at how to perform bulk user management operations in Microsoft 365.

Performing Bulk User Management

While many organizations will deploy a hybrid identity solution and manage accounts on-premises, you may face scenarios where you need to manage cloud identities or guests in bulk (such as when creating bulk guest user invitations or during a tenant-to-tenant migration procedure).

These operations can be performed in several ways, including through the Microsoft 365 admin center, the Azure AD portal, and various PowerShell commands.

Microsoft 365 Admin Center

The Microsoft 365 admin center allows you to perform bulk user additions, either interactively or by uploading a specially-formatted CSV.

To begin the process, select **Add multiple users** on the **Active users** page of the Microsoft 365 admin center, as shown in *Figure 2.32*:

Figure 2.32 – Active users page

On the **Add multiple users** flyout, you can choose to either enter basic details interactively (up to 249 users) or you can download a CSV template with more fields that can be populated. See *Figure 2.33*:

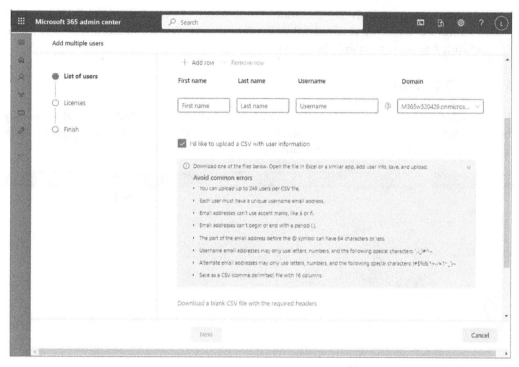

Figure 2.33 – Configuring the bulk user upload

If you choose to work with a bulk user template, you can edit it in any text editor that supports CSV files. You must preserve the first row, which has the fields or header information. You can add up to 249 users, each on its own row. See *Figure 2.34*, where Microsoft Excel is used to edit the user template:

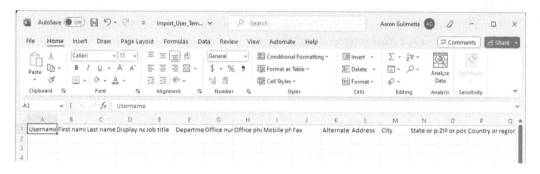

Figure 2.34 – Microsoft 365 admin center bulk user template

After you have either added the users in the admin center flyout or into the CSV and uploaded it, you can click **Next** to go to the next page of the wizard.

On the **Licenses** page, you can assign a **Location**, licensing plan, and optionally, the individual services that will be enabled. When you've completed your selections, click **Next** to proceed to the confirmation page and click **Add users** to submit the operation.

Azure AD Portal

Bulk operations can also be performed through the Microsoft Azure AD portal. In contrast to only the create option provided by the Microsoft 365 admin center, the Azure AD portal supports **Bulk create**, **Bulk invite** (for guest users), and **Bulk delete** operations. See *Figure 2.35*:

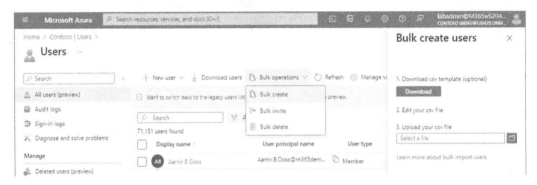

Figure 2.35 – Bulk operations menu in the Azure AD portal

To get started, you'll need to use one of the templates provided in the Azure AD portal. On the **Users** blade, select **Bulk operations** and then choose the appropriate operation.

> **Note**
>
> The templates in the Microsoft 365 admin center and Azure AD portal are *not* interchangeable. You'll need to use the correct template for the interface that you're working with.

On the corresponding flyout, you'll see the **Download** option for the template. Once it's downloaded, you can edit it in any app that supports CSV files. See *Figure 2.36*:

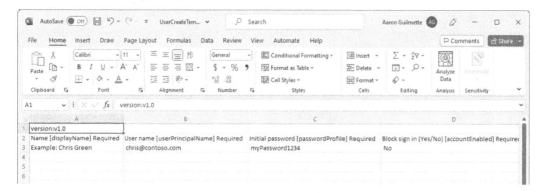

Figure 2.36 – Azure AD bulk user create template

It's important to note that the first two rows of any of the templates must be preserved and not modified in any way. Each identity to be modified is included in a separate row, starting at row 3. The first four fields (**displayName**, **userPrincipalName**, **passwordProfile**, and **accountEnabled**) are required. All other fields are optional.

When finished, you can upload the CSV back to the same flyout in the Azure portal to process the request.

PowerShell

By far the most flexible option for managing bulk users is through Windows PowerShell. There are currently three different PowerShell modules that can be used:

- **MSOnline module**
- **Azure AD Module**
- **Azure AD Graph module**

> **Note**
> Both the MSOnline module and Azure AD Module will eventually be deprecated and replaced by the **Azure AD Graph module**. The modules work similarly, though the cmdlet names, parameters, syntax, and overall capabilities are different.

Installing Modules

- Each of the modules can be installed running the `Install-Module` cmdlet from an elevated PowerShell prompt on your system:

- **MSOnline**: `Install-Module MSOnline`

- **Azure AD**: `Install-Module AzureAD`

- **Microsoft Graph**: `Install-Module Microsoft.Graph`

- Once the modules have been installed, you can begin connecting to Azure AD and performing operations.

Connecting to Azure AD

Each module uses a slightly different syntax for connecting to Azure AD. Let's go over them here:

- **MSOnline**: `Connect-MsolService`

- **Azure AD**: `Connect-AzureAD`

- **Microsoft Graph**: `Connect-MgGraph -Scopes "User.ReadWrite.All"`

In each of these cases, you'll need to provide credentials with the appropriate rights to create users (such as Global Administrator or User Administrator). In the case of the Microsoft Graph cmdlets, you'll also need to consent to the permissions scope.

Working with PowerShell

When working with bulk users via PowerShell, you're free to collect, organize, and manipulate the data in whatever way works best for you. For example, if you need to gather a list of user objects and their properties, you can use one of the modules' `Get-*` cmdlets. You can choose to store, view, or manipulate the data in a variety of ways—for example, saving it to a variable, displaying it to the console (screen), exporting it to a file, or passing the data through to another command.

PowerShell supports a processing concept called **piping**. Piping can be used to redirect the output of one command into another command. It can be used to process intermediary computations or steps without writing data to disk.

Let's look at some common examples of how you might interact with one or more objects in bulk.

Retrieving User Data

Let's say you need to retrieve a list of all users in your organization that meet certain criteria (such as being members of the *Project Management* department).

Using the MSOnline cmdlets, you could accomplish this using the following Get-MsolUser cmdlet:

```
Get-Msoluser -MaxResults 10 -Department "Project Management" | Select
DisplayName,UserPrincipalName,Department
```

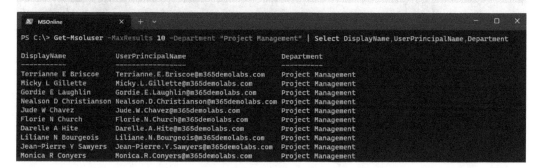

Figure 2.37 – Get-MsolUser cmdlet

To perform the same action with the Azure AD module, you would need to modify the syntax slightly:

```
Get-AzureADUser -Top 10 -Filter "Department eq 'Project Management'" |
Select DisplayName,UserPrincipalName,Department
```

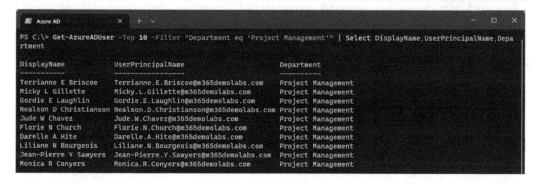

Figure 2.38 – Get-AzureADUser cmdlet

Finally, working with the Microsoft Graph module, you'd need to use the following syntax:

```
Get-MgUser -Filter "Department eq 'Project Management'"
-Top 10 -ConsistencyLevel Eventual -Property
DisplayName,UserPrincipalName,Department | Select
DisplayName,UserPrincipalName,Department
```

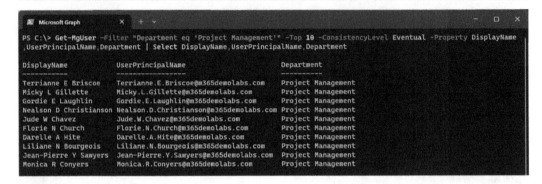

Figure 2.39 – Get-MgUser cmdlet

Updating Users

One of the most common bulk administration tasks, after reporting, is updating objects. Let's say we needed to assign licenses to this group of users, but they didn't have their usage location set. In order to assign the proper license plans and service plans, you'll need to configure the correct location.

Using the MSOnline cmdlets, we could retrieve our list of users and then, through piping, use the output of the Get-MsolUser cmdlet as the input for the Set-MsolUser cmdlet:

```
Get-Msoluser -MaxResults 10 -Department "Project Management" | Set-
MsolUser -UsageLocation US
```

Figure 2.40 – Updating the UsageLocation with Set-MsolUser

The Azure AD cmdlets also support piping input:

```
Get-AzureADUser -Top 10 -Filter "Department eq 'Project Management'" |
Set-AzureADUser -UsageLocation US
```

Figure 2.41 – Updating the UsageLocation with Set-AzureADUser

Finally, you can also use the `Set-MgUser` cmdlet to update user objects with the Microsoft Graph PowerShell, though the pipeline syntax is a little different still. In this example, the piped data is processed using a `Foreach` command, instructing PowerShell to loop through the list of users returned, substituting the actual individual object (represented by `$_`) and the property of the object to be retrieved (represented by the `.id`):

```
Get-MgUser -Filter "Department eq 'Project Management'" -Top 5
-ConsistencyLevel Eventual -Property * | Foreach { Update-MgUser
-UserId $_.id -UsageLocation US }
```

```
Microsoft Graph                    ×  +  ˅                                      —  ☐  ×
PS C:\> Get-MgUser -Filter "Department eq 'Project Management'" -Top 5 -ConsistencyLevel Eventual -Property * | Foreach
{ Update-MgUser -UserId $_.id -UsageLocation US }
```

Figure 2.42 – Updating the UsageLocation with Update-MgUser

Updating Licenses

License management is also a task that is often performed via scripting.

In order to determine the licensing plan to assign with the MSOnline module, you'll need to retrieve the list of valid products using the `Get-MsolAccountSku` cmdlet. After that, you can assign a license using the `tenant:LICENSINGPLAN` syntax:

```
Get-MsolAccountSku
Set-MsolUserLicense -UserPrincipalName Aamir.b.doss@m365demolabs.com
-AddLicenses "M365w520429:TEAMS_EXPLORATORY"
```

```
MSOnline                    ×  +  ˅                                      —  ☐  ×
PS C:\> Get-MsolAccountSku

AccountSkuId                        ActiveUnits WarningUnits ConsumedUnits
------------                        ----------- ------------ -------------
M365w520429:EMSPREMIUM              20          0            20
M365w520429:ENTERPRISEPREMIUM       20          0            20
M365w520429:WINDOWS_STORE           1000000     0            0
M365w520429:TEAMS_EXPLORATORY       100         0            2


PS C:\> Set-MsolUserLicense -UserPrincipalName Aamir.b.doss@m365demolabs.com -AddLicenses "M365w520429:TEAMS_EXPLORATORY"
"
```

Figure 2.43 – Adding a license to a user with the MSOnline module

To assign a license with the Azure AD PowerShell is a bit more complicated, as it involves creating a special licensing object. In this example, you'll assign the user Aamir the TEAMS_EXPLORATORY license:

```
Get-AzureADSubscribedSku
$TeamsSku = Get-AzureADSubscribedSku | ? { $_.SkuPartNumber -eq
"TEAMS_EXPLORATORY" }
$License = New-Object -TypeName Microsoft.Open.AzureAD.Model.
AssignedLicense
$License.SkuId = $TeamsSku.SkuId
$LicenseToAssign = New-Object -TypeName Microsoft.Open.AzureAD.Model.
AssignedLicenses
$LicenseToAssign.AddLicenses = $License
Set-AzureADUserLicense -ObjectId Aamir.E.Cupp@m365demolabs.com
-AssignedLicenses $LicenseToAssign
```

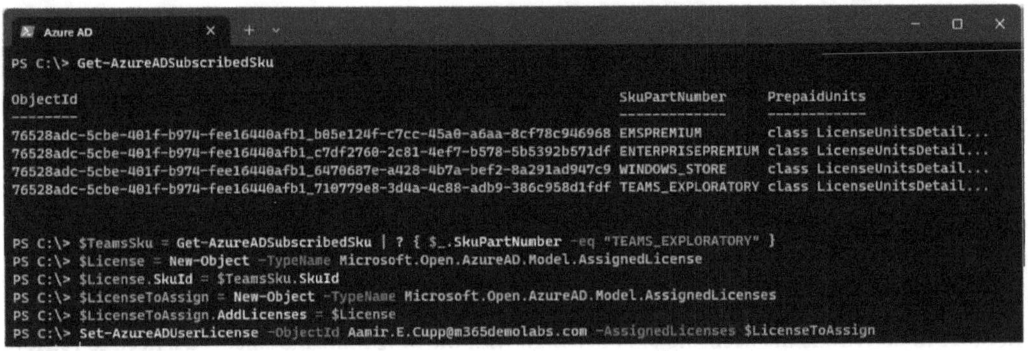

Figure 2.44 – Adding a license with the Set-AzureADUserLicense cmdlet

In the final license example, you'll use the Microsoft Graph PowerShell cmdlets. It works similarly to the Azure AD cmdlet, but the syntax requires a hash table to hold the license SkuId property:

```
$user = Get-Mguser -UserId karenb@M365w520429.OnMicrosoft.com
-Property *
$TeamsSku = Get-MgSubscribedSku -all | Where SkuPartNumber -eq "TEAMS_
EXPLORATORY"
Set-MgUserLicense -UserId $user.Id -AddLicenses @{SkuId = $TeamsSku.
SkuId} -RemoveLicenses @()
```

Figure 2.45 – Adding a license with the Set-MgUserLicense cmdlet

Depending on your scenario, managing licensing through one of the PowerShell interfaces may be the most efficient way to craft custom license configurations.

> **Further Reading**
>
> Managing licenses can be a complex topic, especially when considering options for enabling or disabling individual service plans within a license or replacing licensing options for users. You can see more in-depth information regarding different capabilities of PowerShell-based licensing at `https://learn.microsoft.com/en-us/microsoft-365/enterprise/view-licenses-and-services-with-microsoft-365-powershell`.

Creating Users

There are several scenarios where you may need to bulk-create users or contacts or bulk-invite users to your tenant. Frequently, when these operations are required, you will be working with source data stored in a **comma-separated values (CSV)** text file.

Previously in the *Performing Bulk User Management* section, you used a specially-formatted CSV to import objects into the Microsoft 365 admin center. You can use a similarly-formatted CSV to perform the action with PowerShell.

In this set of examples, we've entered a few names into a CSV file (as shown in *Figure 2.40*) to demonstrate bulk user processing. While some of the administrative interfaces (such as the Microsoft 365 admin center) limit you to a maximum of 249 objects, you can process thousands of objects with PowerShell—the only real limitation is the memory on your computer.

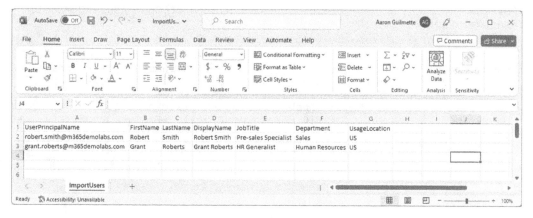

Figure 2.46 – Bulk user template

First, you'll perform the operation with the MSOnline cmdlets. Begin by importing the CSV source file and storing it as a variable. Then, with a `Foreach` command, you'll iterate through the lines in the CSV, using the values stored in the `$User` variable to provide the inputs for each of the parameters:

```
$Users = Import-Csv -Path C:\temp\ImportUsers.csv
Foreach ($User in $Users) { New-MsolUser -UserPrincipalName $User.
UserPrincipalName -FirstName $User.FirstName -LastName $User.LastName
-DisplayName $User.DisplayName -Title $User.JobTitle -Department
$User.Department -UsageLocation $User.UsageLocation -Country US }
```

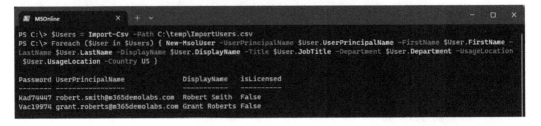

Figure 2.47 – Bulk creating users with New-MsolUser

Next, you'll look at doing the same thing with the Azure AD cmdlets. As with the other examples in this section, you'll see that the syntax follows a pattern, but there are other required parameters that must be specified. In the case of `New-AzureADUser`, it is a `PasswordProfile` object (which is used to specify a password) and `MailNickName` that must be supplied:

```
$Users = Import-Csv C:\temp\ImportUsers.csv
$PasswordProfile = New-Object -TypeName Microsoft.Open.AzureAD.Model.
PasswordProfile
$PasswordProfile.Password = "P@ssw0rd123"
Foreach ($User in $Users) { New-AzureADUser -UserPrincipalName $User.
UserPrincipalName -GivenName $User.FirstName -Surname $User.LastName
-DisplayName $User.DisplayName -JobTitle $User.JobTitle -Department
$User.Department -UsageLocation $User.UsageLocation -Country
$User.UsageLocation -AccountEnabled $True -MailNickname $User.
UserPrincipalName.Split("@")[0] -PasswordProfile $PasswordProfile }
```

Figure 2.48 – Creating new users with New-AzureADUser

Finally, you'll look at bulk user creation with the Microsoft Graph-based cmdlet `New-MgUser`. It has very similar parameters to the `New-AzureADUser` cmdlet, with the main difference being how the `$PasswordProfile` object is created and that the `AccountEnabled` parameter does not require an argument:

```
$Users = Import-Csv C:\Temp\ImportUsers.csv
$PasswordProfile = @{ Password = "P@ssw0rd123" }
PS C:\> Foreach ($User in $Users) { New-MgUser -UserPrincipalName
$User.UserPrincipalName -GivenName $User.FirstName -Surname $User.
LastName -DisplayName $User.DisplayName -JobTitle $User.JobTitle
-Department $User.Department -UsageLocation $User.UsageLocation
-Country $User.UsageLocation -AccountEnabled -MailNickname $User.
UserPrincipalName.Split("@")[0] -PasswordProfile $PasswordProfile }
```

Figure 2.49 – Creating new users with the New-MgUser cmdlet

As you can see, the flexibility and capability of the PowerShell interface allow you to do far more than what's available in the graphical administration centers—with the trade-off that the parameters and syntax for the various modules can vary greatly.

> **Further Reading**
>
> We have only scratched the surface of describing the capabilities of the various PowerShell modules. You can learn more about all of the available modules and their associated cmdlets and best practices at `https://learn.microsoft.com/en-us/powershell/`.

Summary

In this chapter, you learned some of the basics of administering objects on the Microsoft 365 platform, whether those objects were on-premises or cloud only. Managing identity is a large part of the Microsoft 365 administration experience, so it's important to have a firm grasp on the variety of tools and methods for provisioning, licensing, and updating objects.

In the next chapter, you'll learn how to manage roles in Microsoft 365.

Exam Readiness Drill - Chapter Review Questions

Benchmark Score: 75%

Apart from a solid understanding of key concepts, being able to think quickly under time pressure is a skill that will help you ace your certification exam. That's why, working on these skills early on in your learning journey is key.

Chapter review questions are designed to improve your test-taking skills progressively with each chapter you learn and review your understanding of key concepts in the chapter at the same time. You'll find these at the end of each chapter.

> **Before You Proceed**
>
> You need to unlock these resources before you start using them. Unlocking **takes less than 10 minutes, can be done from any device**, and **needs to be done only once**. Head over to the start of *Chapter 7, Managing Security Reports and Alerts by Using the Microsoft 365 Defender Portal* in this book for instructions on how to unlock them.

To open the **Chapter Review Questions** for this chapter, click the following link: `https://packt.link/MS102E1_CH02`. Or, you can scan the following QR code:

Figure 2.50 – QR code that opens Chapter Review Questions for logged-in users

Once you login, you'll see a page similar to what is shown in *Figure 2.51*:

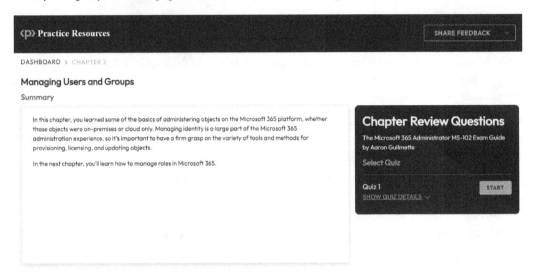

Figure 2.51 – Chapter Review Questions for Chapter 2

Once ready, start the following practice drills, re-attempting the quiz multiple times:

Exam Readiness Drill

For the first 3 attempts, don't worry about the time limit.

ATTEMPT 1

The first time, aim for at least 40%. Look at the answers you got wrong and read the relevant sections in the chapter again to fix your learning gaps.

ATTEMPT 2

The second time, aim for at least 60%. Look at the answers you got wrong and read the relevant sections in the chapter again to fix any remaining learning gaps.

ATTEMPT 3

The third time, aim for at least 75%. Once you score 75% or more, you start working on your timing.

> **Tip**
>
> You may take more than 3 attempts to reach 75%. That's okay. Just review the relevant sections in the chapter till you get there.

Working On Timing

Target: Your aim is to keep the score the same while trying to answer these questions as quickly as possible. Here's an example of how your next attempts should look like:

Attempt	Score	Time Taken
Attempt 5	77%	21 mins 30 seconds
Attempt 6	78%	18 mins 34 seconds
Attempt 7	76%	14 mins 44 seconds

Table 2.1 – Sample timing practice drills on the online platform

> **Note**
>
> The time limits shown in the above table are just examples. Set your own time limits with each attempt based on the time limit of the quiz on the website.

With each new attempt, your score should stay **above 75%** while your time taken to complete should decrease. Repeat as many attempts as you want till you feel confident dealing with the time pressure.

3

Managing Roles in Microsoft 365

In the last chapter, you became familiar with provisioning and managing identities. This chapter will address how to grant those identities roles in the Microsoft 365 platform.

Each of these object types serves a distinct purpose, with one typically better suited to fulfill business requirements than the others.

In this chapter, we're going to look at the following topics as they relate to the MS-102 exam objectives:

- Managing roles in Microsoft 365 and Azure AD
- Managing role groups for Microsoft Defender, Microsoft Purview, and Microsoft 365 workloads
- Managing administrative units
- Planning and implementing privileged identity management

By the end of this chapter, you should be able to describe Azure AD roles and other Microsoft 365 security management concepts. You should also understand how to assign roles.

> **Note**
>
> As has been mentioned elsewhere in this book, Microsoft has recently introduced the umbrella term **Entra** to unify security and identity management products. The product documentation uses both Azure AD and Entra ID terminology, as does this book. While many commercial tenants have been updated to reflect some of the Entra naming conventions, most tenants in the national or sovereign clouds still reflect the old Azure AD branding. For purposes of the exam, you can use the terms **Azure AD** and **Entra ID** interchangeably.

Let's get started!

Managing Roles in Microsoft 365 and Azure AD

Azure AD roles are used to delegate permissions to perform tasks in Azure AD and Microsoft 365. Most people are familiar with the Global Administrator role, as it is the first role that's established when you create a tenant. However, there are dozens of other roles available that can be used to provide a refined level of delegation throughout the environment. As the number of applications and services available in Microsoft 365 has grown, so has the number of security roles.

Roles for applications, services, and functions are intuitively named and generally split into two groups, **Administrator** and **Reader**, though there are some roles that have additional levels of permission associated with them (such as *Printer Technician* or *Attack Simulator Payload Author*).

If you're reading this book chronologically, you'll already be familiar with the **Global Administrator role** (also called the Company Administrator role in some legacy interfaces). If not, you can refer to *Chapter 1, Implementing and Managing a Microsoft 365 Tenant*, to get up to speed. The Global Administrator role is able to administer all parts of the organization, including creating and modifying users or groups and delegating other administrative roles. In most cases, users with the Global Administrator role can access and modify all parts of an individual Microsoft 365 service—for example, editing Exchange transport rules, creating SharePoint Online sites, or setting up directory synchronization.

> **Further Reading**
>
> There are currently over 70 built-in administrative roles specific to Azure AD services and applications. For an up-to-date list of the roles available, see `https://learn.microsoft.com/en-us/azure/active-directory/roles/permissions-reference`.

For the MS-102 exam, you should plan on becoming familiar with the core Microsoft 365 and Azure AD roles:

Role name	Role description
Global Administrator	Can manage all aspects of Azure AD and Microsoft 365 services
Hybrid Identity Administrator	Can manage Azure AD Connect and Azure AD Connect Cloud Sync configuration settings, including Pass-Through Authentication (PTA), Password Hash Synchronization (PHS), Seamless Single Sign-on (Seamless SSO), and federation settings
Billing Administrator	Can perform billing tasks such as updating payment information

Role name	Role description
Compliance Administrator	Can read and manage the compliance configuration and reporting in Azure AD and Microsoft 365
Exchange Administrator	Can manage all aspects of the Exchange Online service
Guest Inviter	Can invite guest users regardless of whether the members can invite guests setting is enabled
Office Apps Administrator	Can manage Office apps, including policy and settings management
Reports Reader	Can read sign-in and audit reports
Security Reader	Can read security information and reports in Azure AD and Office 365
SharePoint Administrator	Can manage all aspects of the SharePoint service
Teams Administrator	Can manage all aspects of the Microsoft Teams service
User Administrator	Can manage all aspects of users and groups, including resetting passwords for limited admins

Table 3.1 – Core Azure AD and Microsoft 365 roles

Planning for Role Assignments

One of the core tenets of security is the use of a **least-privilege model**. Least privilege means delegating the minimum level of permissions to accomplish a particular task. In the context of Microsoft 365 and Azure AD, this translates to using the built-in roles for services, applications, and features where possible instead of granting the Global Administrator role. Limiting the administrative scope for services based on roles is commonly referred to as **role-based access control (RBAC)**.

In order to help organizations plan for a least-privilege deployment, Microsoft currently maintains this list of the least privileged roles required to accomplish certain tasks, grouped by application or content area: `https://learn.microsoft.com/en-us/azure/active-directory/roles/delegate-by-task`.

When planning for role assignments in your organization, you can choose to assign roles directly to users or via a specially designated Azure AD group. If you want to use groups for role assignment, you must configure the `isAssignableToRole` property during the group creation. For example, in *Figure 3.1*, the Azure AD roles cannot be assigned to the group due to the current setting of the **Azure AD roles can be assigned to the group** toggle. To enable roles to be assigned to this group, the toggle will need to be set to **Yes**, thereby setting the `isAssignableToRole` property of the object to `$true` behind the scenes. It cannot be configured afterward. If you make a mistake on this setting for a group, your only option is to delete the group and start over.

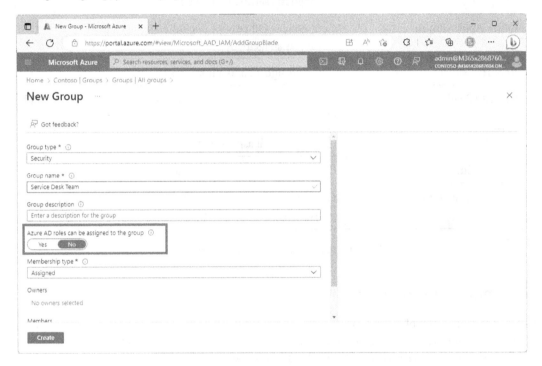

Figure 3.1 – Configuring the isAssignableToRole property on a new group

Azure AD groups that are configured to be role-eligible must have assigned membership. As soon as you move the slider to configure a role-assignable group, the ability to change the membership type to dynamic is grayed out. Role-assignable groups must have assigned membership to prevent unintentionally elevating a user to a privileged role or removing a user's privilege when a group's dynamic membership rules are evaluated.

Managing Roles in the Microsoft 365 Admin Center

Roles can be easily managed within the Microsoft 365 admin center by expanding the navigation menu, expanding **Roles**, and then selecting **Role assignments**, as shown in *Figure 3.2*:

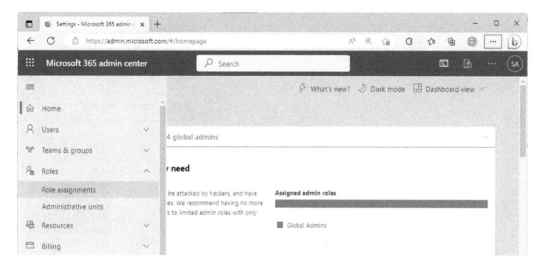

Figure 3.2 – Role assignments

Roles are displayed across four tabs—**Azure AD, Exchange, Intune,** and **Billing**—on the **Role assignments** page, as shown in *Figure 3.3*:

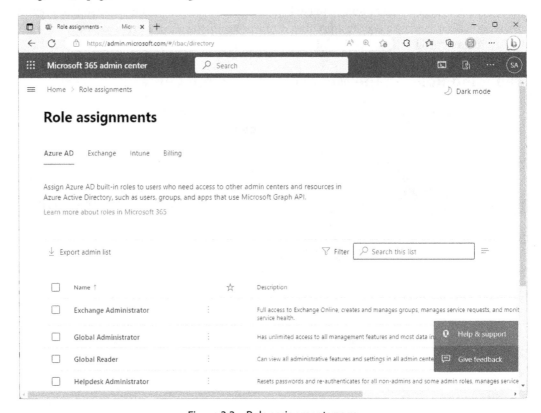

Figure 3.3 – Role assignments page

To add people to a role, simply select the role from the list, choose the **Assigned** tab, and then add either users (click **Add users**) or groups (click **Add groups**) to the particular admin role, as shown in *Figure 3.4*:

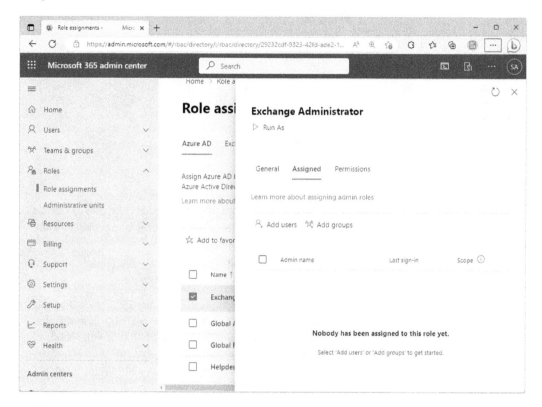

Figure 3.4 – Making role assignments

Depending on the roles being assigned through this interface, you may be able to use Microsoft 365 groups, role-assignable security groups, or mail-enabled security groups.

Managing Role Groups for Microsoft Defender, Microsoft Purview, and Microsoft 365 Workloads

Now that you're familiar with role groups and concepts, let's look at managing roles for some specific workloads and feature areas of Microsoft 365:

- Microsoft Defender
- Microsoft Purview
- Microsoft 365 workloads

You will next look at some of the nuances of managing roles in each of these areas.

Microsoft Defender

All of the Microsoft Defender roles can be administered from the Azure portal (`https://portal.azure.com`). Both the Microsoft 365 Defender and Azure portal interfaces also provide the ability to define custom roles or role groups.

> **Note**
>
> Microsoft 365 Defender also has a new RBAC model available. As of June 2023, the Microsoft 365 Defender RBAC model is in preview and is subject to change. Not all features and rights are present in the new RBAC model and it is not yet suitable for production. If you switch as part of your study program, you may lose out on the opportunity to perform some activities. The exam will focus on the current model that is generally available. You should perform any study exercises with the default RBAC model.

Microsoft 365 Defender users can be configured to use either the global Azure AD roles or custom roles from the Microsoft 365 Defender portal. When using Azure AD's global roles to assign permissions for Microsoft 365 Defender, it's important to note that the Azure AD roles will grant access to multiple workloads.

By default, Global Administrators and Security Administrators have access to the Microsoft 365 Defender features. To delegate administrative duties, you can use custom roles.

To create a custom role, follow these steps:

1. Navigate to the Microsoft 365 Defender portal (`https://security.microsoft.com`) with an account that is either a member of the Global Administrators or Security Administrators group.

2. In the navigation menu, select **Permissions**, as shown in *Figure 3.5*:

Figure 3.5 – Microsoft 365 Defender permissions

3. Click **Create custom role**.

4.   On the **Basics** page, enter a role name and click **Next**.

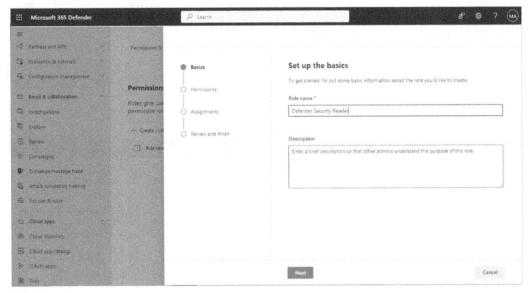

Figure 3.6 – Creating a new custom role

5.   Select permissions from the available permissions groups. For example, select **Security operations**, then choose the **Select all read-only permissions** radio button and click **Apply**, as shown in *Figure 3.7*:

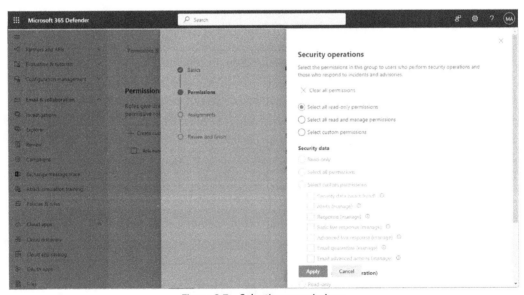

Figure 3.7 – Selecting permissions

6. When you've finished, click **Next**.

7. On the **Assignments** page, click **Add assignment**. See *Figure 3.8*:

Figure 3.8 – Adding user and data assignments

8. On the **Add assignment** page, enter an assignment name for this permissions assignment.

9. On the **Add assignment** page, select which data sources this assignment applies to. You can select **Choose all data sources (including current and future supported data sources)** to make a broadly scoped role or select specific individual data sources.

10. On the **Add assignment** page, select which users or groups will be configured with this assignment. Click **Add** when finished. See *Figure 3.9*:

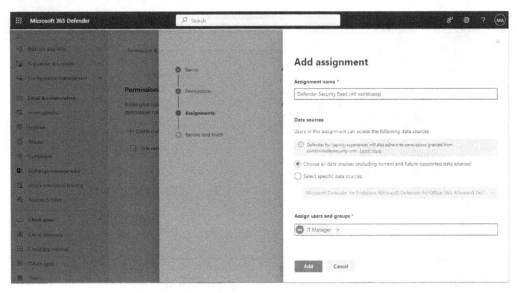

Figure 3.9 – Selecting assignment options

11. Add more assignments if necessary and then click **Next** to continue.

12. On the **Review and finish** page, confirm the selections and then click **Submit**, as shown in *Figure 3.10*:

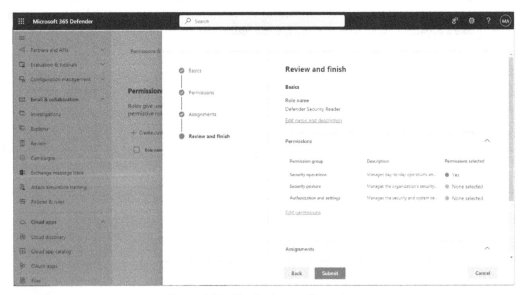

Figure 3.10 – Confirming configuration

Once the roles and assignments have been configured, users can log in and view or manage the features to which they've been assigned.

> **Further Reading**
>
> For more information on the deeper nuances of the Microsoft 365 Defender custom roles and available permissions, see `https://learn.microsoft.com/en-us/microsoft-365/security/defender/custom-permissions-details`.

Next, you'll explore the roles and permissions for Microsoft Purview.

Microsoft Purview

Like Microsoft 365 Defender, Microsoft Purview can leverage both Azure AD global roles as well as more refined role groups specifically designed for Microsoft Purview. Some features (such as eDiscovery) can only be configured using the Purview-specific roles.

You can view the global Azure AD roles by navigating to the Microsoft Purview compliance center, expanding **Roles & scopes**, selecting **Permissions**, and then selecting **Roles** under **Azure AD**. See *Figure 3.11*:

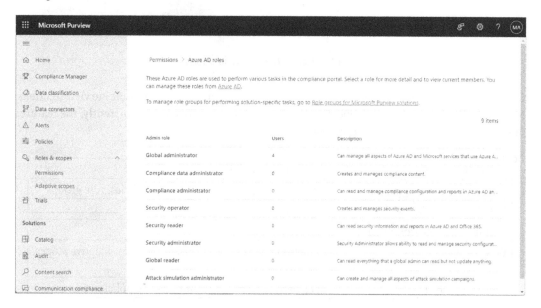

Figure 3.11 – Viewing the Azure AD roles in the Microsoft 365 admin center

By comparison, the Microsoft Purview-specific roles are more detailed. They can be seen in the Microsoft Purview compliance center (https://compliance.microsoft.com) by expanding **Roles & scopes**, selecting **Permissions**, and then selecting **Roles** under **Microsoft Purview solutions**. See *Figure 3.12*:

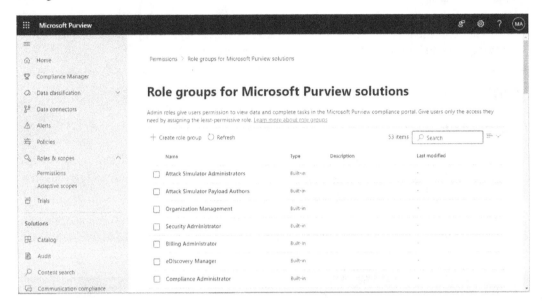

Figure 3.12 – Microsoft Purview solutions roles

Like Microsoft 365 Defender, you can also create custom role groups for Microsoft Purview solutions. Microsoft Purview roles also support scoping with administrative units. Currently, the features described in *Table 3.2* support administrative units:

Solution or feature	Configuration areas
Data lifecycle management	Retention policies, retention label policies, role groups
Data Loss Prevention (DLP)	DLP policies, role groups
Communications compliance	Adaptive scopes
Records management	Retention policies, retention label policies, adaptive scopes, role groups
Sensitivity labels	Sensitivity label policies, auto-labeling policies, role groups

Table 3.2 – Microsoft Purview's support for administrative units

Next, you'll look at managing role groups for Microsoft 365 workloads.

Microsoft 365 Workloads

The core Microsoft 365 workloads, such as Exchange Online and SharePoint Online, have built-in support for a number of role groups.

Figure 3.13 – Microsoft 365 workload roles

In the case of Exchange Online, there are additional management roles that can be assigned within the Exchange admin center's existing RBAC mechanisms. Exchange Online's RBAC model predates the modern Microsoft 365 and Azure role assignments; Exchange Online's roles provide extra security granularity.

While many workloads will have a single role group (such as **Kaizala Administrator** or **SharePoint Administrator**), some, such as Teams, have multiple role groups that can be used to further segment or delegate administration. You can review the current list of roles available in the Microsoft 365 admin center by navigating to the admin center (`https://admin.microsoft.com`), expanding **Roles**, and then selecting **Role assignments**.

Managing Administrative Units

Administrative units are collections of users and devices that can be delegated to certain administrators. In on-premises Active Directory, you may choose to delegate control of administrative functions using the **Delegation of Control wizard** in **Active Directory Users and Computers** or the **Active Directory Administration Center**. Unlike on-premises Active Directory, Azure AD is not hierarchical. Delegation must be achieved by defining boundaries and then controlling which users or devices are placed inside the boundaries.

Administrative units can be role-scoped—that is to say, administrators can both be granted administrative roles (such as Helpdesk Administrator) as well as be limited to administrative tasks only for assigned administrative units.

Creating Administrative Units

In the following example, an administrative unit called *California* (used to hold users in that region) is created. During the creation, administrators are configured to perform role-scoped activities inside that administrative unit:

1. Navigate to the Microsoft 365 admin center (`https://admin.microsoft.com`) and log in with Global Administrator credentials.

2. Expand **Roles | Role assignments** and click **Administrative units**.

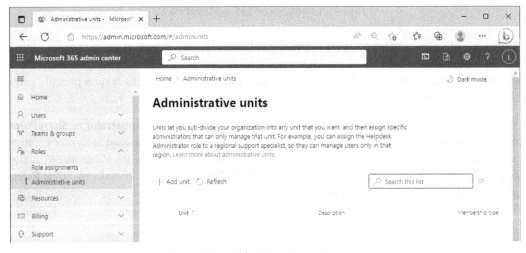

Figure 3.14 – Administrative units page

3. Click **Add unit**.

4. On the **Basics** page, as shown in *Figure 3.15*, enter a name and description and click **Next**.

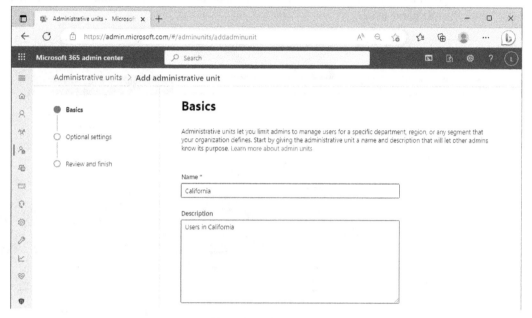

Figure 3.15 – Basics page

5. On the **Optional settings | Add members** page, as shown in *Figure 3.16*, you can add members to the administrative unit or click **Next** to proceed.

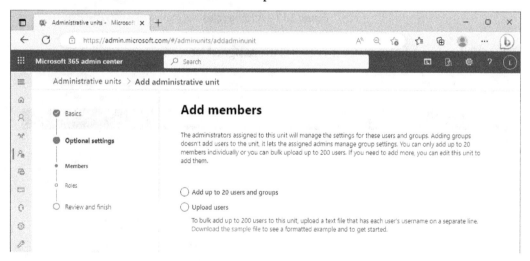

Figure 3.16 – Add members page

6. On the **Assign admins to scoped roles** page, as shown in *Figure 3.17*, review the roles listed. Not all roles can be scoped to administrative units (as it's a relatively new feature and not all roles support it). In this example, select the checkbox next to **User Administrator** and then click the role name itself.

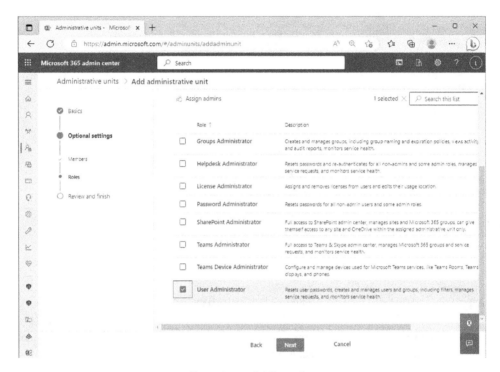

Figure 3.17 – Adding roles

7. On the **User Administrator** flyout, click the **Assigned** tab as shown in *Figure 3.18*:

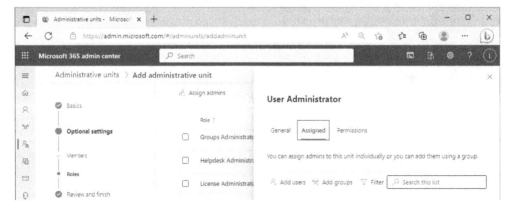

Figure 3.18 – User Administrator flyout

8. Click **Add users** or **Add groups** to assign administrators to this role. Click **Close** when you've finished.

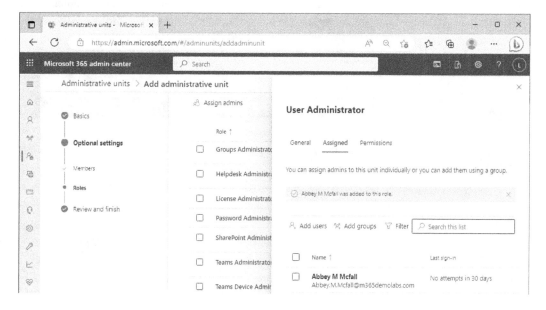

Figure 3.19 – Adding users to role

9. On the **Assign admins to scoped roles** page, click **Next**.

10. On the **Review and finish** page, review your selections, make any changes, and then click **Add**.

11. Click **Done** to return to the **Administrative units** page.

One of the features of role-scoped administration is being able to limit what users or objects can be impacted by a particular administrator. As you noticed during the configuration, only a subset of the roles available in the tenant honor administrative unit scoping.

Viewing and Updating Administrative Units

After creating the administrative units, you can review them and modify their members and administrators from either the Azure portal or the Microsoft 365 admin center under **Roles | Administrative units**. See *Figure 3.20*:

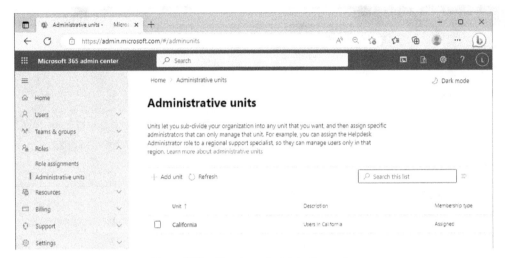

Figure 3.20 – Viewing administrative units

By selecting an administrative unit in the Microsoft 365 admin center, you can view or change its membership.

> **Note**
>
> The user interface for managing administrative units isn't consistent. From the Microsoft 365 admin center, you can view an administrative unit and add users or groups to it, but you can't do the inverse of navigating to a user or group object and adding it to an administrative unit. You can, however, perform both types of membership operations in the Azure portal.

While you can assign groups to administrative units, it does not automatically add the group member objects to the administrative scope—it only enables managing the properties of the group. You need to add the members of the group to the administrative unit directly in order for them to be in scope.

> **Note**
>
> **Dynamic administrative units** are a preview feature that allows you to use filters and queries to automatically populate administrative units. Like dynamic groups, dynamic administrative units can only have one object type (users or devices). Dynamic administrative units can only be configured in the Azure portal at this time.

As you define administrative structures and delegation for your organization, you'll need to understand the limits of scoping controls. For instance, assigning an administrator to both an administrative unit as well as an Exchange or SharePoint Administrator role means that while they can only make modifications to users in their administrative unit, they can potentially make changes to application settings that affect users tenant-wide.

> **Note**
>
> Some applications, such as Exchange Online, support additional RBAC scoping controls to offer finer-grained service administration.

Planning and Implementing Privileged Identity Management

Privileged Identity Management (**PIM**) is the logical next step in RBAC and least-privilege identity management. While RBAC addresses *what amount of privilege is needed to accomplish a task*, PIM addresses the idea of *how long this level of privilege is required.*

Sometimes called **Just-in-Time** (**JIT**) access, PIM is a feature that allows users to request elevation to Azure AD roles or resources for limited periods of time to perform administrative tasks. At the end of the period, the roles and privileges are revoked, returning the user account to their pre-elevation access rights.

> **Note**
>
> PIM is an Azure AD Premium P2 or Enterprise Mobility + Security E5 feature.

PIM has a few key terms that you'll need to understand:

- **Assignment**: This describes *how the user is granted the role*. In the case of **Eligible**, it means a user has to perform an action to use the role, such as requesting elevation or asking for approval. In the case of **Active**, it means the user doesn't have to do anything to request the role.

- **Duration**: This describes *how long a particular assignment is active*. It can be **permanent** (no expiration date) or **time-bound**, meaning it will be active only for a specific period of time.

For example, John is a full-time employee and needs to periodically be able to perform functions in the Exchange Administrator role. His assignment would be **Eligible**, while the duration would be **permanent**.

In another example, Kay is a temporary worker whose contract ends on July 31. She periodically needs to be elevated to be able to perform user administration functions. Her assignment would be **Eligible**, while the duration would have an end date of July 31.

PIM for Azure AD roles and Azure resources can be configured in the Azure portal on the **Identity Governance** blade, as shown in *Figure 3.12*:

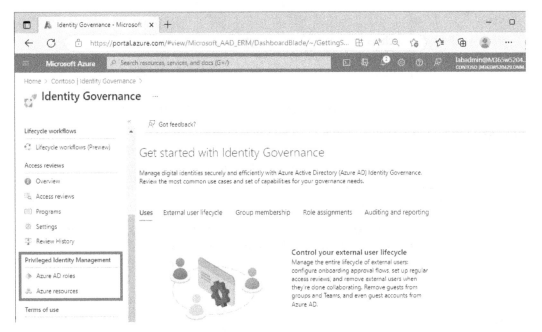

Figure 3.21 – Privileged Identity Management

Next, you'll look at configuring a simple assignment.

Creating a Role Assignment

You can configure PIM for a role by following this procedure:

1. Navigate to the Azure portal (`https://portal.azure.com`). Enter `Identity Governance` into the search bar and select the **Identity Governance** option.

2. Under **Privileged Identity Management**, select **Azure AD roles** (or **Microsoft Entra roles**).

3. Under **Manage**, select **Roles**. See *Figure 3.22*:

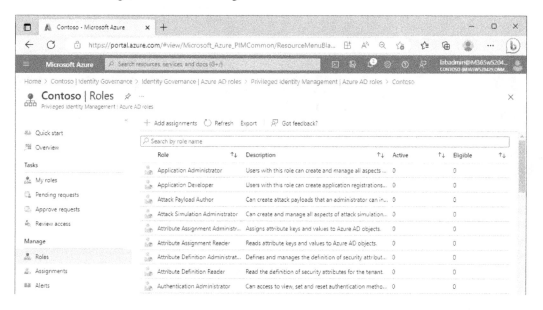

Figure 3.22 – Role assignments

4. Select the role you wish to configure an assignment for, such as the **Exchange Administrator** role.

5. Click **Add assignments**.

6. On the **Membership** tab of the **Add assignments** page, under **Select member(s)**, click **No member selected** to bring up the **Select a member** flyout.

7. On the **Select a member** flyout, choose one or more members and click **Select**, as shown in *Figure 3.23*:

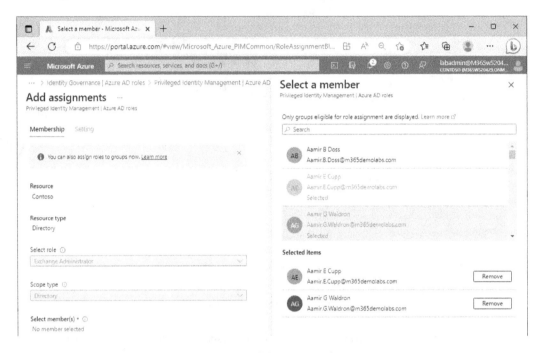

Figure 3.23 – Selecting members

8. On the **Add assignments** page, click **Next**.

9. On the **Setting** tab of the **Add assignments** page, select an assignment type, such as **Eligible**. In this instance, if you want the users to be eligible to request elevation for the duration of the time period their account is enabled, select **Permanently eligible**.

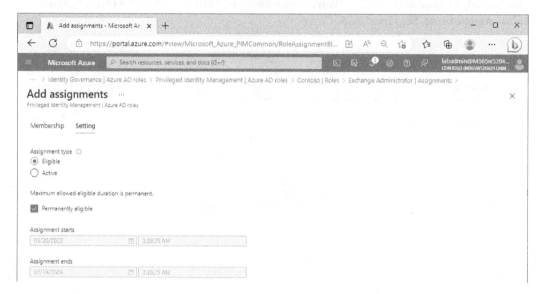

Figure 3.24 – Configuring assignment type and eligibility duration

10. Click **Assign**.

From this point, the users that you have selected can activate their role assignment from the Azure portal.

Reviewing Role Assignments

You can review all of the assignments that you've created in the Azure portal. To view the role assignments, navigate to the **Identity Governance** blade and then select **Azure AD roles | Azure AD roles | Assignments**. See *Figure 3.25*:

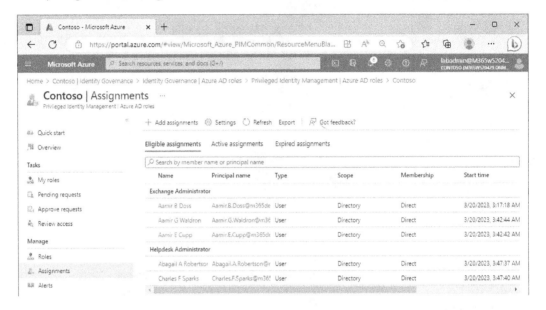

Figure 3.25 – Viewing role assignments

On the **Eligible assignments** tab, assignments are listed under their respective Azure AD role. The **Active assignments** tab lists individuals with various role assignments, including their end dates and whether they're permanent. Review *Figure 3.26* for an example of active assignments.

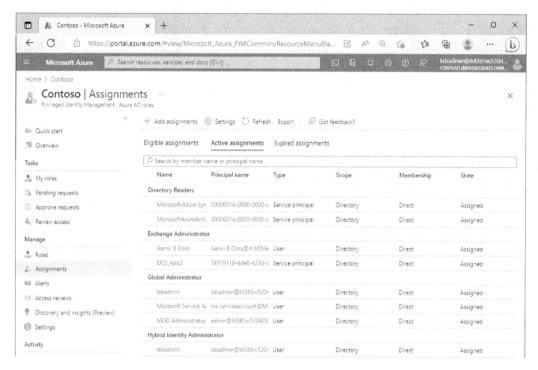

Figure 3.26 – Viewing active assignments

Notice that the assignments can include both users as well as application security principals.

Alerting

PIM also has built-in alerting functions. The alerts are designed to provide notifications if certain risk conditions are detected. Several of the role alerts have sliders for notifications that can be used to tune them for your organization. Alerts are accessed through the Azure portal by going to the **Identity Governance** | **Microsoft Entra roles** | **Alerts** page. By clicking on the gear icon, you can see all of the pre-configured alerts and edit them to your needs, as shown in *Figure 3.27*:

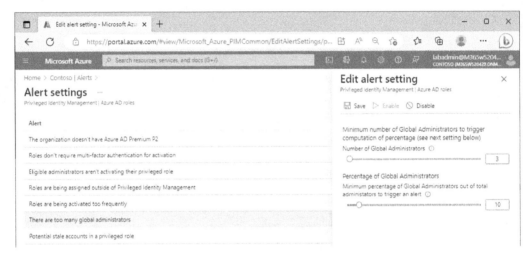

Figure 3.27 – Viewing PIM Alert settings

Note

Users can only edit and manage pre-configured alerts; creating new alerts is not an option.

PIM is a tool to help reduce the surface area of your organization. By reducing the number of accounts with standing privileges, you can greatly reduce the risks presented by compromised administration accounts.

Summary

In this chapter, you learned about what it means to manage Azure AD from a least-privilege perspective. Reducing the scope and privileges used to administer an environment can greatly reduce the possible impacts of administrative actions—whether they are unintentional or targeted attacks by malicious users.

The next chapter will explore authentication options and configurations in the Microsoft 365 platform.

Exam Readiness Drill - Chapter Review Questions

Benchmark Score: 75%

Apart from a solid understanding of key concepts, being able to think quickly under time pressure is a skill that will help you ace your certification exam. That's why, working on these skills early on in your learning journey is key.

Chapter review questions are designed to improve your test-taking skills progressively with each chapter you learn and review your understanding of key concepts in the chapter at the same time. You'll find these at the end of each chapter.

> **Before You Proceed**
>
> You need to unlock these resources before you start using them. Unlocking **takes less than 10 minutes, can be done from any device**, and **needs to be done only once**. Head over to the start of *Chapter 7, Managing Security Reports and Alerts by Using the Microsoft 365 Defender Portal* in this book for instructions on how to unlock them.

To open the **Chapter Review Questions** for this chapter, click the following link: `https://packt.link/MS102E1_CH03`. Or, you can scan the following QR code:

Figure 3.28 – QR code that opens Chapter Review Questions for logged-in users

Once you login, you'll see a page similar to what is shown in *Figure 3.29*:

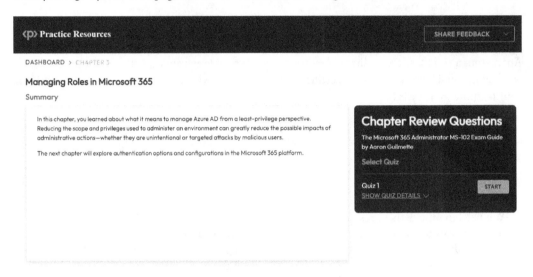

Figure 3.29 – Chapter Review Questions for Chapter 3

Once ready, start the following practice drills, re-attempting the quiz multiple times:

Exam Readiness Drill

For the first 3 attempts, don't worry about the time limit.

ATTEMPT 1

The first time, aim for at least 40%. Look at the answers you got wrong and read the relevant sections in the chapter again to fix your learning gaps.

ATTEMPT 2

The second time, aim for at least 60%. Look at the answers you got wrong and read the relevant sections in the chapter again to fix any remaining learning gaps.

ATTEMPT 3

The third time, aim for at least 75%. Once you score 75% or more, you start working on your timing.

> **Tip**
> You may take more than 3 attempts to reach 75%. That's okay. Just review the relevant sections in the chapter till you get there.

Working On Timing

Target: Your aim is to keep the score the same while trying to answer these questions as quickly as possible. Here's an example of how your next attempts should look like:

Attempt	Score	Time Taken
Attempt 5	77%	21 mins 30 seconds
Attempt 6	78%	18 mins 34 seconds
Attempt 7	76%	14 mins 44 seconds

Table 3.3 – Sample timing practice drills on the online platform

> **Note**
> The time limits shown in the above table are just examples. Set your own time limits with each attempt based on the time limit of the quiz on the website.

With each new attempt, your score should stay **above 75%** while your time taken to complete should decrease. Repeat as many attempts as you want till you feel confident dealing with the time pressure.

4

Implementing and Managing Identity Synchronization with Azure AD

As you've already learned, Microsoft 365 relies on identity. When moving to Microsoft 365, many organizations may want to use their existing on-premises identity as a basis for populating Azure AD.

In this chapter, you will step through the basic configuration and troubleshooting tasks for Azure AD Connect and Azure AD Connect Cloud Sync.

This chapter covers the following exam objectives:

- Preparing for identity synchronization by using IdFix
- Configuring and managing directory synchronization by using Azure AD Connect Cloud Sync
- Monitoring synchronization by using Azure AD Connect Health
- Troubleshooting Azure AD Connect synchronization
- Configuring and managing directory synchronization by using Azure AD Connect
- Troubleshooting Azure AD Connect Cloud Sync synchronization

The topics in this chapter will help you understand *what the directory synchronization options are* and *what it takes to deploy and manage directory synchronization.*

> **Note**
>
> As has been mentioned elsewhere in this book, Microsoft has recently introduced the umbrella term **Entra** to unify security and identity management products. The product documentation uses both the Azure AD and Entra ID terminology, as does this book. While many commercial tenants have been updated to reflect some of the Entra naming conventions, most tenants in the national or sovereign clouds still reflect the older Azure AD branding. For the purposes of the exam, you can use the terms **Azure AD** and **Entra ID** interchangeably.

Azure AD Connect Cloud Sync is the next evolution of Microsoft's directory synchronization product. While it does not yet have full parity with Azure AD Connect features, Azure AD Connect Cloud Sync (sometimes referred to as just **Cloud Sync**) can provide additional features and benefits where Azure AD Connect cannot:

- While Azure AD Connect requires on-premises connectivity between the Azure AD Connect server and all connected forests, Azure AD Connect Cloud Sync can import identities from forests that do not have Site-to-Site connectivity. This makes cloud sync advantageous when dealing with mergers and acquisitions as well as organizations that have multiple, disconnected business units.

- It provides lightweight on-premises provisioning agents with cloud-managed sync configuration. Multiple sync agents can be installed to provide fault tolerance and redundancy for password hash synchronization customers.

- However, cloud sync provides fewer overall features. The following list identifies the core feature gaps:

- Cloud sync does not support on-premises **Lightweight Directory Access Protocol (LDAP)** directories.

- Cloud sync does not support device objects like workstations or servers.

- Pass-through authentication is unavailable with cloud sync.

- Advanced filtering and scoping (such as by using object attributes) are not supported with cloud sync, nor are advanced configurations of custom synchronization rules.

- Azure AD Connect Cloud Sync does not support more than 150,000 objects per AD domain, nor does it support **Azure AD Domain Services (AADDS)**. Since cloud sync is limited to 150,000 objects, it does not support large groups (up to 250,000 members), though it can support groups with up to 50,000 members.

- Cloud sync does not support Exchange hybrid writeback or group writeback.

- Cloud sync cannot merge object attributes from multiple source domains.

As you can see from the list, Azure AD Connect Cloud Sync is potentially a good option for organizations that don't have more than 150,000 objects in any single domain, don't require object or property writeback, and don't need to heavily customize synchronization rules.

> **Further Reading**
>
> A full comparison of features is available at `https://learn.microsoft.com/en-us/azure/active-directory/cloud-sync/what-is-cloud-sync`.

Preparing for Identity Synchronization by Using IdFix

Since the purpose of Azure AD Connect and Azure AD Connect Cloud Sync is to synchronize user, group, contact, and device objects to Azure AD, you'll need to make sure your objects meet the minimum requirements.

Microsoft has guidance surrounding the preparation of user objects for synchronization. Some attributes (specifically those that are used to identify the user throughout the system) must be unique throughout the organization. For example, you cannot have two users that have the same `userPrincipalName` value.

The following attributes should be prepared before synchronizing the directory to Azure AD:

Attribute	Constraints	Must be unique	Required
`displayName`	≤ 256 characters		X
`givenName`	≤ 64 characters		
`mail`	≤ 113 characters ≤ 64 characters before the @ symbol Adheres to the RFC 822/2822/5322 standards	X	
`mailNickName`	≤ 64 characters Cannot start with a . Cannot contain certain characters such as &	X	
`proxyAddresses`	≤ 256 characters per value No spaces Diacritical marks are prohibited	X	
`sAMAccountName`	≤ 20 characters	X	X

Attribute	Constraints	Must be unique	Required
sn	≤ 64 characters		
targetAddress	≤ 256 characters No spaces Includes a prefix (such as SMTP:). Value after prefix adheres to the RFC 822/2822/5322 standards	X	
userPrincipalName	≤ 113 characters Must use a routable domain name Unicode characters are converted to underscores	X	X

Table 4.1 – Azure AD Connect attributes

As you can see, very few attributes are actually required for an object to synchronize. Each attribute that is synchronized has some core requirements around formatting, including length and allowed characters. Several attributes (such as mailNickname, userPrincipalName, mail, sAMAccountName, and proxyAddresses) must contain unique values—that is, no other object in the directory of any type can share the value.

> **Further Reading**
>
> You can learn more about the required and supported values for attributes at https://learn.microsoft.com/en-us/powershell/module/exchange/set-mailbox and https://learn.microsoft.com/en-us/microsoft-365/enterprise/prepare-for-directory-synchronization.

IdFix is Microsoft's tool for detecting common issues with on-premises AD identity data. While it doesn't fix all possible errors, it is able to identify and remediate data formatting errors so that objects have valid data to synchronize.

IdFix supports the following features:

- Transaction rollback
- Verbose logging
- Exporting data to CSV and LDF formats for offline review and editing

To get started with the tool, follow these steps:

1. Navigate to `https://aka.ms/idfix`.

2. Scroll to the bottom of the page and click **Next**.

3. Review the prerequisites for the tool. Scroll to the bottom of the page and click **Next**.

4. Click **setup.exe** to download the file and start the installation.

5. After the installation wizard starts, click **Install**.

6. Acknowledge the IdFix privacy statement by clicking **OK**.

7. IdFix, by default, targets the entire directory. You can select **Settings** (the gear icon) to change the options for IdFix. You can edit the **Filter** option to scope to certain object types. You can also select **Search Base** to specify a starting point for IdFix to begin its query. After modifying any settings, click **OK**, as shown in *Figure 4.1*:

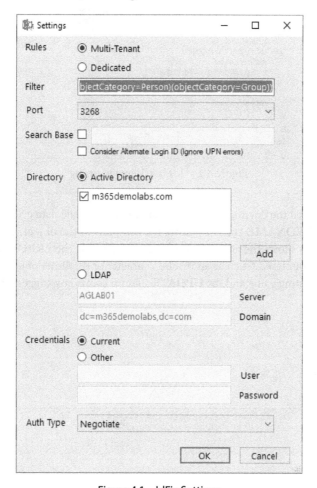

Figure 4.1 – IdFix Settings

8.   Click **Query** to connect to Active Directory and begin the analysis.

Schema Warning

If you receive a schema warning, such as the one in *Figure 4.2*, you can click **Yes** to proceed or **No** to return to the IdFix tool. The schema warning is generally presented when attributes are present in the AD schema but have not been marked for replication (usually because Exchange Server has not been installed or replication hasn't been completed successfully in your organization for an extended period of time). If you receive this error, you should check to ensure that you have at least run the Exchange Server setup with the `/PrepareSchema` and `/PrepareAD` switches and have validated that AD replication is working correctly.

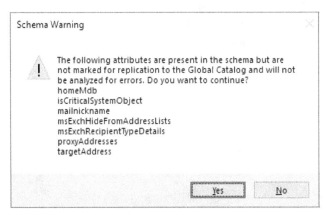

Figure 4.2 – IdFix schema warning

After IdFix has analyzed the environment, results are returned to the data grid, shown in *Figure 4.3*. The **DISTINGUISHEDNAME** column shows the full path to the object in question, while the **ATTRIBUTE** column shows the attribute or property impacted. The **ERROR** column shows what type of error was encountered (such as an invalid character or duplicate object value). The **VALUE** column shows the existing value and the **UPDATE** column shows any suggested value.

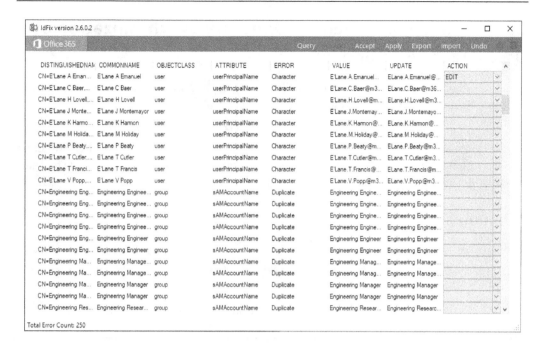

Figure 4.3 – IdFix data grid

After you have investigated an object, you can choose to accept the suggested value in the **UPDATE** column (if one exists). You can also choose to either enter or edit a new value in the **UPDATE** column.

Once you're done investigating or updating an object, you can use the dropdown in the **ACTION** column to mark an object:

- Selecting **EDIT** indicates you want to configure the object attribute with the value in the **UPDATE** column

- Selecting **COMPLETE** indicates you want to leave the object as it is

- Selecting **REMOVE** instructs IdFix to clear the offending attribute

In addition, you can select **Accept** to accept any suggested values in the **UPDATE** column. Choosing this option will configure all objects with a value in the **UPDATE** column to **EDIT**, indicating that the changes are ready to be processed.

Once you have configured an action for each object, select **Apply** to instruct IdFix to make the changes.

IdFix will process the changes. Transactions are written to a log that can be imported and used to roll back any mistakes.

Once you have ensured that your on-premises directory data is ready to synchronize to Azure AD, you can deploy and configure one of the Azure AD Connect synchronization products.

Configuring and Managing Directory Synchronization by Using Azure AD Connect

Azure AD Connect has a long history, originally starting as **DirSync** to support the deployment of Microsoft **Business Productivity Online Suite** (**BPOS**) in 2007.

If you are familiar with **Microsoft Identity Manager** (**MIM**), you'll notice a lot of similarities shared with the current Azure AD Connect platform. Azure AD Connect (rebranded as Microsoft Entra Connect) allows you to connect to multiple directory sources and provision those objects to Azure Active Directory.

Planning and Sizing

Depending on your organization's requirements for onboarding to Microsoft 365, as well as additional features or services that are included with your subscription, you may want (or need) to enable or configure additional Azure AD Connect features.

Table 4.2 illustrates the features that can be enabled through an Azure AD Connect setup:

Feature	Description
Device writeback	Synchronizes Azure AD-joined devices back to on-premises Active Directory
Directory extensions	Enables the synchronization of additional on-premises attributes
Federation	Enables authentication federation with Microsoft AD Federation Services (FS) or PingFederate
Hybrid Azure AD join	Enables on-premises domain-joined devices to be synchronized and automatically joined to Azure AD
Password hash synchronization	Enables the hash of an on-premises password to be synchronized to Azure AD; can be used for authentication, a backup option for authentication, or leaked credential detection
Pass-through authentication	Authentication method where passwords are validated on-premises through the Azure AD Connect service's connection to Azure Service Bus
Unified group writeback	Enables cloud-based Microsoft 365 groups to be written back to on-premises Active Directory

Table 4.2 – Azure AD Connect features

There are several additional features available post-installation for Azure AD Connect, such as managing **duplicate attribute resiliency** and **user principal name soft-matching**, both of which are used to manage how Azure AD handles conflicts and connecting cloud accounts to on-premises accounts.

> **Further Reading**
>
> More detailed information about Azure AD Connect's optional features, such as duplicate attribute resiliency, is available here: `https://learn.microsoft.com/en-us/azure/active-directory/hybrid/how-to-connect-syncservice-features`.

Installing the Synchronization Service

The first step to deploying Azure AD Connect is gathering the requirements of your environment. These requirements can impact the prerequisites for deployment (such as additional memory or a standalone SQL Server environment). As part of the planning process, you'll also want to identify which sign-in method will be employed (password hash synchronization, pass-through authentication, or federation).

> **Exam Tip**
>
> To perform the express installation, you'll need Enterprise Administrator credentials to the on-premises **Active Directory forest** so that the installer can create a service account and delegate the correct permissions. You'll also need an account that has either the Global Administrator or Hybrid Identity Administrator role in Azure AD, which Azure AD Connect will use to create a cloud sync service account.

With that information in hand, it's time to start deploying Azure AD Connect:

1. On the server where Azure AD Connect will be deployed, download the latest version of the Azure AD Connect setup files (`https://aka.ms/aad-connect`) and launch the installer.

2. Agree to the installation terms and select **Continue**. See *Figure 4.4*:

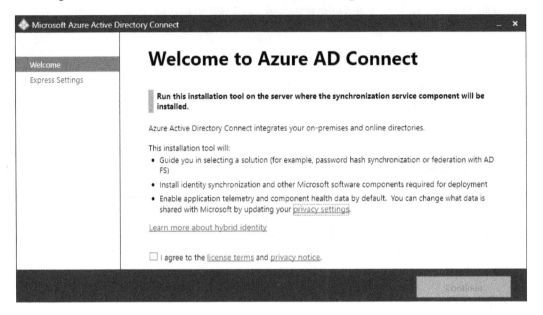

Figure 4.4 – Azure AD Connect welcome page

3. Review the **Express Settings** page, as shown in *Figure 4.5*. You can choose **Customize** if you want to configure Azure AD Connect to use pass-through or federated authentication methods, group-based filtering, or a custom SQL Server installation. *While the sign-in methods and other features can be changed after installation, it is not possible to enable group-based filtering or change the SQL Server location after setup.*

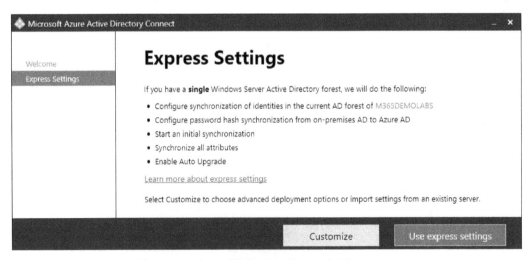

Figure 4.5 – Azure AD Connect Express Settings page

Installation Notes

If you have other domains in your Active Directory forest, they must all be reachable from the Azure AD Connect server or installation will fail. You can perform a custom installation to specify which domains to include in synchronization.

4. On the **Connect to Azure AD** page, enter credentials for either the Global Administrator or Hybrid Identity Administrator role in Azure AD. Click **Next**.

5. On the **Connect to AD DS** page, enter Enterprise Administrator credentials and click **Next**.

6. Verify the configuration settings. By default, the Exchange hybrid scenario is not enabled. If you have an on-premises Exchange environment that you will be migrating to Microsoft 365, select the **Exchange hybrid deployment** option to include the Exchange-specific attributes. If you want to perform additional configuration tasks prior to synchronizing users, clear the **Start the synchronization process when configuration completes.** checkbox.

Figure 4.6 – Azure AD Connect Ready to configure page

7. Click **Install**.

8.   Review the **Configuration complete** page, as shown in *Figure 4.7*, and click **Exit**:

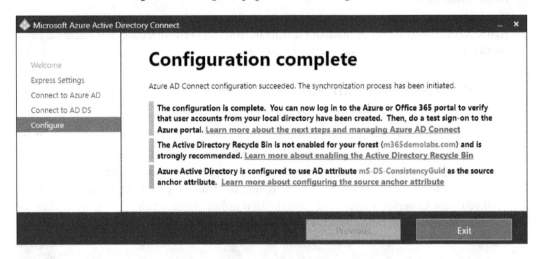

Figure 4.7 – Azure AD Connect Configuration complete page

If you selected the **Start the synchronization process when configuration completes** checkbox, you can review the Azure AD portal to verify that users have been synchronized.

Configuring Azure AD Connect Filters

If you need to exclude objects from Azure AD Connect's synchronization scope, you can do that through a number of different methods:

- Domain and organizational unit-based filtering
- Group-based filtering
- Attribute-based filtering

Let's quickly examine these.

Domain and Organizational Unit-Based Filtering

With this method, you can deselect large portions of your directory by modifying the list of domains or organizational units that are selected for synchronization. While there are several ways to do this, the easiest way is through the **Azure AD Connect setup and configuration tool**:

1. To launch the Azure AD Connect configuration tool, double-click the Azure AD Connect icon on the desktop of the server where Azure AD Connect is installed. After it launches, click **Configure**.

2. On the **Additional tasks** page, as shown in *Figure 4.8*, select **Customize synchronization options** and then click **Next**.

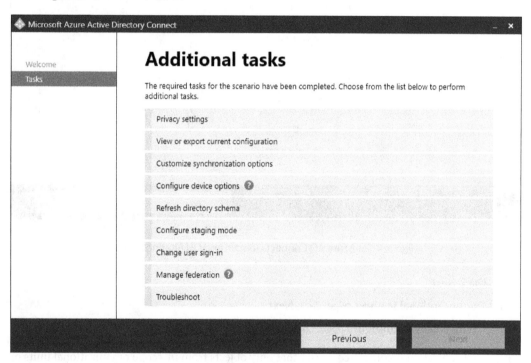

Figure 4.8 – Additional tasks page

3. On the **Connect to Azure AD** page, enter credentials for either the Global Administrator or Hybrid Identity Administrator role and click **Next**.

4. On the **Connect your directories** page, click **Next**.

5. On the **Domain and OU filtering** page, as shown in *Figure 4.9*, select the **Sync selected domains and OUs** radio button and then select or clear objects to include or exclude from synchronization.

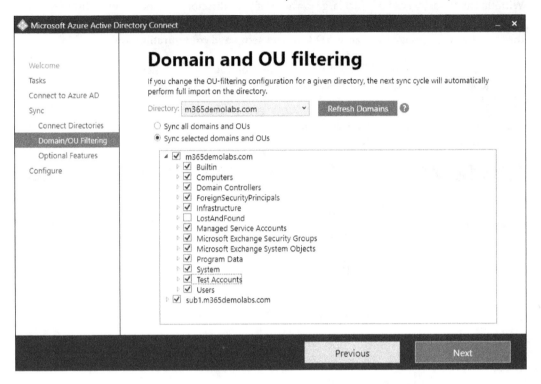

Figure 4.9 – Azure AD Connect Domain and OU filtering page

6. Click **Next**.

7. On the **Optional features** page, click **Next**.

8. On the **Ready to configure** page, click **Configure**.

After synchronization is completed, verify that only objects from in-scope organizational units or domains are present in Azure Active Directory.

Group-Based Filtering

Azure AD Connect only supports the configuration of **group-based filtering** if you choose to customize the Azure AD Connect setup. Group-based filtering is not available if you perform an express installation.

If you've chosen a custom installation, you can choose to limit the synchronization scope to a single group. On the **Filter users and devices** page of the configuration wizard, select the default radio button, **Synchronize all users and devices**, to continue without group filtering. You can also choose the **Synchronize selected** radio button and then enter the name or **distinguishedName (DN)** of a group that contains the users and devices to be synchronized.

Figure 4.10 – Filter users and devices page

With group-based filtering, only direct members of the group are synchronized. Users, groups, contacts, or devices nested inside other groups are not resolved or synchronized.

> **Note**
>
> Microsoft recommends group-based filtering for piloting purposes only.

Attribute-Based Filtering

Another way to prevent objects from being synchronized to Azure AD is using an **attribute filter**. This advanced method requires creating a custom synchronization rule in the **Azure AD Connect Synchronization Rules Editor**.

To create an attribute-based filtering rule, select an attribute that isn't currently being used by your organization for another purpose. You can use this attribute as a scoping filter to exclude objects.

The following procedure can be used to create a simple filtering rule:

1. On the server running Azure AD Connect, launch the Synchronization Rules Editor.

2. Under **Direction**, select **Inbound** and then click **Add new rule**. See *Figure 4.11*:

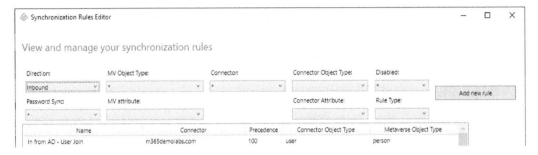

Figure 4.11 – Synchronization rules editor

3. Provide a name and description for the rule.

4. Under **Connected System**, select the object that represents your on-premises Active Directory forest.

5. Under **Connected System Object Type**, select **user**.

6. Under **Metaverse Object Type**, select **person**.

7. Under **Link Type**, select **Join**.

8. In the **Precedence** text field, enter an unused number (such as 50) , as shown in *Figure 4.12*. Click **Next**.

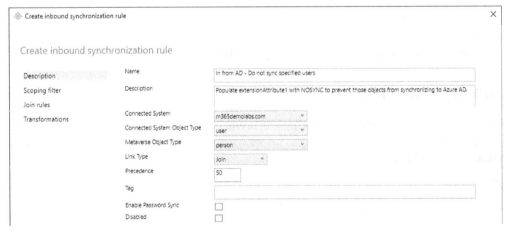

Figure 4.12 – Creating a new inbound synchronization rule

9. On the **Scoping filter** page, click **Add group** and then click **Add clause**.

10. Under **Attribute**, select **extensionAttribute1** (or whichever unused attribute you have selected).

11. Under **Operator**, select **EQUAL**.

12. In the **Value** text field, enter NOSYNC, as shown in *Figure 4.13* and then click **Next**.

Figure 4.13 – Configuring a scoping filter for extensionAttribute1

13. On the **Join rules** page, click **Next** without adding any parameters.

14. On the **Transformations** page, click **Add transformation**.

15. Under **FlowType**, select **Constant**.

16. Under **Target Attribute**, select **cloudFiltered**.

17. In the **Source** text field, enter the value True. Click **Add**.

Figure 4.14 – Adding a transformation for the cloudFiltered attribute

18. Acknowledge the warning that a full import and synchronization cycle will be required by clicking **OK**. See *Figure 4.15*:

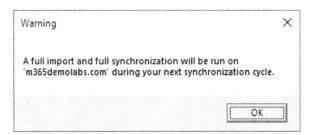

Figure 4.15 – Warning for full import and synchronization

After modifying the synchronization rule, a full import and full synchronization is required. You don't have to perform any special steps, however; Azure AD Connect is aware of the update and will automatically perform the necessary full imports and synchronizations.

Monitoring Synchronization by Using Azure AD Connect Health

Azure AD Connect Health is a premium feature of the Azure AD license. Azure AD Connect Health has separate agent features for Azure AD Connect, Azure AD Health for **Directory Services** (**DS**), and **Azure AD Health for AD FS**.

Azure AD Connect Health

You can browse the Azure AD Connect Health portal at `https://aka.ms/aadconnecthealth`. From there, you will be able to view basic details about your environment as well as obtain agent installation packages. See *Figure 4.16*:

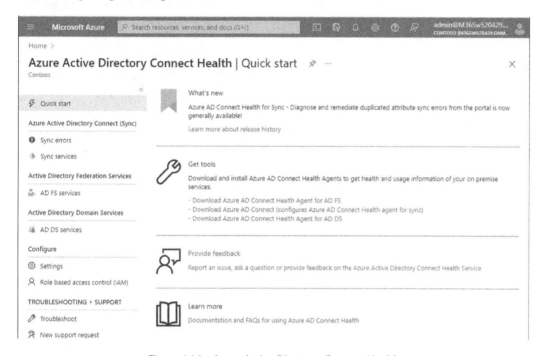

Figure 4.16 – Azure Active Directory Connect Health

While **Azure AD Connect Health Agent for Sync** is included in the Azure AD Connect installation, the health agents for DS and AD FS are separate installations and must be downloaded separately:

- **Azure AD Connect Health Agent for DS**:
  `https://go.microsoft.com/fwlink/?LinkID=820540`

- **Azure AD Connect Health Agent for AD FS**:
  `https://go.microsoft.com/fwlink/?LinkID=518973`

If you do not have AD FS deployed in your environment, you do not need to deploy the AD FS agents.

Azure AD Connect Health for Sync

The core health product, Azure AD Connect Health for Sync, shows the current health of your synchronization environment, including object synchronization problems and data-related errors.

You can view the health status and identified errors by selecting **Sync errors** under **Azure Active Directory Connect (Sync)** in the Azure AD Connect Health portal (`https://aka.ms/aadconnecthealth`), as shown in *Figure 4.17*:

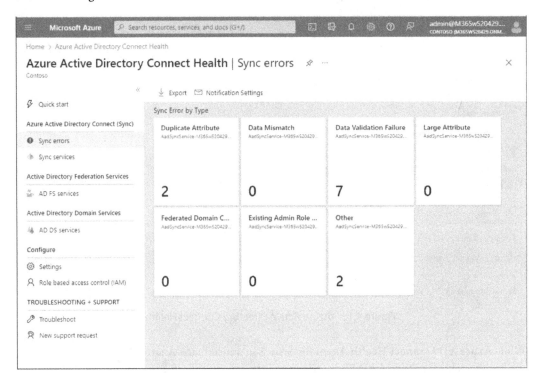

Figure 4.17 – Azure AD Connect Health Sync errors

Selecting an error type will allow you to drill down into individual errors. *Figure 4.18* shows an example where Azure AD Connect Health has detected two objects with the same address:

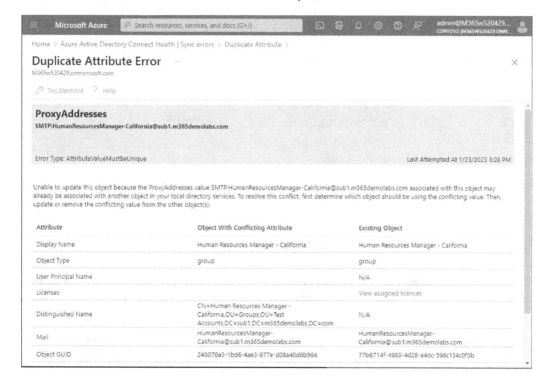

Figure 4.18 – Azure AD Connect Health error details

You can use this information to identify and troubleshoot on-premises objects.

Azure AD Connect Health for Directory Services

Microsoft recommends deploying Azure AD Connect Health for DS agents on all domain controllers you want to monitor, or at least one for each domain.

The Azure AD Connect Health agent deployment is relatively straightforward, asking only for credentials to complete the installation. Once the installation is complete, you can review details about your domain controller's health in the Azure AD Connect Health portal at `https://aka.ms/aadconnecthealth`.

From the **Azure AD Connect Health** page, under **Active Directory Domain Services**, select **AD DS services**, as shown in *Figure 4.19*, and then select a domain to view its details:

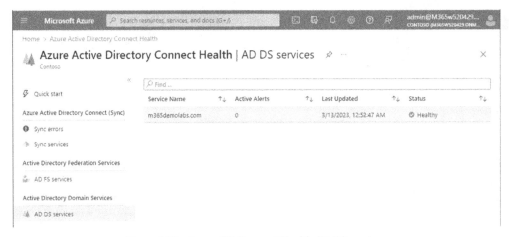

Figure 4.19 – Azure AD Connect Health AD DS services

The health services agents display a variety of details about the environment, including replication errors, LDAP bind operations, NTLM authentication operations, and Kerberos authentication operations. See *Figure 4.20*:

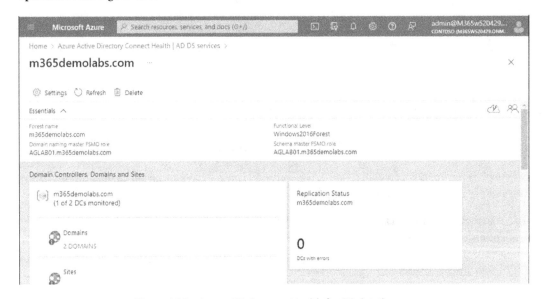

Figure 4.20 – Azure AD Connect Health for DS detail page

Errors that are detected here should be resolved in your on-premises AD environment.

Azure AD Connect Health for Active Directory Federation Services

In addition to gathering and reporting information for your on-premises AD and synchronization services, Azure AD Connect Health also supports AD FS.

To get the most out of Azure AD Connect Health for AD FS, you'll need to enable auditing, which involves three steps:

1. Ensure the AD FS farm service account has been granted the **Generate security audits** right in the security policy (**Local Policies | User Rights Assignment | Generate security audits**).

2. From an elevated command prompt, run the following command: `auditpol.exe /set / subcategory:{0CCE9222-69AE-11D9-BED3-505054503030} /failure:enable /success:enable`.

3. On the AD FS primary farm server, open an elevated PowerShell prompt and run the following command: `Set-AdfsProperties -AuditLevel Verbose`.

Then, you can deploy the agents to your servers.

After deploying the agents to your federation and proxy servers, you will see information reported in the Azure AD Connect Health portal by selecting **AD FS services** under the **Active Directory Federation Services** section, as shown in *Figure 4.21*:

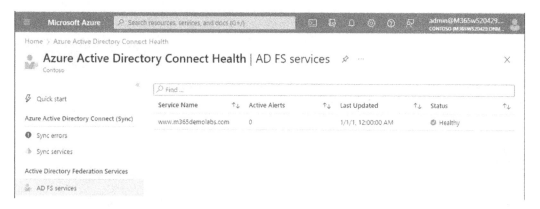

Figure 4.21 – Azure AD Connect Health for AD FS

In addition to diagnostic information, the health services for AD FS can also provide usage analytics and performance monitoring, as well as failed logins and information regarding risky sign-ins. See *Figure 4.22*:

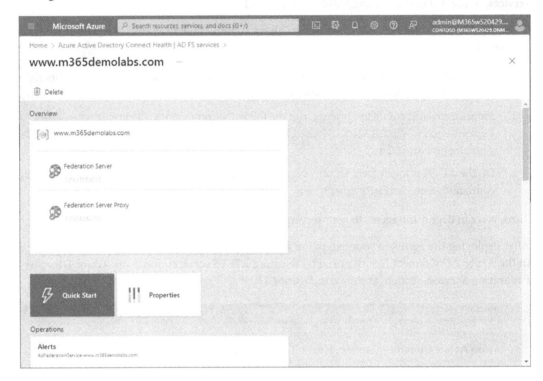

Figure 4.22 – Azure AD Connect Health for AD FS overview

Azure AD Connect Health is a valuable premium service that can help you keep on top of the health and performance aspects of your hybrid identity deployment.

Troubleshooting Azure AD Connect Synchronization

While things normally operate smoothly, there may be times when objects become misconfigured, or services go offline unexpectedly. You can troubleshoot common issues with Azure AD Connect's built-in troubleshooting tool.

To launch the troubleshooting tool, follow these steps:

1.   Launch the Azure AD Connect configuration tool on the desktop of the server where Azure AD Connect is installed.

2.   Click **Configure**.

3. On the **Additional tasks** page, select **Troubleshoot** and then click **Next**.

4. On the **Welcome to AADConnect Troubleshooting** page, select **Launch**, as shown in *Figure 4.23*:

Figure 4.23 – Launching the AADConnect Troubleshooting tool

5. Select the appropriate troubleshooting option from the menu shown in *Figure 4.24*:

```
Administrator: Windows PowerShell                                               —  □  ×

------------------------------------------AADConnect Troubleshooting--------------------------------------------

    Enter '1' - Troubleshoot Object Synchronization
    Enter '2' - Troubleshoot Password Hash Synchronization
    Enter '3' - Collect General Diagnostics
    Enter '4' - Configure AD DS Connector Account Permissions
    Enter '5' - Test Azure Active Directory Connectivity
    Enter '6' - Test Active Directory Connectivity
    Enter 'Q' - Quit

    Please make a selection: _
```

Figure 4.24 – AADConnect Troubleshooting menu

The AADConnect Troubleshooting tool provides several specific troubleshooters, such as diagnosing attribute or group membership synchronization, password hash synchronization, as well as service account permissions.

Most object or attribute troubleshooting routines will require the errored object's distinguished name to continue.

Further Reading

For more information on the tests that can be performed by the AADConnect Troubleshooting tool, see https://learn.microsoft.com/en-us/azure/active-directory/ hybrid/tshoot-connect-objectsync.

Configuring and Managing Directory Synchronization by Using Azure AD Connect Cloud Sync

Azure AD Connect Cloud Sync (rebranded as Microsoft Entra Cloud Sync) is a new synchronization platform that allows you to manage directory synchronization from the Azure portal. Depending on your organization's goals and environments, Azure AD Connect Cloud Sync can be a lightweight, flexible option that allows you to begin directory synchronization quickly.

> **Exam Tip**
>
> To perform the installation, you'll need either Domain Admin or Enterprise Admin credentials to the on-premises Active Directory forest so that the installer can create the **group Managed Service Account (gMSA)**. You'll also need an account that has either the Global Administrator or Hybrid Identity Administrator roles in Azure AD.
>
> Microsoft recommends configuring a unique identity in Azure AD with the Hybrid Identity Administrator role for Azure AD Connect Cloud Sync.

Installing the Provisioning Agent

Before you begin the installation, you should make sure that the server where the provisioning agent will be installed can communicate with the various Azure AD services. *Table 4.3* highlights ports and URLs that are required for the cloud sync agent to function correctly:

Endpoint	Port/Protocol	Description
`*.msappproxy.net` `*.servicebus.windows.net`	443/HTTPS	Azure Application Proxy cloud service endpoints

`crl3.digicert.com`
`crl4.digicert.com`
`ocsp.digicert.com`
`crl.microsoft.com`
`oneocsp.microsoft.com`
`ocsp.msocsp.com`
	80/HTTP	Certificate Revocation List (CRL) endpoints

Endpoint	Port/Protocol	Description
login.windows.net	443/HTTPS	Agent configuration and registration
secure.aadcdn. microsoftonline-p.com		
*.microsoftonline.com		
*.microsoftonline-p.com		
*.msauth.net		
*.msauthimages.net		
*.msecnd.net		
*.msftauth.net		
*.msftauthimages.net		
*.phonefactor.net		
enterpriseregistration. windows.net		
management.azure.com		
policykeyservice.dc.ad. msft.net		
ctldl.windowsupdate.com		
www.microsoft.com/pkiops		
ctldl.windowsupdate.com	80/HTTP	Agent configuration and registration

Table 4.3 – Required endpoints for Azure AD Connect Cloud Sync service

To begin configuring Azure AD Connect Cloud Sync, follow these steps:

1. Log on to a server where you wish to install the Azure AD Connect Cloud Sync provisioning agent.

2. Navigate to the Azure portal (`https://portal.azure.com`) and select **Active Directory | Azure AD Connect**.

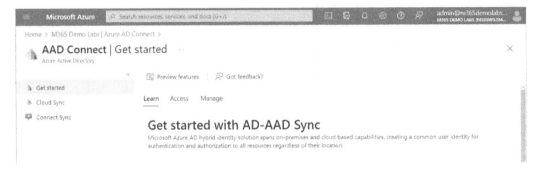

Figure 4.25 – Azure AD Connect in the Azure portal

3. From the navigation menu, select **Cloud Sync**.

4. Under **Monitor**, select **Agents**.

5. Select **Download on-premises agent**.

Figure 4.26 – Download on-premises agent for Azure AD Connect Cloud Sync

6. On the **Azure AD Provisioning Agent** flyout, select **Accept terms & download** to begin the download.

7. Open the `AADConnectProvisioningAgentSetup.exe` file to begin the installation.

8. Agree to the licensing terms and click **Install** to deploy the Microsoft Azure AD Connect provisioning package.

9. After the software installation is complete, the configuration wizard will launch. Click **Next** on the splash page to begin the configuration.

10. On the **Select Extension** page, choose the **HR-driven provisioning (Workday and SuccessFactors) / Azure AD Connect Cloud Sync** radio button and click **Next**. See *Figure 4.27*:

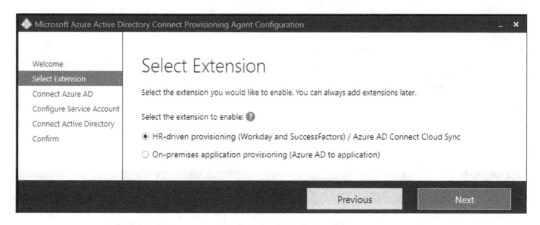

Figure 4.27 – Azure AD Connect Cloud Sync Select Extension page

11. On the **Connect Azure AD** page, click **Authenticate** to sign in to Azure AD.

12. On the **Configure Service Account** page, select the **Create gMSA** radio button to instruct the setup process to provision a new gMSA. Enter either Domain Admin or Enterprise Admin credentials and click **Next**. See *Figure 4.28*:

Figure 4.28 – Configure Azure AD Connect Cloud Sync service account

13. On the **Connect Active Directory** page, click **Add Directory** and provide the domain credentials to add the directory to the configuration. When finished, click **Next**. See *Figure 4.29*:

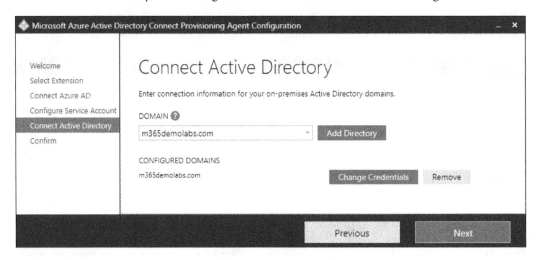

Figure 4.29 – Adding a directory to Azure AD Connect Cloud Sync

14. Review the details on the **Agent configuration** page and click **Confirm** to deploy the provisioning agent. When finished, click **Exit**.

After the agent has been deployed, you will need to continue the configuration in the Azure AD portal.

Configuring the Provisioning Service

In order to complete the Azure AD Connect Cloud Sync deployment, you'll need to set up a new configuration in the Azure portal:

1. Navigate to the Azure portal (https://portal.azure.com) and select **Active Directory | Azure AD Connect**.

2. Select **Cloud sync** from the navigation menu, and then on the **Configurations** tab, select **New configuration**.

3. On the **New cloud sync configuration** page, select which domains you would like to synchronize to Azure AD. If desired, select the **Enable password hash sync** checkbox. The password hash sync checkbox on this page only enables the feature—it does not configure password hash sync as a sign-in method. See *Figure 4.30*.

> **Exam Tip**
> Azure AD Connect Cloud Sync does not support using password hash sync for `InetOrgPerson` objects.

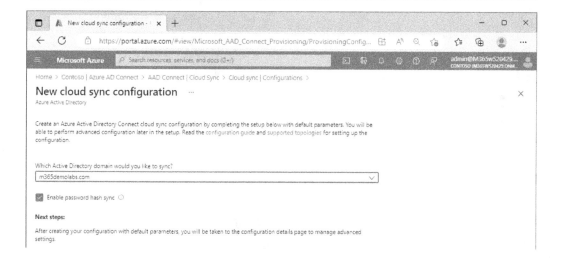

Figure 4.30 – Creating a new Azure AD Connect Cloud Sync configuration

4. Scroll to the bottom of the page and click **Create** to complete the basic configuration.

The Azure AD Connect Cloud Sync configuration has been completed but it is not yet enabled and ready to start provisioning users. In the next series of steps, you can customize the service before fully enabling it.

Customizing the Provisioning Service

Like the on-premises Azure AD Connect service, Azure AD Connect Cloud Sync features the ability to perform scoping (including or excluding objects from synchronization) as well as attribute mapping.

After creating a new configuration, you should be redirected to the properties of the configuration, as shown in *Figure 4.31*:

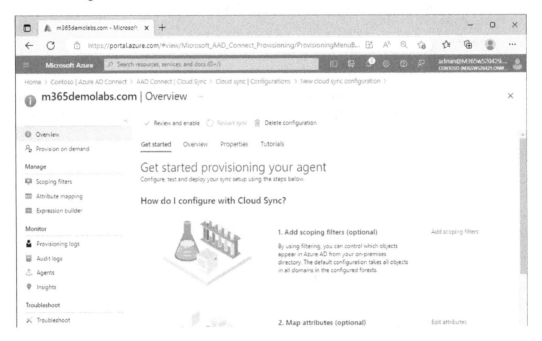

Figure 4.31 – Provisioning agent overview page

From this page, you can set up the **scoping filters** and **attribute mappings** for customizing your environment. By default, Azure AD Connect Cloud Sync will include all objects in the connected forest and domains for synchronization.

Scoping Filters

By selecting **Scoping filters** under **Manage**, you can configure which objects should be synchronized to Azure AD. You can specify a list of security groups or select organizational units, but not both. See *Figure 4.32*:

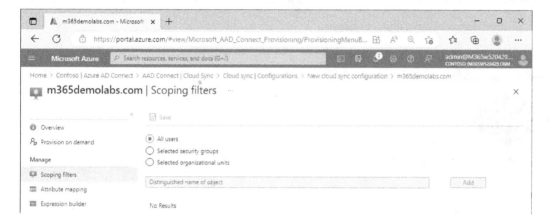

Figure 4.32 – Azure AD Connect Cloud Sync scoping filters

There are a few important caveats when using scoping filters with Azure AD Connect Cloud Sync:

- When using group-based scoping, nested objects beyond the first level will not be included in the scope

- You can only include 59 separate OUs or security groups as scoping filters

It's also important to note that using security groups to perform scoping is only recommended for piloting scenarios.

Attribute Mapping

Another customization option available involves mapping attribute values between on-premises and cloud objects. As with Azure AD Connect, you can configure how cloud attributes are populated—whether it's from a source attribute, a constant value, or some sort of expression.

Azure AD Connect sync comes with a default attribute mapping flow, as shown in *Figure 4.33*:

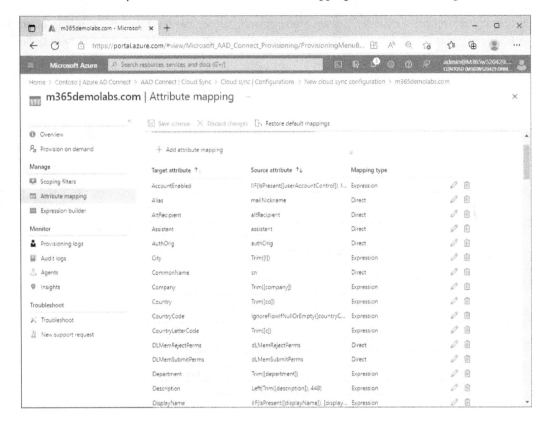

Figure 4.33 – Azure AD Connect Cloud Sync attribute mappings

You can select an existing attribute to modify or create a new attribute flow. One of the basic configuration features for most attributes is to configure a **Default** value (if the on-premises value is blank), allowing you to make certain that cloud attributes are populated with values.

In *Figure 4.34*, the **Country** attribute has been selected and updated with the default value **US**. This ensures that in the event a user's on-premises country attribute is blank, the corresponding cloud attribute will be populated with a valid entry.

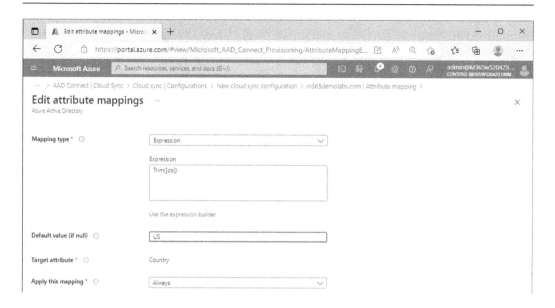

Figure 4.34 – Edit attribute mappings in Azure AD Connect Cloud Sync

Azure AD Connect Cloud Sync also features an expression builder, allowing you to create your own custom attribute flows.

Unlike Azure AD Connect, however, attribute mappings and expressions cannot be used to merge attributes from different domains or forests, nor does Azure AD Connect Cloud Sync support synchronization rules or attribute flow precedence. If you require that level of customization, you should deploy Azure AD Connect instead.

Once you have finished customizing the scoping filters and attribute flows, you can return to the **Overview** page and enable synchronization by selecting **Review and enable**.

Troubleshooting Azure AD Connect Cloud Sync Synchronization

Just as Azure AD Connect may experience issues with synchronizing identity, Azure AD Connect Cloud Sync can as well. Successful synchronization depends on several factors:

- **Agent functionality**: Is the agent installed and functioning normally?
- **Network communications**: Can the agent reach all of the required endpoints and resolve DNS for Azure AD services?
- **Service account issues**: Does the service account have the appropriate rights to the on-premises objects?

When troubleshooting the Azure AD Connect Cloud Sync service, you should start with the Windows Event Viewer to determine whether there are any errors related to the service, such as invalid credentials or missing privileges.

While Microsoft generally recommends bypassing proxy and content filtering services for Microsoft 365 endpoints, your organization may still choose to deploy them. In the event that the server for the Azure AD Connect Cloud Sync agent is located behind a proxy server or appliance, it may become necessary to modify the service configuration file with the proxy's information.

The Azure AD Connect Cloud Sync provisioning agent utilizes a configuration file stored in `C:\Program Files\Microsoft Azure AD Connect Provisioning Agent\ AADConnectProvisioningAgent.exe.config`. To add proxy configuration information, edit this file, and before the closing `</configuration>` tag, enter the following data (replacing `[proxy-server]` and `[proxy-port]`) with the proxy server or appliance address and network port:

```
<system.net>
        <defaultProxy enabled="true" useDefaultCredentials="true">
            <proxy
                usesystemdefault="true"
                proxyaddress="http://[proxy-server]:[proxy-port]"
                bypassonlocal="true"
            />
        </defaultProxy>
    </system.net>
```

If you need to perform deeper troubleshooting for the agent, you can install the **AADCloudSyncTools PowerShell** module. The AADCloudSyncTools module has a number of functions in it for configuring and gathering verbose logging data, configuring the sync schedule, and repairing the service account. For more information on the functions supported by the cmdlet, see `https://learn.microsoft.com/ en-us/azure/active-directory/hybrid/cloud-sync/reference-powershell`.

Summary

In this chapter, you learned how to deploy identity synchronization and authentication solutions. You learned how to configure filtering for both Azure AD Connect and Azure AD Connect Cloud Sync, as well as deploying and managing the health agents for diagnostic and troubleshooting.

The next chapter will discuss methods to manage authentication.

Exam Readiness Drill - Chapter Review Questions

Benchmark Score: 75%

Apart from a solid understanding of key concepts, being able to think quickly under time pressure is a skill that will help you ace your certification exam. That's why, working on these skills early on in your learning journey is key.

Chapter review questions are designed to improve your test-taking skills progressively with each chapter you learn and review your understanding of key concepts in the chapter at the same time. You'll find these at the end of each chapter.

> **Before You Proceed**
>
> You need to unlock these resources before you start using them. Unlocking **takes less than 10 minutes, can be done from any device**, and **needs to be done only once**. Head over to the start of *Chapter 7, Managing Security Reports and Alerts by Using the Microsoft 365 Defender Portal* in this book for instructions on how to unlock them.

To open the **Chapter Review Questions** for this chapter, click the following link: `https://packt.link/MS102E1_CH04`. Or, you can scan the following QR code:

Figure 4.35 – QR code that opens Chapter Review Questions for logged-in users

Once you login, you'll see a page similar to what is shown in *Figure 4.36*:

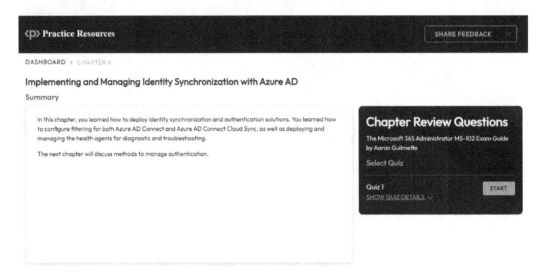

Figure 4.36 – Chapter Review Questions for Chapter 4

Once ready, start the following practice drills, re-attempting the quiz multiple times:

Exam Readiness Drill

For the first 3 attempts, don't worry about the time limit.

ATTEMPT 1

The first time, aim for at least 40%. Look at the answers you got wrong and read the relevant sections in the chapter again to fix your learning gaps.

ATTEMPT 2

The second time, aim for at least 60%. Look at the answers you got wrong and read the relevant sections in the chapter again to fix any remaining learning gaps.

ATTEMPT 3

The third time, aim for at least 75%. Once you score 75% or more, you start working on your timing.

> **Tip**
>
> You may take more than 3 attempts to reach 75%. That's okay. Just review the relevant sections in the chapter till you get there.

Working On Timing

Target: Your aim is to keep the score the same while trying to answer these questions as quickly as possible. Here's an example of how your next attempts should look like:

Attempt	Score	Time Taken
Attempt 5	77%	21 mins 30 seconds
Attempt 6	78%	18 mins 34 seconds
Attempt 7	76%	14 mins 44 seconds

Table 4.4 – Sample timing practice drills on the online platform

> **Note**
>
> The time limits shown in the above table are just examples. Set your own time limits with each attempt based on the time limit of the quiz on the website.

With each new attempt, your score should stay **above 75%** while your time taken to complete should decrease. Repeat as many attempts as you want till you feel confident dealing with the time pressure.

5

Implementing and Managing Authentication

Over the course of the last few chapters, you've learned a lot about identity, synchronization, and sign-in methods—all part of the Microsoft 365 foundation. In this chapter, you'll shift gears from how you configure the service for a sign-in method to how you implement authentication on the user-facing side.

You're going to tackle authentication mechanisms and methods by covering the following topics:

- Implementing and managing authentication methods
- Implementing and managing self-service password reset
- Implementing and managing Azure AD password protection
- Configuring and managing multifactor authentication
- Investigating and resolving authentication issues

By the end of this chapter, you should be able to describe the various authentication methods and supporting tools, as well as understand where to go to troubleshoot authentication issues.

> **Note**
>
> As has been mentioned elsewhere in this book, Microsoft has recently introduced the umbrella term **Entra** to unify security and identity management products. The product documentation reflects both Azure AD and Entra ID terminology, as does this book. While many commercial tenants have been updated to reflect some of the Entra naming conventions, most tenants in the national or sovereign clouds still reflect the older Azure AD branding. For the purposes of the exam, you can use the terms **Azure AD** and **Entra ID** interchangeably.

Implementing and Managing Authentication Methods

After onboarding identity and configuring multifactor authentication requirements, you can begin deployment.

> **Exam Note**
>
> Full deployment and configuration of these methods are outside the scope of the MS-102 exam, but it would be good to spend a little bit of time reviewing the product documentation for deeper dives into how passwordless authentication works. See `https://learn.microsoft.com/en-us/entra/identity/authentication/concept-authentication-passwordless` for further information.

Let's go through an overview of the configurations necessary to enable passwordless authentication methods.

Choosing an Authentication Mechanism

Everyone is familiar with using an identity and a corresponding password to log in to a device, service, application, or website—whether it's a bank website, Facebook, Xbox Live, or even just a local computer. While Microsoft 365 supports traditional username and password authentication mechanisms, there are newer methods that provide fewer opportunities for malicious users to compromise identities, applications, and devices.

Microsoft has long advocated for using multifactor authentication as part of the logon process to help secure identities—that is, using some sort of supplementary logon tool (such as a token, authenticator app, phone call, or text message) to confirm the logon process. The weakest link in this chain is the password—and interfaces unable to leverage the multifactor authentication process are more susceptible to bad actors.

With Microsoft's newest **passwordless** technologies, users get the advantage of multifactor authentication (something you have, something you know, or something you are) without the frustration of remembering complex passwords. Microsoft supports several different approaches to passwordless logon, including **Windows Hello for Business (WHFB)**, the **Microsoft Authenticator app**, and **Fast Identity Online 2 (FIDO2)**-compatible security keys or tokens.

Microsoft passwordless options are based on a **public key infrastructure (PKI)** design, comprising a **private key** (managed and stored by the user's device) and a **public key** saved in Azure AD. The keys are linked and only work with each other. When an entity (be it a user or device) establishes a public/private **key pair**, the public key can be broadly distributed to all other entities that the owner of the key pair wishes to communicate with.

Each key has two purposes:

- The public key is used to *encrypt* data. Only the corresponding private key can *decrypt* it.

- The private key is used to *sign* data. Only the corresponding public key can *authenticate* or verify the signature, offering proof that a particular private key produced it.

For example, let's say you establish a public/private key pair and you wish to conduct secure email communication. You distribute the public key to everyone you will communicate with. You might even add it to your email signature, post it on a blog, or store it in a directory where others can look it up.

The following examples demonstrate possible uses for public key cryptography in the context of email:

- You're sending out an important product announcement update on behalf of your organization and you want people to be certain it's authentic. You sign the email with your private key. Recipients who already have your public key (or who can retrieve it from your website or a directory) can use the public key to check the signature on your email. Since only your private key matches that well-known public key, recipients can be assured that your private key was used to sign the content.

- You're in the process of acquiring financing for a new business venture. The lender has prepared documents for you to review. Since they contain sensitive financial information, the lender wants to make sure that only you can open them. They encrypt the content with your public key and email you the documents. Since only your private key is able to decrypt the content, both entities can be assured that the content will be unreadable to anyone else.

Those types of scenarios are very analogous to what happens when using PKI-based sign-on methods such as Windows Hello—but instead of signing and encrypting email, it's used for authentication data.

In this section, you'll explore a little bit about each of these mechanisms to help you decide which is appropriate for your organization.

Windows Hello for Business

Microsoft's recommended solution for passwordless authentication is **Windows Hello for Business (WHFB)**. It's designed for users that have their own dedicated PC. When logging on, the user presents a biometric or PIN code to unlock the device.

WHFB supports a variety of biometric logons, including facial recognition and fingerprint scanners. Devices configured to use Windows Hello (such as the one shown in *Figure 5.1*) can be recognized because they have the Windows Hello smiley face greeting at the top:

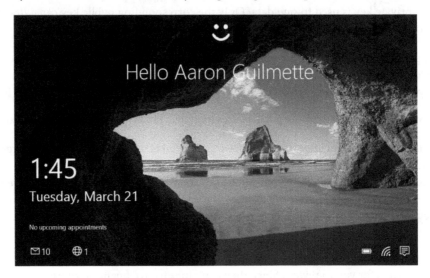

Figure 5.1 – Windows Hello for Business sign-on screen

After configuring Windows Hello, the sign-in flow follows this sequence, as depicted in *Figure 5.2*:

Figure 5.2 – Windows Hello authentication sequence

1. The user signs in with either a biometric or PIN (if the configured biometric input can't be accessed), which unlocks the WHFB private key. The key is then passed to the **Cloud Authentication security support provider**, also known as the **Cloud AP**, part of the on-device security package.

2. The Cloud AP requests a **nonce** (single-use random number) from Azure AD.

3. Azure AD sends the nonce to the Cloud AP on the endpoint.

4. The Cloud AP signs the nonce with the user's private key and returns the signed nonce to Azure AD.

5. Azure AD decrypts and validates the signed nonce with the user's public key. After it's validated, Azure AD issues a **primary refresh token (PRT)** with the session key, encrypts it using the device's public transport key, and sends that to the Cloud AP.

6. The Cloud AP decrypts the PRT/session key using the device's transport private key and then uses the **Trusted Platform Module (TPM)** to store the session key.

7. The Cloud AP returns a success response to Windows, allowing the user to log in to complete.

WHFB is available to be deployed as a cloud-only or hybrid identity solution and can be used for both Windows logon as well as logon to Microsoft 365 services. Windows Hello-based authentication is tied to a unique device, meaning you have to set it up individually for each device that you will be using.

Microsoft Authenticator App

Many administrators and users are already familiar with the Microsoft Authenticator mobile device app, after using it for multifactor authentication. The Authenticator app can also be used as a passwordless sign-in option. When used as a passwordless option, Microsoft Authenticator can use number-matching, where the sign-in screen displays a number that the user enters and confirms with their PIN or biometric data. See *Figure 5.3*:

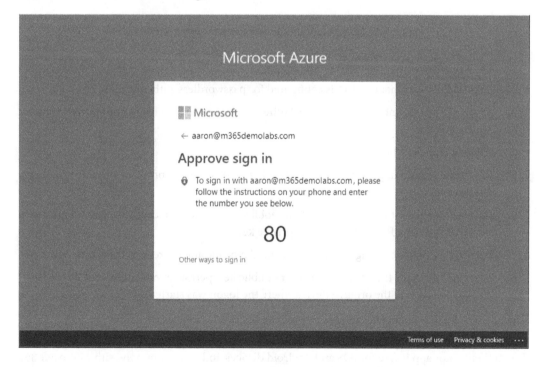

Figure 5.3 – Passwordless authentication dialog with Microsoft Authenticator

The data flow using the Authenticator app follows the same general pattern as Windows Hello, as shown in *Figure 5.4*:

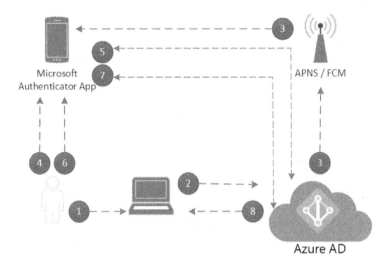

Figure 5.4 – Microsoft Authenticator authentication sequence

1. The user enters their username on the device.
2. Azure AD detects that the user is configured for passwordless authentication.
3. Azure AD sends a notification to the Authenticator app on the user's configured Apple or Android device.
4. The user launches the Authenticator app.
5. The Authenticator app connects to Azure AD and receives the proof-of-presence challenge and the nonce.
6. The user completes the challenge on their mobile device and then confirms their identity with biometric data or a PIN, unlocking the private key.
7. The private key is used to sign the nonce and the Authenticator app returns the data to Azure AD.
8. Azure AD decrypts the data with the user's public key, performs validation, and then returns the sign-in token to the original device where the logon was started.

Whereas WHFB has specific hardware requirements (such as a Windows Hello-compatible camera or fingerprint reader), passwordless using Microsoft Authenticator has a very low barrier to entry. The Authenticator app is free for iOS and Android devices and works not only with Microsoft 365 services but also any service that supports a soft-token app or device.

> **Further Reading**
>
> In addition to the traditional Microsoft Authenticator application, Microsoft has also released Authenticator Lite as part of Outlook. For more information, see `https://learn.` `microsoft.com/en-us/azure/active-directory/authentication/how-` `to-mfa-authenticator-lite`.

FIDO2 Security Keys

Physical tokens, such as the **Fast Identity Online 2 (FIDO2)**-based token or security key, are another passwordless option that can be used. While the Microsoft Authenticator app is a soft token, FIDO2 tokens are physical pieces of hardware that are typically either connected to the computer (in the form of a USB device) or that communicate wirelessly (via Bluetooth or NFC).

You can access the security key logon process during a browser session by selecting the **Sign in with Windows Hello or a security key** option from the sign-in page, as shown in *Figure 5.5*:

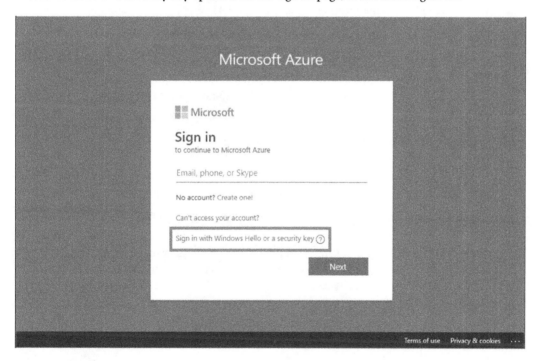

Figure 5.5 – Passwordless authentication dialog with a FIDO2 security token

The data flow for a FIDO2-based logon follows a similar pattern as both WHFB and the Microsoft Authenticator app. For example, to log in to a device using FIDO2, this process outlined in *Figure 5.6* is followed:

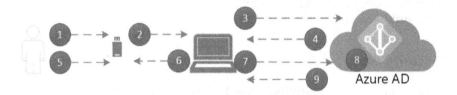

Figure 5.6 – FIDO2 authentication sequence

1. The user plugs in a FIDO2 security key.

2. Windows detects the security key.

3. Windows sends an authentication request to Azure AD.

4. Azure AD responds by sending a nonce back to the logon device.

5. The user authenticates to the FIDO2 key, unlocking the secure storage area containing the private key.

6. The FIDO2 key signs the nonce with the private key and sends it to Windows.

7. Windows generates a PRT request and sends it with the signed nonce to Azure AD.

8. Azure AD verifies the signed nonce with the FIDO2 device's public key.

9. Azure AD returns the PRT to the logon device.

FIDO2, like Windows Hello, has specific requirements for supported hardware.

> **Supported FIDO2 Security Tokens**
>
> You can see an up-to-date list of supported FIDO2 security keys or tokens here: `https://learn.microsoft.com/en-us/azure/active-directory/authentication/concept-authentication-passwordless#fido2-security-key-providers`.

As you've seen from the diagrams, each of the passwordless options (Windows Hello, Microsoft Authenticator App, and FIDO2) follows a similar authentication workflow, based on public key infrastructure.

Comparison

Now that you have explored the different passwordless options available for Microsoft 365, let's look at some information that will help you choose the appropriate solution. *Table 5.1* describes some basic features and requirements for each authentication scheme.

	Windows Hello for Business	Authenticator app	FIDO2 security keys
Prerequisite requirement	A device with a built-in TPM and biometric recognition running Windows 10 (1809 or later) or Windows 11; Azure AD	Authenticator app for iOS or Android; a device supporting biometric recognition	Windows 10 (1903 or later) or Windows 11; Azure AD
Authentication mode	Platform	Software/soft token	Hardware
User experience	Sign in to the supported device using a PIN or biometric data	Sign in to supported applications and browsers using a PIN or biometric data	Sign in using a FIDO2 device with a supported PIN or biometric data
Scenarios	Passwordless sign-in with a Windows device and supported applications	Multi-platform passwordless solution for web applications	Passwordless sign-in for single or multiuser scenarios or where soft tokens are not suitable

Table 5.1 – Authentication method comparison table

It's also important to consider the various end user scenarios that your organization utilizes to ensure you're recommending an appropriate mechanism based on your real-world use cases. *Table 5.2* describes a few example scenarios:

Role/persona	Scenario/use case	Platform	Suitable or recommended passwordless methods
Administrator	Secure device access for administrative tasks	Assigned Windows 10 or Windows 11 device	WHFB; FIDO2
Administrator	Administrative tasks on down-level or non-Windows devices	Mobile, down-level, or non-Windows devices	Microsoft Authenticator app
Information/knowledge worker	Productivity work	Assigned Windows 10 or Windows 11 device	WHFB; FIDO2
Information/knowledge worker	Productivity work	Mobile, down-level, or non-Windows devices	Microsoft Authenticator app
Frontline worker	Kiosks, Azure Virtual Desktop (preview)	Shared Windows 10 or Windows 11 devices; Azure Virtual Desktop (preview)	FIDO2

Table 5.2 – Passwordless logon scenarios

With that information in hand, it's time to look at the implementation aspects.

Configuring Windows Hello

WHFB supports cloud-only, hybrid Azure AD, and on-premises deployments. The easiest method to deploy Windows Hello is in a cloud-only model since the Microsoft 365 organization is set up for it automatically. You'll look at that scenario in this section.

During the **out-of-box experience** (**OOBE**), users are prompted for credentials. After providing an Azure AD credential, if the Intune enrollment policy has not been configured to block WHFB, the user will be prompted to enroll with their biometric data (such as a facial scan with a compatible camera) and set a PIN.

Devices will be joined to Azure AD during the initial sign-in process and WHFB will be enabled.

If your subscription supports it, Microsoft recommends creating a WHFB policy to configure settings for your organization:

1. Navigate to the Intune admin center (`https://intune.microsoft.com` or `https://endpoint.microsoft.com`).

2. Expand **Devices** and, under **Device enrollment**, select **Enroll devices**, as shown in *Figure 5.7*:

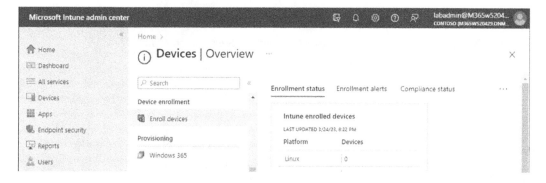

Figure 5.7 – Enroll devices

3. Select **Windows enrollment** and then choose **Windows Hello for Business**, as shown in *Figure 5.8*:

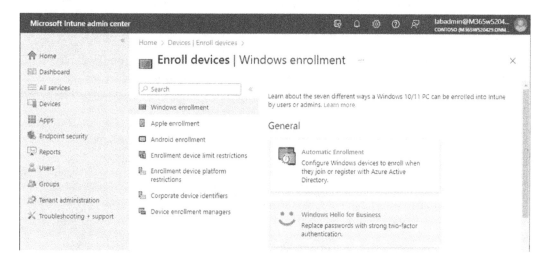

Figure 5.8 – Windows Hello for Business

4. Under **Assigned to**, select a group (if scoping the enrollment policy to a subset of users).

5. Configure the options for Windows Hello for Business (*italics* options are the default settings for the enrollment policy):

- **Configure Windows Hello for Business**: *Enabled*, Disabled, Not Configured

- **Use a Trusted Platform Module (TPM)**: *Required*, Preferred

- **Minimum PIN length**: Configure a numeric value between *4* and 127.

- **Maximum PIN length**: Configure a numeric value between 4 and *127*.

- **Lowercase letters in PIN**: *Not allowed*, Allowed, Required

- **Uppercase letters in PIN**: *Not allowed*, Allowed, Required

- **Special characters in PIN**: *Not allowed*, Allowed, Required

- **PIN expiration (days)**: *Never*, a numeric value between 1 and 730

- **Remember PIN history**: *Never*, a numeric value between 1 and 50

- **Allow biometric authentication**: *Yes,* No

- **Use enhanced anti-spoofing, when available**: *Not configured*, Yes, No

- **Allow phone sign-in**: *Yes*, No

- **Use security keys for sign-in**: *Not configured*, Enabled, Disabled

6. Click **Save** to update the enrollment policy.

With the policy configured, new device enrollments (for the configured user group) will receive the Windows Hello for Business setup prompt to begin enrollment, as shown in *Figure 5.9*:

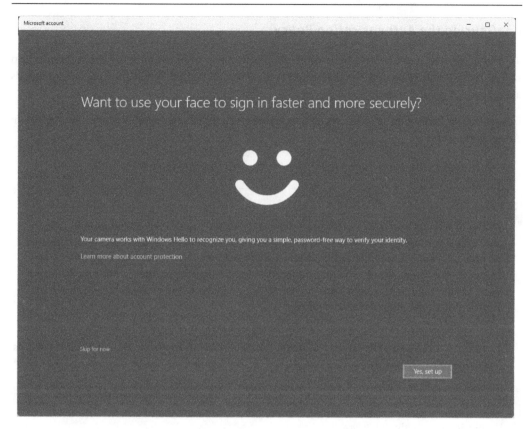

Figure 5.9 – Windows Hello for Business enrollment

After completing enrollment, users will be able to unlock and log in to devices using supported biometrics or their PIN.

Users that are already connected to Azure AD can also trigger the Windows Hello setup wizard, by either navigating to the **Account protection** blade in the **Windows Settings** app or by pressing Win+R and entering ms-cxh://nthaad in the **Run** dialog box.

Next, you'll look at configuring Microsoft Authenticator for passwordless sign-in.

Configuring Microsoft Authenticator

The Microsoft Authenticator app provides a convenient way to sign in to any Azure AD account with a supported mobile device. Before users can sign in using the method, however, it will need to be enabled in your tenant through the authentication policy.

Configuring the Authentication Policy

To enable users to sign in with Microsoft Authenticator, you need to configure the authentication policy. The authentication policy is shared across the tenant, though different authentication methods are scoped for groups of users.

Configuring and managing the policy requires an account with the Global Administrator or Authentication Administrator role:

1. Navigate to the Azure portal (`https://portal.azure.com`).

> **Exam Tip**
>
> While the current (as of this writing) version of the exam was developed before full parity of the Entra admin center was delivered, it's important to understand that interim exam updates may include references to the Entra admin center (`https://entra.microsoft.com`). Things such as menu items or configuration options are located in slightly different locations (from the left-hand menu navigation perspective), though they render the current Azure portal information in the main content window.

2. Select **Azure Active Directory | Security | Authentication methods** and then select **Policies**, as shown in *Figure 5.10*:

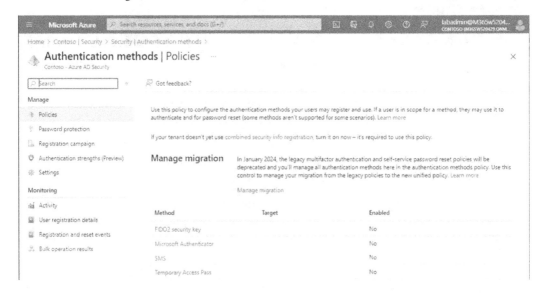

Figure 5.10 – Authentication methods

3.   Select **Microsoft Authenticator**.

4.   On the **Enable and Target** tab of the **Microsoft Authenticator settings** page, slide the **Enable** toggle to **On**, as shown in *Figure 5.11*:

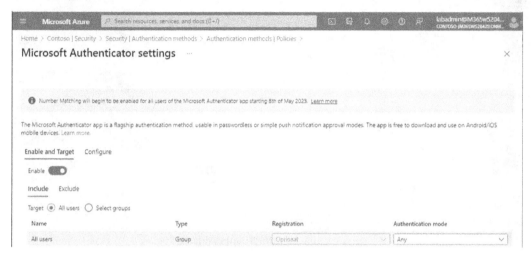

Figure 5.11 – Enabling Microsoft Authenticator

5.   Using the **Include** and **Exclude** tabs, specify which users the policy settings will apply to. Select the **All users** radio button to include all users in the policy or choose the **Select groups** radio button to specify which groups will be included or excluded. Each group can have a separate **Authentication mode** value selected, including **Any** (default), **Passwordless**, or **Push**. Choosing **Push** as the option prevents the use of the passwordless phone sign-in credential.

6.   Click **Save** to update the policy configuration.

After configuring the policy, users will need to register any devices to be used for passwordless authentication.

Registering Devices

Before users can log in to the service using Microsoft Authenticator, they will need to register their devices. If they've already registered for multifactor authentication, nothing else needs to be done.

If a user who has not registered signs in to the Microsoft 365 portal, they are greeted with a **More information required** dialog as part of the sign-in process, as shown in *Figure 5.12*:

Figure 5.12 – More information required

During the process, they are redirected to download the Microsoft Authenticator app, as shown in *Figure 5.13*:

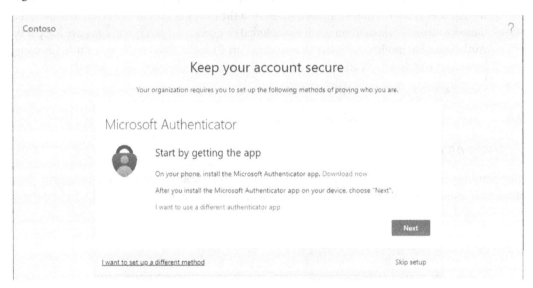

Figure 5.13 – Keep your account secure page

After they click **Next**, they are prompted to launch the Microsoft Authenticator app and add an account. Following the directions on the mobile device, they should launch a camera window that allows them to take a picture of a unique QR code, linking their device to their account, as shown in *Figure 5.14*:

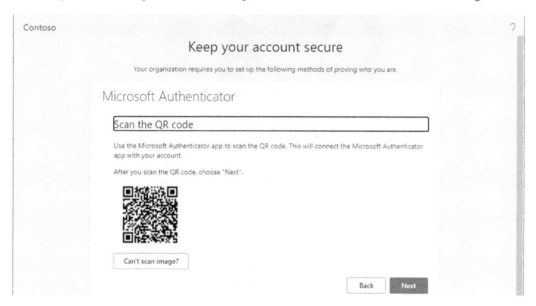

Figure 5.14 – Registering a device

Once the device has been linked, the enrollment process will ask the user to confirm a code between the registration screen and their Microsoft Authenticator app. After completing the challenge, users should be presented with a confirmation screen, similar to the one shown in *Figure 5.15*:

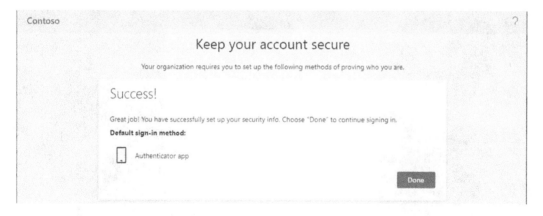

Figure 5.15 – Authenticator registration screen

The final step for the user for full passwordless sign-in from the Microsoft Authenticator app is to configure the device itself. In Microsoft Authenticator, the user can open the app and select **Enable phone sign-in**, as shown in *Figure 5.16*:

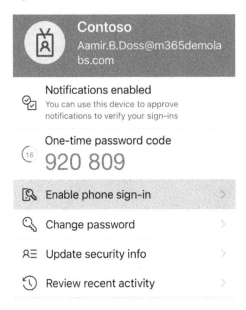

Figure 5.16 – Microsoft Authenticator Enable phone sign-in

This will start a process to configure the device for passwordless sign-in. After configuration, the user can choose to log in with an app instead, triggering the phone authentication notification on their device. See *Figure 5.17*:

Figure 5.17 – Launching passwordless sign-in

The user then completes the logon challenge in the Microsoft Authenticator app to finish logging in to Microsoft 365.

Configuring FIDO2

When setting up FIDO2-based authentication, you'll follow a similar process as with Microsoft Authenticator—updating the authentication policy to allow the method and then instructing users to self-register their security keys.

Configuring the Authentication Policy

To enable users to sign in with FIDO2 security keys, you need to configure the authentication policy. Configuring the policy requires an account with the Global Administrator or Authentication Administrator role:

1. Navigate to the Azure portal (`https://portal.azure.com`).

2. Select **Azure Active Directory | Security | Authentication methods** and then select **Policies**.

3. Select **Microsoft Authenticator**.

4. On the **Enable and Target** tab of the **FIDO2 security key settings** page, slide the **Enable** toggle to **On**. See *Figure 5.18*:

Figure 5.18 – Enabling Microsoft Authenticator

5. Using the **Include** and **Exclude** tabs, specify which users the policy settings will apply to. Select the **All users** radio button to include all users in the policy or choose the **Select groups** radio button to specify which groups will be included or excluded.

6. Click **Save** to update the policy configuration.

The next step is to instruct users to register the security keys.

Registering Devices

Like Microsoft Authenticator-based authentication, FIDO2 authentication requires end users to register the compatible device they wish to use for authentication.

> **Note**
>
> In order to register a FIDO2 security key, the user must already have an Azure AD multifactor authentication method configured. If they do not have one, they must add one (such as Microsoft Authenticator or SMS). If that is not possible, an administrator can issue a **Temporary Access Pass** (**TAP**) to allow the user to complete registration. For more information on configuring a TAP, please see `https://learn.microsoft.com/en-us/azure/active-directory/ authentication/howto-authentication-temporary-access-pass`.

To register a FIDO2 security key, users must follow these steps:

1. Navigate to `https://myprofile.microsoft.com` or, from the Microsoft 365 portal, expand the profile icon and select **View account**:

Figure 5.19 – Accessing My account

2. Click **Security Info**.

3. Select **Add method** and click **Security key**.

4. Select either **USB device** or **NFC device**.

5. Ensure the key is ready and click **Next**.

6. In the dialog box, create and enter a PIN for the security key and then perform the required gesture (biometric/touch) to confirm.

7. Enter a **Name** value for the key and click **Next**.

8. Click **Done.**

After the key has been registered, users can sign in to Azure AD, Entra ID, or Microsoft 365 using their security key. At the sign-in page, after entering a username, users can select the **Use Windows Hello or a security key** option, which will cause the browser to issue a prompt to insert the key, as shown in *Figure 5.20*:

Figure 5.20 – Sign in with Windows Hello or a security key

Next, you'll look at configuring a self-service password reset.

Implementing and Managing Self-Service Password Reset

Self-service password reset (SSPR) is a feature that allows users to change or reset passwords without administrator or service desk involvement. Self-service passwords can be configured for Azure AD cloud-only environments as well as enabling SSPR of hybrid identity through the **Azure AD Connect Password Writeback** feature.

Configuring SSPR

Enabling SSPR is a straightforward task. Like many other features in Azure AD, it can be scoped to a group of users.

To enable SSPR, follow these steps:

1. Navigate to the Azure portal (`https://portal.azure.com`) and select **Azure Active Directory**.

2. Under **Manage**, select **Password reset**.

3. On the **Properties** page, as shown in *Figure 5.21*, click **Selected** if you want to be able to select one or more groups to enable SSPR. Click **All** if you want to enable all users for SSPR:

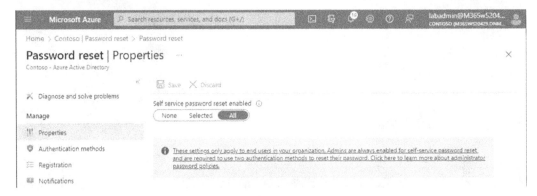

Figure 5.21 – Enabling self-service password reset

4. Click **Save**.

Now that SSPR has been enabled, you can manage and configure the features.

Managing SSPR

The SSPR service has a number of configuration options, including **Authentication methods**, **Registration** settings, **Notifications** options, **Customization** portal, and **On-premises integration**. Each of those options can be configured on the **Password reset** configuration blade of the Azure portal.

Authentication Methods

Authentication methods are used to define how a user proves their identity, such as multifactor authentication or answering security questions. The **Authentication methods** page lets you select which options a user can register, as well as the number of methods needed to perform a reset. See *Figure 5.22*:

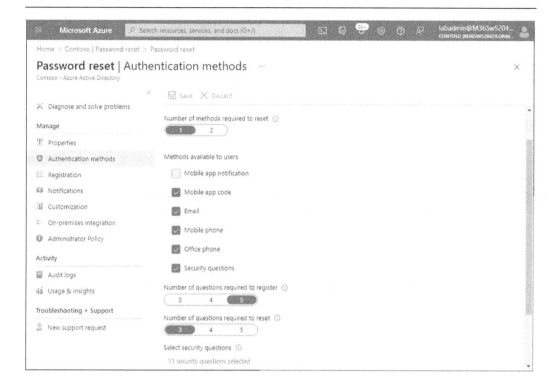

Figure 5.22 – Authentication methods

If you choose **Security questions**, additional options are configurable:

- The number of questions a user must supply when they select that option
- The number of security questions they must answer to prove their identity

You can choose up to 20 security questions from a list of predefined options or create your own security questions. Administrators are unable to pre-populate or retrieve answers to end user security questions; users must select their own questions.

> **Exam Tip**
>
> Using the **Office phone** registration option requires an Azure AD Premium license (either P1 or P2) and can be pre-populated with a phone number in Active Directory under the `telephoneNumber` attribute (if using Azure AD Connect to synchronize data). Other fields that can be pre-populated for SSPR include a user's alternate email address and mobile phone number. Alternate email does not synchronize from the on-premises Active Directory and must be set using `Set-AzureADUser -OtherMails`, `Set-MsolUser -AlternateEmailAddresses`, or `Set-MgUser -OtherMails`.

Registration

Options on this page allow you to configure a workflow to force users to register for SSPR the first time they log in to the Microsoft 365 portal (or any other Azure AD-backed service), as well as the interval in days in which users are asked to reconfirm their details.

Notifications

The **Notifications** page allows you to configure options for alerting on password changes. You can select **Notify users on password resets**, which sends users an email when their own password is reset via SSPR. The **Notify all admins when other admins reset their password** setting determines whether all Global Administrators receive a notification when any Global Administrator resets their password via SSPR.

> **Note**
> SSPR can be disabled on a per-user basis. In addition, SSPR can be disabled for administrator accounts using the `Update-MgPolicyAuthorizationPolicy` cmdlet. For more information, see `https://learn.microsoft.com/en-us/powershell/module/microsoft.graph.identity.signins/update-mgpolicyauthorizationpolicy`.

Customization

The **Customization** page allows you to display a custom URL or email address for support-related requests.

On-premises integration

If you have configured Azure AD Connect or Azure AD Connect Cloud sync with your organization, you can manage SSPR integration features, as shown in *Figure 5.23*:

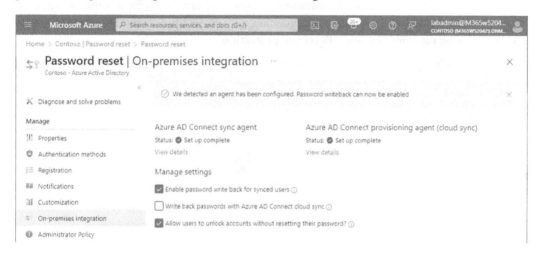

Figure 5.23 – On-premises integration

It's important to note that the **Enable password write back for synced users** option only modifies the behavior of Azure AD sending password reset data back to the on-premises environment, effectively stopping on-premises integration. It *does not* modify the on-premises Azure AD Connect configuration.

Next, you'll look at the features of Azure AD password protection.

Implementing and Managing Azure AD Password Protection

Azure AD password protection is a set of features designed to limit the effects of common password attacks. To view the password protection configuration, navigate to **Azure Active Directory | Security | Authentication methods** and select **Password protection**. See *Figure 5.24*:

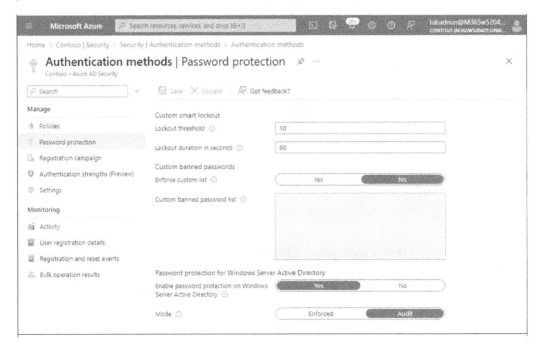

Figure 5.24 – Password protection

There are three groups of settings to configure:

- **Custom smart lockout**
- **Custom banned passwords**
- **Password protection for Windows Server Active Directory**

Let's briefly examine each set of configurations.

Custom smart lockout

The smart lockout settings determine how Azure Active Directory handles failed login attempts. **Lockout threshold** is the number of times in a row a user can enter a bad password before getting locked out. By default, **Lockout threshold** is set to 10 in Azure Worldwide (sometimes referred to as Commercial or Public) and Azure China 21Vianet tenants, while it is set at 3 for Azure US for Government customers. *Figure 5.25* depicts the error message displayed when the bad password threshold is met:

Figure 5.25 – Account lockout

Lockout duration in seconds only specifies the initial lockout duration after the lockout threshold has been reached. Each subsequent lockout increases the lockout duration. As a security mechanism, Microsoft does not publish the rate at which the duration increases.

Custom banned passwords

While Microsoft recommends moving toward passwordless authentication as a primary mechanism, passwords are still required to be configured in a number of scenarios. To help minimize using well-known, weak, or easily guessable passwords, you can choose to specify a custom list of words that you want to exclude from being used as passwords. For example, you may wish to include your organization's name or abbreviation, products or services offered by your organization, or local sports teams.

To enable the option, slide the **Enforce custom list** toggle to **Yes**, and then add up to 1,000 banned words in the **Custom banned password list** text area. The list is not case-sensitive. Azure AD automatically performs common substitutions (such as *0* and *o* or *3* and *e*), so you do not need to think of all of the possible ways a word can be represented.

Password protection for Windows Server Active Directory

This settings area allows you to extend the custom banned password list to your on-premises infrastructure. There are two components:

- **Azure AD Password Protection DC agent**, which must be installed on domain controllers.
- **Azure AD Password Protection proxy**, which must be installed on at least one domain-joined server in the forest. As a security best practice, Microsoft recommends deploying it on a member server since it requires internet connectivity.

In this configuration, the Azure AD Password Protection proxy servers periodically retrieve the custom banned password list from Azure AD. The DC agents cache the password policy locally and validate password change requests accordingly.

If **Enable password protection on Windows Server Active Directory** is configured as **Yes**, then you can choose what mode to process password change requests. They can be processed in **Audit** mode (where changes or logged) or **Enforced** mode, where password resets are actively evaluated against the banned password list and rejected if they do not meet the requirements.

> **Further Reading**
>
> To view detailed steps for deploying password protection on-premises, see `https://learn.`
> `microsoft.com/en-us/azure/active-directory/authentication/`
> `concept-password-ban-bad-on-premises`.

Configuring and Managing Multifactor Authentication

Configuring users for multifactor authentication can increase the security posture of your Microsoft 365 environment, in addition to protecting any apps that use Azure AD for identity and authentication.

In this section, you'll look at configuring multifactor authentication for your tenant.

Per-User Multifactor Authentication

If multifactor authentication was configured in your tenant prior to October 2019, it may have been configured using the legacy multifactor authentication scheme. Prior to newer technologies, Legacy Azure MFA was enabled on a per-user basis by manually updating each user's account to enforce the use of MFA.

Prior to implementing either Microsoft-managed security defaults or Conditional Access policies, you will need to disable the legacy per-user MFA. Having per-user MFA enabled while configuring a Conditional Access policy that prompts for MFA may cause unintended or unexpected MFA prompts.

> **Note**
>
> You should only configure one mechanism for multifactor authentication to avoid unexpected behaviors, such as users being prompted for MFA in scenarios where they previously satisfied multifactor authentication requirements or were accessing resources from trusted locations. Microsoft recommends discontinuing the use of per-user MFA and using Conditional Access policies instead.

To disable per-user multifactor authentication, follow these steps:

1. Navigate to the Microsoft 365 admin center (`https://admin.microsoft.com`).

2. Expand **Users** and select **Active users**.

3. Select **Multi-factor authentication**:

Figure 5.26 – Active users page

4. If your tenant already has Conditional Access policies, you may need to select the **Legacy per-user MFA** link to launch the legacy **multi-factor authentication** page.

5. On the **multi-factor authentication** page, as shown in *Figure 5.27*, configure the per-user MFA status to **Disabled** for users that have **Enforced** or **Enabled** set. You can select multiple users, but can only multi-select users that have the same MFA status type:

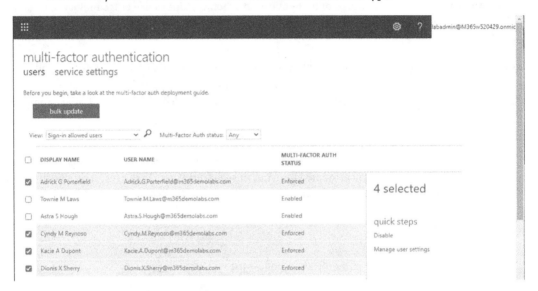

Figure 5.27 – Selecting users

Once per-user MFA is disabled, you can configure security defaults or Conditional Access policies.

Security Defaults

For most organizations, **security defaults** are a good choice for configuring broad baseline security policies. Security defaults make the following security changes:

- Requiring all users to register for multifactor authentication
- Requiring administrators to perform multifactor authentication upon sign-in
- Requiring users to do multifactor authentication when necessary
- Blocking basic authentication and other legacy authentication protocols
- Requiring administrators to perform multifactor authentication when accessing privileged resources, such as the Azure portal, Azure PowerShell, or the Azure CLI

Security defaults can be modified by users with the Global Administrator, Conditional Access administrator, or Security administrator roles. Security defaults can be enabled or disabled using the following process:

1. Navigate to the Azure portal (`https://portal.azure.com`).

2. Select **Azure Active Directory**.

3. Under **Manage**, click **Properties**.

4. Scroll to the bottom of the page and click **Manage security defaults**.

5. On the **Security defaults** flyout, select either **Enabled** or **Disabled** and click **Save**.

If you are going to configure Conditional Access policies, you should disable security defaults. If you are not going to configure Conditional Access policies, you should enable security defaults.

Further Reading

For more information on the impact of security defaults, see `https://learn.microsoft.com/en-us/azure/active-directory/fundamentals/concept-fundamentals-security-defaults`.

Conditional Access

Conditional Access provides the most fine-grained control when managing the multifactor authentication requirements for your organization. Conditional Access policies can be configured from the Azure portal.

To access the **Conditional Access** configuration page, follow these steps:

1. Navigate to the Azure portal (`https://portal.azure.com`).

2. Select **Azure Active Directory** | **Security** | **Conditional Access**, and then choose **Policies**.

You can create new policies or use one of the Microsoft-provided 14 sample Conditional Access policy templates. Policies created with a template can be modified once they have been deployed to your tenant.

To configure a template-based policy, follow these steps:

1. From the **Conditional Access | Policies** page, as shown in *Figure 5.28*, select **New policy from template (Preview)**:

Figure 5.28 – Creating a new Conditional Access policy from a template

2. Select one of the templates, such as **Require multifactor authentication for all users**, and click **Review + create**, as shown in *Figure 5.29*:

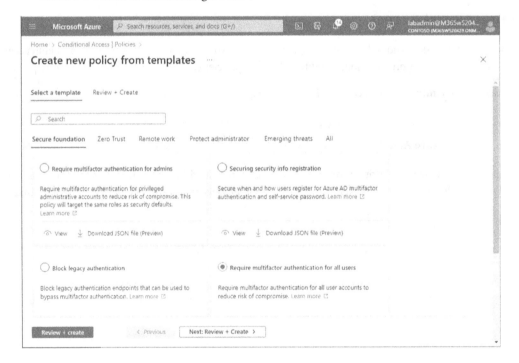

Figure 5.29 – Selecting a template

3. Review the settings and click **Create**.

Policies created through the templates cannot be modified during creation, with the exception of **Enforcement** mode. All template-based policies are configured in **Report only** mode, which can be toggled during creation. The user creating the policy is excluded from the policy to prevent accidental lockout.

After the template policies have been configured, you can edit the scope and conditions for the policy like manually created policies.

Further Reading

For more information on Conditional Access templates, see `https://learn.microsoft.com/en-us/azure/active-directory/conditional-access/concept-conditional-access-policy-common`.

With the exception of Windows Hello, passwordless sign-in methods (such as the Microsoft Authenticator app or FIDO2 security keys) will require users to register for multifactor authentication.

Additional Multifactor Authentication Behavior Settings

In addition to the core options for the methods and types of multifactor authentication, Azure AD also supports a number of settings, as given in *Table 5.3*, to further modify the behavior of multifactor authentication. These properties are located under **Azure Active Directory | Security | Multi-Factor authentication** in the Azure portal:

Area	Description	Setting
Account lockout	Temporarily lock accounts from using MFA if there are too many denied authentication attempts in a row.	Number of multifactor authentication denials to trigger lockout Default: <none>, Valid range: 1-99
		Minutes until the lockout counter is reset Default: <none>, Valid range: 1-1440
		Minutes until the account is automatically unblocked Default: <none>, Valid range: 1-9999

Area	Description	Setting
Block/unblock users	Maintain a list of users to block from receiving multifactor authentication requests	Add or remove users from the Blocked users list
Fraud alert	Allow users to report fraud if they receive MFA requests that they did not initiate	Allow users to submit fraud alerts Default: `Off`
		Automatically block users who report fraud Default: `<grayed out>`
		Code to report fraud during initial greeting Default: 0, Valid range: `1-99999`
Notifications	Notify this address of multifactor authentication requests	Recipient's Email Address `<none>`
OATH tokens	Upload OATH token data for end users	Upload OATH token CSV data
Phone call settings	Customize the verification phone calls for users who choose an MFA method that supports calling	Multifactor authentication caller ID number (US phone number only) Default: `<none>`, Valid range: `1-12` digits
		Operator required to transfer extensions Default: `<grayed out>`
		Add greeting Record a custom voice greeting

Table 5.3 – Additional multifactor authentication settings

Investigating and Resolving Authentication Issues

Resolving authentication issues in Azure AD can be tricky due to the number of authentication methods, sign-in methods, and other configurations that may be put in place.

The first step when attempting to troubleshoot an issue is to review any available sign-in logs in the Azure portal. To locate the sign-in logs, navigate to the Azure portal (`https://portal.azure.com`) and then select **Azure Active Directory** | **Sign-in logs**. See *Figure 5.30*:

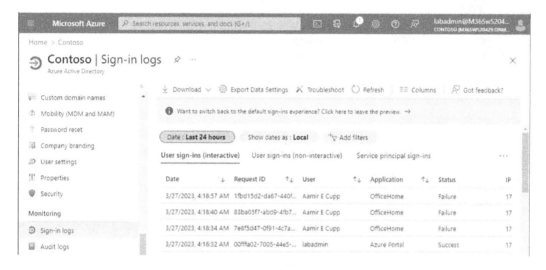

Figure 5.30 – Sign-in logs

Each authentication failure generates an individual entry. You can select an entry to see expanded details, as shown in *Figure 5.31*:

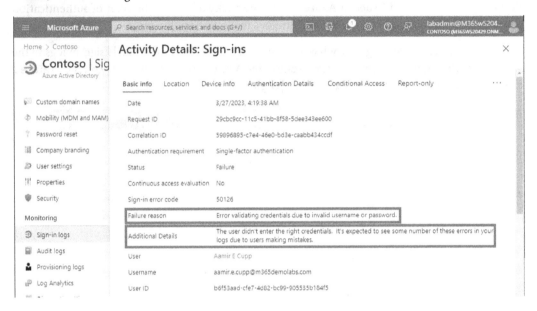

Figure 5.31 – Activity details

The **Basic info** tab displays high-level information about this particular event. The critical piece of information will typically be listed next to **Failure reason**, and some expanded explanation may be available in the **Additional Details** property. In the example shown in *Figure 5.31*, the reason for the failure of authentication is that the user entered an incorrect password. If the user has entered an incorrect password multiple times in a row, it may be a sign of a forgotten password or an attempted identity breach. *Figure 5.32* shows the same account after it has met the smart lockout threshold:

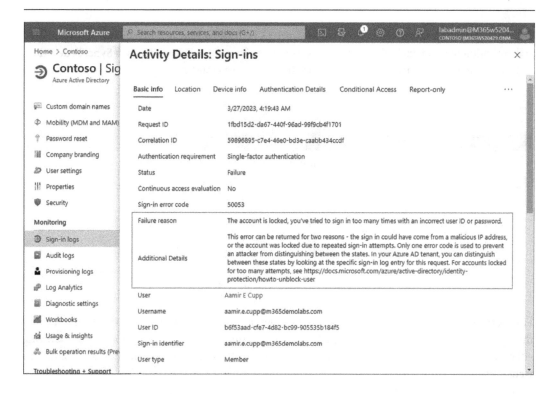

Figure 5.32 – Sign-in detail showing locked-out account

The **Location** tab will show detailed information regarding the source IP address, and, if possible, resolution to a particular geographic location.

The **Device info** tab displays information regarding the device that was attempting a logon, such as a Windows 10 device with the Edge browser.

> **Note**
>
> Other browsers can also provide device information or interact with the Microsoft 365 logon process if they have the **Windows Accounts** extension installed. For example, Chromium-based browsers can install the Windows Accounts extension from the Chrome Web store: `https://chromewebstore.google.com/detail/windows-accounts/ppnbnpeolgkicgegkbkbjmhlideopiji`.

The **Authentication Details** tab, shown in *Figure 5.33*, provides additional information regarding the authentication method, including whether the user is configured for **Password Hash Sync**, **Federation**, or **Pass-through Authentication**, or whether they're using a cloud-managed identity:

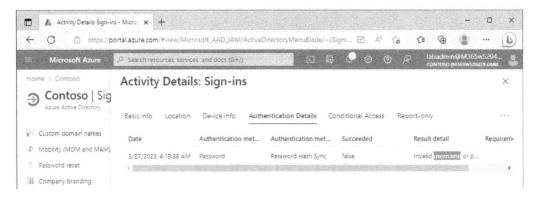

Figure 5.33 – Authentication details

Finally, the last two tabs, **Conditional Access** and **Report-only**, show what policies took effect during the sign-in process. You can review these tabs for the status of Conditional Access policies, showing either what was applied or would have been applied during the logon process and how any conditions were satisfied.

Resolving an authentication issue sometimes requires examining several logs to determine the source of the error. In many cases, however, the detailed data provided on each of the tabs of an event's activity details should provide adequate information to pinpoint the source of the error.

Summary

In this chapter, you learned how to evaluate passwordless sign-in options for your organization and deploy the ones that best suit your needs. Some passwordless options, such as Windows Hello or FIDO2 keys, may require specialized hardware such as cameras, USB devices, or fingerprint readers, while the Microsoft Authenticator app method requires only the Microsoft Authenticator app on any supported Android or iOS-based device.

You also learned about deploying features such as self-service password reset and Azure AD password protection to further reduce administrative overhead, helping your organization comply with security policies.

In the next chapter, you'll learn about implementing secure access in the context of Microsoft 365.

Exam Readiness Drill - Chapter Review Questions

Benchmark Score: 75%

Apart from a solid understanding of key concepts, being able to think quickly under time pressure is a skill that will help you ace your certification exam. That's why, working on these skills early on in your learning journey is key.

Chapter review questions are designed to improve your test-taking skills progressively with each chapter you learn and review your understanding of key concepts in the chapter at the same time. You'll find these at the end of each chapter.

> **Before You Proceed**
>
> You need to unlock these resources before you start using them. Unlocking **takes less than 10 minutes, can be done from any device**, and **needs to be done only once**. Head over to the start of *Chapter 7, Managing Security Reports and Alerts by Using the Microsoft 365 Defender Portal* in this book for instructions on how to unlock them.

To open the **Chapter Review Questions** for this chapter, click the following link: `https://packt.link/MS102E1_Ch05`. Or, you can scan the following QR code:

Figure 5.34 – QR code that opens Chapter Review Questions for logged-in users

Once you login, you'll see a page similar to what is shown in *Figure 5.35*:

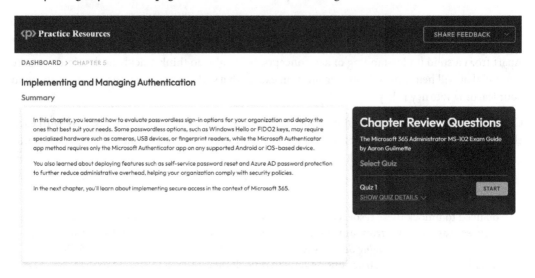

Figure 5.35 – Chapter Review Questions for Chapter 5

Once ready, start the following practice drills, re-attempting the quiz multiple times:

Exam Readiness Drill

For the first 3 attempts, don't worry about the time limit.

ATTEMPT 1

The first time, aim for at least 40%. Look at the answers you got wrong and read the relevant sections in the chapter again to fix your learning gaps.

ATTEMPT 2

The second time, aim for at least 60%. Look at the answers you got wrong and read the relevant sections in the chapter again to fix any remaining learning gaps.

ATTEMPT 3

The third time, aim for at least 75%. Once you score 75% or more, you start working on your timing.

> **Tip**
>
> You may take more than 3 attempts to reach 75%. That's okay. Just review the relevant sections in the chapter till you get there.

Working On Timing

Target: Your aim is to keep the score the same while trying to answer these questions as quickly as possible. Here's an example of how your next attempts should look like:

Attempt	Score	Time Taken
Attempt 5	77%	21 mins 30 seconds
Attempt 6	78%	18 mins 34 seconds
Attempt 7	76%	14 mins 44 seconds

Table 5.4 – Sample timing practice drills on the online platform

> **Note**
>
> The time limits shown in the above table are just examples. Set your own time limits with each attempt based on the time limit of the quiz on the website.

With each new attempt, your score should stay **above 75%** while your time taken to complete should decrease. Repeat as many attempts as you want till you feel confident dealing with the time pressure.

Implementing and Managing Secure Access

Securing access and identity is one of the most important parts of managing a Microsoft 365 tenant.

As an administrator, you may need to configure the environment to restrict application and data access from secure locations or devices. Planning an access strategy for both internal and external access is critical to maintaining a secure operating environment.

This chapter will look at the following areas:

- Planning for Identity Protection
- Implementing and managing Azure AD Identity Protection
- Planning Conditional Access policies
- Implementing and managing Conditional Access policies

By the end of this chapter, you should be able to describe and configure Identity Protection and Conditional Access policies.

Planning for Identity Protection

Azure Identity Protection is an Azure AD Premium P2 feature (with a few limited features available in P1) that allows organizations to identify several types of risks in the Azure AD environment based on signals received and processed, including the following:

- Impossible or atypical travel (logging in from two geographically distant areas in a very short amount of time)
- Usage of anonymous IP addresses or address ranges
- Usage of malware-linked IP addresses

- Leaked credentials, such as end user or workload identity client ID or secret values

- Password spray attempts

These risks are categorized into three tiers: low, medium, and high. While Microsoft doesn't provide exact details on what signals or combinations of signals are used as the basis of categorization, it does provide reporting and workflows that can mitigate the risks.

> **Note**
>
> Identity Protection features are based on machine learning and need to gather at least 30 days' worth of baseline data before it can be used to provide information.

When these types of activities or events are detected, notifications are generated for administrators. For example, users attempting to log in when impossible travel is detected may be presented with a dialog to re-confirm their identity using an already-established multifactor authentication method.

Depending on how your security organization is structured, you may be able to delegate certain levels of responsibility. *Table 6.1* describes the roles and access available to Identity Protection users:

Role	Identity Protection Actions allowed	Identity Protection Actions prohibited
Global Administrator	All	
Security Administrator	• View all Identity Protection reports • Dismiss user risk, confirm safe sign-in, confirm compromise • Create Conditional Access policies that use risk as a sign-in condition	Reset user passwords
Security Operator	• View all Identity Protection reports • Dismiss user risk, confirm safe sign-in, confirm compromise	• Configure policies • Reset user passwords • Configure alerts

Role	Identity Protection Actions allowed	Identity Protection Actions prohibited
Security Reader	View all Identity Protection reports	• Configure policies • Reset user passwords • Configure alerts • Give feedback on detections
Global Reader	Read-only access to Identity Protection	
Conditional Access Administrator	Create Conditional Access policies that use risk as a sign-in condition	All Identity Protection actions

Table 6.1 – Identity Protection roles

Identity Protection data is contained in four reports:

- Risky users
- Risky workload identities
- Risky sign-ins
- Risk detections

Figure 6.1 shows examples of risk items:

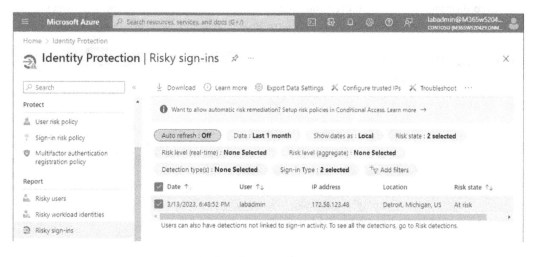

Figure 6.1 – Identity protection reports

Using the data in these reports, you can review details of risk events in the tenant. Before implementing Identity Protection policies, you should review the existing Identity Protection reports.

Investigating Risks

You can review risks by reviewing the various risk detection reports on the **Identity Protection** blade (`https://aka.ms/identityprotection`). For example, you can expand the **Risky users** report and select an individual user, as shown in *Figure 6.2*:

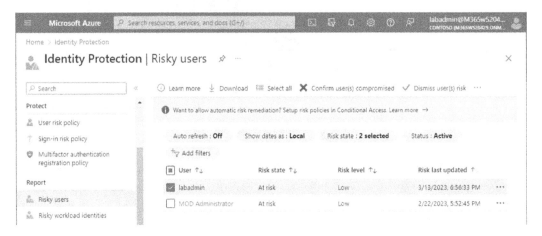

Figure 6.2 – Risky users report

By clicking on the user, you can view details regarding the items contributing to the risk level for the user as well as historical data for risk-related events. You can perform additional actions for a user, such as confirming that a user has been compromised, dismissing risk, blocking the user from logging in, or opening the corresponding events in Microsoft 365 Defender, as shown in *Figure 6.3*:

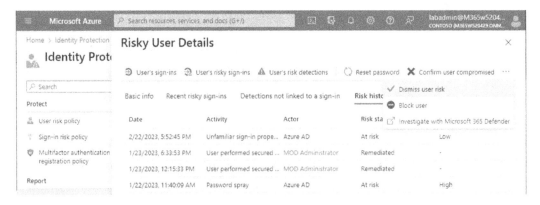

Figure 6.3 – Risky User Details pane

The **Risk info** page of the **Risky Sign-in Details** pane allows you to further understand the types of risks associated with the user, as shown in *Figure 6.4*:

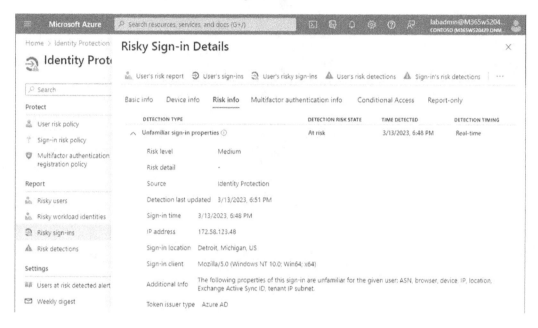

Figure 6.4 – Risky Sign-in Details page

After reviewing the risky sign-in data and confirming safe or compromised logins, you can move on to remediating the risks.

Remediating risks

All active, non-dismissed risks contribute to an individual user's risk level, which equates to the probability that a user has been compromised. Risk remediation involves reviewing the logs and reports available and then making decisions on how to proceed: reset passwords, block accounts from logging in, disable the users' devices, revoke any sign-in tokens, or confirm that the account is safe.

Implementing and Managing Azure Identity Protection

Identity Protection has three policy configuration nodes on the **Identity Protection** blade:

- User risk policy
- Sign-in risk policy
- Multifactor authentication registration policy

The Identity Protection **User risk policy** pane, depicted in *Figure 6.5*, is used to scope the Identity Protection features and enable the settings to control access enforcement:

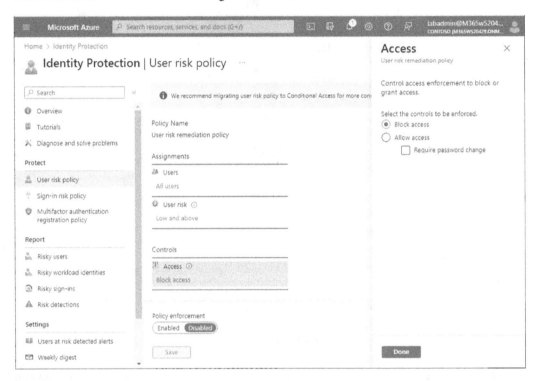

Figure 6.5 – User risk policy

The term **user risk** represents the likelihood that an identity (user account, service, or workload identity) is somehow compromised. User risk is determined based on all available signal data.

Sign-in risk, while similar to user risk, is a more restricted view of the signal data. Sign-in risk assertions are used to represent the likelihood that a sign-in or authentication request wasn't authorized by the identity owner. The **Sign-in risk policy** pane features similar scoping and control policy settings, as shown in *Figure 6.6*:

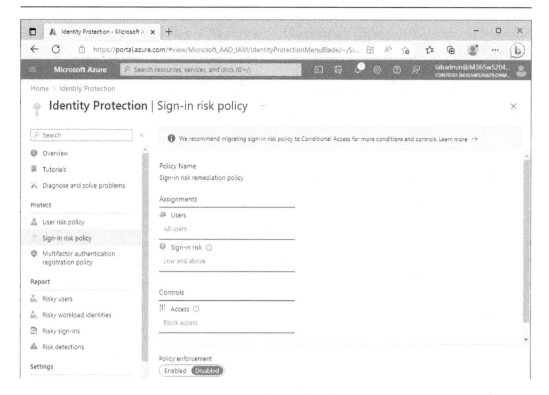

Figure 6.6 – Sign-in risk policy

Finally, the **Multifactor authentication registration policy**, as shown in *Figure 6.7*, is used to require users to configure Azure AD multifactor authentication as part of self-remediation for at-risk users:

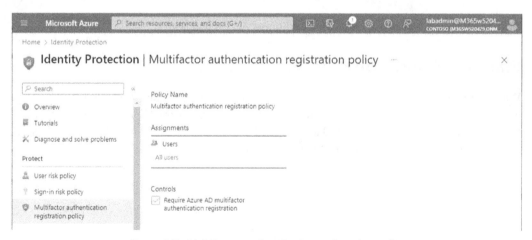

Figure 6.7 – Multifactor authentication registration policy

Microsoft recommends migrating the native Identity Protection policies (configured through the Identity Protection blade) to the newer **Conditional Access policies**, as shown in *Figure 6.8*:

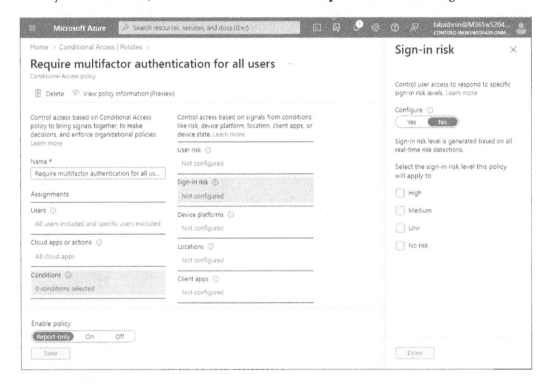

Figure 6.8 – Migrating Identity Protection policies to Conditional Access

Next, you'll look at securing access with Conditional Access policies.

Planning Conditional Access Policies

With the increase in hybrid and remote work, it is important to ensure that users can securely access organizational resources. Conditional Access policies, part of Azure AD Premium Plans P1 and P2, Enterprise Mobility + Security E3 and E5, and Microsoft 365 F1, E3, and E5, are Microsoft's recommended tools for providing identity security for Microsoft 365 users.

In this section, you'll look at planning and configuring Conditional Access to secure identity and resources.

Conditional Access policies can be used to secure both Microsoft 365 workloads as well as applications that are federated with Azure AD. See *Figure 6.9*:

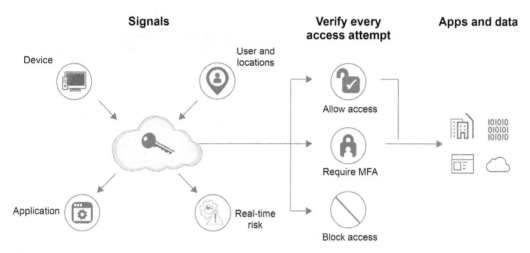

Figure 6.9 – Conditional Access signals

Conditional Access requires an Azure AD Premium P1 plan for all features, with the exception of risk-based Conditional Access, which requires an Azure AD Premium P2 plan. Administering and configuring Conditional Access requires either the Global Administrator, Conditional Access Administrator, or Security Administrator role.

A Conditional Access policy is made up of the following components:

- Assignments
- Conditions
- Access controls

Let's explore each of these areas.

Assignments

Assignments are used to control the scoping of a policy. The **Users** assignment control, shown in *Figure 6.10*, allows you to include or exclude a mix of **Users and groups**, **Guest or external users**, and **Directory roles**.

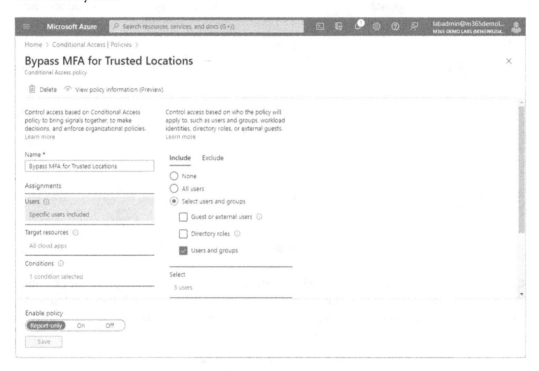

Figure 6.10 – Conditional Access policy user assignments

You can select items from both the **Include** and **Exclude** tabs in a single policy to fine-tune the individuals that will be impacted by a policy.

The **Target resources** assignment, shown in *Figure 6.11*, is used to select which **Cloud apps**, **User actions**, or **Authentication contexts** are included in or excluded from the policy scope:

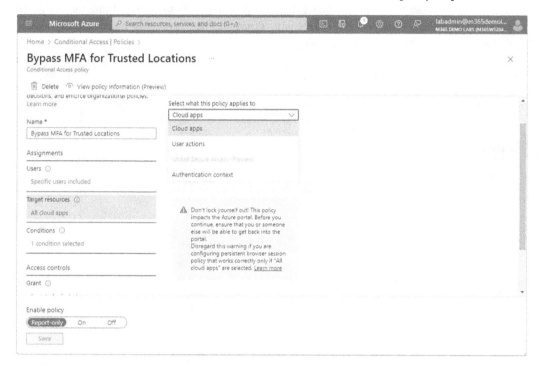

Figure 6.11 – Conditional Access policy target resources assignments

> **Note**
>
> You can only select one target resource type per Conditional Access policy. For example, you cannot select an application and a user action in the same policy. Policies can only be scoped to user identities or groups that contain user identities. Devices cannot be members of groups used for Conditional Access policy assignment, though device filters can be implemented as part of a condition.

If you select **Cloud apps** as the target resource type, you can choose from any of the applications that are connected to Azure AD. This includes both out-of-the-box Microsoft first-party applications, any third-party applications configured as Azure AD Enterprise applications, and applications configured to use Azure AD Application Proxy in your tenant. *Figure 6.12* shows multiple native and third-party applications selected for inclusion in a policy:

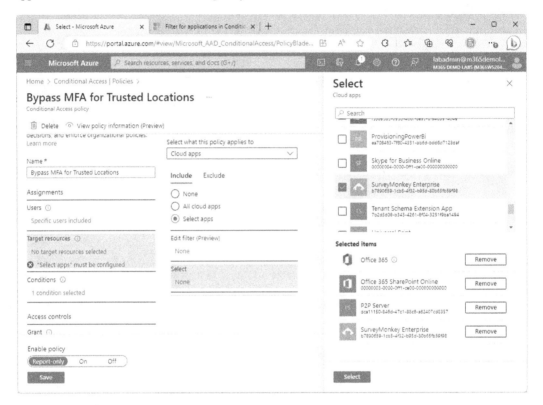

Figure 6.12 – Conditional Access policy cloud apps

Further Reading

Conditional Access application filters are in public preview, which allow you to create search filters for selecting which applications will be included or excluded from the policy. To work with attribute filters, you must be delegated one of the following roles: **Attribute Assignment Administrator**, **Attribute Assignment Reader**, **Attribute Definition Administrator**, or **Attribute Definition Reader**. Global administrators are not automatically granted access to this feature, though users with the Global administrator role can assign these roles to themselves. For more information on configuring attribute filters, see `https://learn.microsoft.com/en-us/azure/active-directory/conditional-access/concept-filter-for-applications`.

If you select **User actions** as the **Target resources** assignment, you can include the **Register security information** and **Register or join devices** actions. You can also select an **authentication context**—a configuration object that is used to identify and secure content inside SharePoint.

> **Further Reading**
>
> For more information on authentication contexts, see https://aka.ms/authentication-context.

Conditions

Conditions are the scenarios under which access will be granted or blocked. Conditions include **User risk**, **Sign-in risk**, **Device platforms**, **Locations**, **Client apps**, and **Filter for devices**. You can configure one or more conditions as part of a policy. See *Figure 6.13*:

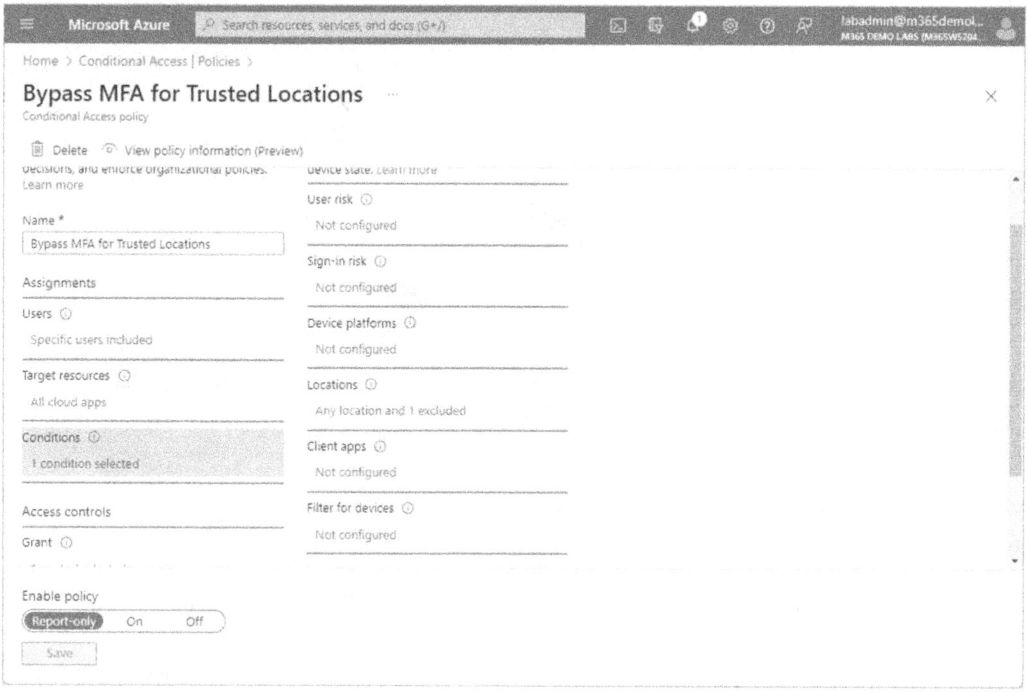

Figure 6.13 – Conditional Access policy conditions

Access Controls

Access controls are used to specify how access is granted and what experiences are allowed for the users. Access controls are divided between **Grant** and **Session**.

The **Grant** configuration node is used to either block access if the conditions are met or grant access with certain stipulations: **Require multifactor authentication**, **Require authentication strength**, **Require device to be marked as compliant**, **Require Hybrid Azure AD joined device**, **Require approved client app**, **Require app protection policy**, or **Require password change**. You can choose to require only a single control or require all of the selected controls. *Figure 6.14* depicts some of the **Grant access** control options:

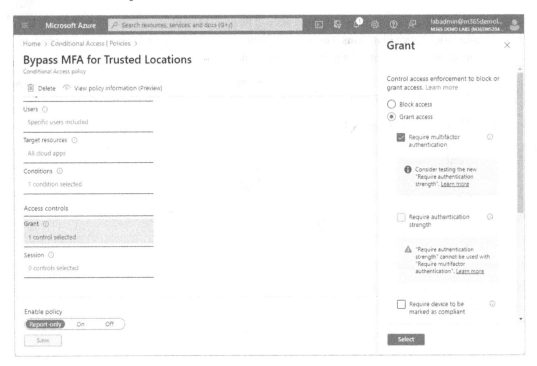

Figure 6.14 – Granting access control with the Conditional Access policy

The **Session** configuration node controls are used to enable or manage limited experiences in supported cloud applications. You can choose from **Use app enforced restrictions** (only available in Office 365, Exchange Online, and SharePoint Online), **Use Conditional Access App Control**, **Sign-in frequency**, **Persistent browser session**, **Customize continuous access evaluation**, **Disable resilience defaults**, and **Require token protection for sign-in sessions (Preview)**. See *Figure 6.15* for an example of the **Session** controls:

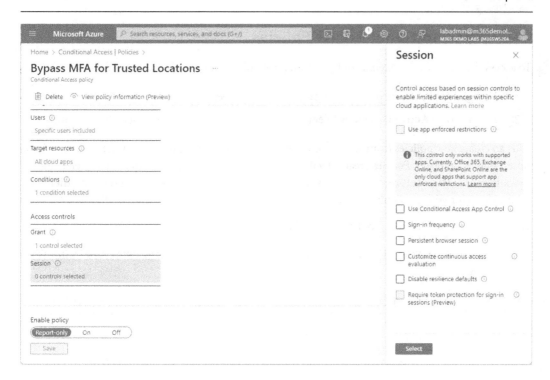

Figure 6.15 – Conditional Access policy session controls

You can configure both **Grant** and **Session** access controls in the same policy.

Further Reading

For more information on session controls, see https://aka.ms/caapprestrictions.

Finally, as part of the planning process, you can choose to enable a policy in **Report-only** mode (see *Figure 6.14* and *Figure 6.15*). That way, you can configure the settings and then review the sign-in logs to see whether the policy had been applied during a particular sign-in or access attempt.

Implementing and Managing Conditional Access Policies

Conditional Access provides the most fine-grained control when managing the multifactor authentication requirements for your organization. Conditional Access policies can be configured from the Azure portal.

Creating Conditional Access Policies

To access the Conditional Access configuration page, follow these steps:

1. Navigate to the Azure portal (`https://portal.azure.com`).

2. Select **Azure Active Directory** | **Security** | **Conditional Access**, and then choose **Policies**.

You can create new policies from scratch or use one of the Microsoft-provided 14 sample Conditional Access policy templates. Policies created by the template can be modified once they have been deployed to your tenant. Microsoft recommends using the policy templates as a starting point and then fine-tuning them for your particular use case.

To configure a template-based policy, follow these steps:

1. From the **Conditional Access** | **Policies** page, as shown in *Figure 6.16*, select **New policy from template (Preview)**:

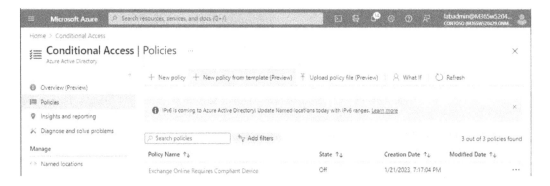

Figure 6.16 – Creating a new Conditional Access policy from a template

2. Select one of the templates, such as **Require multifactor authentication for all users**, and click **Review + create**. See *Figure 6.17*:

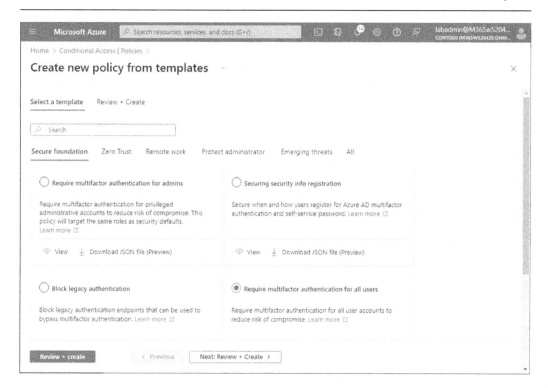

Figure 6.17 – Selecting a template

3. Review the settings and click **Create**.

Policies created through the templates cannot be modified during creation, with the exception of the enforcement mode. All template-based policies are configured in **Report only** mode, which can be toggled during creation. The user creating the policy is excluded from the policy to prevent accidental lock-out.

After the template policies have been configured, you can edit the scope and conditions for the policy like any other manually created policy.

> **Further Reading**
>
> For more information on Conditional Access templates, see `https://learn.microsoft.com/en-us/azure/active-directory/conditional-access/concept-conditional-access-policy-common`.

Reporting on Conditional Access Policies

The insights and reporting workbook for Conditional Access offers a detailed analysis of how Conditional Access policies affect your organization. When a user signs in, their login might be impacted by one or more Conditional Access policies. These policies can either allow or deny access based on specific grant controls. By processing the Entra ID sign-in logs, the insights and reporting workbook can be used to determine the impact of policies.

> **Note**
>
> The insights and reporting workbook requires an Azure subscription with a Log Analytics workspace in addition to either Azure AD Premium P1 or P2 or Entra ID P1 or P2. While configuring and using the insights and reporting workbook is not part of the MS-102 exam, it is definitely worth reviewing as you progress through your Microsoft 365 administration journey.

Before you can use the insights and reporting workbook, you need to set up a Log Analytics workspace and connect the Microsoft Azure AD or Entra ID logs to the workspace.

Configuring a Log Analytics Workspace

The Log Analytics workspace will be used to process the logs from Azure AD. To configure a Log Analytics workspace, follow these steps:

1. Navigate to the Azure portal (`https://portal.azure.com`).
2. In the **Search** box, enter `Log Analytics` and select **Log Analytics workspaces**.
3. Click **Create**.
4. Under **Project details**, select a subscription and a resource group.
5. Under **Instance details**, enter a name and select a region.
6. Click **Review + Create** to skip to the end of the wizard.
7. On the **Review + Create** page, click **Create**.

Once you have a Log Analytics workspace provisioned, you can proceed to the next step.

Integrating Azure AD or Entra ID Logs

In order for Log Analytics to be able to work with Entra ID logs, you need to configure log integration with Azure Monitor. To configure the integration, follow these steps:

1. Navigate to the Entra admin center (`https://entra.microsoft.com`).

2. Expand **Identity | Monitoring & health | Diagnostic settings**. See *Figure 6.18*:

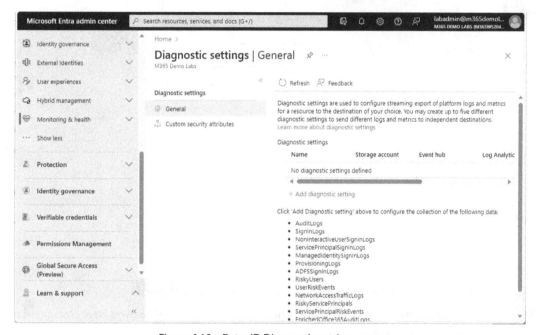

Figure 6.18 – Entra ID Diagnostic settings page

3. Click **Add diagnostic setting**.

4. Enter a diagnostic setting name.

5.   Under **Logs**, select **SignInLogs**, **NonInteractiveUserSignInLogs**, **ServicePrincipalSignInLogs**, **ManagedIdentitySignInLogs**, and **ADFSSignInLogs** at a minimum, as shown in *Figure 6.19*:

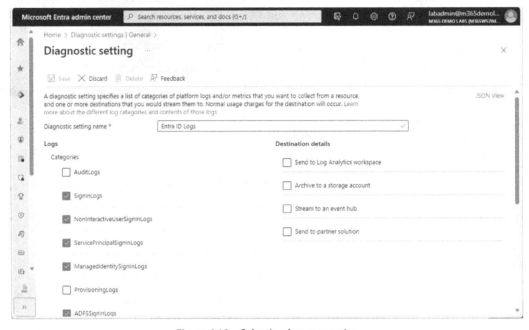

Figure 6.19 – Selecting log categories

6.   Under **Destination details**, select **Send to Log Analytics workspace**.

7.   In the **Subscription** dropdown, select the Azure subscription where you have configured a Log Analytics workspace.

8.   In the **Log Analytics workspace** dropdown, select the **Log Analytics workspace**.

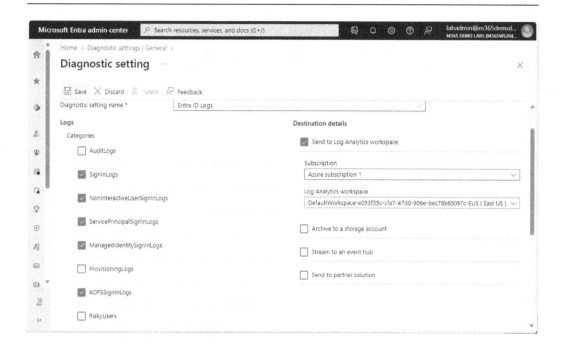

Figure 6.20 – Selecting the destination

9. Click **Save**.

After the settings take effect, log events will begin flowing into the Log Analytics workspace.

Reviewing the Workbook

After logs have begun showing up in Log Analytics, you can use the insights and reporting workbook to view the details. To access the workbook, follow these steps:

1. Navigate to the Azure portal (`https://portal.azure.com`).
2. In the **Search** box, enter `Conditional Access` and select **Conditional Access**.
3. Select **Insights and reporting**.

4. Adjust the filters to select the data to display, as shown in *Figure 6.21*:

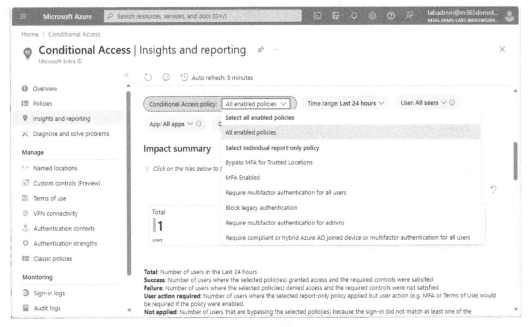

Figure 6.21 – Setting filters to display data

By adjusting the filter criteria, you can gain insights into what Conditional Access policies were applied to what users, which were excluded, and what applications, device platforms, and other condition criteria were applied.

Summary

In this chapter, you learned about Identity Protection features and Conditional Access policies. You also learned about Identity Protection features such as risk-based access policies and how to investigate and remediate risks.

In the next chapter, you will learn about configuring application access.

Exam Readiness Drill - Chapter Review Questions

Benchmark Score: 75%

Apart from a solid understanding of key concepts, being able to think quickly under time pressure is a skill that will help you ace your certification exam. That's why, working on these skills early on in your learning journey is key.

Chapter review questions are designed to improve your test-taking skills progressively with each chapter you learn and review your understanding of key concepts in the chapter at the same time. You'll find these at the end of each chapter.

> **Before You Proceed**
>
> You need to unlock these resources before you start using them. Unlocking **takes less than 10 minutes, can be done from any device**, and **needs to be done only once**. Head over to the start of *Chapter 7, Managing Security Reports and Alerts by Using the Microsoft 365 Defender Portal* in this book for instructions on how to unlock them.

To open the **Chapter Review Questions** for this chapter, click the following link: `https://packt.link/MS102E1_CH06`. Or, you can scan the following QR code:

Figure 6.22 – QR code that opens Chapter Review Questions for logged-in users

Once you login, you'll see a page similar to what is shown in *Figure 6.23*:

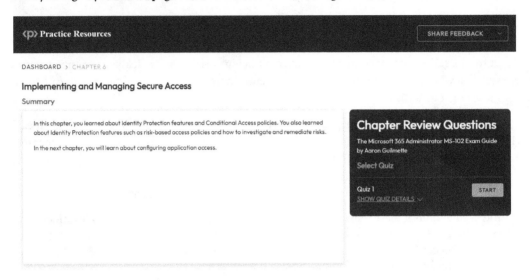

Figure 6.23 – Chapter Review Questions for Chapter 6

Once ready, start the following practice drills, re-attempting the quiz multiple times:

Exam Readiness Drill

For the first 3 attempts, don't worry about the time limit.

ATTEMPT 1

The first time, aim for at least 40%. Look at the answers you got wrong and read the relevant sections in the chapter again to fix your learning gaps.

ATTEMPT 2

The second time, aim for at least 60%. Look at the answers you got wrong and read the relevant sections in the chapter again to fix any remaining learning gaps.

ATTEMPT 3

The third time, aim for at least 75%. Once you score 75% or more, you start working on your timing.

> **Tip**
>
> You may take more than 3 attempts to reach 75%. That's okay. Just review the relevant sections in the chapter till you get there.

Working On Timing

Target: Your aim is to keep the score the same while trying to answer these questions as quickly as possible. Here's an example of how your next attempts should look like:

Attempt	Score	Time Taken
Attempt 5	77%	21 mins 30 seconds
Attempt 6	78%	18 mins 34 seconds
Attempt 7	76%	14 mins 44 seconds

Table 6.2 – Sample timing practice drills on the online platform

> **Note**
>
> The time limits shown in the above table are just examples. Set your own time limits with each attempt based on the time limit of the quiz on the website.

With each new attempt, your score should stay **above 75%** while your time taken to complete should decrease. Repeat as many attempts as you want till you feel confident dealing with the time pressure.

Managing Security Reports and Alerts by Using the Microsoft 365 Defender Portal

Instructions to Unlock the Free Practice Resources

To access the free online content that comes with the book, you'll need to unlock it first. Unlocking **takes less than 10 minutes, can be done from any device, and needs to be done only once**. Follow these 5 easy steps to complete the process:

STEP 1

Open the link `https://packt.link/ms102ed1unlock` OR scan the following QR code:

Figure 7.1 – QR code for page that lets you unlock this book's free online content

Either of those links will lead to the following page as shown in *Figure 7.2*:

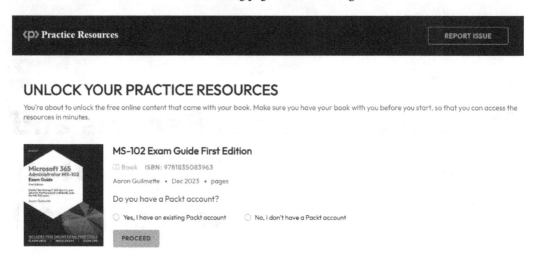

Figure 7.2 – Unlock page for MS-102 Exam Guide First Edition Practice Resources

STEP 2

If you already have a Packt account, select the option "**Yes, I have an existing Packt account**". If not, select the option "**No, I don't have a Packt account**".

If you don't have a Packt account, you'll be prompted to create a new Packt account on the next page. It's free and takes just a minute to create.

Click **Proceed** after selecting one of those options.

> **Forgot your password?**
>
> If you have a Packt account but have forgotten your password, you can reset it from this link before proceeding to the next step. You can reset your password here
> `https://www.packtpub.com/forget-password`.

STEP 3

After you've created your account or logged in to an existing one, you'll be directed to the following page as shown in *Figure 7.3*:

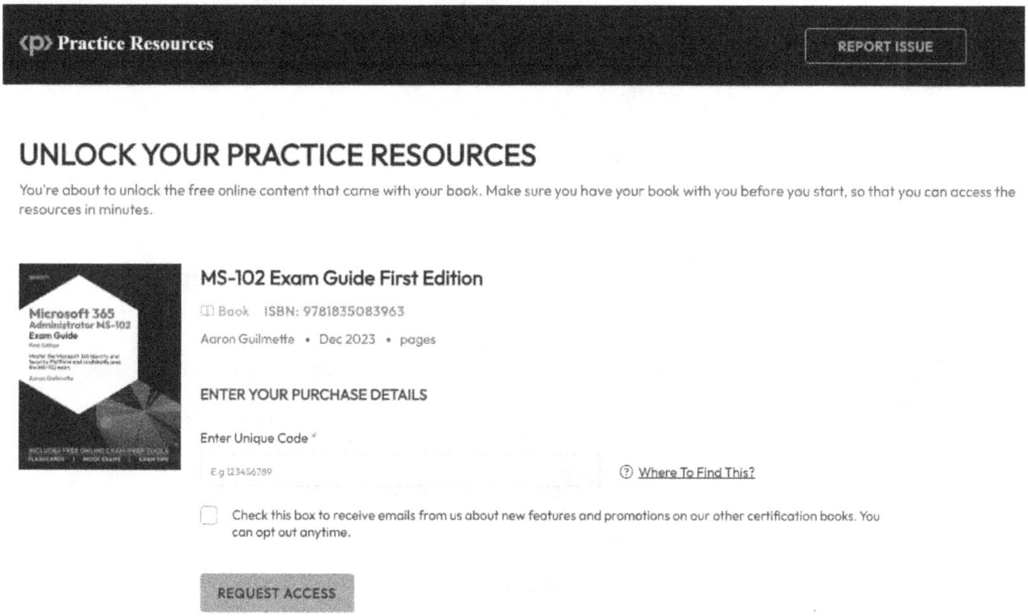

Figure 7.3 – Enter your unique sign-up code to unlock the resources

STEP 4

Enter the following unique code:

HUJ8067

Optional: You may choose to opt into promotions regarding other certification books. We don't spam, only send the best deals, and it's easy to opt out at any time.

Click **Request Access**.

STEP 5

If the code you entered is correct, you'll see a button that says, **OPEN PRACTICE RESOURCES**, as shown in *Figure 7.4*:

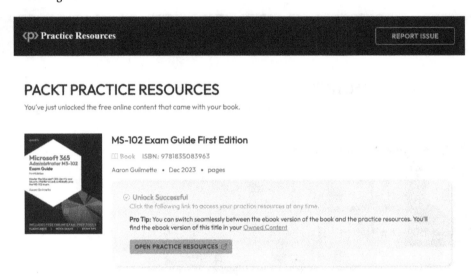

Figure 7.4 – Page that shows up when you've successfully unlocked the free online content

Click the **OPEN PRACTICE RESOURCES** link to start using your free online content. You'll be redirected to the Dashboard that looks similar to *Figure 7.5*.

Figure 7.5 – Dashboard page upon successful unlock of practice resources

Refer to the *Practice Resources – A Quick Tour* section of the *Preface* for a quick tour of these Practice Resources.

Bookmark this link

Now that you've unlocked the resources, you can come back to them anytime by visiting this link: `https://packt.link/ms102ed1practice`

Or by scanning the following QR code:

Figure 7.6 – QR code for your free practice resources

Troubleshooting Tips

If you're facing issues unlocking, here are 3 things you can do:

1. Double-check your unique code. All unique codes in our books are case sensitive and your code needs to match exactly as it is shown in *STEP 5*.

2. If that doesn't work, use the "**Report Issue**" button located at the top-right corner of the page.

3. If you're not able to open the unlock page at all, write to `customercare@packt.com` and mention the name of the book.

Microsoft 365 Defender is an advanced cloud-based **Extended Detection and Response (XDR)** suite that harnesses vast datasets within the Microsoft 365 environment, delivering insights and capabilities to detect, prevent, investigate, and respond to cybersecurity threats. This comprehensive solution ingests data from across various workloads, including the following:

- **Endpoints**: Personal computer workstations, mobile devices, and servers

- **Office 365**: Exchange email messages, Teams chats, and files stored in SharePoint Online/ OneDrive for Business

- **Identity**: User and workload sign-in data and credentials

- **Cloud apps**: First and third-party **Software as a Service (SaaS)** solutions

The hub to manage Microsoft 365 Defender is the **Microsoft 365 Defender portal**, previously known as the Microsoft 365 Security Center. This unified portal offers a user-friendly experience designed to help organizations investigate and respond to threats across the entire Microsoft 365 ecosystem. The portal consolidates various tools and resources from different security domains, including threat monitoring, hunting, attack simulation, alerting policies, email message tracing, threat investigation, and auditing functionalities.

Further Learning

With Microsoft 365 Defender safeguarding these workloads, security administrators can seamlessly integrate it with **Security Information and Event Management (SIEM)** and **Security Orchestration, Automation, and Response (SOAR)** tools such as **Microsoft Sentinel**. While Microsoft Sentinel is outside the scope of the MS-102 exam, you can learn more about it here: `https://learn.microsoft.com/en-us/azure/sentinel/overview`.

This chapter covers the following exam objectives:

- Reviewing and taking action to improve the Microsoft Secure Score in the Microsoft 365 Defender portal
- Reviewing and responding to security incidents and alerts in Microsoft 365 Defender
- Reviewing and responding to issues identified in security and compliance reports in Microsoft 365 Defender
- Reviewing and responding to threats identified in threat analytics

It's a big objective, so let's dive in!

Reviewing and Taking Action to Improve the Microsoft Secure Score in the Microsoft 365 Defender Portal

Microsoft 365 has several security features that can be configured in different ways, depending on an organization's requirements. However, many organizations aren't up to date on all the settings, the order in which the settings need to be addressed, and how they might impact the user experience.

Additionally, organizations are faced with the following questions:

- How can they understand the current security best practices?
- How does their current deployment compare to the best practices?
- What are the steps necessary to proactively configure security controls?

Secure Score is a Microsoft 365 capability that contains a list of security-focused features and configuration recommendations. Each recommendation or setting is assigned a point value. Secure Score compares an organization's current settings against the Microsoft-recommended best practices for the available (licensed) applications and services, assigning the tenant a score.

Secure Score provides a view of your organization's security posture and helps you determine which actions need to be taken to improve the current score. Microsoft Secure Score can be accessed through the Microsoft 365 Defender portal at `https://security.microsoft.com` under the **Secure Score** navigation item.

The **Overview** page is shown in *Figure 7.7*:

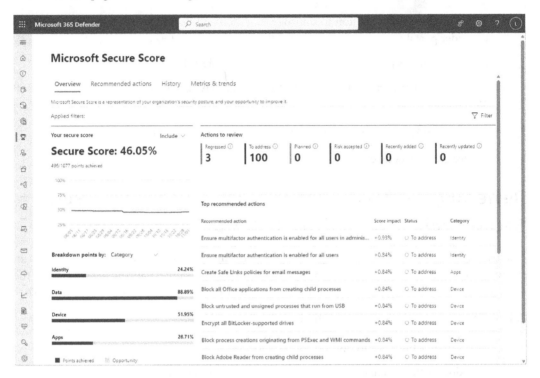

Figure 7.7 – Microsoft Secure Score

Possible actions are organized according to the following categories:

- **Identity**
- **Data**
- **Device**
- **Apps**

Figure 7.8 shows various **Recommended actions** (previously called **Improvement actions**), sorted by rank (the highest score impact):

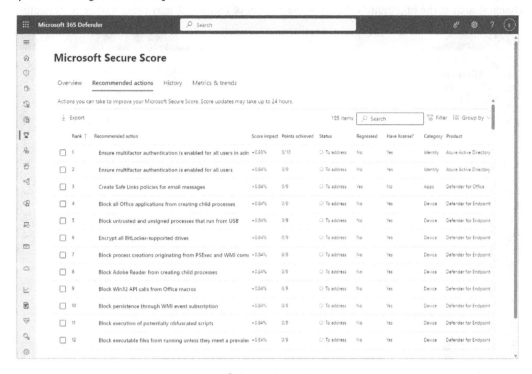

Figure 7.8 – Microsoft Secure Score improvement actions

> **Note**
>
> The term **Improvement actions** has been replaced with **Recommended actions** in the Microsoft 365 Defender portal. Look out for either term on the exam.

For each recommended action, you can review a description and see which attacks or risks it mitigates, understand the related compliance controls, and review the impact of its implementation on users. The score is updated (typically after 48 hours), and the refreshed score is shown on the dashboard on the **Overview** page.

The dashboard provides links to the various admin centers where actions need to be taken. It also includes an acknowledgment toggle that lets you indicate whether a mitigation has been implemented in a third-party system that isn't tracked by Secure Score, thus allowing them to maintain a more accurate tally.

As you make changes (including remediations and adding services or features to the environment), the **History** tab (shown in *Figure 7.9*) shows how those actions taken have impacted the score. Some changes, such as the highlighted change at the bottom of *Figure 7.9*, may cause a score regression:

Figure 7.9 – Viewing the Secure Score history

Microsoft recommends reviewing Secure Score frequently to make sure you implement current best practices, as well as enabling and configuring new security controls as features become available or you change subscriptions. This will help you to continuously improve the security of your Microsoft 365 environment.

The **Metrics & trends** tab displays information about historical changes in your Secure Score, as well as providing a comparison of how your score relates to other organizations of similar size or industry.

Reviewing and Responding to Security Incidents and Alerts in Microsoft 365 Defender

Alerts represent individual risk items or threats, such as an email that triggers a **data loss prevention** (**DLP**) policy action or a macro that queries a computer's filesystem. When threats are detected in the organization through any of the Microsoft 365 Defender signals, they will show up on the **Alerts** page of Microsoft 365 Defender.

When working with incidents and alerts in the Microsoft 365 platform, Microsoft recommends a three-phased approach – **Triage**, **Investigate**, and **Respond** – as shown in *Figure 7.10*:

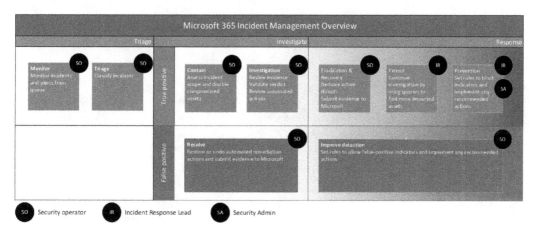

Figure 7.10 – The Microsoft 365 Incident Management phases

The first phase, **Triage**, involves determining whether the alerts generated are indeed real (true positives) or not (false positives). In the **Investigate** phase, potentially affected assets are isolated or disabled (or, if automation is already in place that has disabled and isolated assets, you review those assets and determine whether you need to adjust the scope). If the alert was a false positive and automated incident response activities were activated, you may need to restore functionality for those assets. The final phase, **Response**, includes any recovery actions (e.g., removing malware, restoring data, resetting devices, or other activities related to eradicating the threat) as well as implementing protections to guard against the threat in the future.

Over the next few sections, you'll look at the Microsoft 365 Defender interface components that are used during the **Triage**, **Investigate**, and **Response** phases of incident management.

Reviewing alerts and incidents

To locate the **Alerts** page, navigate to the Microsoft 365 Defender portal (`https://security.microsoft.com`), expand **Incidents & alerts**, and then select **Alerts**. *Figure 7.11* depicts the **Alerts** page:

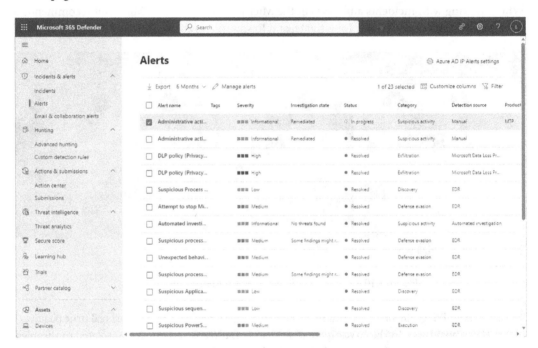

Figure 7.11 – Viewing the Alerts page in the Microsoft 365 Defender portal

Incidents are collections of alerts and other signal data that the Microsoft 365 Defender platform has correlated together. See *Figure 7.12* for an example incident:

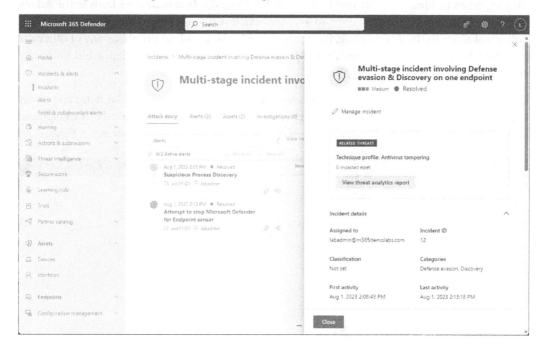

Figure 7.12 – Reviewing an incident

There are a number of tabs to navigate when reviewing the details of an incident, specifically **Attack story**, **Alerts**, **Assets**, **Investigations**, and **Evidence and Response**.

Expanding Notifications

By default, Microsoft 365 Defender doesn't generate email alerts. All alerts and incidents are visible in the Microsoft 365 Defender portal. Depending on the types of incidents your organization tends to see or the goals of your **Security Operations Center** (**SOC**), you may wish to create email notifications whenever new types of activities come in. You can create new email alerts under **Settings | Microsoft 365 Defender | Email notifications** in the Microsoft 365 Defender portal or by navigating directly to the settings panel at `https://security.microsoft.com/securitysettings/defender/email_notifications`.

You'll examine these alerts in this section.

Attack story

Clicking on an incident from the main Microsoft 365 Defender **Incidents** page leads to the **Attack story** view of an incident. In this view, you have the flexibility to pivot on various elements, including individual alerts in the **Alerts** pane, items displayed in the **Incident graph,** or any of other the available tabs that are part of the incident (**Alerts**, **Assets**, **Investigations**, **Evidence and Response**, and **Summary**).

The **Incident graph** section in the **Attack story** tab automatically groups similar items and nodes together, although you can toggle this feature off to view each item node separately. The graph can be useful for gaining a clearer understanding of interactions between events, as shown in *Figure 7.13*:

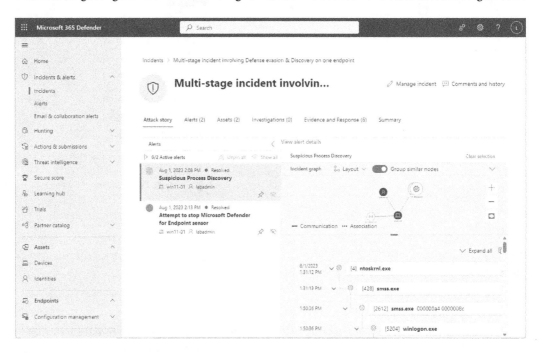

Figure 7.13 – Reviewing the Incident graph as part of an Attack story

Each item within this context provides relevant details and actionable options. For instance, you can access URL details that a malicious process attempted to contact or examine the code executed within a script. Clicking on an item in the **Alerts** pane of the **Attack story** refocuses the details pane on that specific item within the **Incident graph** and displays related events in the chain. For instance, clicking on the **Attempt to stop Microsoft Defender for Endpoint sensor** alert item (*Figure 7.14*) causes the **Attack story** to pivot, highlighting the processes and devices in the **Incident graph**:

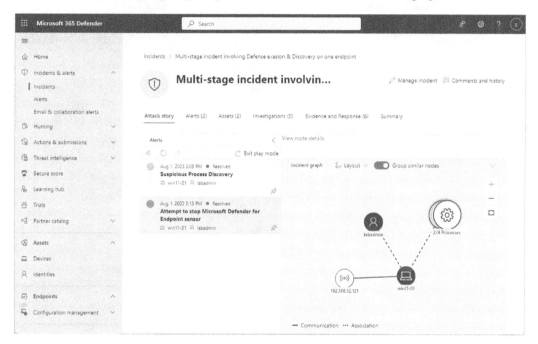

Figure 7.14 – Reviewing an alert in the Attack story

Clicking on the individual nodes in the **Incident graph** presents additional details, such as the IP address, commands executed, or processes started and stopped.

Alerts

Switching to the **Alerts** tab within an incident displays all associated alerts. Individual alerts can be selected to access more information, including details related to files, IP addresses, devices, or processes, depending on the alert type. Users have the option to modify the **Classification** of the alert state (setting it to **New**, **In progress**, or **Resolved**), assign it to an individual for further investigation or triage, specify a classification, and add comments (as depicted in *Figure 7.15*):

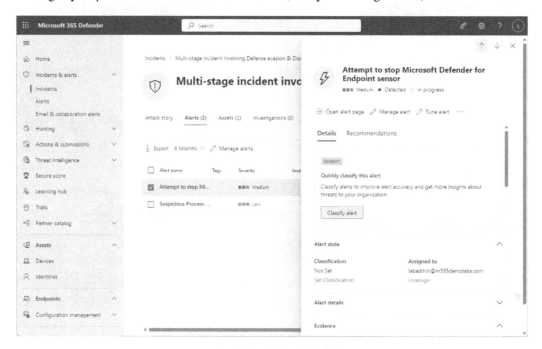

Figure 7.15 – Reviewing an alert's details

The classification feature aids in distinguishing genuine risks. This classification informs others in the organization about how to appropriately respond to such alerts.

Assets

The **Assets** tab within an incident provides a comprehensive view of all organizational assets impacted by the incident. These assets encompass **Devices**, **Users**, **Mailboxes**, and **Apps**. When a specific asset category is chosen, it reveals all the affected items within that category that are linked to the ongoing incident. Furthermore, selecting an individual item within this list will navigate you to the corresponding asset page, such as the **Assets** page for devices and users or the **Threat Explorer** for mailboxes.

Investigations

The **Investigations** tab is used to track an incident's triggering alerts. After selecting an alert to view its details, you can click **Open investigation page** to explore the event. This area also shows any automated actions that Defender has taken on your organization's behalf. An investigation is shown in *Figure 7.16*:

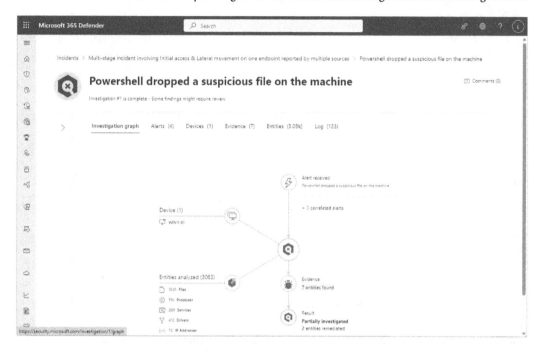

Figure 7.16 – Reviewing an investigation

The **Investigation graph** tab can show many details, depending on the type of alert being reviewed. Typically, an investigation will center around activities on a device or identity, with connectors branching out to items correlated from the graph (such as a script that creates a file or items currently loaded in memory on the device).

Evidence and Response

Like the **Investigations** tab, the **Evidence and Response** tab presents a view of correlated items that were identified as part of the event. Evidence is categorized, and each item can be expanded to provide additional context and detail, as shown in *Figure 7.17*:

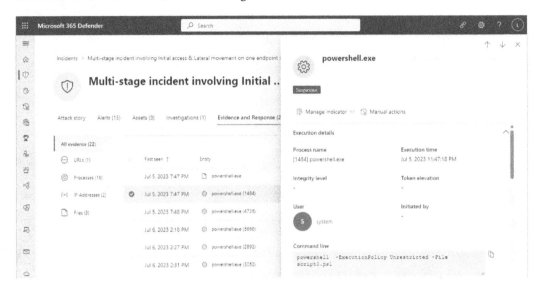

Figure 7.17 – Reviewing data on the Evidence and Response tab

The details of an individual evidence item can be used to learn about all the data gathered regarding an identity, device, URL, process, IP address, file, or other artifact.

> **Further Reading**
>
> For a deep dive into incident investigation techniques based on threat types, see `https://learn.microsoft.com/en-us/microsoft-365/security/defender/investigate-incidents`.

Responding to Alerts and Incidents

Now that you've seen where you can gather data regarding an incident during the triage phase, you'll shift to looking at how to respond.

The Microsoft 365 Defender suite has many automated actions that may be triggered – such as isolating processes or quarantining devices. You can also undertake your own tasks to further respond to incidents.

For example, when viewing the **Attack story**, you may deduce that a particular user account is responsible for attempting to extract privileged information. By selecting the identity, you can see details about what that account has been doing from an Entra ID activity perspective, mark the identity as compromised, disable the account, or force the user to sign in again and be re-prompted for MFA, see *Figure 7.18*:

Figure 7.18 – Taking action on a user in the Attack story

Alternatively, perhaps your investigation revealed that a particular device was used as an attack vector for other events. By selecting the device and expanding the actions pane, you may be able to take action to isolate that device and prevent it from causing further problems, see *Figure 7.19*:

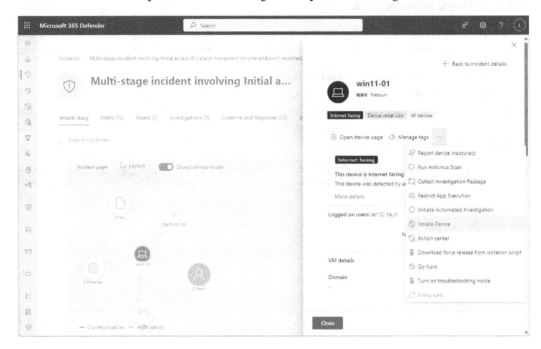

Figure 7.19 – Responding to a problematic device

Isolating the potential risks in the environment is key to limiting the scope of impact.

> **Further Reading**
>
> You'll look at Microsoft 365 Defender for Endpoint in more detail in *Chapter 9, Implementing and Managing Endpoint Protection by Using Microsoft Defender for Endpoint*.

As you work through alerts and incidents, you can use the Microsoft 365 Defender portal to apply **tags** to incidents (labels that help you group or classify incidents for your organization), assign incident tasks to others, track notes through **Comments**, update the **Status**, and apply a **Classification** from a taxonomical list to help keep others in your organization's **Security Operations Center (SOC)** informed, as shown in *Figure 7.20*:

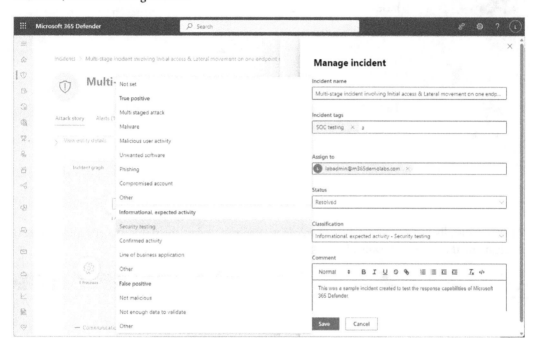

Figure 7.20 – Updating incident details

As a SOC operator, you can use the Microsoft 365 **Incidents** page to filter incidents assigned to you, helping you focus on the most important activities, see *Figure 7.21*:

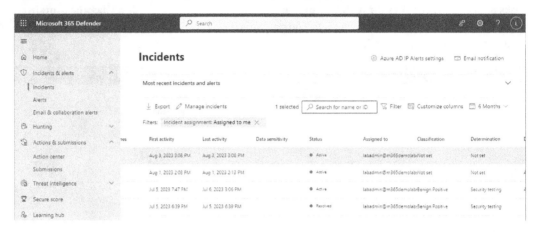

Figure 7.21 – Viewing assigned incidents

After successfully triaging and resolving incidents, you can update the status of alerts and incidents by changing the status to **Resolved**, as shown in *Figure 7.22*:

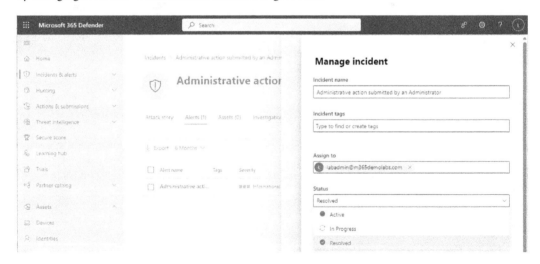

Figure 7.22 – Updating an incident status

Next, you'll shift to looking at other issues identified in Microsoft 365 Defender.

Reviewing and Responding to Issues Identified in Security and Compliance Reports in Microsoft 365 Defender

While responding to alerts and incidents is important to remove potential risks from your organization, arguably, the best way to limit the impact of security risks is to put the technologies and processes in place, addressing vulnerabilities as soon as possible before they're exploited.

The **Reports** section of the Microsoft 365 Defender portal is a great way to get both high-level and very detailed information about the overall health of your environment, gaps identified in your defenses, and recommendations to protect your environment. To access the reports, navigate to the Microsoft 365 Defender portal (`https://security.microsoft.com`) and select **Reports** from the navigation menu, see *Figure 7.23*:

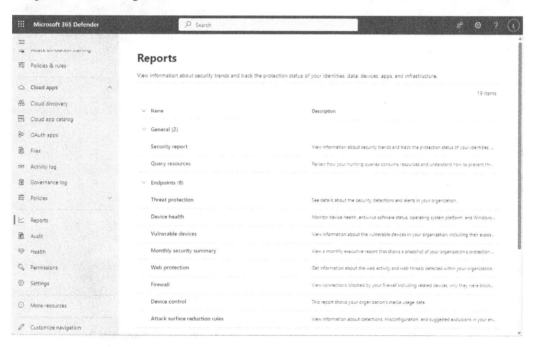

Figure 7.23 – Viewing the available Microsoft 365 reports

Each of these reports contains information critical to the security or potential vulnerability of every facet of your Microsoft 365 deployment, including a managed endpoint, email, identity, and apps. You'll examine a few reports in each of these areas to help you understand the depth and breadth of information available.

General

In the **General** section, there are two reports:

1. **Security report**: This report displays information about the general state of identity, devices, data, apps, and infrastructure connected to your Microsoft 365 tenant, see *Figure 7.24*:

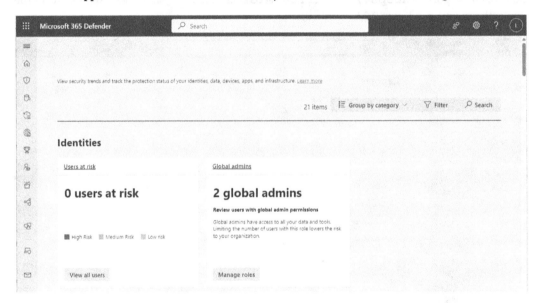

Figure 7.24 – Viewing the security report

2. **Query resources**: These reports display information on how threat hunting and query activities are performing across your organization

Endpoints

The endpoints section has the most reports (eight in total), covering a wide range of endpoint configuration and assessment data:

1. **Threat protection**: This Defender for Endpoint report lists alerts generated across your devices. You can filter the available reports by **Detection source**, **Category**, **Severity**, **Classification**, **Determination**, and **Device group**.

> **Note**
>
> The threat protection report is scheduled to be deprecated on December 11, 2023, but it may appear on the exam until the next refresh cycle.

2. **Device health**: This report displays information about the operating system versions and the Defender Antivirus health where Defender for Endpoint is deployed.

3. **Vulnerable devices**: This report shows information about what devices Defender for Endpoint determines are vulnerable—such as the availability of exploits for installed applications. Clicking through vulnerabilities redirects to other areas in the Microsoft 365 Defender portal, such as Endpoint vulnerability recommendations (`https://security.microsoft.com/security-recommendations`).

> **Further Reading**
>
> You'll look more at managing vulnerabilities and recommendations for Microsoft 365 Defender for Endpoint in *Chapter 9, Implementing and Managing Endpoint Protection by Using Microsoft Defender for Endpoint*.

4. **Monthly security summary**: The monthly security summary shows the overall Secure Score status, as well as how many devices are onboarded to MDE, stats for ransomware and phishing protection, how many clicks or URLs were blocked by endpoint web filtering, and how many incidents and alerts were resolved during the period.

5. **Web protection**: The web protection report provides information about the web filtering component of Microsoft Defender for Endpoint. The report displays data points regarding the number of requests, the percentage of activity change, and activity targeted to malicious URLs and blocked domains or categories.

One key area is located by clicking on the **Configure the security baseline** button, as shown in *Figure 7.25*:

Figure 7.25 – Viewing the web protection report

The **Configure the security baseline** button redirects you to the Microsoft Intune admin center (https://intune.microsoft.com or https://endpoint.microsoft.com). From there, you have the option to create a number of baseline security profiles, such as one that configures basic settings for each of the Windows 10 management categories, or the Microsoft 365 Defender for Endpoint categories, as shown in *Figure 7.26*:

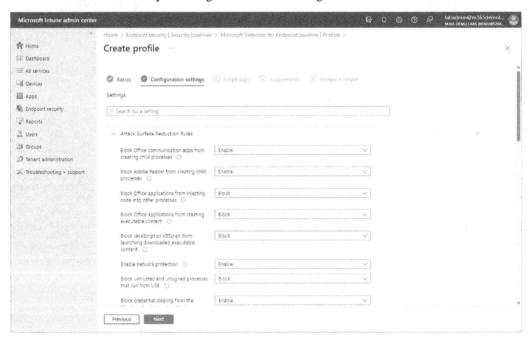

Figure 7.26 – Creating a baseline security policy

These baselines are easy, one-stop shops to implement strong security posture enhancements across your entire managed environment. The Windows baseline contains settings for many built-in Windows settings (which are normally managed via GPO), while the MDE baseline contains the **Attack Surface Reduction rules**, **BitLocker**, **Device Guard**, **Device Installation**, **DMA Guard**, **Firewall**, **Microsoft Defender** (Antivirus), and **Smart Screen** sections, with recommended default settings.

6. **Firewall**: The Firewall report shows information regarding inbound and outbound requests that were blocked by the endpoint firewall configuration.

7. **Device control**: The device control report can be used to discover information regarding media usage (e.g., the insertion and removal of disk drives or USB memory sticks, printing, CD/DVD access, or usage of other removable storage devices). It can be useful for investigating data exfiltration concerns.

8. **Attack surface reduction rules**: The **Attack Surface Reduction (ASR)** rules report displays information about actions that detected activities matching specific ASR rules (such as blocking JavaScript, Win32 API access, Windows Management Instrumentation subscription, and driver exploits). See *Figure 7.27*:

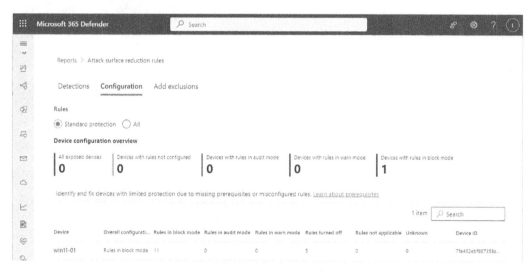

Figure 7.27 – Viewing the Attack surface reduction rules overview

Tip

If you want to get a jump on getting ASR rules deployed, click the **Configure the security baseline** button in the web reports to create a Windows 10 and later policy, and consider each of the defaults selected.

Email and Collaboration

These reports are intended to highlight information regarding overall mail flow, including detected threats and mitigated risks (such as risky URLs identified and blocked by Defender for Office 365, spoof detections, and malware detections):

- **Email & collaboration reports**: This option is actually a dashboard featuring a set of data cards, each displaying an overview graph of a different mail-related report. The dashboard widgets link to the **Mailflow status summary**, **Threat protection status**, **Post-delivery activities**, **URL protection**, **Top malware**, **Spoof detections**, **Compromised users**, **Mail latency**, **User reported messages**, **Submissions**, and **Top senders and recipients** reports, see *Figure 7.28*:

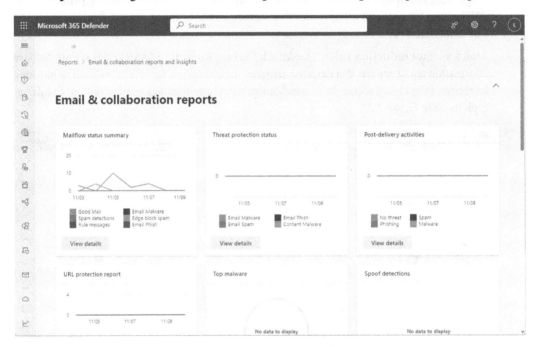

Figure 7.28 – Viewing the Email & collaboration reports dashboard

---

Exam Tip

If you've started a trial tenant as part of your exam study process, you should take time to examine each of the reports. While they may not show a lot of actual data in your trial scenario, it's good to get a feel for how the data cards take you through the various reports of the Microsoft 365 Defender portal. The reports linked on this page are all in the Microsoft 365 Defender portal, but they aren't easy to find outside of the **Email & collaboration reports** dashboard.

If you have access to a Microsoft 365 tenant with a lot of traffic, it may be worthwhile to see some of these reports with more data (possibly by viewing under the supervision of a SOC analyst) explaining that you are studying for the MS-102 exam), as long as you're staying within your organization's security policy.

For more information on each of the reports presented, you can learn more at `https://learn.microsoft.com/en-us/microsoft-365/security/office-365-security/reports-defender-for-office-365`.

Many of the reports linked through the various cards on this page can be scheduled by clicking the **Create schedule** button on the details page, as shown in *Figure 7.29*:

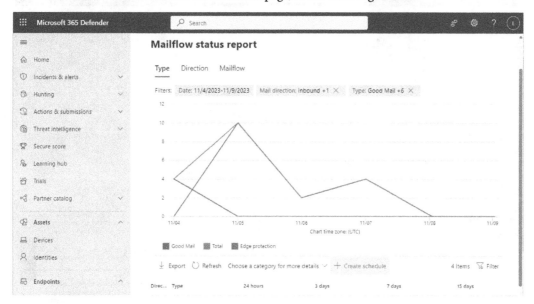

Figure 7.29 – Creating a scheduled Mailflow status report

Clicking on **Create schedule** will initiate a wizard where you can choose the frequency, start and end dates, and recipients for scheduled reports.

- **Manage schedules**: On this page, you can manage the schedules for reports that you have configured.

- **Reports for download**: This page features reports that are available to download – namely, mail reports that are generated from the legacy Exchange admin center reporting console.

- **Exchange mail flow reports**: This is a link to the **Mail flow reports** section of the Exchange admin center, as shown in *Figure 7.30*:

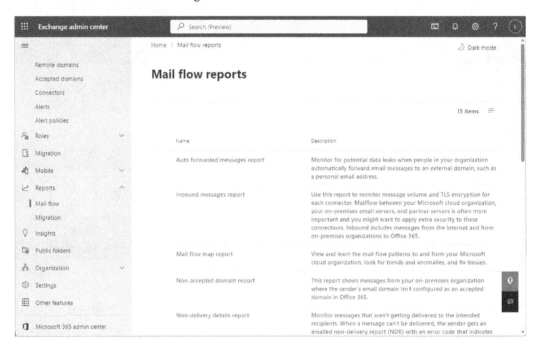

Figure 7.30 – Viewing the Mailflow reports in the Exchange admin center

When working with the reports on this page, you generally have two options – download the dataset that is displayed to a CSV by clicking **Export**, or use the request report to specify a custom report to be generated and delivered, see *Figure 7.31*:

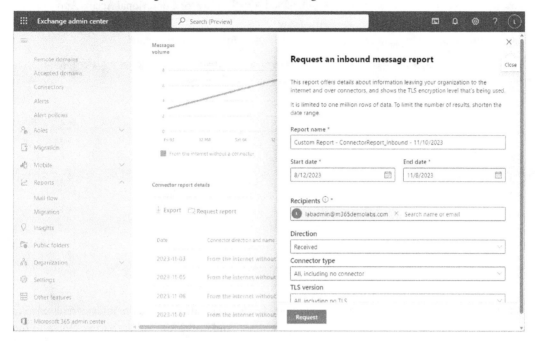

Figure 7.31 – Requesting a custom report

After specifying the details for the report, a copy will be sent to the recipient listed, and it will also be available on the **Reports for download** page of the Microsoft 365 Defender portal.

Cloud Apps

In the **Cloud Apps** section, there is a single link for **Exported reports**. This page is used to view and download reports that you generated through Cloud App Security for Conditional Access App Control, Cloud App Discovery, and other Cloud App security policies. *Figure 7.32* depicts the **Exported reports** page, containing two reports generated from the Cloud App security console:

Figure 7.32 – Viewing the Cloud Apps' Exported reports page

The Microsoft 365 Defender reports act like a bit of a two-way mirror – you are informed of existing data (such as vulnerable devices or phishing attempts) and also provided with direct links to the relevant Endpoint sections of the portal where you can make remediations, pre-emptively mitigating the reach of threats.

These real-life examples might help you understand the value of the reporting available in Microsoft 365 Defender:

- When viewing the **Mailflow status** report, (**Email & collaboration | Email & collaboration reports | Mailflow status report**), you may determine that you're getting a lot of spoof or phishing attempts from particular domains or IP addresses, which can lead you to create Exchange transport rules to filter out inbound mail from those sources.

- When viewing the **Vulnerable devices** report (**Endpoints | Vulnerable devices**), you may notice that you have a large number of devices that have a version of Adobe Acrobat deployed with a known exploit in the wild, prompting you to create a package to update those endpoints.

- While reviewing the **Web protection** report (**Endpoints | Web protection**), you might see that there was a lot of web activity on sites listed under the **Legal Liability** or **Adult Content** categories, both of which might present a variety of issues for your organization. You can select the **Policies** button on that page to directly navigate to the Microsoft Defender for Endpoint **Web content filtering rules** page, allowing you to quickly create a policy to enforce restrictions and block problematic content.

Next, you'll move on to managing Microsoft Defender 365 from a threat analytics perspective.

Reviewing and Responding to Threats Identified in Threat Analytics

Microsoft **threat analytics** is a security product that is focused on combining data captured in the wild and analysis by Microsoft security and threat researchers, with proactive remediation guides and information about your potentially vulnerable assets.

Threat analytics is accessed from the Microsoft 365 Defender portal (`https://security.microsoft.com`) by expanding **Threat intelligence** and selecting **Threat analytics**, as shown in *Figure 7.33*:

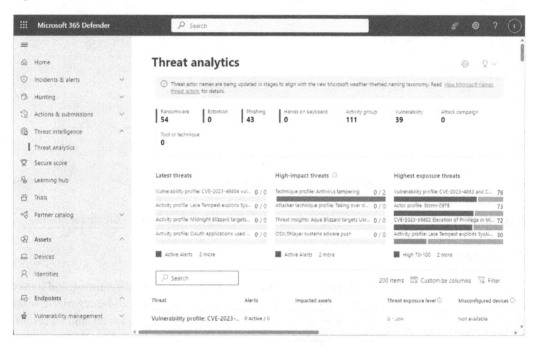

Figure 7.33 – Viewing the Threat analytics dashboard

The dashboard highlights three areas:

- **Latest threats**: The most recent emerging threats found in the wild, including updated threat reports

- **High-impact threats**: The most active threats in your organization

- **Highest exposure threats**: Threats with the highest exposure risk levels, as calculated by how severe the vulnerabilities are and how many devices could potentially be exploited

When you click on a threat, you'll be directed to the **threat's vulnerability profile** with several different sections, as shown in *Figure 7.34*:

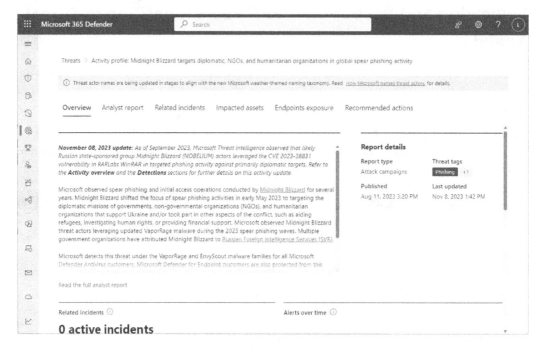

Figure 7.34 – Viewing a threat's vulnerability profile

Over the next few sections, you'll explore each of the tabs or pages available in the threat profile.

Overview

The **Overview** page (as shown in *Figure 7.34*), gives a high-level assessment of the threat, and it may include data about how the threat was discovered, how it's been monitored and categorized, what products may be vulnerable, and whether there are available mitigation measures or recommendations. The **Overview** page also provides a snapshot of information available on the other tabs or pages of the vulnerability profile.

Analyst Report

The **Analyst report** provides clear details about the nature of the threat or vulnerability, including known historical information regarding the threat's development, tracking, targeting, and the **Common Vulnerabilities and Exposures (CVE)** reference ID. The reports frequently provide examples caught in the wild and are used to identify the threat, as well as information on what exploits are used to invoke the threat and who may be targeted. A sample analysis from a spear-phishing threat is shown in *Figure 7.35*:

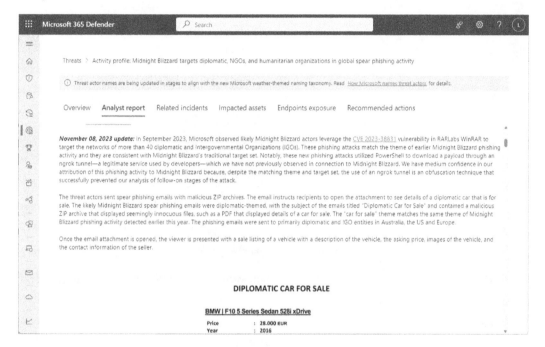

Figure 7.35 – Reviewing the Analyst report

A report may have detailed information about the **attack chain** (as shown in *Figure 7.35*) as well as examples of the code executed, sample email artifacts, targeting information, **attribution** (who is likely responsible for the threat), and **recommendations** for addressing vulnerabilities.

The recommendations listed in the Analyst report include all the products that the threat can potentially exploit (including products that may not be in use by managed devices or organizations). The recommendations can cover both Microsoft and non-Microsoft products, as shown in *Figure 7.36*:

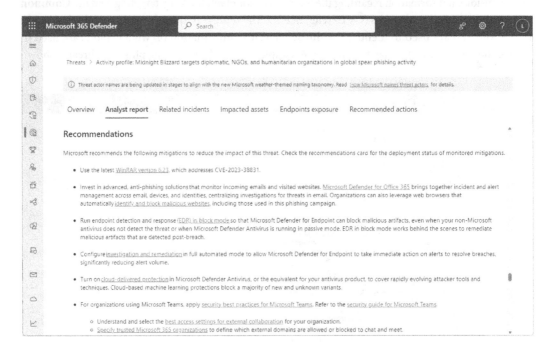

Figure 7.36 – Reviewing recommendations for non-Microsoft products in the Analyst report

Related Incidents

The **Related incidents** page will list any incidents in your Microsoft 365 tenant that Microsoft 365 Defender associates with this threat. Selecting an incident item will allow you to open the related incident on the **Incidents** page.

Impacted Assets

The **Impacted assets** page is used to display organizational assets (**Devices**, **Users**, **Mailboxes**, and **Apps**) that have been affected by incidents related to this threat. Selecting an asset will redirect you to its page in Microsoft 365 Defender, where you can learn more about the individual vulnerabilities and exposures.

Endpoints Exposure

The **Endpoints exposure** page, as shown in *Figure 7.37*, lists the managed endpoints where vulnerabilities exploited by the threat might exist:

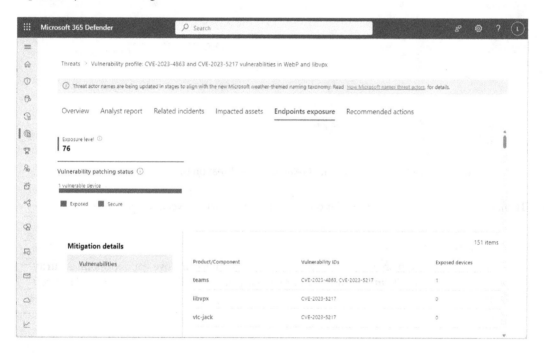

Figure 7.37 – Viewing the exposed endpoints

By selecting a value in the **Vulnerability IDs** column for a line item, you will be directed to the **Weaknesses** page under **Vulnerability management**, as shown in *Figure 7.38*. From here, you can filter the list based on the **Product/Component** column value from the **Endpoints exposure** page, allowing you to home in on exactly what needs to be mitigated.

Figure 7.38 – Searching for the product related to the threat on the Endpoint exposures page

Then, you can follow the recommendations to address the specific weakness identified.

> **Further Reading**
>
> For more information on using vulnerability management to improve your endpoint security posture, see *Chapter 9, Implementing and Managing Endpoint Protection by Using Microsoft Defender for Endpoint.*

Recommended Actions

The **Recommended actions** page, as shown in *Figure 7.39*, provides guidance on specific steps you can take to reduce exposure using the tools in Microsoft 365 Defender. These recommendations are filtered from the broader list of Microsoft 365 Defender security recommendations, specifically tailored to mitigate the risk of the selected threat.

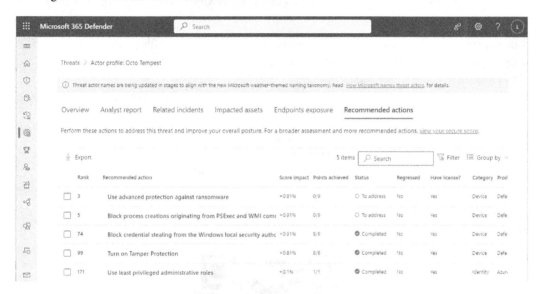

Figure 7.39 – Reviewing Recommended actions

As you can see in *Figure 7.33*, several mitigating actions have already been completed for this tenant. These actions are pulled from both Microsoft Secure Score and Vulnerability Management, so as you complete tasks through either path, you'll improve your organizational security for threats.

Summary

In this chapter, you learned about the Microsoft 365 Defender portal and some of the specific capabilities around incident and threat management. Using the insights from Secure Score and Vulnerability Management's recommendations, you can quickly build a list of high-impact actions that will dramatically improve your overall security posture and reduce threat exposure.

In the next chapter, you'll learn about the Microsoft 365 Defender for Office features, which are used to protect threats targeting the Microsoft 365 email and collaboration tools.

Exam Readiness Drill - Chapter Review Questions

Benchmark Score: 75%

Apart from a solid understanding of key concepts, being able to think quickly under time pressure is a skill that will help you ace your certification exam. That's why, working on these skills early on in your learning journey is key.

Chapter review questions are designed to improve your test-taking skills progressively with each chapter you learn and review your understanding of key concepts in the chapter at the same time. You'll find these at the end of each chapter.

> **Before You Proceed**
>
> You need to unlock these resources before you start using them. Unlocking **takes less than 10 minutes, can be done from any device**, and **needs to be done only once**. Head over to the start of this chapter in this book for instructions on how to unlock them.

To open the **Chapter Review Questions** for this chapter, click the following link: `https://packt.link/MS102E1_CH07`. Or, you can scan the following QR code:

Figure 7.40 – QR code that opens Chapter Review Questions for logged-in users

Once you login, you'll see a page similar to what is shown in *Figure 7.41*:

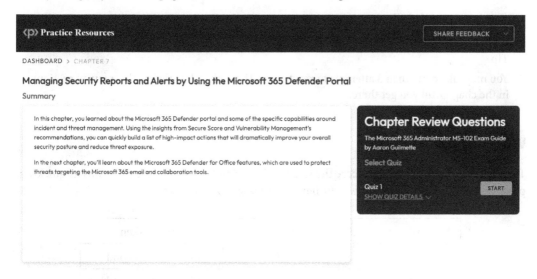

Figure 7.41 – Chapter Review Questions for Chapter 7

Once ready, start the following practice drills, re-attempting the quiz multiple times:

Exam Readiness Drill

For the first 3 attempts, don't worry about the time limit.

ATTEMPT 1

The first time, aim for at least 40%. Look at the answers you got wrong and read the relevant sections in the chapter again to fix your learning gaps.

ATTEMPT 2

The second time, aim for at least 60%. Look at the answers you got wrong and read the relevant sections in the chapter again to fix any remaining learning gaps.

ATTEMPT 3

The third time, aim for at least 75%. Once you score 75% or more, you start working on your timing.

> **Tip**
> You may take more than 3 attempts to reach 75%. That's okay. Just review the relevant sections in the chapter till you get there.

Working On Timing

Target: Your aim is to keep the score the same while trying to answer these questions as quickly as possible. Here's an example of how your next attempts should look like:

Attempt	Score	Time Taken
Attempt 5	77%	21 mins 30 seconds
Attempt 6	78%	18 mins 34 seconds
Attempt 7	76%	14 mins 44 seconds

Table 7.1 – Sample timing practice drills on the online platform

> **Note**
> The time limits shown in the above table are just examples. Set your own time limits with each attempt based on the time limit of the quiz on the website.

With each new attempt, your score should stay **above 75%** while your time taken to complete should decrease. Repeat as many attempts as you want till you feel confident dealing with the time pressure.

8

Implementing and Managing Email and Collaboration Protection by Using Microsoft Defender for Office 365

The Microsoft 365 Defender suite has a lot to offer. In this chapter, you're going to look at the features of **Microsoft Defender for Office 365 (MDO)**—a set of tools that provides protection for the Office 365 collaboration platform (Exchange Online, Teams, SharePoint, and OneDrive for Business).

MDO, a cloud-based service, enhances your organization's security by filtering emails and safeguarding against sophisticated threats targeting email and collaboration platforms. This includes protection from phishing, business email compromise, and malware. Additionally, MDO equips security teams with tools for effective investigation, threat hunting, and remediation, enabling them to swiftly detect, prioritize, and address potential threats.

In addition to protecting content in the collaboration platform, **MDO Plan 2** also boasts a competitive training package that allows you to run phishing campaigns against your users and then offer reinforcement training to help them better respond to threats in the future.

This chapter covers the following exam objectives:

- Implementing policies and rules in Defender for Office 365
- Reviewing and responding to threats identified in Defender for Office 365
- Creating and running campaigns
- Unblocking users

Microsoft Defender for Office 365 is a comprehensive suite of tools that builds on the **Exchange Online Protection (EOP)** platform for message hygiene and adds additional heuristic scanning capabilities, as well as enhanced functionality for detecting threats inside message attachments, including URL-based attacks. MDO has the ability to protect from threats at time-of-click or time-of-access, helping protect against latent threats that are activated after content has been delivered to recipients.

By the end of this chapter, you should be able to describe the capabilities of Defender for Office 365 and implement core policies.

Implementing Policies and Rules in Defender for Office 365

Before you dive into configuring policies, it's important to understand the features and capabilities available across the Microsoft Defender for Office 365 service plans. MDO is available at three different subscription levels: Microsoft Defender for Office 365 Plan 1, Microsoft Defender for Office 365 Plan 2, and as part of Microsoft 365 E5 or Microsoft 365 E5 Security.

> **Note**
> Microsoft Defender for Office 365 was previously called Advanced Threat Protection. You shouldn't see that reference on the current or future versions of the MS-102 exam, but it may periodically surface in Microsoft product documentation.

Table 8.1 lists the capabilities that are part of each subscription level:

	Defender for Office 365 P1	Defender for Office 365 P2	Microsoft 365 A5/ E5/F5/G5 and A5/E5/F5/G5 Security
Configuration, protection, and detection features			
Preset security policies and Configuration analyzer	Yes	Yes	Yes
Safe Attachments (Outlook, Microsoft 365 apps)	Yes	Yes	Yes
Safe Attachments (Teams)	Yes	Yes	Yes
Safe Links	Yes	Yes	Yes
Safe Links in Teams	Yes	Yes	Yes
Safe Documents	No	No	Yes
Report Message add-in	Yes	Yes	Yes
Protection for documents in SharePoint, OneDrive, and Microsoft Teams	Yes	Yes	Yes

	Defender for Office 365 P1	Defender for Office 365 P2	Microsoft 365 A5/ E5/F5/G5 and A5/E5/F5/G5 Security
Anti-phishing	Yes	Yes	Yes
Real-time reporting	Yes	Yes	Yes
Automation, investigation, remediation, and training			
Advanced protection for internal email	Yes	Yes	Yes
Threat trackers	No	Yes	Yes
Campaign views	No	Yes	Yes
Threat investigation	(through Real-time detections only)	Threat Explorer	Threat Explorer
Automated investigation and response (AIR)	No	Yes	Yes
Attack simulation training	No	Yes	Yes
Integration with Microsoft 365 Defender	No	Yes	Yes

Table 8.1 – Microsoft Defender for Office 365 feature matrix

While most of the features are available across all service plans, there are a handful of features that are only available with higher subscriptions.

> **Further Reading**
>
> For the latest information on available features across service plans, see `https://learn. microsoft.com/en-us/office365/servicedescriptions/office-365- advanced-threat-protection-service-description`.

Deploying the Preset Security Policies

MDO includes a group of preconfigured policies known as the **preset security policies**. These policies are configured with Microsoft's recommended settings. The policies are scoped to users or groups and are divided into two policy sets: **Standard** and **Strict**.

> **Note**
>
> One of the advantages of preset security policies is that they are continually updated and managed by Microsoft, based on the evolving threat landscape.

The strict policies feature a more aggressive setting and may result in higher false positives. These policies are designed to be applied to individuals and groups that are highly targeted (such as the executive team members and their staff). Since the strict policies may result in more false positives, you should ensure that you have enough support coverage to manage the increase in service tickets or support calls to review and release messages from the quarantine.

The standard policies are designed to be assigned to the broad user base.

> **Further Reading**
>
> The table at `https://learn.microsoft.com/en-us/microsoft-365/security/office-365-security/recommended-settings-for-eop-and-office365` details the Microsoft EOP and MDO default policy values, as well as the policy values for the Standard and Strict preset security policies.

In either case, it's important to note that *preset security policies will override any custom policies*. You can also exclude users or groups.

To configure the preset policies, follow these steps:

1. Determine the users that will be assigned or scoped to the Standard or Strict security presets.

2. Navigate to the Microsoft 365 Defender portal (`https://security.microsoft.com`). Expand **Email & collaboration**, select **Policies & rules**, and then select **Threat policies**, as shown in *Figure 8.1*:

Figure 8.1 – Navigating to Threat policies

3. Under **Templated policies**, select **Preset Security Policies**, as shown in *Figure 8.2*:

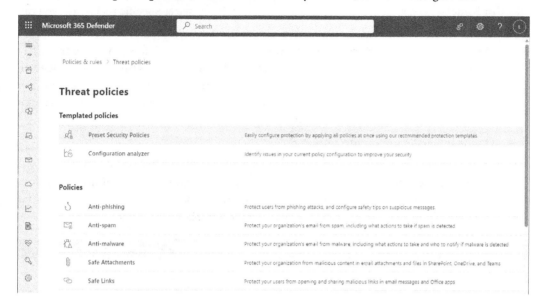

Figure 8.2 – Configuring preset security policies

4. On the **Preset security policies** page, as shown in *Figure 8.3*, under **Standard protection**, select **Manage protection settings**:

Figure 8.3 – Configuring Standard protection settings

5. On the **Exchange online protection** page, select the recipients (**All recipients**, **Specific recipients**, or **None**) to which the EOP settings will be applied. If you select **Specific recipients**, you can add individual users, groups, and domains. Click **Next**.

6. On the **Defender for Office 365 protection** page, select the recipients to which the MDO settings will be applied. You can select **Previously selected recipients** (recipients specified on the **Exchange online protection** page), **All recipients**, **Specific recipients**, or **None**. You can also select **Exclude these recipients** to filter out users, groups, or domains that you don't want to receive the MDO settings. Click **Next**.

7. On the **Impersonation protection** page, click **Next**.

8. On the **Protected custom users** page, as shown in *Figure 8.4*, enter the names and addresses of up to 350 senders who might be impersonated when trying to trick your users. This may include executives, individuals in key roles, or even external human resources applications (such as well-known payroll processing or benefits coordination email addresses). Click **Next**.

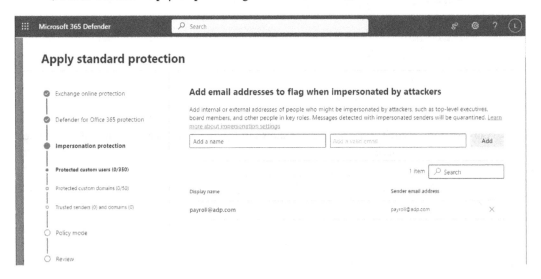

Figure 8.4 – Configuring impersonation settings

9. On the **Protected custom domains** page, enter up to 50 domains where malicious users may attempt to impersonate users when communicating with your organization. Click **Next**.

10. On the **Trusted senders and domains** page, add addresses and domains not to flag for impersonation. Click **Next**.

11. On the **Policy mode** page, choose either **Turn on the policy when finished** or **Leave it turned off**. Click **Next**.

12. On the **Review** page, click **Confirm**.

13. Click **Done** to leave the wizard.

The **Standard protection** preset template has been deployed. If at any time you need to modify the recipients or disable the policy for troubleshooting, you can return to the **Preset security policies** page and slide the **Standard protection is on** toggle to **Off**.

To deploy the **Strict protection** template, click the **Manage protection** settings link under **Strict protection** and follow the same steps as you did for the **Standard protection** preset security policy template.

Configuring Standalone Policies

While the preset policies provide Microsoft's recommended protections, there may be instances when you need to configure different options or add additional processing steps. For these scenarios, you can configure custom policies.

You can configure custom policies along with the preset configuration policies, but you need to exclude the users, groups, or domains to whom you want the custom policies to apply. The preset policies have the highest priority and will take action over lower-priority policies.

All of the standalone policies are accessible through the **Threat policies** page (shown previously in *Figure 8.2*), including **Anti-phishing**, **Anti-spam**, **Anti-malware**, **Safe Attachments**, and **Safe Links**.

Anti-Phishing

Microsoft 365 Exchange Online Protection includes built-in protection for protecting against phishing attacks. The default Exchange Online Protection features include **spoof intelligence**, authenticated senders visual indicators, and spoof-specific actions for messages that fail **Domain-based Message Authentication, Reporting, and Conformance (DMARC)**.

Deep Dive

Spoof intelligence is a Microsoft **Exchange Online Protection** (EOP) feature that detects messages that appear to originate from one entity while actually coming from another. EOP uses a number of checks, such as checking against **Sender Policy Framework** (SPF) records, to validate the contents of the FROM header in messages. If EOP determines that there is a high likelihood that the FROM field was forged, then the message is identified as spoofed. For more information, see https://learn.microsoft.com/en-us/microsoft-365/security/office-365-security/anti-phishing-protection-spoofing-about and https://www.undocumented-features.com/2019/08/13/exchange-online-protection-eop-best-practices-and-recommendations/.

The additional anti-phishing protections that Defender for Office 365 layers on top of that include the following:

- Impersonation protection settings for specific senders and domains
- Campaign views to help you understand coordinated attacks against your organization
- Attack simulation training that focuses on end user responses to phishing attacks

Microsoft Defender for Office 365's phishing protection allows you to customize protections and policies, including configuring multiple policies (each with a maximum of 350 protected recipients) to protect against phishing attacks.

> **Note**
> Remember, if you have configured one of the preset policies, then this will take precedence over any other custom policy for any of the users, groups, or domains that overlap.

To configure a custom anti-phishing policy for Microsoft Defender for Office 365, follow these steps:

1. Navigate to the Microsoft 365 Defender portal (`https://security.microsoft.com`). Expand **Email & collaboration**, select **Policies & rules**, and then select **Threat policies**.

2. Under **Policies**, select **Anti-phishing**.

3. Click **Create**.

4. On the **Policy name** page, enter a **Name** value for the policy and click **Next**.

5. On the **Users, groups, and domains** page, enter the individual users, groups, and domains to which the policy will apply, and then click **Next**.

6. On the **Phishing threshold & protection** page, choose the settings that will apply to this policy, including the **Phishing email threshold** aggressiveness, **Impersonation**, and **Spoof** settings. See *Figure 8.5*:

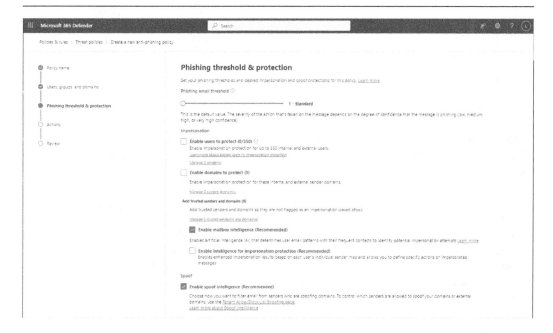

Figure 8.5 – Phishing threshold & protection page

> **Note**
>
> If you have already configured a preset policy, these options will look very familiar. They're the same settings—the difference being that the preset policy process combines all of the Microsoft 365 threat protection policies (**Anti-phishing**, **Anti-spam**, **Anti-malware**, **Safe attachments**, and **Safe links**) into a single wizard.

7. Click **Next**.

8. On the **Actions** page, choose which actions you will apply for messages detected as user impersonation or domain impersonation.

9. Choose whether to **Honor DMARC record policy** when the message is detected as spoof. You also have the options of **Show first contact safety tip** (a warning/tooltip message to recipients when they receive messages from a new sender or someone they don't receive mail from often), **Show (?) for unauthenticated senders for spoof** (adds a question mark to the sender's photo in the **From** box if the message fails SPF or DKIM and doesn't pass DMARC or Microsoft **Composite Authentication**), and **Show "via" tag** (displays a tooltip if the sender's FROM address doesn't match the domain in the **DomainKeys Identified Mail (DKIM)** signature).

10. Click **Next**.

11. On the **Review** page, review the settings and click **Submit** when complete.

12. Click **Done** to leave the wizard.

Anti-Spam

Microsoft 365 Exchange Online Protection includes built-in protection against spam, though none of the features of EOP are specifically associated with MDO. Anti-spam policies are available under the **Threat policies** section of the Microsoft 365 Defender portal.

> **Note**
>
> Remember, if you have configured one of the preset policies, then this will take precedence over any other custom policy for any of the users, groups, or domains that overlap. For more information on EOP's anti-spam settings, see `https://learn.microsoft.com/en-us/microsoft-365/security/office-365-security/anti-spam-protection-about`.

Anti-Malware

Microsoft Exchange Online Protection also includes built-in signature-based malware protection, which is separate from the heuristic-based detections available with Microsoft Defender for Office 365.

> **Note**
>
> Remember, if you have configured one of the preset policies, then this will take precedence over any other custom policy for any of the users, groups, or domains that overlap. For more information on EOP's anti-malware settings, see `https://learn.microsoft.com/en-us/microsoft-365/security/office-365-security/anti-malware-protection-about`.

Safe Attachments

Microsoft Defender for Office 365's **Safe Attachments** feature adds an extra security layer for email attachments. This feature complements the anti-malware scanning already done by EOP. Safe Attachments uses a virtual sandbox environment to analyze attachments in emails before they reach the intended recipients.

Safe Attachments protection of emails is enforced through Safe Attachments policies. A policy called *Built-in protection (Microsoft)* extends Safe Attachments protection to all recipients not covered by either the Standard or Strict preset security policies or by customized Safe Attachments policies.

> **Note**
>
> Remember, if you have configured one of the preset policies, then that will take precedence over any other custom policy for any of the users, groups, or domains that overlap.

To configure a Safe Attachments policy, follow these steps:

1. Navigate to the Microsoft 365 Defender portal (`https://security.microsoft.com`). Expand **Email & collaboration**, select **Policies & rules**, and then select **Threat policies**.

2. Under **Policies**, select **Safe Attachments**.

3. Click **Create**.

4. On the **Name your policy** page, enter a **Name** value for the policy and click **Next**.

5. On the **Users and domains** page, enter the individual users, groups, and domains to which the policy will apply, and then click **Next**.

6. On the **Settings** page, under **Safe Attachments unknown malware response**, choose how to manage mail delivery for protected users, as shown in *Figure 8.6*:

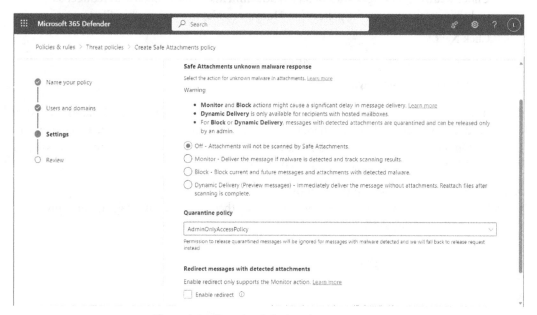

Figure 8.6 – Choosing Safe Attachments options

- **Off**: Safe Attachments will not process attachments

- **Monitor**: Scan attachments, deliver regardless of the outcome, and log the results

- **Block**: Block the affected attachments

- **Dynamic Delivery**: Immediately deliver the body of the message without attachments; scan attachments and reconnect to the message inside the mailbox

7. Under **Quarantine policy**, select from **DefaultFullAccessPolicy**, **AdminOnlyAccessPolicy**, and **DefaultFullAccessWithNotificationPolicy**.

> **Further Reading**
>
> For more information on the values contained in DefaultFullAccessPolicy, AdminOnlyAccessPolicy, and DefaultFullAccessWithNotificationPolicy, see `https://learn.microsoft.com/en-us/microsoft-365/security/office-365-security/quarantine-policies`.

8. Under **Redirect messages with detected attachments**, you can choose to redirect suspected malware attachments (if the policy is in **Monitor** mode) to a specified mailbox.

9. Click **Next**.

10. On the **Review** page, confirm the settings and click **Submit**.

11. Click **Done** to leave the wizard.

One of the important things to note (that isn't spelled out in the wizard) is that **Dynamic Delivery** functions differently, depending on where the intended recipient is. If the intended recipient is in Exchange Online, it works as described. If the recipient is an on-premises recipient, the message is delayed until processing is complete and then delivered to the recipient.

Normally, Safe Attachments with the **Dynamic Delivery** option processes things very quickly. It is possible, however, that users may see a message telling them that their message is currently being processed, as shown in *Figure 8.7*:

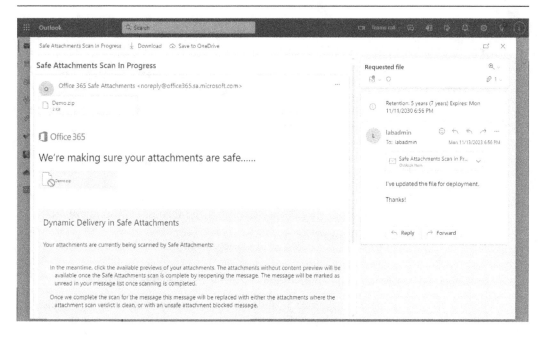

Figure 8.7 – Viewing a Safe Attachments message

A message like this is normal and is not a cause for concern. The message will be updated as soon as processing is finished.

> **Note**
>
> If a user receives a message that is currently being processed by dynamic processing (without its attachment) and then forwards that message to other users, the copies of the message that other individuals receive will not be updated with the attachment after it completes scanning.

Safe Links

Organizations using Microsoft Defender for Office 365 benefit from the **Safe Links** feature, which safeguards against harmful links commonly found in phishing and various cyber attacks. Safe Links actively scans and rewrites URLs in incoming email messages as they are processed, and it also verifies these URLs and links at the time they are clicked in email messages, Teams, and other supported Office 365 applications. This scanning by Safe Links is conducted alongside the standard anti-spam and anti-malware defenses.

Like Safe Attachments, Safe Links has a built-in policy that applies to users who are not members of any other policy and have a Microsoft 365 Defender license.

> **Note**
>
> Remember, if you have configured one of the preset policies, then this will take precedence over any other custom policy for any of the users, groups, or domains that overlap.

To configure a Safe Attachments policy, follow these steps:

1. Navigate to the Microsoft 365 Defender portal (`https://security.microsoft.com`). Expand **Email & collaboration**, select **Policies & rules**, and then select **Threat policies**.

2. Under **Policies**, select **Safe Links**.

3. Click **Create**.

4. On the **Name your policy** page, enter a **Name** value for the policy and click **Next**.

5. On the **Users and domains** page, enter the individual users, groups, and domains to which the policy will apply, and then click **Next**.

6. On the **URL & click protection settings**, configure the appropriate settings for this policy, as shown in *Figure 8.8*:

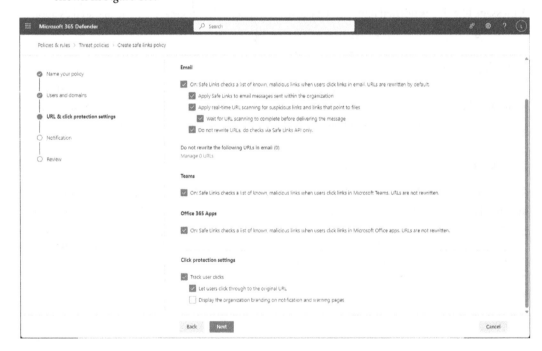

Figure 8.8 – Configuring a Safe Links policy

- Under **Email**, configure the options for managing Safe Links, including URL rewriting.

- Under **Teams**, select to enable Safe Links click-time protection settings.

- Under **Office 365 Apps**, select to enable Safe Links checking for links inside documents. Documents must be opened on a device with Microsoft 365 Apps deployed and the user accessing the document must have an MDO license applied.

- Under **Click protection settings**, choose the tracking user settings, such as **Let users click through to the original URL** or **Display the organization branding on notification and warning pages**.

7. Click **Next**.

8. On the **Notification** page, choose either **Use the default notification text** or **Use custom notification text**. If selecting **Use custom notification text**, fill out the text area with the custom notification text you want users to see. Click **Next**.

9. On the **Review** page, review the settings and click **Submit**.

10. Click **Done** to leave the wizard.

Congratulations! You've configured the Microsoft Defender for Office policies!

Configuring Rules

In this section, you'll examine a number of configuration options that are available for email protection.

> **Exam Note**
>
> These additional settings and configuration options, however, are not related explicitly to Microsoft Defender for Office 365, as they're part of the default Exchange Online Protection settings. They may, however, show up on the MS-102 exam (especially as part of multipart scenario questions), so it's important to familiarize yourself with them.

Figure 8.9 depicts some of the Exchange Online Protection standard features and configuration options:

Figure 8.9 – Exchange Online Protection standard features

Let's quickly go through them so you have an awareness of their usage.

Tenant Allow/Block Lists

In organizations using Microsoft 365 Exchange Online Protection (with either cloud-hosted or on-premises mailboxes), there might be instances where you disagree with the filtering decisions made by EOP or Microsoft Defender for Office 365. This could be cases where legitimate messages are incorrectly flagged as harmful (false positives) or harmful messages are mistakenly allowed (false negatives).

To address this, the **Tenant Allow/Block List** in the Microsoft 365 Defender portal allows you to manually override these filtering decisions made by Defender for Office 365 or EOP. This list is actively utilized during the processing of incoming emails from external senders.

It's important to note that the Tenant Allow/Block List does not affect internal messaging within your organization. However, any domains and email addresses added to the block section of the list will restrict users in your organization from sending emails to those specified blocked domains and addresses:

- The **Domains & addresses** page allows you to add entries blocking email to or from certain domains or external email addresses.

- Data is entered on the **Spoofed senders** page as a pair denoting the spoofed user or domain, and the second value references the sending infrastructure (such as a DNS PTR record, IP subnet, or domain).

- By adding entries to the **URLs** page, you can block users from following links to URLs. New messages containing those URLs are blocked as high-confidence phishing.

- The **Files** page is used to add the SHA256 hashes of files that you want to block.

Email Authentication Settings

The **Email authentication settings** page is used to manage the **Authenticated Received Chain** (ARC) and DKIM settings for the tenant.

The **ARC** page allows you to specify intermediate hosts (called **trusted sealers**) that you trust to examine messages and modify content (header or body) along the delivery path and allows Exchange Online Protection to honor the original DKIM signature.

The **DKIM** page allows you to manage the DKIM keys for your verified domains. Once you've generated DKIM keys and added them to your organization's DNS, your outbound mail will be authenticated and recipient systems can verify the signature on the message with the public key published in your organization's DNS.

Advanced Delivery

The **Advanced delivery** page helps you manage special mailboxes used for security and training purposes. The **SecOps** page contains a list of mailboxes that your security team uses for threat management. Mail delivered to these mailboxes is delivered unfiltered. The **Phishing simulation** page allows you to configure special rules to allow third-party phishing training messages to get through EOP.

Enhanced Filtering

The **Enhanced Filtering for Connectors** feature (also called **skip-listing**) allows you to configure filters for inbound messages that may have passed through additional filters that you don't want to explicitly trust.

For example, if you have partner systems that deliver mail to EOP or you have another layer of email filtering in front of EOP, you may want to configure EOP to ignore certain hops on the email route and determine spam and phishing scoring based on an IP address or system from earlier in the routing process.

Quarantine Policies

Quarantine is where EOP and MDO place potentially harmful messages. By delivering to the quarantine, you can keep potentially harmful messages or attachments out of user mailboxes and examine them in a safe place before releasing them to the intended recipient or deleting them.

Using the Configuration Analyzer

The **Configuration analyzer** reviews your policy settings and makes recommendations based on Microsoft best practices. You can access the Configuration analyzer by navigating to the Microsoft 365 Defender portal (`https://security.microsoft.com`), expanding **Policies & rules** under **Email and collaboration**, and then selecting **Threat policies**.

The Configuration analyzer has policy recommendations for both **Standard** and **Strict** deployments, and it also provides a feature called **Configuration drift analysis and history** to track policy changes over time. See *Figure 8.10*:

Figure 8.10 – Viewing the Configuration analyzer's recommendations

Each recommendation displays information regarding the policy where the setting is found, what the current configuration setting is, and what the recommended setting is. You can select any policy item and then click **Apply recommendation** to have Microsoft 365 Defender make the change for you, as shown in *Figure 8.11*:

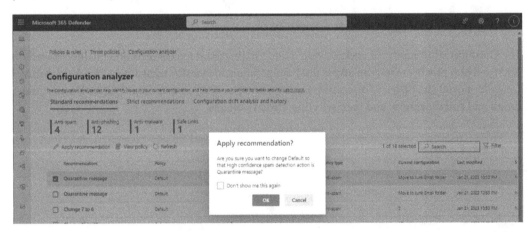

Figure 8.11 – Applying a Microsoft 365 Defender recommendation

The Configuration analyzer is a great tool for helping organizations ensure they are deploying the most effective recommendations.

Reviewing and Responding to Threats Identified in Defender for Office 365

Email-based threats are some of the most common that organizations face. In this section, you'll look at the various panes where email threats can be viewed and processed.

Email & Collaboration Alerts

You can review alerts and notifications under the **Email & collaboration alerts** section of **Incidents & alerts**, as shown in *Figure 8.12*:

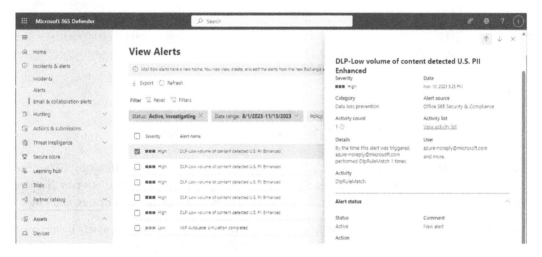

Figure 8.12 – Viewing Email & collaboration alerts

A wide variety of alerts can show up here, including alerts that have to do with email-borne threats as well as information protection alerts. If warranted, Microsoft 365 Defender will aggregate alerts and create an incident for them.

> **Further Reading**
>
> For more on overall incident management, see *Chapter 7, Managing Security Reports and Alerts by Using the Microsoft 365 Defender Portal.*

Investigations

The **Investigations** page is used to track and manage AIR cases. Many times, the investigation will already be resolved and the artifacts will be available for you to review and use for creating new rules, configuring actions for **Indicators of Compromise (IOCs)**, or running a user education campaign.

To access the **Investigations** page, navigate to the Microsoft 365 Defender portal (`https://security.microsoft.com`), expand **Email & collaboration**, and select **Investigations**. See *Figure 8.13*:

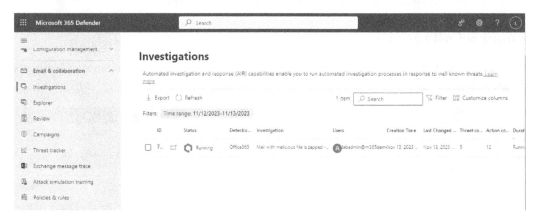

Figure 8.13 – Viewing the Investigations page

Like the **Incident** view in *Chapter 7, Managing Security Reports and Alerts by Using the Microsoft 365 Defender Portal*, an investigation presents a summary, a graph, and various tabs that give you perspective on different parts of the activity (**Alerts**, **Mailboxes**, **Evidence**, **Entities**, and **Log**).

Each of these areas can be used to further explore the incident and connected assets inside your organization. See *Figure 8.14* for an example of the **Investigation graph** page:

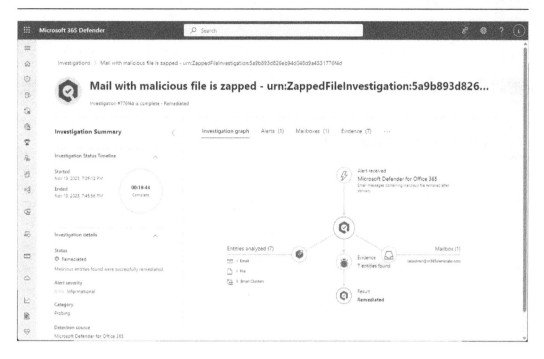

Figure 8.14 – Viewing the Investigation graph

By selecting the **Alerts** tab, you can see the related alerts and also a link to view the incident queue (where you'll be able to view the overall **Attack story** as well). The views are very similar and offer much of the same information, though an incident's **Attack story** will have a little bit more detail on all of the detected activities.

The investigation's **Mailboxes**, **Evidence**, and **Entities** pages show similar information as the corresponding incident's **Assets** and **Evidence and Response** pages, while the investigation's **Log** page shows similar information to the **Attack story** (though not laid out in the same hierarchical fashion).

As with investigating an incident, you can use the actions on items in the **Evidence** or **Entities** pages to pivot to managing indicators or adding items to the tenant block list, as shown in *Figure 8.15*:

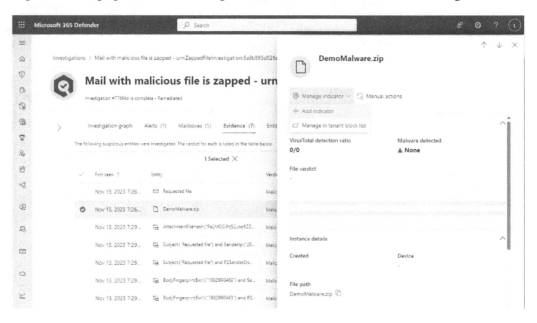

Figure 8.15 – Reviewing actions for evidence in an investigation

Explorer and Real-Time Detections

Explorer (formerly **Threat Explorer**) and **Real-time detections** are essentially two sides of the same coin. Which Microsoft 365 Defender license you have (P1 or P2) will determine which dashboard you see. Real-time detections is part of P1, while Explorer is part of P2.

The core differences are as follows:

- Real-time detections is a reporting tool, while Explorer is a hunting and remediation tool.

- Explorer allows you to not only view detections but also view attack campaign details and give the **Security Operations Center** (**SOC**) the ability to initiate an AIR investigation.

- Explorer also has an **All email** view available, whereas Real-time detections only shows various threats.

- Explorer features rich filtering and remediation capabilities, whereas Real-time detections does not.

Let's look at some of the features available as part of Explorer.

As you can see in *Figure 8.16*, Explorer has a variety of pages that can be used to pivot to different views of email.

All Email

Each page has a filtering bar that allows you to create custom searches and views. Views or filters can be saved and pulled up under the **Threat tracker**, as shown in *Figure 8.16*:

Figure 8.16 – Viewing the Explorer dashboard

Selecting the **Open in new window** icon in the **Subject** column of a message item directs you to a page containing detailed information about the item. In the case of *Figure 8.17*, this view features an alert, showing additional detailed information about the message delivered, attachments, any analyzed URLs that were part of the message, and similar emails (which are useful for investigating campaigns or finding other potentially impacted users).

The **Attachments** tab, shown in *Figure 8.17*, provides details on items detected and what the sandbox or detonation chain looks like:

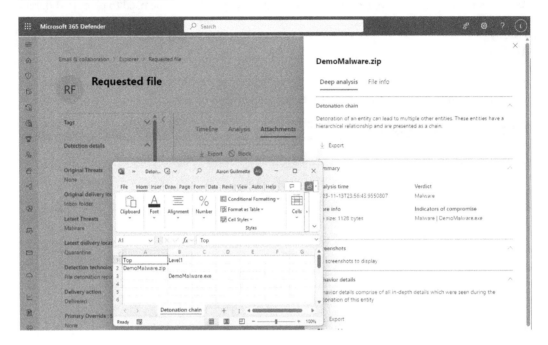

Figure 8.17 – Viewing the details of an attachment

Depending on the type of content you're working with through Explorer, you may be presented with opportunities to block content or create IOCs so Microsoft 365 Defender can take action even more quickly in the future if this threat re-emerges.

You can also click the subject value on any message on any page and be presented with additional options, such as viewing a preview of the message, using the message as a basis to start threat hunting, or even instantiating one of several actions. See *Figure 8.18*:

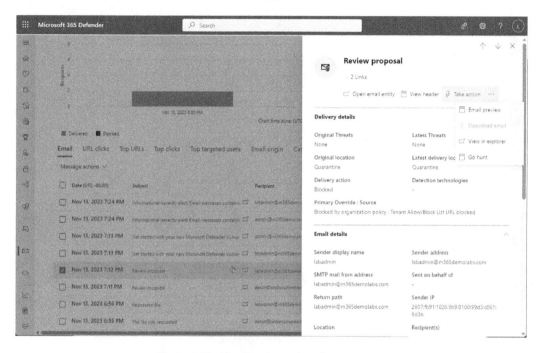

Figure 8.18 – Viewing the actions for a message

When selecting **Take action**, as shown in *Figure 8.19*, from the context menu of a message item, you can choose how to handle the message (such as moving it to a different folder, updating the classification if you think it was classified incorrectly, or initiating an automated investigation).

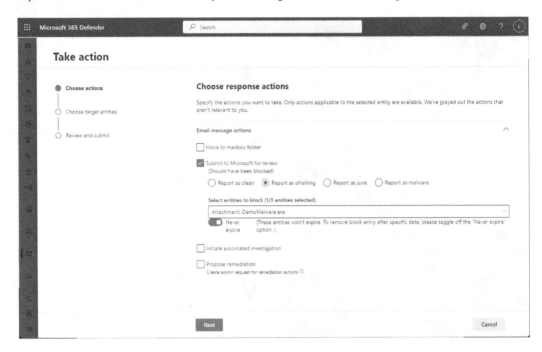

Figure 8.19 – Taking action on a message

Malware

Explorer also features a **Malware** view, as shown in *Figure 8.20*, which is essentially a pre-canned filter highlighting malicious file detections. You can use the controls on the chart to provide different views of the data.

Figure 8.20 – Reviewing the malware page in Explorer

Phish

Like the **Malware** page, the **Phish** page provides a pre-canned view of messages identified as phishing candidates in your tenant. You can filter and search for content and messages and use the **Take action** context menu option to initiate remediation activities.

Campaigns

If you find your organization under attack from spam, malware, or phishing campaigns, the messages will be collected on this page. The **Campaigns** page is useful for identifying trends across content and users to help you understand who is being targeted.

Content Malware

The **Content Malware** page shows files that MDO has detected in the collaboration workloads—such as through Teams channels and chat, SharePoint sites, and OneDrive for Business. *Figure 8.21* shows a file's detail on the **Content Malware** page:

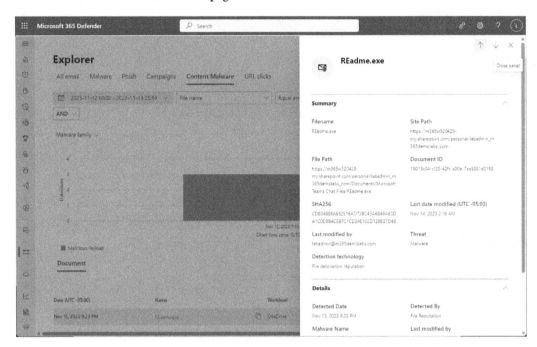

Figure 8.21 – Reviewing a malicious file detection on the Content Malware page

URL Clicks

The **URL clicks** page can be used to understand malicious links that were protected by Defender for Office 365. Whether links show up here organically through the normal MDO evaluation process or through adding URLs to the tenant allow/block list, you can get information about who was targeted and what URLs were detected. See *Figure 8.22*:

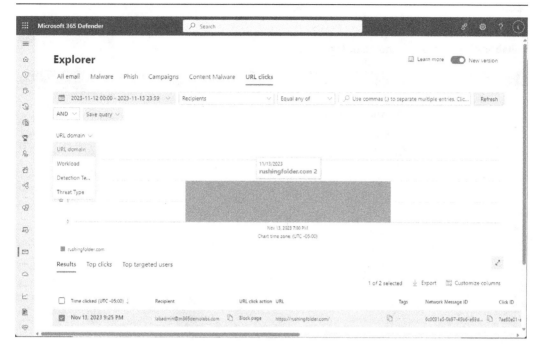

Figure 8.22 – Reviewing the URL clicks page

Now that you've seen how the Microsoft Defender for Office 365 tools work in terms of detection and protection, let's shift gears to looking at how **Attack simulation training** can help prepare users to respond to phishing attempts.

Creating and Running Campaigns

Nearly everyone has been the victim of a phishing email attempt at some point. The results can be devastating—both personally and professionally. Given the constant assault and ever-evolving threat landscape, *how can you help your organization's users not fall prey?*

Microsoft's solution for this is **Defender for Office 365 Attack simulation training**. Available as part of Defender for Office 365 P2, this feature helps you run phishing simulation campaigns against your users—and then provide them with valuable follow-up training to help improve their ability to detect future threats.

Attack simulation training is available in the Microsoft 365 Defender portal under the **Email & collaboration** section, as shown in *Figure 8.23*:

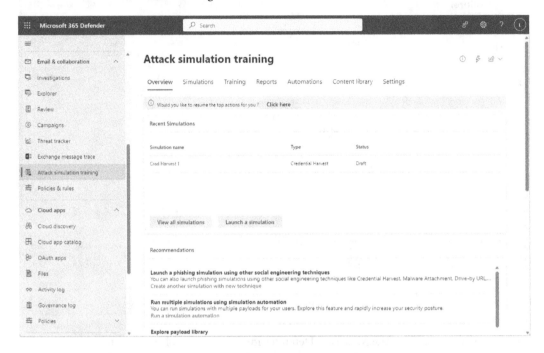

Figure 8.23 – Attack simulation training overview

Attack simulation training is comprised of five components:

- **Simulations**: The actual testing component that attempts to trick users into clicking links or supplying information

- **Training**: Content that can be used to teach good security behaviors

- **Content library**: The content that is used in a simulation to lure users, such as the following:

- **End user notifications**: Message templates used when users have been phished or they have been assigned training

- **Login pages**: Designed to lure users into thinking they are accessing a legitimate website

- **Payloads**: Content that attempts to instill urgency or otherwise trick users into giving away information

- **Phish landing pages**: Templated pages used during a simulation when users have failed

- **Training modules**: Custom training exercises to reinforce good security practices

- **Automations**: Scaling tools to allow you to run more simulations against more users with randomized options
- **Reports**: Information on how users performed throughout the training exercises

In this next section, you'll examine how to create different types of campaigns.

Creating a Phishing Campaign

Campaigns are one of the original **Attack simulation training** capabilities. The campaigns utilize a variety of social engineering methods and techniques, each designed to convince the user to supply some sort of information or click some sort of link to download and install malicious software.

> **Further Reading**
>
> The tactics used by **Attack simulation training** follow the **MITRE ATT&CK** patterns, a global repository for adversarial tactics and threat models compiled and used by researchers all over the world. For more information, see `https://attack.mitre.org/`.

Attack simulation training features the following types of threat simulations:

- **Credential Harvest**: A message with a URL that will direct users to a web page—commonly, a page that looks like a familiar login web page—and asks users to enter credentials
- **Malware Attachment**: A message with an attachment that executes code such as a macro or keylogger
- **Link in Attachment**: A hybrid attack featuring an attachment with a link inside that attempts to gather credentials or deploy malicious software
- **Link to Malware**: A message with a link to a site with a malicious download
- **Drive-by URL**: A message with a URL that takes the recipient to a website that attempts to run information-gathering processes
- **OAuth Consent Grant**: A malicious application that asks the target to grant access to their data

> **Note**
>
> The phishing modules of **Attack simulation training** depends on using a wide variety of URLs to make the exercises seem believable. You'll need to ensure that your web content filtering applications aren't blocking the URLs that the system uses. You can find a complete list of the URLs used by Attack simulation training here: `https://learn.microsoft.com/en-us/microsoft-365/security/office-365-security/attack-simulation-training-get-started`.

To create a phishing simulation campaign, follow these steps:

1. Navigate to the Microsoft 365 Defender portal (`https://security.microsoft.com`). Expand **Email & collaboration** and then select **Attack simulation training**.

2. Select the **Simulations** tab.

3. Click **Launch a simulation**. See *Figure 8.24*:

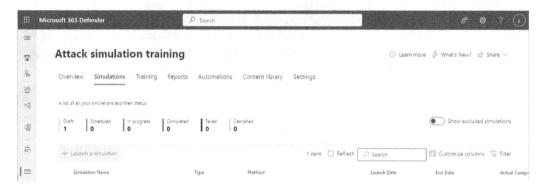

Figure 8.24 – Launching a phishing campaign

4. On the **Select technique** page, as shown in *Figure 8.25*, choose a technique from the presented options:

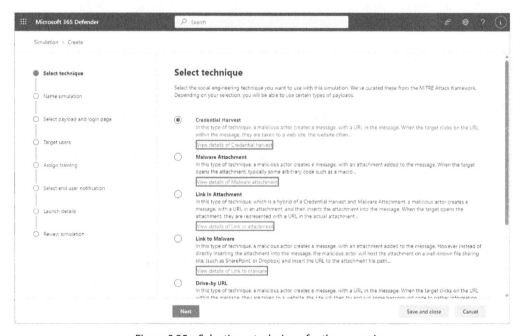

Figure 8.25 – Selecting a technique for the campaign

5. Click **Next**.

6. On the **Name simulation** page, enter a **Name** value and click **Next**.

7. On **Select payload and login page**, as shown in *Figure 8.26*, select a payload that will be used for the simulation. Depending on the technique you chose in *step 4*, you'll have a variety of options.

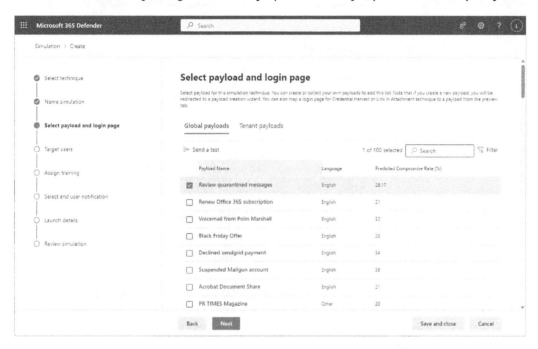

Figure 8.26 – Selecting a payload

You can click the actual payload name to view the sample content that will be sent to your users.

8. Click **Next**.

9. On the **Target users** page, select the users or groups that will be part of the simulation. Click **Next**.

10. On the **Exclude users** page, you can choose to exclude users from the simulation. Click **Next**.

11. On the **Assign training** page, as shown in *Figure 8.27*, you can choose which content to assign to users who fail the simulation exercise. You can use Microsoft-provided training options or links to your own content. Click **Next**.

Figure 8.27 – Selecting training options

12. On the **Phish landing page**, select a landing page that will be shown to users if they fail the simulation training exercise. You can select from built-in templates or create your own to be stored in the tenant for later simulations, as well as redirect to a custom URL. Click **Next**.

13. On the **Select end user notification** page, select the options to notify users of their training requirements or other follow-up information. Click **Next**.

14. On the **Launch details** page, select a schedule for launching the training. Click **Next**.

15. On the **Review simulation** page, review the settings and make any changes. Click **Submit** when finished.

16. Click **Done**.

As the simulation ramps up, messages will be delivered to the selected targets.

Creating a Training Simulation

MDO also includes security-themed training content (such as password security techniques, identifying social engineering attempts, and data over-sharing) that can be used as part of a campaign. The training campaigns can be used to help grow and reinforce users' knowledge.

Configuring a training campaign works much like creating a phishing simulation campaign.

> **Further Reading**
>
> There are currently 89 training modules available as part of Attack simulation training. You can view the available modules here by navigating to `https://security.microsoft.com/attacksimulator?viewid=contentlibrary` and selecting **Training modules**.

To create a training campaign, follow these steps:

1. Navigate to the Microsoft 365 Defender portal (`https://security.microsoft.com`). Expand **Email & collaboration** and then select **Attack simulation training**.

2. Select the **Training** tab.

3. Click **Create new**.

4. On the **Name campaign** page, enter a **Training name** value and click **Next**.

5. On the **Target users** page, select the users or groups that will be part of the simulation. Click **Next**.

6. On the **Exclude users** page, you can choose to exclude users from the simulation. Click **Next**.

7. On the **Select training modules** page, select a content source option (either the built-in **Training catalog** option or **Redirect to a custom URL**). Click **Add trainings**:

8. If using the built-in modules, select from the list of training objectives. Select as many objectives as necessary. When finished, click **Add**. See *Figure 8.28*:

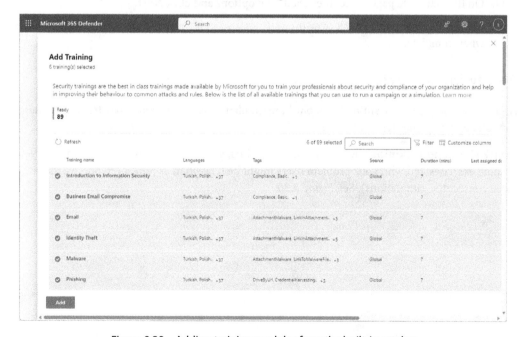

Figure 8.28 – Adding training modules from the built-in catalog

9. If using the custom training option, enter a **Custom Training URL** and **Custom Training Name** value. Click **Add**. See *Figure 8.29*:

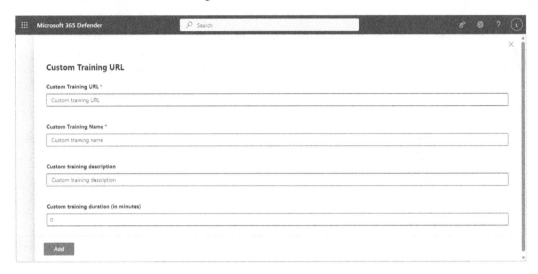

Figure 8.29 – Adding custom training options

10. On the **Select end user notification** page, choose the notification options for users to be informed about their assignment and any follow-up tasks. Click **Next**.

11. On the **Schedule** page, select the scheduling options and click **Next**.

12. On the **Review** page, check over the settings and make any modifications. Click **Submit** when complete.

Reviewing Reports

As the users complete the training (both phishing simulation as well as standalone training modules), you can begin to gather reporting data.

Attack simulation training shows critical data points, such as how many users have completed training exercises and who your problem users might be (classified as repeat offenders—those who failed consecutive simulations). See *Figure 8.30*:

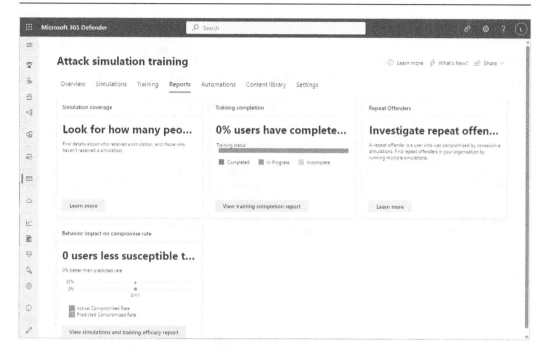

Figure 8.30 – Reviewing training reports

By periodically sending training campaigns to your users, you can help them improve their detection capabilities and limit the risk to your organization and data.

Next, you'll look at how to resolve situations regarding users being blocked from sending messages.

Unblocking Users

Despite your best efforts, you may encounter a compromised user or device that is being used to send high volumes of messages. When that happens, the user may be blocked and prohibited from sending more messages.

Configuring Alerts

While blocked sender alerts are configured automatically in Microsoft 365, you can modify the configuration in the Microsoft 365 Defender portal. To configure the alerts, follow these steps:

1. Navigate to the Microsoft 365 Defender portal (`https://securtiy.microsoft.com`), expand **Email & collaboration**, select **Policies & rules**, and then select **Alert policy**.

2. Locate the **User restricted from sending email** alert.

Figure 8.31 – Locating the alert policy

3. Click **Edit policy**.

4. On the **Set your recipients** page, under **Email recipients**, enter any additional recipients who should receive notifications for blocked senders. Click **Next**.

5. On the **Review your settings** page, click **Submit**.

Depending on how your organization handles alerting and actions, it may be advisable to add a recipient for the service desk ticketing system.

Removing Restrictions

To investigate blocked users, you can use the **Microsoft 365 Defender Restricted Entities** page (`https://security.microsoft.com/restrictedentities`) or navigate to the Microsoft 365 Defender portal (`https://security.microsoft.com`), expand **Email & collaboration**, select **Review**, and then select **Restricted entities**.

To unblock a user, follow these steps:

1. Navigate to the Microsoft 365 Defender portal (`https://security.microsoft.com`), expand **Email & collaboration**, select **Review**, and then select **Restricted entities**.

2. Locate the mailbox to unblock.

3. Select the checkbox next to the user's name and then select the **Unblock** action.

4. On the **Unblock user** flyout, review the details and recommendations. When ready, click **Next**.

5. On the **Unblock user** page, specify whether you want to enforce MFA or reset the user's password. When ready, click **Submit**.

6. Click **Yes** to confirm.

The user should be able to send emails shortly.

Summary

In this chapter, you learned about the advanced email protection features of Microsoft Defender for Office 365, including Safe Links and Safe Attachments, and how to use threat management tools such as Explorer to investigate and remediate risks. You also learned about the education component, Attack simulation training.

In the next chapter, you'll continue learning about the Microsoft Defender platform by exploring Defender for Endpoint.

Exam Readiness Drill - Chapter Review Questions

Benchmark Score: 75%

Apart from a solid understanding of key concepts, being able to think quickly under time pressure is a skill that will help you ace your certification exam. That's why, working on these skills early on in your learning journey is key.

Chapter review questions are designed to improve your test-taking skills progressively with each chapter you learn and review your understanding of key concepts in the chapter at the same time. You'll find these at the end of each chapter.

Before You Proceed

You need to unlock these resources before you start using them. Unlocking **takes less than 10 minutes, can be done from any device**, and **needs to be done only once**. Head over to the start of *Chapter 7, Managing Security Reports and Alerts by Using the Microsoft 365 Defender Portal* in this book for instructions on how to unlock them.

To open the **Chapter Review Questions** for this chapter, click the following link: `https://packt.link/MS102E1_CH08`. Or, you can scan the following QR code:

Figure 8.32 – QR code that opens Chapter Review Questions for logged-in users

Once you login, you'll see a page similar to what is shown in *Figure 8.33*:

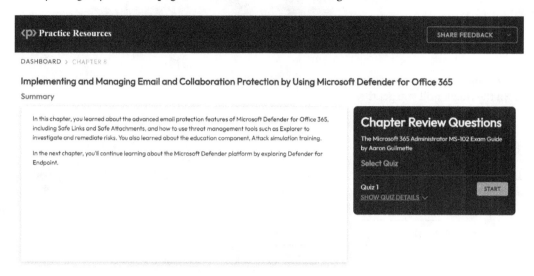

Figure 8.33 – Chapter Review Questions for Chapter 8

Once ready, start the following practice drills, re-attempting the quiz multiple times:

Exam Readiness Drill

For the first 3 attempts, don't worry about the time limit.

ATTEMPT 1

The first time, aim for at least 40%. Look at the answers you got wrong and read the relevant sections in the chapter again to fix your learning gaps.

ATTEMPT 2

The second time, aim for at least 60%. Look at the answers you got wrong and read the relevant sections in the chapter again to fix any remaining learning gaps.

ATTEMPT 3

The third time, aim for at least 75%. Once you score 75% or more, you start working on your timing.

> **Tip**
> You may take more than 3 attempts to reach 75%. That's okay. Just review the relevant sections in the chapter till you get there.

Working On Timing

Target: Your aim is to keep the score the same while trying to answer these questions as quickly as possible. Here's an example of how your next attempts should look like:

Attempt	Score	Time Taken
Attempt 5	77%	21 mins 30 seconds
Attempt 6	78%	18 mins 34 seconds
Attempt 7	76%	14 mins 44 seconds

Table 8.2 – Sample timing practice drills on the online platform

> **Note**
> The time limits shown in the above table are just examples. Set your own time limits with each attempt based on the time limit of the quiz on the website.

With each new attempt, your score should stay **above 75%** while your time taken to complete should decrease. Repeat as many attempts as you want till you feel confident dealing with the time pressure.

Implementing and Managing Endpoint Protection by Using Microsoft Defender for Endpoint

Devices (especially those connected to the internet) are continuously under attack from malicious actors. These threat actors may attempt to compromise a device or system and use it either to gain access to an environment's resources or for use as part of a larger system to attack other targets.

Whatever the scenario, **Microsoft Defender for Endpoint** (MDE) can be used to secure organizations against ransomware, file-less malware, credential compromise, and more advanced attacks.

MDE has several key features, including **attack surface reduction** (**ASR**), **automatic investigation and remediation** (**AIR**), and **endpoint detection and response** (**EDR**). These components, as well as next-generation virus detection and comprehensive threat management, are brought together as a comprehensive platform to protect Windows, macOS, iOS, Linux, and Android devices.

This chapter covers the following MS-102 exam objectives:

- Onboarding devices to Defender for Endpoint
- Configuring Defender for Endpoint settings
- Reviewing and responding to endpoint vulnerabilities
- Reviewing and responding to risks

By the end of this chapter, you should understand the features of Defender for Endpoint as well as how to deploy it and use it to respond to risks.

This objective has a lot of parts, so let's get started!

Overview of Microsoft Defender for Endpoint

Before we dive into configuration and planning topics, it's important to understand the features and requirements associated with MDE.

> **Tip**
>
> This chapter features a lot of hands-on exercises and demonstrations. The best way to experience these features is to follow along as much as possible with trial subscriptions to the Microsoft 365 Defender suite.

Features

As mentioned earlier, MDE is a collection of several related security features:

- **Attack surface reduction** (**ASR**): This advanced feature is used to limit the potential attack vectors on a particular device. ASR includes concepts such as **controlled folder access**, code integrity audits, preventing child processes from spawning, and blocking executable content from executing.

> **Further Reading**
>
> For a detailed list of all of the ASR rules and platform capabilities, see `https://learn.microsoft.com/en-us/microsoft-365/security/defender-endpoint/attack-surface-reduction-rules-reference` and `https://learn.microsoft.com/en-us/microsoft-365/security/defender-endpoint/attack-surface-reduction`.

- **Endpoint detection and response** (**EDR**): This advanced feature is activated through the use of behavioral telemetry looking for anomalous patterns of file access, memory access, registry changes, and more. *EDR is an MDE P2 feature.*

- **Automated investigation and response** (**AIR**): Upon detection of a threat, AIR can take actions to isolate and remove threats. Actions taken include removing registry keys, quarantining files, disabling drivers, stopping services or processes, and removing scheduled tasks. *AIR is an MDE P2 feature; manual response actions are part of MDE P1.*

- **Vulnerability management**: MDE provides total device vulnerability assessment and management, including measuring compliance against **Center for Internet Security (CIS)** and **Security Technical Implementation Guides (STIG)** benchmarks, software inventory and vulnerability assessment, browser extension assessment, certificate assessment, applied updates, as well as bios and firmware assessment. *Vulnerability management is an MDE P2 feature.*

- **Next-generation protection**: MDE provides behavior, heuristic, and definition-based virus detection as well as cloud integration to detect emerging threats.

- **Microsoft Threat Experts**: Threat Experts is a managed threat-hunting service. *Microsoft Threat Experts is an MDE P2 feature.*

- **Secure Score for Devices**: Taking its cues from the broader Secure Score framework, Secure Score for Devices provides a holistic view of the device environment that identifies unprotected systems and provides steps to improve the overall security posture of the organization.

- **Threat analytics**: This feature tracks emerging threats worldwide and categorizes them based on prevalence, impact, and exposure. *Threat analytics is an MDE P2 feature.*

These components are brought together through a set of administration portals and **application programming interfaces (APIs)**, facilitating the seamless integration of Microsoft Defender security products with cloud analytics and threat intelligence services. MDE is part of the Microsoft 365 Defender family of products, along with Microsoft Defender for Office 365 (which you learned about in *Chapter 8, Implementing and Managing Email and Collaboration Protection by Using Microsoft Defender for Office 365*), Microsoft 365 Defender for Identity, and Microsoft 365 Defender for Cloud Apps.

> **Further Reading**
>
> You can learn more about the entire suite of Microsoft 365 Defender products, including Defender for Cloud, Defender for Servers, Defender for Storage, and Defender for IoT, here: `https://learn.microsoft.com/en-us/defender/`.

Requirements

MDE is unique among threat protection products for Windows in that it uses the sensors built into Windows 10 and Windows 11 to communicate with the Defender cloud analytics services. The MDE agent is available as a standalone application for Android, Linux, macOS, and iOS devices.

The following table lists the supported versions of various platforms (though not all features or capabilities are available across all platforms):

Operating System	Version(s)
Windows client (current) Pro, Enterprise	10, 11
Windows client (previous versions) Pro, Enterprise	7, 8.1
Windows Server (current)	2012 R2, 2016, 2019, 2022
Windows Server (previous versions)	2008 R2 SP1
macOS	11 (Big Sur), 12 (Monterey), 13 (Ventura)
iOS	14.0+
Linux	RHEL 6.7+, 7.2+, 8.x, 9.x
	CentOS 6.7+, 7.2+
	Ubuntu 16.04+
	Debian 9+
	SUSE ES 12+
	Oracle Linux 7.2+, 8.x
	Amazon Linux 2
	Fedora 33+
Android	8.0+

Table 9.1 – MDE-supported platforms

Deployment of MDE on platforms besides Windows 10 or Windows 11 will require additional software, such as the **MDE client** for iOS or Android, **Microsoft Monitoring Agent** (**MMA**) for down-level Windows devices, or the **Defender for Endpoint deployment packages** for macOS or Linux.

> **Further Reading**
>
> There are many features available as part of EDR or AIR that may not be available on all platforms. Also, there may be differences in feature performance or capability based on whether MDE P1 or P2 is used. To review the differences, see the following resources:
>
> • **Defender for Endpoint-supported capabilities by platform**: `https://learn.microsoft.com/en-us/microsoft-365/security/defender-endpoint/supported-capabilities-by-platform`.
>
> • **Vulnerability management plans and capabilities**: `https://learn.microsoft.com/en-us/microsoft-365/security/defender-vulnerability-management/defender-vulnerability-management-capabilities`.

Next, you'll briefly look at the deployment architectures.

Deployment Architectures

MDE can be deployed in a variety of ways, depending on how your organization is currently configured, what type of infrastructure is in use, and what management tools are available.

For example, your infrastructure architecture may fall into one of the following categories:

- Cloud-first or cloud-native
- Co-management or hybrid
- On-premises

From a management perspective, you may be able to deploy using one or more of the following methods:

- Local scripting (recommended for up to 10 devices)
- Group policy
- Microsoft Intune or another **mobile device management** (**MDM**) platform
- Microsoft Configuration Manager or a third-party software deployment platform
- **Virtual desktop infrastructure** (**VDI**) platform servicing

Before you begin planning deployment and onboarding activities, you will need to understand how your environment is currently designed and what your strategy for management is going to be, as well as what licensing subscription level you will use. Once you have identified those requirements and components, it's time to start planning a deployment and what Defender for Endpoint settings will be configured.

Configuring Defender for Endpoint Settings

MDE has a myriad of settings that allow you to manage features across multiple platforms and software features.

Configuring Defender for Endpoint Options

There are many potential MDE options to configure—especially if you have subscribed to MDE P2.

In this section, you'll take a look at the high-level options that you can configure for MDE.

> **Tip**
> You'll definitely want to spend a little bit of time reviewing all of the available options in the Intune admin center (`https://intune.microsoft.com`). Focus on the middle pane of the **Endpoint security** page. Each feature has its own configuration node (**Antivirus**, **Disk encryption**, **Firewall**, and so forth). Everything is in scope for the MS-102 exam, so you'll need a good understanding of the names of the options and the types of policy items that can be configured. Even though these configuration options *appear* in the Intune admin center, they're part of Defender for Endpoint. The **Manage Endpoint Security configuration** link from the Microsoft 365 Defender portal (under **Endpoints | Device configuration**) redirects to the Intune Endpoint security page.

Before we begin exploring, though, it's worth noting the terminology that the Intune admin center uses:

- **Policy**: A policy is a group of settings that are applied as a set to one or more devices.

- **Platform**: A platform represents a device type. Depending on the feature being configured, you may have different platform choices, such as **Windows 10 and later**, **macOS**, **Windows 10, Windows 11, and Windows Server**, **Android**, or **iOS/iPadOS**. Since different platforms have different options that can be managed per Defender feature, you'll need to create at least one policy for every platform. For example, if you are configuring the **MDE disk encryption** feature and have both macOS and Windows 11 devices, you'll need to create at least two disk encryption policies—one for Windows 11 devices and one for macOS devices.

- **Profile**: A profile is used to determine the types or categories of settings per feature, per platform. Some features have multiple settings areas and may require multiple policies (each with its own platform/profile selections) to ensure you have configured all of the feature options. For example, if you select the **Windows 10, Windows 11, and Windows Server** platform for the Antivirus feature, you'll notice the profile has options for **Microsoft Defender Antivirus exclusions**, **Microsoft Defender Antivirus**, and **Windows Security Experience**. If you need to configure settings in each of those profile areas, you'll need to create a policy with the same platform but different profile settings for each configuration area.

- **Scope tag**: A scope tag is used to group administrative control in the context of **role-based access control (RBAC)**.

- **Assignments**: Each policy can be configured and assigned to groups. This allows you to configure different policy settings based on departments, use cases, or other business requirements.

This terminology will be used when working through the Defender for Endpoint configuration.

Integrating Defender for Endpoint with Intune

As components of the Microsoft 365 suite, MDE and Intune are designed to be able to work together. With the integration of the two products, you can activate advanced features, such as automatically onboarding new devices to Defender for Endpoint and using Defender's health data as part of your Conditional Access policies. For more information on Conditional Access policies, refer to *Chapter 6, Implementing and Managing Secure Access*.

Android, iOS, and Windows 10/11 (configured as either Azure AD Joined or Hybrid Azure AD Joined) devices support using Intune with Defender.

To use the two products together successfully, you need to complete the following tasks:

1. Establish a service-to-service connection between Defender for Endpoint and Intune.
2. Configure an Intune compliance policy to assign a risk level to devices.
3. Configure a Conditional Access policy to prevent users from accessing resources from devices marked as risky or non-compliant.
4. Configure a device configuration profile for onboarding new devices to Defender for Endpoint.

Let's look at the steps in more detail.

Establishing a Service-to-Service Connection

The first step in integrating Defender for Endpoint with Intune is to connect the services together. They are not natively integrated; you can purchase each service subscription individually or use different tools to manage your devices.

To enable the integration, follow these steps:

1. Navigate to the Intune admin center (`https://endpoint.microsoft.com` or `https://intune.microsoft.com`).

2. Select **Endpoint security** from the navigation menu pane, as shown in *Figure 9.1*:

Figure 9.1 – Intune admin center

3. Under **Setup** in the middle pane, select **Microsoft Defender for Endpoint**, as shown in *Figure 9.2*:

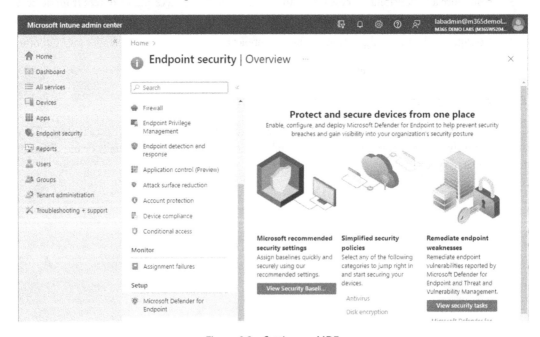

Figure 9.2 – Setting up MDE

4. In the details pane, note the connection status. If your tenant has not yet been configured for integration, the connection status will be **Unavailable**. See *Figure 9.3*:

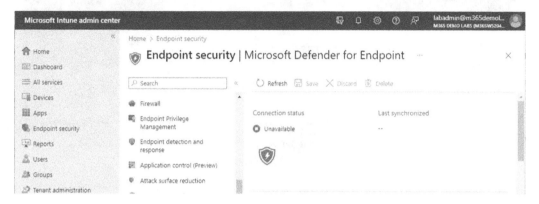

Figure 9.3 – Viewing Intune and Defender connection status

5. If the integration is not configured, scroll to the **Configuring Microsoft Defender for Endpoint** section and select **Connect Microsoft Defender for Endpoint to Microsoft Intune in the Microsoft Defender Security Center**, as shown in *Figure 9.4*, to launch the Microsoft 365 Defender portal in a new window:

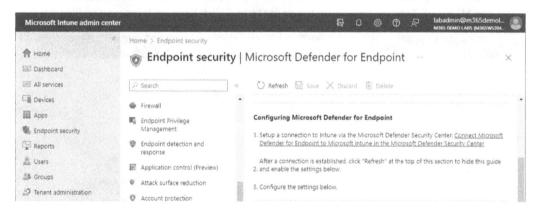

Figure 9.4 – Connecting to the Microsoft 365 Defender Security Center

6. In the navigation pane of the Microsoft 365 Defender portal, scroll down toward the bottom and select **Settings**.

7. On the **Settings** page, select **Endpoints**, as shown in *Figure 9.5*:

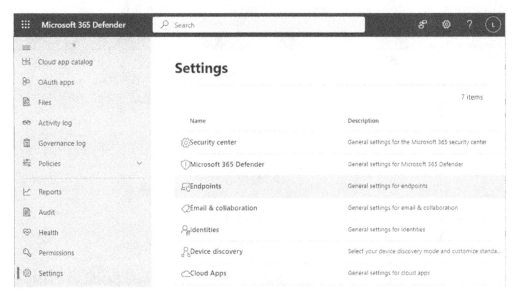

Figure 9.5 – Microsoft 365 Defender portal Settings page

8. On the **Endpoints** page, under **General**, select **Advanced features**. In the details pane, slide the **Microsoft Intune connection** toggle to **On** and click **Save preferences**. See *Figure 9.6*:

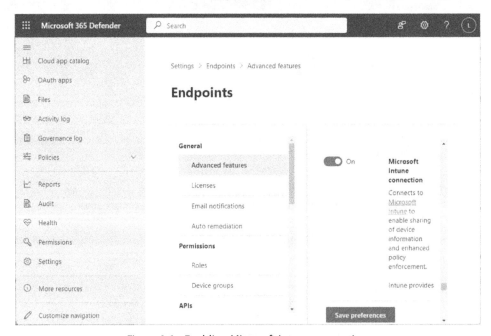

Figure 9.6 – Enabling Microsoft Intune connection

This will enable the service-to-service connection between Intune and Defender.

9. Switch back to the Microsoft Intune admin center and click **Refresh**. The connection status should update to **Available**. See *Figure 9.7*:

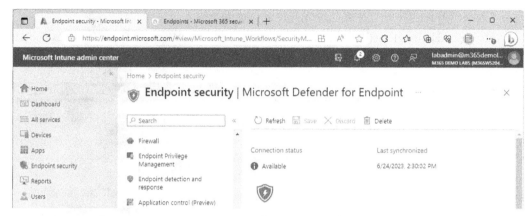

Figure 9.7 – Intune admin center after connection has been established

The integration between Intune and Defender for Endpoint has been completed. By default, the services should sync at least once every 24 hours.

> **Tip**
>
> You can configure a threshold for Microsoft Intune to consider the connection unresponsive by setting the **Number of days until partner is unresponsive** value. The default value is *7*. If the service shows as unresponsive, open a service ticket with Microsoft to troubleshoot the issue.

Next, you'll look at configuring Defender for Endpoint to use compliance and app protection policies.

Enabling Compliance Policy Evaluation

In this sequence, you'll configure Defender for Endpoint to use compliance and app protection policies configured in Intune.

To complete the configuration, follow these steps:

1. Navigate to the Intune admin center (`https://endpoint.microsoft.com` or `https://intune.microsoft.com`).

2. Select **Endpoint security** from the navigation menu pane.

3. In the middle pane, scroll down to the **Setup** section and select **Microsoft Defender for Endpoint**.

4. In the details pane, scroll to the **Compliance policy evaluation** section, as shown in *Figure 9.8*:

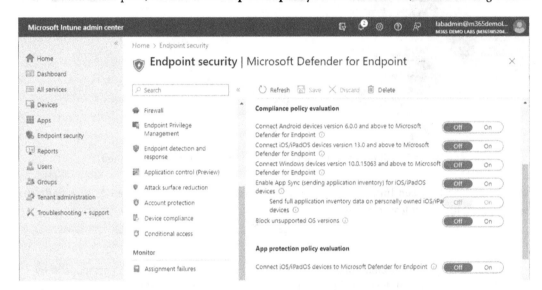

Figure 9.8 – Compliance policy evaluation section

5. Enable the policy toggles that apply to your organization, such as **Connect Android devices version 6.0.0 and above to Microsoft Defender for Endpoint**, **Connect iOS/iPadOS devices version 13.0 and above to Microsoft Defender for Endpoint**, and **Connect Windows devices version 10.0.15063 and above to Microsoft Defender for Endpoint**.

    When enabling these settings, Intune will use the device threat level information sent by MDE to determine whether the device is compliant or not.

6. Click **Save** when you've finished.

This will enable both current and future Intune-enrolled devices to integrate with MDE.

Enabling App Protection Policy Evaluation

In addition to using Defender for Endpoint for compliance policy evaluation, you can also integrate app protection policies.

To enable the app protection policy integration, follow these steps:

1. Navigate to the Intune admin center (`https://endpoint.microsoft.com` or `https://intune.microsoft.com`).

2. Select **Endpoint security** from the navigation menu pane.

3. In the middle pane, scroll down to the **Setup** section and select **Microsoft Defender for Endpoint**.

4. In the details pane, scroll to the **App protection policy evaluation** section.

5. Enable the policy toggles that apply to your organization, such as **Connect Android devices to Microsoft Defender for Endpoint** and **Connect iOS/iPadOS devices to Microsoft Defender for Endpoint**. *Depending on your tenant, you may not have both of these settings available.*

6. Click **Save** when you've finished.

You've now configured the integration between Intune and Defender!

Configuring a Compliance Policy

If you want to use the device health and risk level as part of Conditional Access, you should configure a compliance policy. To configure a compliance policy, follow these steps:

1. Navigate to the Intune admin center (`https://endpoint.microsoft.com` or `https://intune.microsoft.com`).

2. From the navigation menu pane, click **Devices** and then select **Compliance policy**. See *Figure 9.9*:

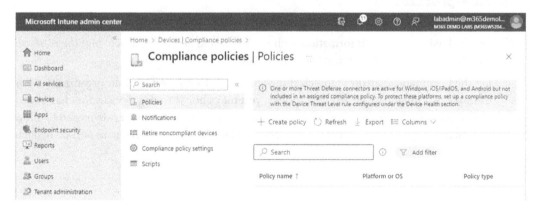

Figure 9.9 – Device Compliance policy page

3. In the details pane, click **Create policy**.

4. Select a platform such as Android Enterprise, iOS/iPadOS, or Windows 10 and later. See *Figure 9.10*:

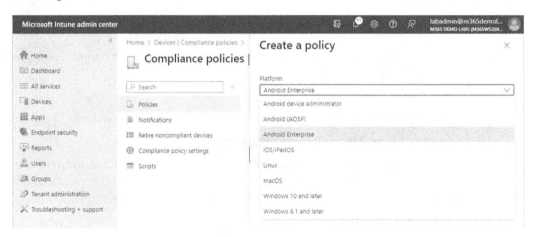

Figure 9.10 – Creating a device compliance policy

5. Select a profile. Depending on the platform you select you will have different options available. Click **Create**. The policy wizard will start.

> **Further Reading**
>
> There are a vast number of platform and profile options available, so you'll need to review which ones will be best for your organization. For more information on the device profile options, see https://learn.microsoft.com/en-us/mem/intune/configuration/device-profiles.

6. On the **Basics** tab, enter information such as a name and description. *Note that the Platform and Profile type options are grayed out.* Click **Next**.

7. On the **Compliance settings** tab, select the options that work best for your organization. For example, if configuring an Android policy, you may choose to flag devices that have been rooted (devices that have had the vendor-supplied boot image parameters bypassed to allow non-standard apps or configurations) or devices older than a certain version as non-compliant.

Device Health and Risk

There are two options on the **Compliance settings** tab that may appear confusing: **Microsoft Defender for Endpoint | Require the device to be at or under the machine risk score** and **Device health | Require the device to be at or under the Device Threat Level**. The first option, **Require the device to be at or under the machine risk score,** uses the MDE data to compute a risk score across the application, operating system, network, accounts, and security controls categories. The combined results from those categories result in a **machine risk score**. Devices exceeding the selected level are marked as non-compliant. The second option, **Require the device to be at or under the Device Threat Level,** evaluates current threats on the device using the information provided by a connected mobile threat management defense (such as Defender for Endpoint, Lookout for Work, Better Mobile, or Zimperium).

When you've finished, select **Next**. See *Figure 9.11*:

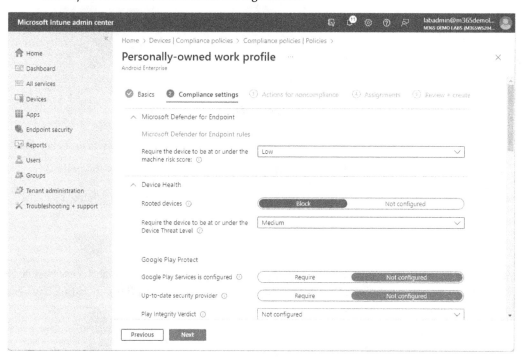

Figure 9.11 – Configuring Compliance settings

8. On the **Actions for noncompliance** tab, select any additional actions such as **Send email to end user**, **Send push notification to end user**, **Remotely lock the noncompliant device**, or **Add device to retire list**. You can configure multiple instances of each action type, if desired. Fill out the additional fields as necessary and click **Next** when finished. See *Figure 9.12*:

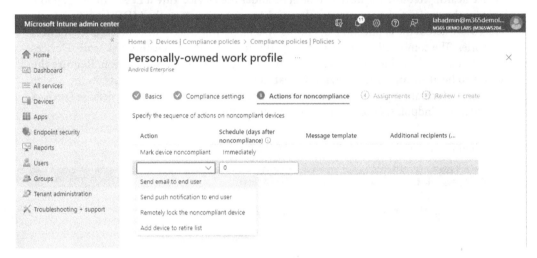

Figure 9.12 – Configuring Actions for noncompliance

9. On the **Assignments** tab, select which users or devices to apply this policy to and click **Next**.

10. On the **Review + create** tab, confirm the settings and click **Create** to save the policy.

Now that you have a compliance policy configured, you can use device compliance as part of a Conditional Access policy.

Configuring a Conditional Access Policy

You can leverage device health and compliance data as part of a Conditional Access policy. In *Figure 9.13*, you can see that the **Require device to be marked as compliant** checkbox has been selected as a **Grant** access control:

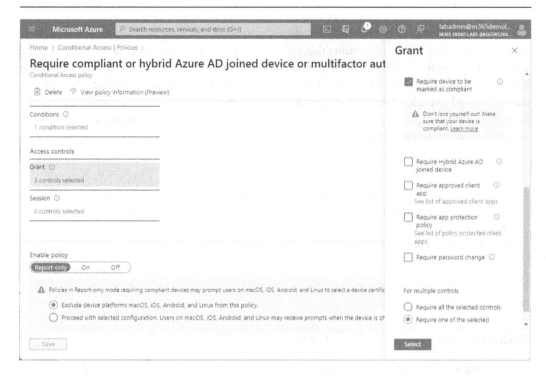

Figure 9.13 – Enabling device compliance as a requirement for Conditional Access policy

Devices are marked compliant using the integration between Intune and Defender for Endpoint to report on whether the device meets compliance standards (such as current antimalware software or no unresolved threats). For more information on configuring Conditional Access policies, refer to *Chapter 6, Implementing and Managing Secure Access*.

The final step for integration is onboarding devices to Defender to Endpoint. We'll look at that next.

Onboarding Devices to Defender for Endpoint

Onboarding devices can take many forms, depending on both the type (mobile versus computer device) and the operating system (current versions of Windows, previous or legacy versions of Windows, Android, Linux, macOS, or iOS). The latest Windows clients have the software built in and merely have to be instructed to connect to the Defender service, while others may require agents or client software to be installed.

Microsoft recommends using Intune as the deployment method, which typically requires newer devices and operating systems. This helps ensure that you're using systems that are under current maintenance or support agreements and have security updates regularly published. Newer devices and operating systems are also able to take advantage of the latest advances in management tooling. You can also onboard using Intune, local scripts, Group Policy, or third-party management platforms that leverage the scripting or packages supplied by Microsoft. It is not supported, however, to re-package the MDE deployment as it may trigger tampering alerts.

> **Note**
>
> You'll notice from the supported requirements that systems as far back as Windows 7, Android 8, and iOS 13 are supported. Many of those platforms, however, are out of vendor support and no longer receive security updates. Microsoft recommends using the latest supported operating system platforms and applications.

In this section, you'll focus on using Intune to deploy MDE, but you'll see some high-level information on other methods as well.

Onboarding Windows Devices

With Intune and Defender for Endpoint integration, onboarding Windows devices is relatively simple. After the connectivity between Intune and MDE is established, Intune can begin receiving the onboarding package configuration from Defender for Endpoint. Intune, in turn, uses a device configuration profile to deploy the configuration to Windows devices.

Onboarding with Intune

Microsoft's preferred method for onboarding Defender for Endpoint is through Microsoft Intune. The integration between Intune, MDE, and the rest of the Microsoft 365 platform helps automate onboarding, configuration, and standardization across your organization.

If you have already configured the service-to-service integration between Intune and MDE, there's nothing else to do. If you haven't done that yet, turn a few pages back and read the *Integrating Defender for Endpoint with Intune* section earlier in this chapter.

The process of either hybrid-joining devices (via Azure AD Connect synchronization, signing in to a new device with an Entra ID identity, or using the **Add a work or school account** wizard) will onboard your device to Intune and Defender for Endpoint. You can view your device's status by opening **Accounts | Access work or school**, as shown in *Figure 9.14*:

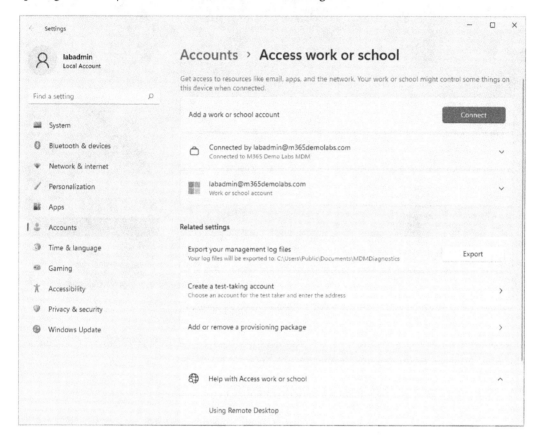

Figure 9.14 – Access work or school screen

You can also view your device's status using the `dsregcmd /status` command, as shown in *Figure 9.15*:

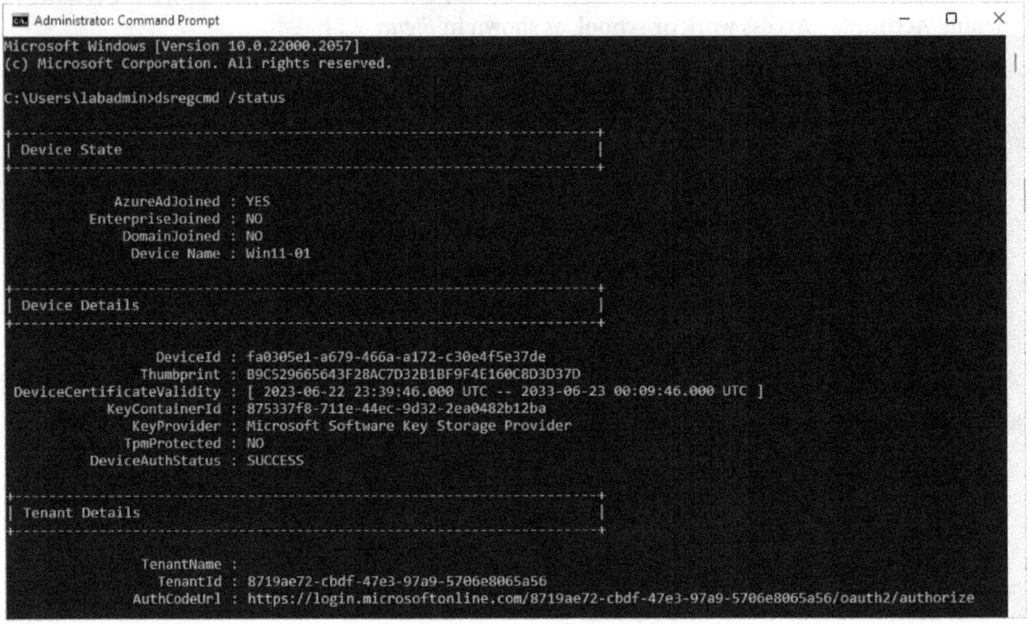

```
Administrator: Command Prompt                                                          —  □  ×
Microsoft Windows [Version 10.0.22000.2057]
(c) Microsoft Corporation. All rights reserved.

C:\Users\labadmin>dsregcmd /status

+----------------------------------------------------------------------+
| Device State                                                         |
+----------------------------------------------------------------------+

            AzureAdJoined : YES
         EnterpriseJoined : NO
             DomainJoined : NO
              Device Name : Win11-01

+----------------------------------------------------------------------+
| Device Details                                                       |
+----------------------------------------------------------------------+

                 DeviceId : fa0305e1-a679-466a-a172-c30e4f5e37de
               Thumbprint : B9C529665643F28AC7D32B1BF9F4E160C8D3D37D
  DeviceCertificateValidity : [ 2023-06-22 23:39:46.000 UTC -- 2033-06-23 00:09:46.000 UTC ]
           KeyContainerId : 875337f8-711e-44ec-9d32-2ea0482b12ba
              KeyProvider : Microsoft Software Key Storage Provider
             TpmProtected : NO
           DeviceAuthStatus : SUCCESS

+----------------------------------------------------------------------+
| Tenant Details                                                       |
+----------------------------------------------------------------------+

               TenantName :
                 TenantId : 8719ae72-cbdf-47e3-97a9-5706e8065a56
              AuthCodeUrl : https://login.microsoftonline.com/8719ae72-cbdf-47e3-97a9-5706e8065a56/oauth2/authorize
```

Figure 9.15 – Viewing device join status

Once you've onboarded to Intune in an environment with the service-to-service connection enabled, you'll need to wait for the policy refresh cycle to configure the device.

Endpoint Detection and Response (EDR) Policy

You can also create an EDR policy to enable MDE settings. To configure an EDR policy, use the following procedure:

1. Navigate to the Intune admin center (`https://intune.microsoft.com`).

2. Select **Endpoint security**, and then under **Manage** in the middle pane, select **Endpoint detection and response**.

3. Click **Create policy**. See *Figure 9.16*:

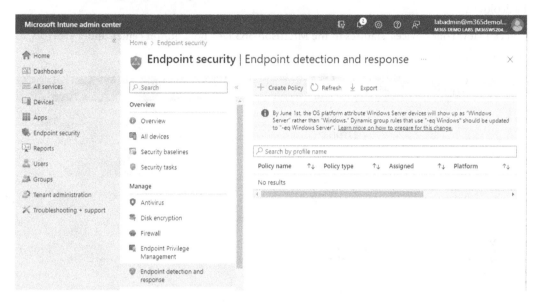

Figure 9.16 – Creating an EDR policy

4. Under **Platform**, select **Windows 10, Windows 11, and Windows Server**.

5. Under **Profile**, select **Endpoint detection and response** and click **Create**.

6. On the **Basics** tab, enter a name and a description, and then click **Next**.

7. On the **Configuration settings** tab, under **Microsoft Defender for Endpoint**, select a **Microsoft Defender for Endpoint client configuration package type** setting. You can select from **Auto from connector**, **Onboard**, **Offboard**, and **Not configured**. For integrated deployments, Microsoft recommends choosing **Auto from connector**.

8. Click **Next**.

9. On the **Scope tags** tab, assign any scope tags for your environment and click **Next**.

10. On the **Assignments** tab, under **Included groups**, select what will be in scope for this policy. For the purpose of this configuration, you can select **Add all devices** and click **Next**.

11. Click **Create**.

After Intune has refreshed the policy against the devices in scope, the onboarding package will be deployed.

You can view your devices' statuses in the Microsoft 365 Defender admin center under **Devices**, as shown in *Figure 9.17*:

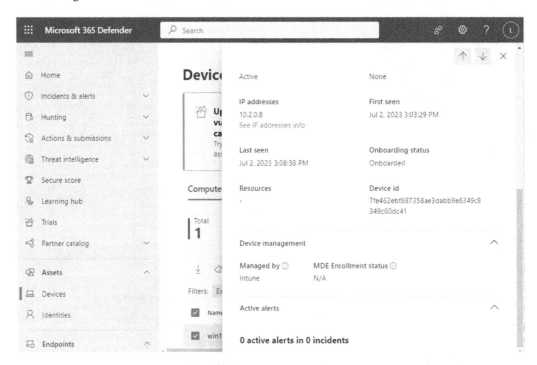

Figure 9.17 – Microsoft 365 Defender admin center device onboarding status

If you've configured and deployed MDE through both the Intune integration as well as an EDR policy for the same devices, you may end up with a conflict. While it's not a critical issue per se, you may get error conditions displayed, as shown in *Figure 9.18*:

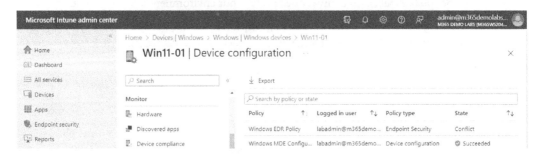

Figure 9.18 – Defender for Endpoint policy conflict

Microsoft recommends you only use one method for deploying or configuring MDE per device.

Other Onboarding Alternatives

In addition to using Intune's device configuration profile to onboard devices, you can also onboard using the following methods:

- **Group policy**: `https://learn.microsoft.com/en-us/microsoft-365/security/defender-endpoint/configure-endpoints-gp`

- **Local script**: `https://learn.microsoft.com/en-us/microsoft-365/security/defender-endpoint/configure-endpoints-script`

Whichever method you choose to use, after you have successfully onboarded your first device, you can check to see that Defender for Endpoint recognizes that the first device has been onboarded. In addition to the **Devices** page shown previously in *Figure 9.17*, you can also check to make sure your first device has been onboarded under the **Settings | Endpoints | Onboarding** section of the Microsoft 365 Defender admin center, as shown in *Figure 9.19*. **First device onboarded** (as well as view directions for other onboarding mechanisms) will display **Completed** if your configuration has been successful.

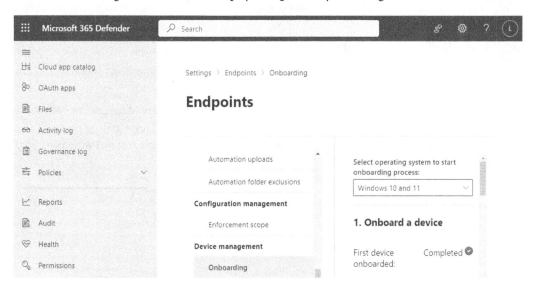

Figure 9.19 – Reviewing endpoint onboarding status

> **Further Reading**
>
> Microsoft provides an excellent reference on all the avenues available for onboarding devices in the online documentation as well. See `https://github.com/MicrosoftDocs/ microsoft-365-docs/raw/public/microsoft-365/security/defender-endpoint/downloads/mdatp-deployment-strategy.pdf` for the supported deployment methods.

Onboarding macOS Devices

Similar to Windows devices, Defender for Endpoint can be deployed to macOS devices using Intune, local scripts and commands, third-party software deployment tools that leverage the Microsoft-provided packaging, or direct user download and activation. The deployment method for MDE will depend largely on what technologies are currently in use to manage devices.

For devices that have already been enrolled in Intune, you can use the following process to deploy MDE for macOS:

1. Navigate to the Microsoft 365 Defender portal (`https://security.microsoft.com`), select **Settings**, and then select **Endpoints**.

2. Under **Device management** in the middle pane, select **Onboarding**.

3. In the details pane, under the **Select operating system to start onboarding process** dropdown, select **macOS**.

4. To download the onboarding package for Intune, select **Mobile Device Management / Microsoft Intune** under **Deployment method** and then select **Download onboarding package**. The browser will begin downloading `WindowsDefenderATPOnboardingPackage.zip`. See *Figure 9.20*:

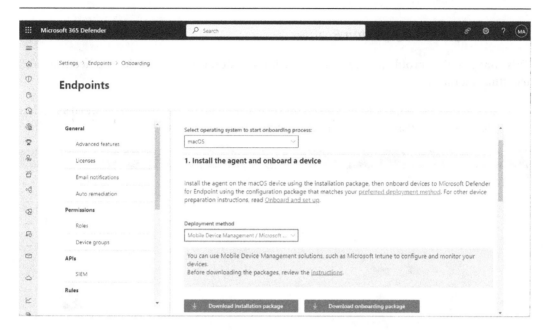

Figure 9.20 – Downloading the onboarding package for macOS

Other Methods

You can also download the installation media for a single device by selecting **Download installation package**.

---

5. Extract the downloaded ZIP file to a temporary location, such as `C:\Intune\macOS`.

Next, you'll create the several configuration profiles necessary to support macOS deployment.

Onboarding a Configuration Profile

This configuration profile provides the basic information for MDE, including licensing and reporting information:

1. Navigate to the Intune admin center (`https://endpoint.microsoft.com`) and select **Devices**. In the **Policy** section, select **Configuration profiles**. See *Figure 9.21*:

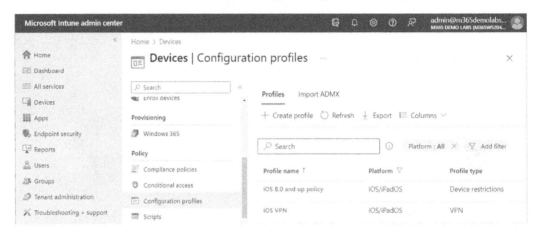

Figure 9.21 – Setting up a new configuration profile

2. Click **Create profile**.

3. On the **Create a profile** flyout, under **Platform**, select **macOS**. Under **Profile type**, select **Templates**.

4. Under **Template name**, select **Custom**. Click **Create**.

5. On the **Basics** tab, enter a name and description and click **Next**.

6. On the **Configuration settings** tab, enter a **Custom configuration profile name** to identify this configuration.

7. Under **Deployment channel**, select **Device channel**.

8. Under **Configuration profile name**, click the folder icon and browse to the folder containing the extracted onboarding package ZIP file. Select the **Intune** subfolder and then select the `WindowsDefenderATPOnboarding.xml` file, as shown in *Figure 9.22*:

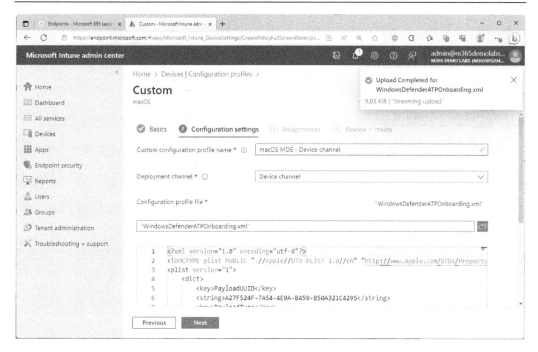

Figure 9.22 – Configuration settings tab

9. Click **Next**.

10. On the **Assignments** tab, under **Included Groups**, choose to add groups containing devices that will be in scope for the policy.

11. Click **Next**.

12. On the **Review + create** tab, verify the settings and click **Create**.

Next, you'll create the extension settings.

Extensions Configuration Profile

This profile enables settings for macOS 11 (Big Sur) and later. Earlier versions, such as macOS 10 (High Sierra), will ignore these settings. To create the configuration profile follow these steps:

1. After returning to the **Devices | Configuration profiles** page, click **Create profile**.

2. On the **Create a profile** flyout, under **Platform**, select **macOS**. Under **Profile type**, select **Templates**.

3. Under **Template name**, select **Extensions**. Click **Create**.

4. On the **Basics** tab, enter a name and description. Click **Next**.

5. On the **Configuration settings** tab, expand **System extensions**.

6. In the **Allowed system extensions** section, enter the following data:

Bundle Identifier	Team Identifier
com.microsoft.wdav.epsext	UBF8T346G9
com.microsoft.wdav.netext	UBF8T346G9

Table 9.2 – Extension configuration settings

1. Confirm the settings and click **Next**. See *Figure 9.23*:

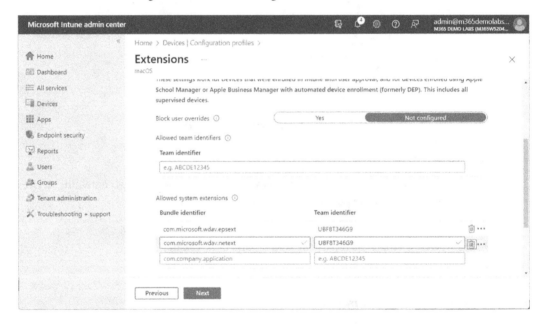

Figure 9.23 – Extension configuration settings

2. On the **Assignments** tab, under **Included Groups**, choose to add groups containing devices that will be in scope for the policy.

3. On the **Review + create** tab, verify the settings and click **Create**.

Next, you'll configure settings for disk access.

Full Disk Access Configuration Profile

1. **Full disk access** and authorization are necessary for Intune and MDE to protect macOS devices. The configuration profile enables **transparency, consent, and control** (TCC) to grant full disk access to MDE. To create the configuration profile, follow these steps:

2. Download the configuration file from `https://raw.githubusercontent.com/microsoft/mdatp-xplat/master/macos/mobileconfig/profiles/fulldisk.mobileconfig` and save it to the temporary location where you stored the macOS onboarding package.

3. On the **Devices | Configuration profiles** page in the Intune admin center (`https://endpoint.microsoft.com`), click **Create profile**.

4. On the **Create a profile** flyout, under **Platform**, select **macOS**. Under **Profile type**, select **Templates** and then choose **Custom**. Click **Next**.

5. On the **Basics** tab, enter a name and description and click **Next**.

6. On the **Configuration settings** tab, enter a custom configuration profile name to identify this configuration.

7. Under **Deployment channel**, select **Device channel**.

8. Under **Configuration profile name**, click the folder icon and browse to the folder containing the downloaded configuration file. Select the `fulldisk.mobileconfig` file and click **Next**.

9. On the **Assignments** tab, under **Included Groups**, choose to add groups containing devices that will be in scope for the policy.

10. On the **Review + create** tab, verify the settings and click **Create**.

Next, you'll create a configuration profile for managing the device's network traffic from an EDR perspective.

Network Filter Configuration Profile

MDE can inspect network traffic and report back to the Microsoft 365 Defender portal. Use the following steps to create a configuration profile that allows the network extension to perform this activity:

1. Download the configuration file from `https://raw.githubusercontent.com/microsoft/mdatp-xplat/master/macos/mobileconfig/profiles/netfilter.mobileconfig` and save it to the temporary location where you stored the macOS onboarding package.

2. On the **Devices | Configuration profiles** page in the Intune admin center (`https://endpoint.microsoft.com`), click **Create profile**.

3. On the **Create a profile** flyout, under **Platform**, select **macOS**. Under **Profile type**, select **Templates** and then choose **Custom**. Click **Next**.

4. On the **Basics** tab, enter a name and description and click **Next**.

5. On the **Configuration settings** tab, enter a custom configuration profile name to identify this configuration.

6. Under **Deployment channel**, select **Device channel**.

7. Under **Configuration profile name**, click the folder icon and browse to the folder containing the downloaded configuration file. Select the `netfilter.mobileconfig` file and click **Next**.

8. On the **Assignments** tab, under **Included Groups**, choose to add groups containing devices that will be in-scope for the policy.

9. On the **Review + create** tab, verify the settings and click **Create**.

Next, you'll create a configuration profile to manage device notifications.

Notifications Configuration Profile

This configuration profile is necessary to allow Intune and MDE to display notifications in the macOS interface. To create the configuration profile, follow these steps:

1. Download the configuration file, `https://raw.githubusercontent.com/microsoft/mdatp-xplat/master/macos/mobileconfig/profiles/notif.mobileconfig`, and save it to the temporary location where you stored the macOS onboarding package.

2. On the **Devices | Configuration profiles** page in the Intune admin center (`https://endpoint.microsoft.com`), click **Create profile**.

3. On the **Create a profile** flyout, under **Platform**, select **macOS**. Under **Profile type**, select **Templates** and then choose **Custom**. Click **Next**.

4. On the **Basics** tab, enter a name and description and click **Next**.

5. On the **Configuration settings** tab, enter a custom configuration profile name to identify this configuration.

6. Under **Deployment channel**, select **Device channel**.

7. Under **Configuration profile name**, click the folder icon and browse to the folder containing the downloaded configuration file. Select the `notif.mobileconfig` file and click **Next**.

8. On the **Assignments** tab, under **Included Groups**, choose to add groups containing devices that will be in scope for the policy.

9. On the **Review + create** tab, verify the settings and click **Create**.

Finally, you'll create the configuration profile to enable MDE to run in the background.

Background Services Configuration Profile

Starting with macOS 13 (Ventura), the operating system contains a new privacy design that prevents applications from running in the background (in daemon mode) without explicit consent. This configuration profile enables MDE to run as a background process. To create the configuration profile, follow these steps:

1. Download the configuration file, `https://raw.githubusercontent.com/microsoft/mdatp-xplat/master/macos/mobileconfig/profiles/background_services.mobileconfig`, and save it to the temporary location where you stored the macOS onboarding package.

2. On the **Devices | Configuration profiles** page in the Intune admin center (`https://endpoint.microsoft.com`), click **Create profile**.

3. On the **Create a profile** flyout, under **Platform**, select **macOS**. Under **Profile type**, select **Templates** and then choose **Custom**. Click **Next**.

4. On the **Basics** tab, enter a name and description and click **Next**.

5. On the **Configuration settings** tab, enter a custom configuration profile name to identify this configuration.

6. Under **Deployment channel**, select **Device channel**.

7. Under **Configuration profile name**, click the folder icon and browse to the folder containing the downloaded configuration file. Select the `background_services.mobileconfig` file and click **Next**.

8. On the **Assignments** tab, under **Included Groups**, choose to add groups containing devices that will be in scope for the policy.

9. On the **Review + create** tab, verify the settings and click **Create**.

As new macOS devices are enrolled in Intune, the MDE deployment package will automatically be sent to them. The Intune admin center displayed in *Figure 9.24* shows a macOS device that has been automatically configured with MDE:

Figure 9.24 – macOS enrolled in Intune

Figure 9.25 shows a newly onboarded macOS device that has a FileVault encryption policy configured. As it is a policy requirement, the user must click **Enable Now** to be able to log in.

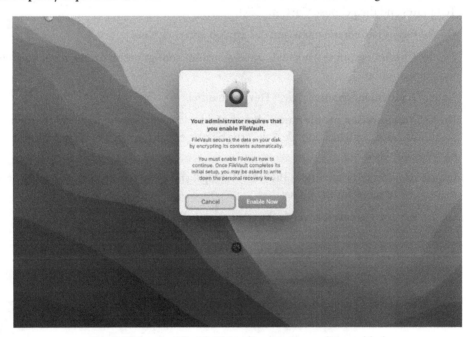

Figure 9.25 – macOS with FileVault encryption policy enabled

Next, you'll shift focus to mobile devices.

Onboarding iOS Devices

iOS devices (such as iPhones and iPads) can run in two modes—the normal user mode (also referred to as **unsupervised**) and **supervised** mode—a special enterprise configuration that allows more control over organization-managed devices.

Out of Scope

Intune and Defender for Endpoint can be deployed to devices in either normal (unsupervised) or supervised mode. Supervised mode requires additional configuration with Apple Configurator and must be set up prior to a device being activated. Most organizations working with device supervision typically deploy Apple School Manager, Apple Business Manager, or Apple Business Essentials. Configuring supervised mode through Apple School Manager, Apple Business Manager, or Apple Business Essentials is outside the scope of the MS-102 exam. You can learn more about Apple Configurator here: `https://support.apple.com/guide/apple-configurator-mac`.

MDE on iOS can still be deployed with Intune through the Intune Company Portal app—even if the device isn't in supervised mode. It can also be individually installed and activated by end users through the Apple App Store.

All Devices

Users who have devices (whether they are supervised or not) can receive MDE as an application through Intune if they are enrolled. To configure MDE for deployment through the Intune Company Portal app, follow these steps:

1. Navigate to the Intune admin center (`https://intune.microsoft.com`).

2. From the navigation menu, select **Apps** and then select **iOS/iPadOS** under **By platform**. See *Figure 9.26*:

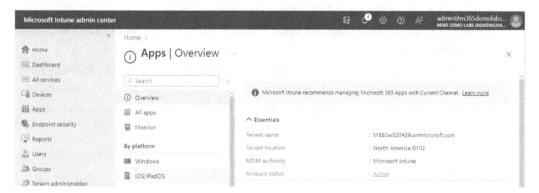

Figure 9.26 – Configuring an iOS app

3. Select **Add**.

4. On the **Select app type** flyout, choose **iOS store app** and click **Select**.

5. On the **App information** tab, click the **Search the App Store** link and locate the **Microsoft Defender** app. Click **Select**.

6. Under the **Minimum operating system** dropdown, select **iOS 14.0**. That is the minimum operating system that the Defender app supports. Click **Next**.

7. On the **Assignments** tab, under **Required**, click **Add group** to specify which users will get the app deployed.

8. Click **Next**.

9. Click **Create**.

As devices are enrolled (either supervised or unsupervised), Defender will be automatically deployed as long as the user has a MDE license assigned.

Supervised Devices

In addition to the core MDE settings, supervised devices can also enforce network monitoring and safe browsing experiences. Much like the custom macOS configuration profiles deployed earlier, the MDE network settings for supervised devices are deployed as configuration profiles. To create the configuration profile, follow these steps:

1. Download the configuration file from `https://aka.ms/mdatpiossupervisedprofile` and save it to a temporary location.

2. On the **Devices | Configuration profiles** page in the Intune admin center (`https://endpoint.microsoft.com` or `https://intune.microsoft.com`), click **Create profile**.

3. On the **Create a profile** flyout, under **Platform**, select **iOS/iPadOS**. Under **Profile type**, select **Templates** and then choose **Custom**. Click **Next**.

4. On the **Basics** tab, enter a name and description and click **Next**.

5. On the **Configuration settings** tab, enter a custom configuration profile name to identify this configuration.

6. Under **Configuration profile name**, click the folder icon and browse to the folder containing the downloaded configuration file. Select the `Microsoft_Defender_for_Endpoint_Control_Filter.mobileconfig` file and click **Next**.

7. On the **Assignments** tab, under **Included Groups**, choose to add groups containing devices that will be in scope for the policy.

8. On the **Review + create** tab, verify the settings and click **Create**.

As supervised devices are onboarded, they will be configured with the networking profile.

Unsupervised Devices

For personal mobile devices or even organization-owned devices that aren't configured for supervision, users can use the Company Portal app to self-enroll (as a personal device) and then download the MDE app from inside Company Portal or just go straight to the App Store and download MDE. It will require the user to sign in, at which point they'll get the settings you've configured for the organization.

You can also create a deployment profile that manages the settings for users who are either logged in through Company Portal or who just download and deploy the app to their individual devices.

Exam Tip

Microsoft identifies targeting devices for assignment, as opposed to users. Policies applied to users aren't processed until the user logs in.

Onboarding Android Devices

Android devices support both user-based installations as well as administrator-initiated installations for Intune-enrolled devices. MDE for Android, like MDE for iOS, also supports managing settings through Intune.

Like iOS, Android devices have several configuration modes and features for managed or Intune-enrolled devices. Android has the legacy Device Administrator and modern Android Enterprise modes. In addition, personally owned and corporate-owned devices can be managed with a work profile.

And, for devices that will not be enrolled and using Intune as an MDM platform, MDE settings can still be configured to send risk signals via an app protection policy.

Note

The MS-102 exam doesn't focus on Intune configuration and deployment for MDM and provisioning. Configuring for Android Enterprise is outside the scope of the MS-102 exam.

In the upcoming sections, you'll look at configuring Android, focusing on **bring-your-own-device** (**BYOD**) and enterprise enrollment scenarios.

Bring Your Own Device

To configure an onboarding package for Intune-enrolled BYOD Android devices, follow these steps:

1. Navigate to the Intune admin center (`https://endpoint.microsoft.com`).

2. Select **Apps** from the navigation menu, and then select **Android apps** from the middle pane.

3. In the details pane, click **Add**.

4. On the **Select app type** flyout, under **App type**, select **Android store app**. See *Figure 9.27*:

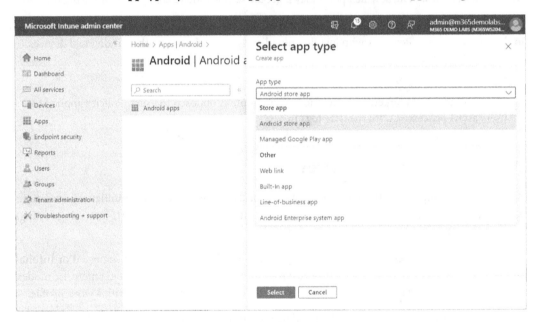

Figure 9.27 – Selecting the Android store app type

5. Click **Select**.

6. On the **App information** tab, populate the required fields of **Name**, **Description**, and **Publisher**.

7. In the **Appstore URL** field, enter the URL for the Microsoft Defender app in the Google Play Store: `https://play.google.com/store/apps/details?id=com.microsoft.scmx`. See *Figure 9.28*:

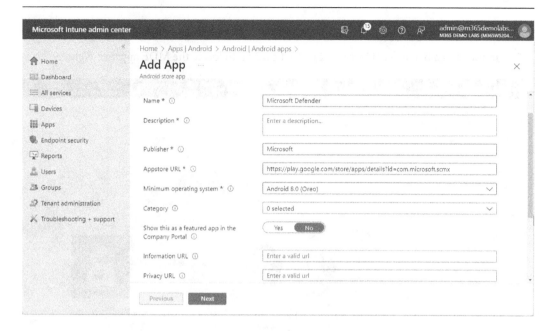

Figure 9.28 – App information tab

8. Click **Next**.

9. On the **Assignments** tab, under **Required**, choose to add groups containing devices that will be in scope for the policy.

10. On the **Review + create** tab, verify the settings and click **Create**.

Once the MDE app has been deployed, the user will need to launch the app and sign in to it.

Enterprise Enrolled Devices

You can also configure MDE as an enterprise-managed app for Android devices. *These settings are designed for devices with a work profile and assume you have already completed the Intune connection to the Google Play Store with a Google Play account.* To configure MDE as an enterprise-managed app, follow these steps:

1. Navigate to the Intune admin center (`https://endpoint.microsoft.com`).

2. Select **Apps** from the navigation menu, and then select **Android apps** from the middle pane.

3. In the details pane, click **Add**.

4. On the **Select app type** flyout, under **App type**, select **Managed Google Play app**.

5. In the search bar, enter `Microsoft Defender` to locate the MDE app. See *Figure 9.29*:

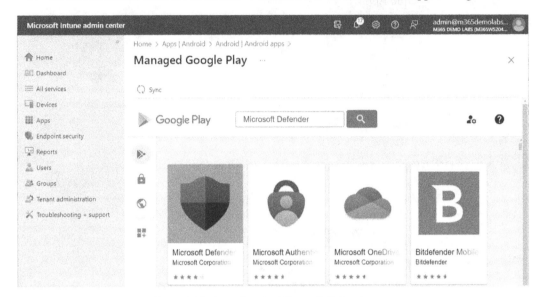

Figure 9.29 – Locating the Microsoft Defender app

6. Select the **Microsoft Defender** app.

7. In the details pane, click **Approve**.

8. On the permissions dialog, confirm the allowed permissions and click **Approve**.

9. On the **Approval Settings** tab, select **Keep approved when app requests new permissions** and click **Done**.

10. At the top of the details pane, click the **Sync** button to update the app configuration policy.

11. After the sync has completed, you should see the Microsoft Defender app listed as a managed Google Play Store app. See *Figure 9.30*:

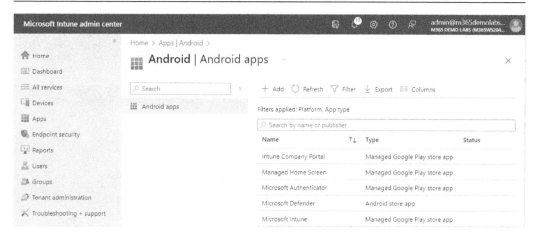

Figure 9.30 – Managed Google Play Store apps

You can manage additional settings for the app by creating an app configuration policy.

> **Further reading**
>
> For more information on **mobile application management (MAM)**, see `https://learn.microsoft.com/en-us/mem/intune/apps/app-management#mobile-application-management-mam-basics`.

Next, you'll learn how to detect and manage endpoint vulnerabilities.

Reviewing and Responding to Endpoint Vulnerabilities

Microsoft 365 Defender, as part of Plan 2, includes the **Vulnerability Management** feature. Vulnerability management, in the context of the environment's threat landscape, means the following:

- **Asset inventory and discovery**: Cataloging of assets (such as identities, certificates, browser extensions, network shares, devices, and applications) across the organization

- **Vulnerability and configuration assessment**: Reviewing the asset inventory for exposure to known or emerging threats and reporting on it

- **Risk-based intelligent prioritization**: Reviewing the assessed threats and categorizing them based on exposure

- **Remediation and tracking**: Taking and monitoring actions to reduce or resolve the risks, such as installing software updates, uninstalling applications or unwanted programs, or making device configuration changes

The **Vulnerability Management** dashboard (`https://security.microsoft.com/tvm_dashboard`), shown in *Figure 9.31*, offers a high-level view of organizational assets, risks, and recommendations:

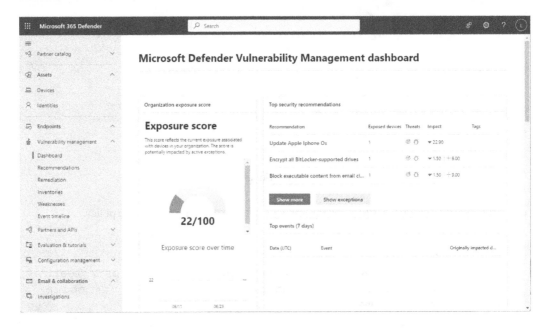

Figure 9.31 – Vulnerability Management dashboard

From here, you can select cards that display statistics or graphs of the various risk areas. You can also use the navigation menu to move between the different vulnerability management pages:

- **Recommendations**

- **Remediation**

- **Inventories**

- **Weaknesses**

- **Event timeline**

Let's look at each of these areas.

Recommendations

This page lists current threats in the organization along with corresponding security recommendations.

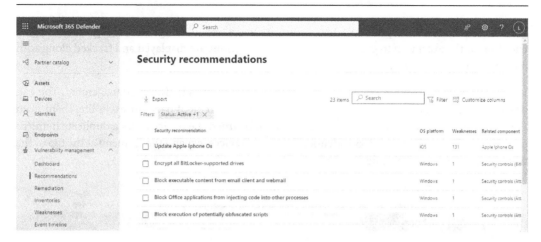

Figure 9.32 – Recommendations page

Selecting an item displays a flyout with information and activities. From here, you can select individual security recommendations to view detailed information about devices or other areas that might be exposed, relevant items tracked in the **Common Vulnerabilities and Exposures** (**CVE**) system, and possible remediation measures.

You can select **Request remediation** (see *Figure 9.33*) to start the process of creating a remediation assignment or task:

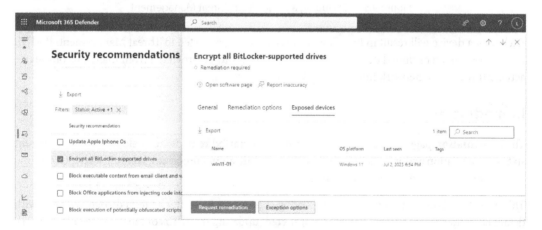

Figure 9.33 – Request remediation

When creating a remediation assignment, you have the option of just creating a tracked remediation item or creating a task in the Intune admin center.

You can also create an exception to acknowledge risk and alternate mitigations, along with setting an end date for the exception to expire (up to 1 year). Exceptions are displayed and tracked along with remediation assignments.

Items marked for exception still show up as open vulnerabilities in Threat Management. You can prevent devices from being included in reporting and management pages by excluding them from the view. You might do this, for example, if you've offboarded the device or it's a duplicate item. To do this, navigate to **Microsoft 365 Defender | Assets | Devices**, expand the **...** menu at the top of the device page, and select **Exclude**. See *Figure 9.34*:

Figure 9.34 – Excluding a device from Threat Management

Excluding a device will result in its vulnerabilities not being reported to Threat Management. If MDE is still active on an excluded device, however, it continues to be protected from malicious on-device activity through the network filtering component.

Remediation

The **Remediation** page lists any currently assigned or started remediations along with their current status. Remediation actions might include stopping or disabling processes, running a script, resetting a password, or sending files to quarantine.

This page also allows you to manage any existing exceptions. Selecting an item displays a flyout with details and allows you to sekect **Mark as completed**, updating the status of the item (see *Figure 9.35*):

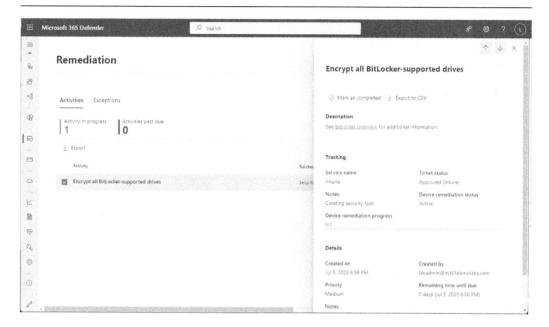

Figure 9.35 – Remediation page

Items marked as completed will continue to show up in the dashboard for 180 days. You can filter items on the **Remediation** page using any combination of the selectable attributes shown in *Table 9.3*:

Remediation Type	Mitigation Type	Device Remediation Progress
Software update	Block	Active
Software upgrade	Warn	Completed
Software uninstall	None	
Configuration change	Workaround	
Attention required		
Firmware update		

Table 9.3 – Filter parameters

Next, you'll look at the threat vulnerability management view of the asset inventory.

Inventories

The **Inventories** page catalogs discovered items, as shown in *Figure 9.36*:

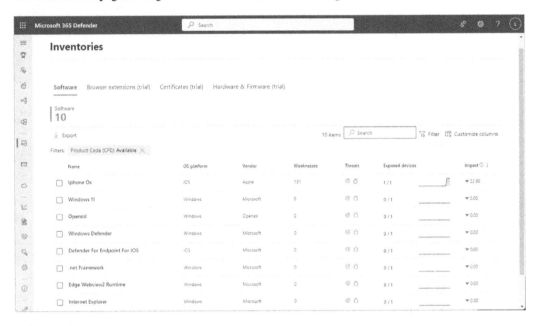

Figure 9.36 – Inventories page

Each tab displays different categories of information. You must have a Plan 2 license, however, to see data on the **Browser extensions**, **Certificates**, and **Hardware & Firmware** tabs.

The **Software** tab is used to show a high-level overview of software (both components and applications) identified in your organization, along with information about the platform, the number of known threats across all the devices with the associated software, the number of exposed devices in relationship to the number of total devices, and the relative impact on your exposure and Secure Score.

The **Browser extensions** tab displays information gathered about installed browser extensions along with the browser, the operating system the browser is running on, the highest risk level generated by the extension based on what access or sites the extension requested, and the version information.

The **Certificates** tab displays information regarding certificates that are potentially vulnerable. Certificates are identified for risk based on whether they have expired or will expire within 60 days, as well as potential vulnerabilities due to key length or algorithm and self-signed certificates.

The **Hardware & Firmware** tab displays inventoried information regarding what types of devices have been discovered (laptop, desktop, and servers), what types of processors are identified, and which BIOS or firmware levels are in place. Vulnerability and risk information is available for Lenovo, Dell, and HP models only.

You can drill down into items on each of the pages, eventually arriving at a device's inventory page. A device's inventory page displays all of the connected risks, vulnerabilities, incidents, and other details associated with a device. Depending on the type of device, you may see information about missing updates, security baseline information, and other policies applied to it. You also have the ability to add your own categorization to the device based on its **device value**.

About Device Value

Device value is a subjective assignment of value. By default, all devices are configured with a value of **Normal**. You can adjust a device's value (**Low, Normal**, and **High**) based on any number of factors you determine are important. For example, you may want to categorize an executive's laptop or the server containing payroll data with a **High** value, while a shared computer in a lab might be downgraded to a **Low** value. The categorization value impacts your organization's overall exposure score (**High**-value devices have more impact than **Normal**-value devices, and **Normal**-value devices have more impact than **Low**-value devices).

Weaknesses

Like other pages in **Vulnerability Management**, the **Weaknesses** page categorizes threats to your environment. This page, however, approaches it from a different perspective by displaying the combined list of unique vulnerabilities across all devices and then highlights the important data points such as which are exploitable, zero-day exploits, and whether updates are available. See *Figure 9.37*:

Figure 9.37 – Weaknesses page

You can sort the vulnerabilities by a variety of properties, including software name, CVE item ID, severity, and the number of exposed devices. Selecting a vulnerability item surfaces a flyout with a link to the corresponding item on the **Recommendations** page.

Event Timeline

The **Event timeline** page displays vulnerabilities in the order they were discovered or affected your environment. See *Figure 9.38* for an example timeline:

Figure 9.38 – Event timeline page

Selecting an item on the timeline will display the corresponding CVE information as well as links to any security recommendations. Clicking on the associated security recommendation will take you to the **Recommendations** page, where you can implement the steps suggested.

Baseline Assessment

A new feature of **Vulnerability Management**, **Baseline assessment** relies on security profiles to continuously evaluate your endpoints against benchmarks. Security profiles mapping to CIS benchmarks are available for Windows 10 and later client endpoints and Windows 2008 R2 and later server endpoints. Security profiles mapping to STIG benchmarks are available for Windows 10 and Windows Server 2019.

Baseline assessment is available as either part of the Microsoft Defender Vulnerability Management Standalone plan or the Defender Vulnerability Management add-on for MDE P2. Assessments are deployed via **Group Policy Object (GPO)** configurations.

Creating a Security Profile

To create a profile, follow these steps:

1. Navigate to the Microsoft 365 Defender portal (https://security.microsoft.com). Expand **Vulnerability management** and select **Baselines assessment**.

2. Select the **Profiles** tab, and then select **Create profile**.

3. On the **Name profile** page, enter a name and a description. The **Activate profile** button is selected by default.

4. On the **Baseline profile** scope page, under **Software**, select the version of Windows to which this profile will apply.

5. In the **Benchmark** section, select which base benchmark to use.

6. Under **Compliance level**, select which compliance level you want this profile to measure against. See *Figure 9.39*:

Figure 9.39 – Configuring Baseline profile scope

Note

Depending on the benchmark selected, you will see different compliance level options. While specific information about compliance levels isn't required for the MS-102 exam, you should know that they exist. You can learn more about CIS benchmark compliance levels here: https://www.cisecurity.org/cis-benchmarks. You can learn more about the STIG compliance levels here: https://www.titania.com/resources/guides/disa-stig-compliance-explained/.

7. Click **Next**.

8. On the **Add configuration settings** page, select which items from the benchmark and compliance scope you want to validate against and click **Next**. Some configuration settings, as shown in *Figure 9.40*, present a **Customize** option. Since many of the configurations check local device policies or registry settings, you can customize the values that the baseline checks against.

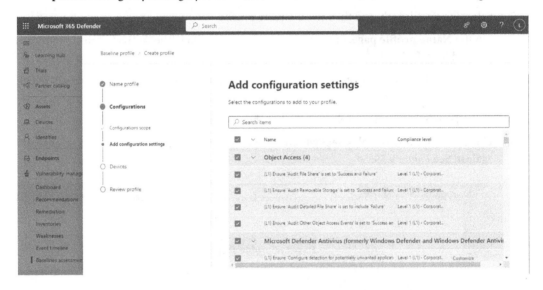

Figure 9.40 – Profile configuration settings

9. On the **Devices to assess** page, select which devices will be in scope for the baseline profile. You can select **All device groups**, **Selected device groups**, and **Filter by device tags**. The page will show you how many devices are in scope based on your selection criteria.

10. On the **Review profile** page, click **Submit** to create the profile.

After the profile has been created, you'll be returned to the **Profiles** tab of **Baselines assessment**.

Reviewing Assessment Results

Once the **Security baselines assessment | Profiles** tab has been updated, you can check your organization's compliance against that profile. On the **Profiles** tab, after the profile data has been updated, you will see how the devices in the baseline score against the baseline assessment and compliance settings chosen in the profile. *Figure 9.41* displays a high-level overview:

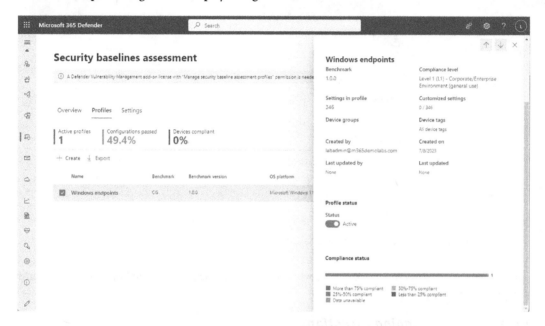

Figure 9.41 – Profile assessment

You can select the name of the profile to view its details page, which will show information regarding compliance against the selected policy configurations as well as each individual in-scope device's rating. The **Configurations** tab shows each selected profile configuration ID. You can drill further down by selecting a particular configuration ID to see the supporting details, such as the rationale, what local device configuration setting is being validated, the configuration category, and steps to bring an item into compliance.

Figure 9.42, the **Devices** tab, shows individual devices that are in scope for the profile and their compliance against the profile:

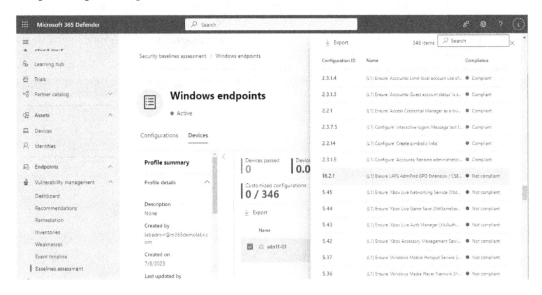

Figure 9.42 – Viewing an individual device's compliance against a baseline profile

This detailed view allows you to see exactly which device policy settings need to be adjusted to become compliant with the profile.

Creating and Managing Exceptions

As with other features in Vulnerability Management, you may have devices that need to be excluded from being included in a particular policy or configuration item for various reasons—such as a policy item being mitigated by a third-party piece of software or alternate control. To configure an exception for a device, follow these steps:

1. Navigate to the Microsoft 365 Defender portal (`https://security.microsoft.com`), expand **Vulnerability management**, select **Baselines assessment**, and then choose the **Exceptions** tab.

2. Select **Create**.

3. Add the details of the justification, including the reason and duration. Click **Next**.

4. On the **Configuration scope** page, choose the software, benchmark, and compliance level where the policy item(s) to be excepted occur and click **Next**.

5. On the **Select configurations** page, select the configuration IDs to be included in the exception. Click **Next**.

6. On the **Devices** page, select the devices to be accepted from the configuration. Click **Next**.

7. Click **Submit**.

Exceptions are applied on a per-configuration ID, per-device basis. That is, if a device appears in multiple profiles, is in scope, and is tracking against the same baseline and compliance configuration ID, it will be excluded from reporting for all of the profiles.

As you can see, all of it items in the Threat Management area are connected—each giving you a different view into various pieces of your organization's infrastructure and assets, linking back to the same devices. This helps you get a holistic view of impacted devices, applications, data, and users as well as the relative risk levels that each item presents.

Now that you're familiar with some of the vulnerability management pages, let's switch gears to threat and risk management.

Reviewing and Responding to Risks

When threats are detected, Microsoft 365 Defender will create incidents and alerts. You can monitor and manage alerts and incidents from the Microsoft 365 Defender portal.

> **Tip**
> Microsoft 365 Defender provides sample files that you can use to understand how to detect and process risks. The examples in this section were generated using the automated investigation (backdoor) simulation, available for download at `https://security.microsoft.com/tutorials/simulations`. We recommend deploying a simulation to a test environment so you can more deeply understand the vulnerability management experience and interface.

Microsoft Defender 365 has some basic terminology you'll need to understand in order to be successful—both on the MS-102 exam as well as managing security operations:

- **Alert**: A detected event that generates a notification. In the context of Microsoft 365 Defender, an alert is specific to some sort of suspicious or threat-like activity. An alert may be generated by a single event (such as the detection of malware) or a series of similar, related events (such as multiple bad password attempts from multiple geographic locations or malicious script activity).

- **Incident**: A group of correlated events that are aggregated together. Incidents are used to provide context and timelines for attacks.

- **Alerts queue**: Shows the alerts across various Microsoft solution areas, including Defender for Endpoint, Defender for Office 365, Defender for Cloud Apps, and Defender for Identity.

- **Attack story**: A multifaceted way of displaying an incident's corresponding alerts and events. Stories can have timelines, graphs, and other data objects to represent how a threat or threat actor is moving across your organization—whether it's contained on a single endpoint, what processes were invoked, what other endpoints were contacted, what content was downloaded, and more.

- **Indicators of compromise (IOCs)**: Signals used to generate alerts. An IOC might be a particular file or file hash, an IP address, a device, an identity, a URL, or any other piece of information used in determining whether something is a threat or risk.

Incidents and alerts are depicted in the Microsoft 365 Defender interface in *Figure 9.43*:

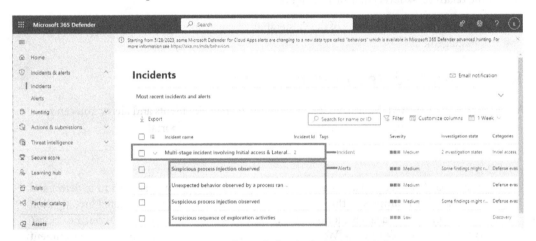

Figure 9.43 – Microsoft 365 Defender incidents and alerts

The alerts queue is displayed by selecting **Alerts** under **Incidents & alerts**. Like other pages in vulnerability management, you can filter the alerts by various criteria, including **Severity**, **Status**, **Categories**, and which service sources were responsible for generating the alert.

When working with security incidents, you may find it best to use a standard approach to triaging. A helpful approach is to examine the current incidents and prioritize them according to **Severity** (the risk level assigned by Microsoft 365 Defender) and **Impact** (a description of how widespread or business-affecting an issue might be, the number of affected users or applications, or the types of alerts).

Investigate

Once an incident has been generated, you can begin investigating all of the related alerts. Like the other pieces in Vulnerability management, each file, process, device, and activity is linked to the related items.

Attack Story

By clicking on the incident (using the incident highlighted in *Figure 9.43* as an example), you're taken to the **Attack story** tab of the incident, shown in *Figure 9.44*:

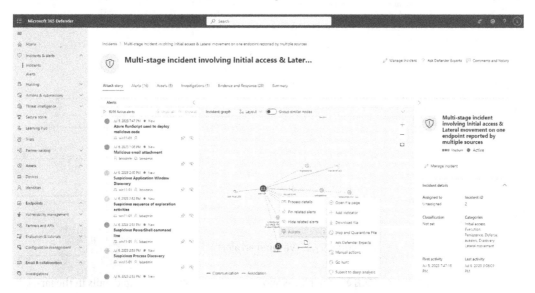

Figure 9.44 – Attack story

From here, you can pivot on any item, be it an individual alert in the **Alerts** pane, an item displayed in the **Incident graph** pane, or any of the tabs (**Alerts**, **Assets**, **Investigations**, **Evidence and Response**, or **Summary**). The attack story's incident graph automatically groups similar items and nodes together, but you can slide the toggle to off to display each item node on its own (as it is in *Figure 9.44*). This may help you further see interactions between events.

Each item will display relevant details and contextual actions that you can take, such as listing out the URL details that a malicious process attempted to contact or seeing the code that was executed inside of a script.

Clicking an item in the **Alerts** pane will cause the details pane to focus on that item in the incident graph and show the other corresponding events that were happening in the chain. For example, by clicking on the **Suspicious behavior by Microsoft Word was observed** item in the **Alerts** pane (see *Figure 9.45*), the attack story pivoted to show the user identity and device highlighted in the incident graph and the process tree, including the application lineage and command line that generated the alert.

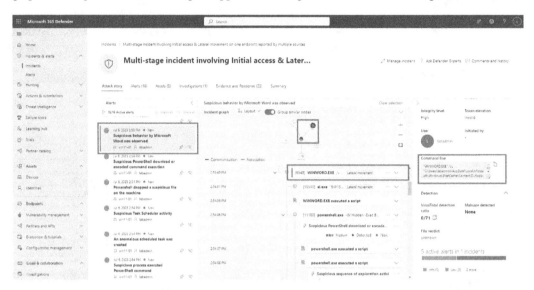

Figure 9.45 – Viewing an alert's details

Clicking on the `WINDWORD.EXE` executable, as shown in *Figure 9.45*, brings up details in the far-right pane, including the process ID, the exact command line that was invoked, publishing details of the file, and more. You can further investigate items in the process tree, looking for any other clues that might aid your investigation.

Alerts

Switching to the **Alerts** tab shows all of the alerts related to an incident. Again, you can select an individual alert to see additional details about the alert. Depending on the type of alert, you may see details about a file, an IP address contacted, a device, or processes. You can edit the classification of the alert state (setting it to **New**, **In progress**, or **Resolved**), assign the alert to an individual for triage or investigation, set a classification, as well as provide a comment. See *Figure 9.46*:

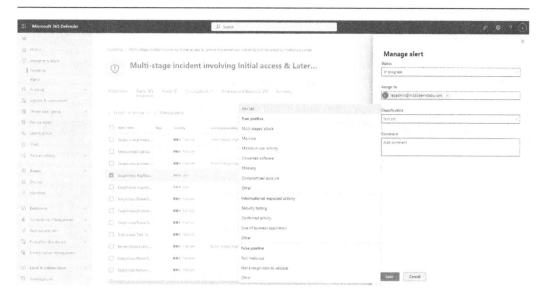

Figure 9.46 – Manage alert details

Alert classification helps your team identify genuine risks. For example, you may have hired a penetration testing firm to assess the security of your organizational processes and tools. When an alert is generated, you might classify that particular alert as **Informational expected activity | Security testing**. That informs others in the organization how they should respond to an alert.

After you have begun classifying alerts, the **Recommendations** tab on the **Alert details** flyout will start to provide additional insights about threats in your organization, such as whether this type of alert has been marked or classified before.

Assets

The **Assets** tab of an incident shows all of the organizational assets that are affected. This could include **Devices**, **Users**, **Mailboxes**, and **Apps**. Selecting an asset category will display all of the affected items in that category that have been associated with the current incident. Selecting an individual item will take you to its associated asset page (such as the **Assets** page for devices and users or **Threat Explorer** for mailboxes).

Investigations

The **Investigations** tab is used to track the triggering alerts for the incident. After selecting an alert to view its details, you can select **Open investigation page** to get a deep insight into the event, as shown in *Figure 9.47*:

Figure 9.47 – Triggering alert investigation

The **Investigations** page for an alert shows details much like the **Attack story** tab, highlighting the correlated alerts and entities that were analyzed. See *Figure 9.48*:

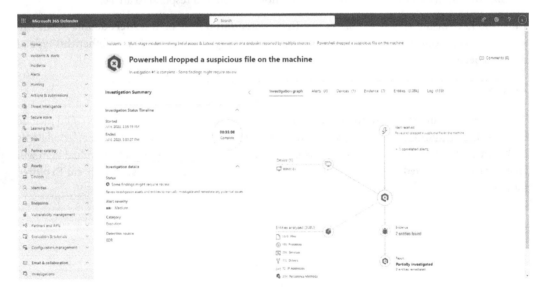

Figure 9.48 – Investigations page

You can further investigate the items by clicking on the relevant tabs. While many of the tabs are familiar, three tabs stand out on this page: **Evidence**, **Entities**, and **Log**.

The **Evidence** tab provides details about specific files that were detected and processes that were executed. You can investigate these items to learn more about automated actions that Defender has taken, view additional details about the file, or even start a threat hunt in your organization based on the item. See *Figure 9.49*:

Figure 9.49 – Evidence details

The **Entities** tab shows all of the items that were scanned or included as part of the investigation, including **Files**, **Processes**, **Services**, **Drivers**, and **IP Addresses**. Additionally, the **Entities** tab also shows **Persistence Methods**—a view that reports the ways that a threat may attempt to hide itself or evade detection and removal and whether Defender located the threat at any of those locations.

The **Log** tab shows the activities that Defender has taken automatically, such as locating files, listing network connections, listing active services and processes, and taking an inventory of the device's memory.

Evidence and Response

The **Evidence and Response** tab for the incident shows much of the same information as the **Evidence** tab in an investigation—the main difference being the absence of the **Persistence Methods** information from the **Evidence** tab.

Just like the **Evidence** tab in an investigation, you can select individual items to dive deeper into each one. Depending on the context and type of evidence, you may be able to download files, examine IP address ownership, look at file header information, quarantine files, or submit the evidence (files or other captured content) for analysis. See *Figure 9.50*:

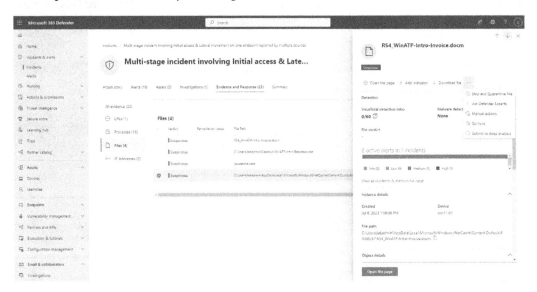

Figure 9.50 – Incident evidence

Other options include invoking help from Microsoft Defender Threat Experts (available as a separate subscription) or using the item to pivot into threat hunting (using the **Go hunt** option).

Respond

Once you have begun analyzing and working on an incident, you may have several options on how to respond.

Taking Actions

Depending on the Microsoft 365 Defender subscription, you may have different options for automated or manual remediation. The types of actions Defender can take are generally divided into two categories: actions that can be performed on devices and actions that can be performed on files.

Let's look into each of those areas.

Devices

Once you have identified devices that are impacted, you can choose how to respond. See *Figure 9.51* for the potential actions:

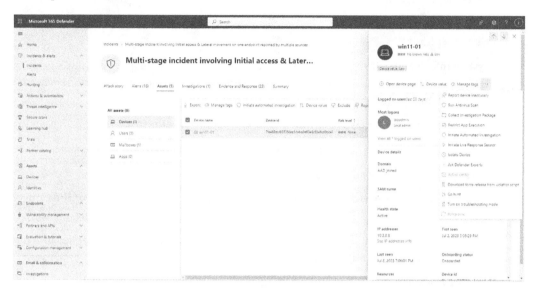

Figure 9.51 – Device remediation actions

The available remediation actions on a device, shown in *Figure 9.51*, include the following:

- **Run Antivirus Scan**: Initiate a Microsoft Defender **Antivirus** (**AV**) scan (whether or not Defender AV is the active solution or not).

- **Collect Investigation Package**: Selecting this initiates data collection on the target device. The device must be online and connected to Microsoft 365 Defender for this action to take effect. Once completed, the resultant file (MDE_Investigation_Package.zip) contains core information about the device, including the following:

- **Autoruns**: Registry output of various startup registry keys

- **Installed Programs**: Text and CSV files containing registry information regarding installed programs

- **Network connections**: Output of various network statistics commands, including IP configuration, DNS cache, ARP table, active network connections, and firewall activity

- **Prefetch files**: File header information that is stored whenever a file is executed for the first time

- **Processes**: CSV listing of active processes

- **Scheduled Tasks**: CSV listing of scheduled tasks

- **Security Event Log**: Export of the security event log

- **Services**: CSV listing of installed or configured services

- **SMB Session**: Summary of established **Server Message Block (SMB)** communications sessions with other hosts

- **System Information**: Text export of basic system information, including device name, operating system version, BIOS and processors, installed hotfixes, domain membership, locale data, and memory configuration

- **Temp Directories**: Contents of any identified temporary files directories

- **Users and Groups**: Lists of locally configured users, groups, and group memberships

- **WdSupportLogs**: Windows Defender support logs

- **Forensics Collection Summary**: List of the types of data collected as part of the Collect Information Package task, including the local commands used to gather the data

- **Restrict App Execution**: This invokes a protection mechanism that prevents applications not signed by Microsoft from running.

- **Initiate Automated Investigation**: Start a general-purpose automated investigation to look for any other potential issues. Any alerts generated on this device during the investigation will automatically be added to this investigation, as well as other instances of the same threats detected on other devices.

- **Initiate Live Response Session**: Launch a remote PowerShell session to the device to run additional scripts or gather additional data.

- **Isolate Device**: Immediately block all traffic on the device except to Microsoft 365 Defender. This is also sometimes referred to as **Contain Device**.

- **Ask Defender Experts**: An additional available service, Microsoft 365 Defende Experts allows you to ask Microsoft security personnel to help provide context around threats. For more information on Threat Experts, see `https://learn.microsoft.com/en-us/ microsoft-365/security/defender/onboarding-defender-experts- for-hunting`.

- **Download force release from isolation script**: This script, executed locally on an isolated device, can be used to un-isolate a device not responding to Microsoft 365 Defender. The script is valid for 3 days, after which time, a new script must be generated to run on the device.

When executing the **Collect Information Package** option, you may need to navigate away from the view where it was activated. To avoid accidentally re-running the collection, you can use the **Action center** context menu item to see the results of pending actions (such as a collection file available for download).

Files

You can also take actions on files involved in an alert or incident. *Figure 9.52* shows the actions available for files:

Figure 9.52 – File actions

The remediation actions listed in *Figure 9.52* include the following:

- **Download file**: Package up the identified file and download it. This may expose your device to risk, so use it with caution.

- **Stop and Quarantine File**: Depending on the type of file, you may stop its execution, quarantine it to prevent it from being accessed, or both.

- **Ask Defender Experts**: An additional service available, Microsoft 365 Defender Experts allows you to ask Microsoft security personnel to help provide context around threats. For more information on Threat Experts, see https://learn.microsoft.com/en-us/ microsoft-365/security/defender/onboarding-defender-experts- for-hunting.

- **Submit to deep analysis**: Examine the file in a Microsoft 365 Defender sandbox. The analysis may take up to 3 hours.

Security analysts working with Microsoft 365 Defender have many options for investigating and remediating issues inside the platform.

Resolve

After you are done investigating an incident and resolving the problems, you can determine the disposition of the incidents and alerts.

To close out an incident, you can select the incident on the **Incidents** page and then click **Manage incidents**, as shown in *Figure 9.53*:

Figure 9.53 – Incident flyout

The **Manage incident** flyout appears, which allows you to update the incident name, add any incident tags, assign the incident to a security analyst, update the status, set a classification, and add any comments, as shown in *Figure 9.54*:

Figure 9.54 – Manage incident flyout

After updating the incident properties, you can click **Save**. Updating an incident's status to **Resolved** automatically resolves all the active alerts associated with it. You can still view the story, alerts, and other associated information for further post-mortem analysis.

Tuning

You can tune the parameters for specific alerts (**Alert details | Tune alert**). Tuning alerts helps your **security operations center** (**SOC**) team focus on alerts that are specifically important to your organization. While you can tune alerts at any time during an incident, you may wish to wait until after an incident has been resolved and all of the relevant information has been analyzed.

Tuning alerts helps streamline the alert queue by hiding or resolving alerts automatically if certain parameters are met—leaving the security analysts time to triage and respond to priority issues.

> **Exam Tip**
>
> **Alert tuning** was previously known as **alert suppression**, so look out for both terms in the exam.

Alerts are tuned through the use of rule conditions. Alerts can be tuned from the **Settings** page (which allows you to specify alerts) as well as from the **Alerts** page (which allows you to work with tuning parameters for a particular alert). The steps look very much the same, so you'll only dive into one of them.

To tune an alert from the **Settings** page, follow these steps:

1. Navigate to the Microsoft 365 Defender portal (`https://security.microsoft.com`), select **Settings**, and then select **Microsoft 365 Defender**. Under **Rules**, select **Alert tuning**, as shown in *Figure 9.55*:

Figure 9.55 – Microsoft 365 Defender rules

2. Click **Add new rule**.
3. On the **Tune alert** flyout, select the service sources to which this rule will apply.

4. Under **IOCs**, select which IOCs or conditions will cause this rule to apply. Depending on which service sources you choose, you may see different options available. In this example, the IOC is configured to be an IP address, as shown in *Figure 9.56*:

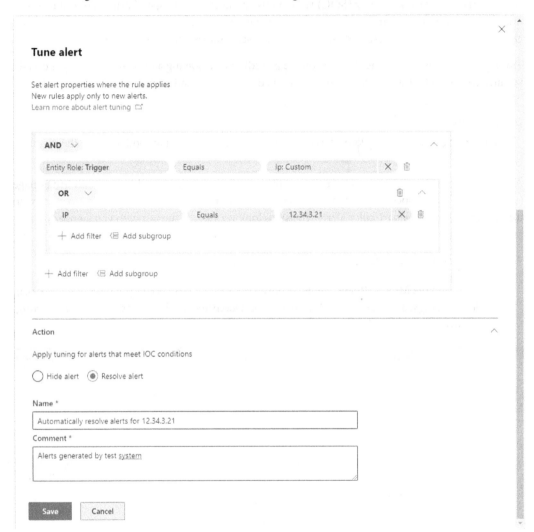

Figure 9.56 – Alert condition parameters

5. Choose how to handle the alerts matching the condition (such as **Hide alert** or **Resolve alert**).

6. Add a name and comment.

7. Click **Save** to add the rule condition.

8. Select the scope of the devices that will be impacted by this rule (either **All organization** or **Device groups**) and click **Save**.

9. Click **Finish**.

10. Alerts generated that meet this particular rule condition will now be automatically resolved (in this case). Microsoft recommends using these judiciously, as it may inhibit you from seeing threats if configured incorrectly.

You can also tune Defender by adding or updating **indicators** (also known as IOCs). You may determine that the presence of a particular file or accessing a particular IP address is a precursor to an exploit or threat.

1. The example file shown in *Figure 9.50*, RS4_WINATP-Intro-Invoice.docm, was flagged as a suspicious file once the code in it was executed. In this example, you'll create an indicator that quarantines that file as soon as it's seen in the environment, since we know it has led to an incident already.

2. To create an indicator based on the evidence in this investigation, follow these steps:

3. From the Microsoft 365 Defender portal (https://security.microsoft.com), expand **Incidents & alerts**, select **Incidents**, select the incident, and then choose the **Evidence and Response** tab.

4. Under **All evidence**, select **Files**.

5. Select the RS4_WINATP-Intro-Invoice.docm file (or another file, if you are not using the same incident simulation), as shown in *Figure 9.57*:

Figure 9.57 – Selecting the evidence to be used as an indicator

6. On the flyout, select **Add indicator**.

7. On the **Indicator** page, add a title and description for the indicator. The **File hash** value is automatically inserted.

8. Click **Next**.

9. On the **Action** page, select an action to take when the file is detected. In this example, **Block and remediate** was chosen, as shown in *Figure 9.58*:

Figure 9.58 – Selecting the Block and remediate action

10. Click **Next**.

11. On the **Alert details** page, choose **Generate alerts** (if desired). Assign a severity, select a category for this indicator, and add any recommended actions. You can also choose **Perform historical matching**, which will look back over data collected and remediate any hosts if needed. Click **Next**.

12. Click **Next** on the **Organizational scope** page.

13. Click **Submit** to finish adding the indicator.

After adding the indicator, you'll be taken back to the **Evidence and Response** page with the item details open. It will be updated to reflect that there is now an indicator rule created for it, as shown in *Figure 9.59*:

Figure 9.59 – Indicator rule has been created

> **Further Reading**
>
> For more information on managing indicators, see https://learn.microsoft.com/en-us/microsoft-365/security/defender-endpoint/manage-indicators.

Automate

In addition to the manual remediation actions that you can take inside Microsoft 365 Defender, you can also configure different levels of automated responses, both integrated within Microsoft 365 Defender and other automation tools.

Automated Investigation and Response

If you have subscribed to MDE P2 or MDB, you have native options for automated remediation. If your organization has MDE P2 or MDB, fully automated remediation is enabled by default in tenants created after August 16, 2020. Automated remediation only supports devices later than Windows 2012 R2 and Windows 10, version 1709.

If you want to limit the amount of automated remediation performed by Microsoft 365 Defender, you can create device groups to limit the level of automated remediation.

> **Note**
>
> You can only use device groups to limit remediation in MDE P2. MDB customers have fully automated remediation enabled by default and cannot use device groups to manage it.

To create and manage remediation levels using device groups, use the following steps:

1. From the Microsoft 365 Defender portal (`https://security.microsoft.com`), go to **Settings | Endpoints**. Under **Permissions**, select **Device groups**, as shown in *Figure 9.60*:

Figure 9.60 – Device groups

2. Click **Add device group**.

3. On the **General** page, specify a device group name.

4. Under **Remediation level**, select the level of automated remediation to apply to this group. Options include **Full – remediate threats fully** (default), **Semi – require approval for core folders**, **Semi – require approval for non-temp folders**, **Semi – require approval for all folders**, and **No automated response**.

5. Enter a description.

6. Click **Next**.

7. On the **Devices** page, use the filters to craft matching rules that will be used to define the membership of the group. You need to specify at least one matching criterion. Click **Next**.

8. On the **Preview devices** page, click **Show preview** to return a sample list of devices that will be included in the group. Click **Next**.

9. On the **User access** page, select groups to which you want to restrict access. If you don't want to limit access to these devices inside Microsoft 365 Defender, leave this blank.

10. Click **Submit**.

After at least one device group has been defined, you can go to **Settings | Endpoints | General | Auto remediation** to update the parameters for auto-remediation for custom device groups and the default device group named **Ungrouped devices**.

Power Automate

In addition to working with native automated remediation features inside Microsoft 365 Defender, you can also create Power Automate flows based on Microsoft Defender triggers.

Microsoft Defender provides three triggers to Power Automate:

- **When a new remediation activity is created**

- **When an alert is generated**

- **When a new WDATP alert occurs**

You can use these notifications to create a variety of flows using Microsoft 365 Defender actions, Azure AD actions, or any other actions supported in the Power Automate service. For example, you could create a flow that automatically runs the **Collect Information Package** action on a device, retrieves statistics for an IP address, executes the **Restrict app execution** remediation task, or blocks a user account.

> **Further Reading**
>
> For more information on configuring Power Automate flows with Microsoft 365 Defender, see https://learn.microsoft.com/en-us/microsoft-365/security/defender-endpoint/api-microsoft-flow.

Summary

In this chapter, you learned about the Microsoft 365 Defender for Endpoint product, including how to deploy it to a variety of platforms, configure basic protection features, and use the Vulnerability management tools to investigate and remediate risks.

These tools are critical for maintaining a secure operating environment and allow organizations to confidently support a wide range of devices. Microsoft 365 Defender for Endpoint can be used as part of Conditional Access policies to ensure only trusted devices are accessing your organization's data as well as creating baselines to validate endpoint configurations.

In the next chapter, you'll start learning about Microsoft Purview information protection and data lifecycle management.

Exam Readiness Drill - Chapter Review Questions

Benchmark Score: 75%

Apart from a solid understanding of key concepts, being able to think quickly under time pressure is a skill that will help you ace your certification exam. That's why, working on these skills early on in your learning journey is key.

Chapter review questions are designed to improve your test-taking skills progressively with each chapter you learn and review your understanding of key concepts in the chapter at the same time. You'll find these at the end of each chapter.

> **Before You Proceed**
>
> You need to unlock these resources before you start using them. Unlocking **takes less than 10 minutes, can be done from any device**, and **needs to be done only once**. Head over to the start of *Chapter 7, Managing Security Reports and Alerts by Using the Microsoft 365 Defender Portal* in this book for instructions on how to unlock them.

To open the **Chapter Review Questions** for this chapter, click the following link: `https://packt.link/MS102E1_CH09`. Or, you can scan the following QR code:

Figure 9.61 – QR code that opens Chapter Review Questions for logged-in users

Once you login, you'll see a page similar to what is shown in *Figure 9.62*:

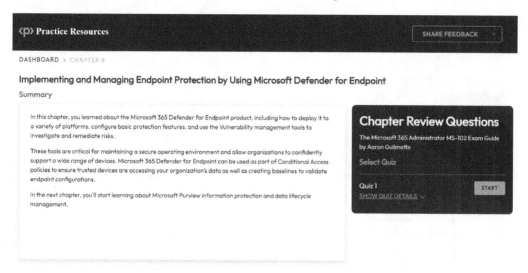

Figure 9.62 – Chapter Review Questions for Chapter 9

Once ready, start the following practice drills, re-attempting the quiz multiple times:

Exam Readiness Drill

For the first 3 attempts, don't worry about the time limit.

ATTEMPT 1

The first time, aim for at least 40%. Look at the answers you got wrong and read the relevant sections in the chapter again to fix your learning gaps.

ATTEMPT 2

The second time, aim for at least 60%. Look at the answers you got wrong and read the relevant sections in the chapter again to fix any remaining learning gaps.

ATTEMPT 3

The third time, aim for at least 75%. Once you score 75% or more, you start working on your timing.

> **Tip**
> You may take more than 3 attempts to reach 75%. That's okay. Just review the relevant sections in the chapter till you get there.

Working On Timing

Target: Your aim is to keep the score the same while trying to answer these questions as quickly as possible. Here's an example of how your next attempts should look like:

Attempt	Score	Time Taken
Attempt 5	77%	21 mins 30 seconds
Attempt 6	78%	18 mins 34 seconds
Attempt 7	76%	14 mins 44 seconds

Table 9.4 – Sample timing practice drills on the online platform

> **Note**
> The time limits shown in the above table are just examples. Set your own time limits with each attempt based on the time limit of the quiz on the website.

With each new attempt, your score should stay **above 75%** while your time taken to complete should decrease. Repeat as many attempts as you want till you feel confident dealing with the time pressure.

10
Implementing Microsoft Purview Information Protection and Data Lifecycle Management

Data is one of the key assets of any organization. Data can be anything: from schematics for a new product, internal sales literature, status reports, and contracts with vendors and customers, to financial forecasts and employee reviews. Data encompasses the breadth and depth of information that an organization produces and consumes to be successful.

Governing this data is key to ensuring that it's available to the right people or systems at the right time.

In this chapter, you'll cover the following data lifecycle management exam concepts:

- Implementing and managing sensitive info types using keywords, keyword lists, or regular expressions
- Implementing retention labels, retention label policies, and retention policies
- Implementing sensitivity labels and sensitivity label policies

It's a big objective, so dive in!

Implementing and managing sensitive info types using keywords, keyword lists, or regular expressions

Sensitive information types (commonly referred to in the **Microsoft 365 (M365)** interface as **sensitive info types** or **SITs**) are classification tools that are used to identify content based on patterns. A pattern can be anything from a simple list of words to formulas and complex expressions that determine whether a piece of content looks like a credit card number, a driver's license number, a physical address, an access or security token, or any other pattern of letters, numerals, and words.

SITs are used across the M365 Purview space, including labels and data loss prevention policies. You can create custom sensitive information types to match organization-specific content, use built-in sensitive information type entities, or a combination of those.

> **Further reading**
>
> The list of built-in sensitive information types is ever-expanding. There are currently 311 SITs defined, with more being added. For a complete list of current sensitive information types and their definitions, see `https://learn.microsoft.com/en-us/purview/sensitive-information-type-entity-definitions`.

SITs can be made of several components and utilize a number of concepts, as described in *Table 10.1*:

Term	Definition
Function	A complex computation used to validate content. For example, a function might include a formula to determine whether a number is a credit card.
Pattern	A pattern describes a sequence of characters (numerals, letters, symbols, or words) and functions that are used to identify content.
Element	One or more identified patterns. Elements can be considered primary (the main thing the sensitive information type is trying to identify) or supporting (additional elements used to help correctly identify matching data).
Proximity	The distance, in characters, between elements. For example, a sensitive information type might be configured to detect two patterns within 100 characters of each other.

Term	Definition
Supporting evidence	Factors used in evaluating whether or not content matches a sensitive information type. For example, suppose a sensitive information type is being used to identify a US telephone number (format ###-###-####). If the primary element is a regular expression with 10 digits, supporting evidence might be the telephone keyword being located within 30 characters of the numeric pattern element.
Confidence level	Confidence is a mathematical representation of how likely it is that content matches a particular sensitive information type. Confidence can be increased by the presence of supporting evidence.

Table 10.1 – Sensitive information type terminology

In this section, we'll explore how to create and manage sensitive information types using a variety of methods.

Managing sensitive information types

You can create and manage custom sensitive information types to detect a variety of data across your organization. In this section, we'll look at creating these classifiers.

Using keywords

The simplest configuration for sensitive information types involves using keywords. Keywords are exactly that—simply words that are used to identify content as sensitive. When using keywords to compose a sensitive information type, you have two options:

- Keyword lists
- Keyword dictionaries

Both of these are functionally the same—the only real difference is in the number of words represented.

You can create sensitive information types based on keyword dictionaries and lists through the Microsoft Purview compliance portal by following these steps:

1. Navigate to the Microsoft Purview compliance portal (`https://compliance.microsoft.com`), expand **Data classification**, select **Classifiers**, and then select **Sensitive info types**, as shown in *Figure 10.1*.

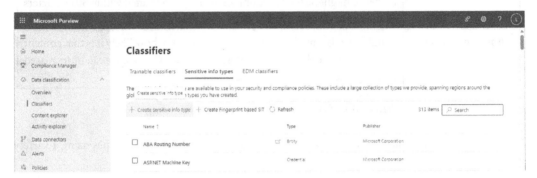

Figure 10.1 – Classifiers page with Sensitive info types tab selected

2. Click **Create sensitive info type**.

3. On the **Name your sensitive info type** page, enter values for the **Name** and **Description** fields. Click **Next**.

4. On the **Patterns** page, select either **Create pattern** or **Create one now**.

Figure 10.2 – Define a pattern

5. On the **New pattern** flyout, set **Confidence level**, choosing from either **High confidence**, **Medium confidence**, or **Low confidence**.

6. Under **Primary element**, click **Add primary element** and select either **Keyword list** or **Keyword dictionary**.

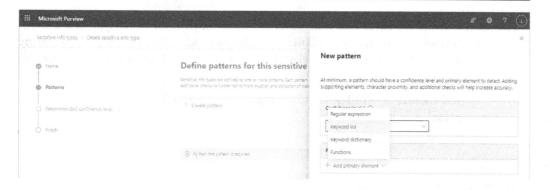

Figure 10.3 – Primary element selection

7. Configure the list or dictionary.

   If configuring a keyword list, follow these steps:

8. Enter an element ID (name).

9. In the **Keyword group #1** area, enter a list of keywords separated by a new line character (with the *Return* key). You can enter up to 50 keywords in a group and specify them as either case-sensitive or case-insensitive by placing them in the respective area, as depicted in *Figure 10.4*:

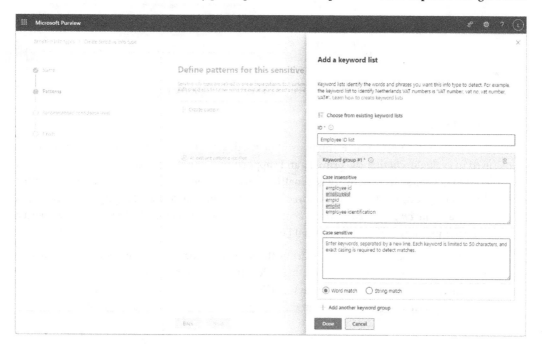

Figure 10.4 – Creating a keyword list

10. Select either **Word match** (recommended) or **String match** as the match type. **Word match** matches whole words only (*slid* will match *slid* but not *slide*, *slides*, or *sliding*), while **String match** will match substrings inside of larger words or strings (for example, *slid* will match *slid*, *slide*, *slides*, and *sliding*).

11. Click **Add another keyword group** to configure another set of keywords to be added to this keyword list.

12. Click **Done** when finished.

    If configuring a keyword dictionary, follow these steps:

13. Enter a **Name** value for the keyword dictionary.

14. In the **Keywords** area, enter the keywords that will appear in the dictionary. Alternately, select **Upload a dictionary** and browse to a TXT or CSV file containing a large list of terms, as shown in *Figure 10.5*:

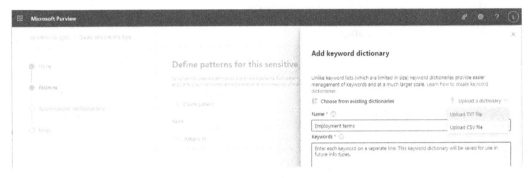

Figure 10.5 – Creating a keyword dictionary

15. Click **Done**.

16. If secondary or supporting elements will be used, set the **Character proximity** value to be used to evaluate whether the primary and supporting elements are close enough to each other to count as a match. **Proximity** is a mathematical distance calculation. For example, with a character proximity of *40*, the *employee* keyword would match the *id* supporting element in the phrase *The employee entered her company-issued id number in the form*. However, with a character proximity of *10*, there would be no match.

17. If supporting elements will be used to define this sensitive information type, click **Add supporting elements or group of elements**, and then select the appropriate types of objects. You can add individual elements (such as more keyword lists, keyword dictionaries, regular expressions, or functions) as well as groups that contain multiple element types and configurations.

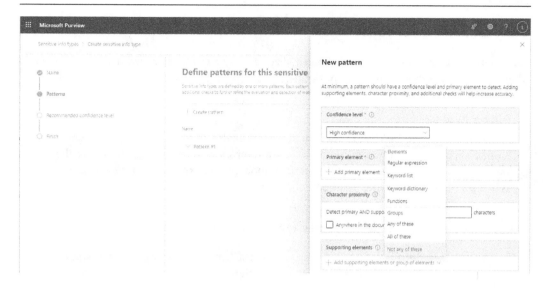

Figure 10.6 – Adding supporting elements

> **Supporting Element Deep-dive**
>
> Supporting elements can be simple (as in just additional keywords, keyword dictionaries, or built-in functions) or complex regex queries that can also have an additional concept of **validators** applied to them. Validators are special functions that perform calculations (such as the Luhn check for credit cards) that aren't necessarily easily expressed with text strings or pattern matches. All supporting elements support proximity as well.

18. Use **Additional checks** to make any required customizations to the rules. Customizations might include requiring or excluding certain patterns, requiring or excluding duplicate characters or items, or requiring or excluding particular suffixes.

19. Select **Create**.

20. Click **Create pattern** to add another pattern for this sensitive information type, repeating *steps 4* through *11*. When finished, click **Next**.

21. On the **Recommended confidence level** page, select a confidence level and click **Next**.

22. On the **Finish** page, verify that everything meets your requirements and click **Create**.

You can now use the sensitive information type throughout the M365 Purview solution.

Using regular expressions

You can use **regular expressions** (sometimes stylized as **RegEx** or **regex**) to detect and match content when simple keywords or strings will not suffice.

> **Further Reading**
>
> Neither this book nor the MS-102 exam focuses much on the construction of regular expressions. Regular expressions can become quite deep and complex with concepts such as look aheads, look behinds, and grouping. You can learn more about regular expressions using resources such as `https://www.regex101.com` and `https://www.regexpal.com`.

To create a sensitive info type using a regular expression, follow these steps:

1. Navigate to the Microsoft Purview compliance portal (`https://compliance.microsoft.com`), expand **Data classification**, select **Classifiers**, and then select **Sensitive info types**.

2. Click **Create sensitive info type**.

3. On the **Name your sensitive info type** page, enter values for **Name** and **Description**. Click **Next**.

4. On the **Patterns** page, select either **Create pattern** or **Create one now**.

5. On the **New pattern** flyout, set **Confidence level**, choosing from either **High confidence**, **Medium confidence**, or **Low confidence**.

6. Under **Primary element**, click **Add primary element** and select **Regular expression**.

7. Enter an element **ID** (name).

8. In the **Regular expression** area, enter a pattern for the regular expression, as shown in *Figure 10.7*:

Figure 10.7 – Configuring a regular expression

> **Note**
>
> The default match type is **String match** (which will take your supplied regular expression). If you switch to **Word match**, M365 will automatically insert $(?:\^|[\backslash\backslash s,;\backslash\backslash:\backslash\backslash(\backslash\backslash)\backslash\backslash [\backslash\backslash]\backslash"'])$ before and $(?:\$|[\backslash\backslash s,\backslash\backslash;\backslash\backslash:\backslash\backslash(\backslash\backslash)\backslash\backslash[\backslash\backslash]\backslash"']|\backslash\backslash.\backslash\backslash s|\backslash\backslash.\$)$ after your pattern to ensure it gets matched as a word.

9. If desired, you can also select **Add validators** (validators are functions used to perform complex computations) to support the regular expression and ensure you're getting quality matches.

10. Click **Done** when finished.

11. If secondary or supporting elements will be used, set a **Character proximity** value that will be used to evaluate whether the primary and supporting elements are close enough to each other to count as a match. **Proximity** is a mathematical distance calculation. For example, with a character proximity of *40*, the *employee* keyword would match the *id* supporting element in the phrase *The employee entered her company-issued id number in the form.* However, with a character proximity of *10*, there would be no match.

12. If supporting elements will be used to define this sensitive information type, click **Add supporting elements or group of elements**, and then select the appropriate types of objects. You can add individual elements (such as more keyword lists, keyword dictionaries, regular expressions, or functions) as well as groups that contain multiple element types and configurations.

13. Use **Additional checks** to make any customizations to the rules. Customizations could be things such as including or excluding certain patterns, duplicate characters or items, or particular suffixes.

14. Select **Create**.

15. Click **Create pattern** to add another pattern for this sensitive information type, repeating *steps 4* through *14*. When finished, click **Next**.

16. On the **Recommended confidence level** page, select a confidence level and click **Next**.

17. On the **Finish** page, verify that everything meets your requirements and click **Create**.

You can now use the sensitive information type throughout the M365 Purview solution. Next, we'll look at using some of the built-in functions as part of the sensitive information type.

Using built-in functions

Microsoft currently supports 185 built-in functions that can be used as part of custom sensitive information types. Functions, as mentioned previously, are more complex computations that are used to detect the presence of certain data types, such as driver's license numbers, social security or taxpayer identification numbers, and financial data.

To create a sensitive information type using one of the predefined functions, follow these steps:

1. Navigate to the Microsoft Purview compliance portal (`https://compliance.microsoft.com`), expand **Data classification**, select **Classifiers**, and then select **Sensitive info types**.

2. Click **Create sensitive info type**.

3. On the **Name your sensitive info type** page, enter values for **Name** and **Description**. Click **Next**.

4. On the **Patterns** page, select either **Create pattern** or **Create one now**.

5. On the **New pattern** flyout, set **Confidence level**, choosing from either **High confidence**, **Medium confidence**, or **Low confidence**.

6. Under **Primary element**, click **Add primary element** and select **Functions**.

7. On the **Add function** flyout, select **Choose functions**.

Figure 10.8 – Creating a function-based sensitive information type

8. On the **Choose functions** flyout, select one of the predefined functions to add to the sensitive information type and click **Add**.

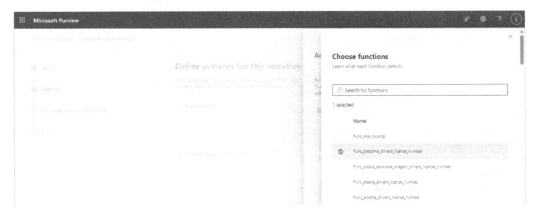

Figure 10.9 – Adding a function

9. If secondary or supporting elements will be used, set a **Character proximity** value that will be used to evaluate whether the primary and supporting elements are close enough to each other to count as a match. **Proximity** is a mathematical distance calculation. For example, with a character proximity of *40*, the *employee* keyword would match the *id* supporting element in the phrase *The employee entered her company-issued id number in the form*. However, with a character proximity of *10*, there would be no match.

10. If supporting elements will be used to define this sensitive information type, click **Add supporting elements or group of elements**, and then select the appropriate types of objects. You can add individual elements (such as more keyword lists, keyword dictionaries, regular expressions, or functions) as well as groups that contain multiple element types and configurations.

11. Use **Additional checks** to make any customizations to the rules. Customizations could be things such as including or excluding certain patterns, duplicate characters or items, or particular suffixes.

12. Select **Create**.

13. Click **Create pattern** to add another pattern for this sensitive information type, repeating *steps 4* through *12*. When finished, click **Next**.

14. On the **Recommended confidence level** page, select a confidence level and click **Next**.

15. On the **Finish** page, verify that everything meets your requirements and click **Create**.

You can now use the sensitive information type throughout the M365 Purview compliance portal.

Using document fingerprinting

Document fingerprinting is a classification method that's used to detect data where the content matches a recognizable pattern.

> **Note**
> Document fingerprinting is not part of the MS-102 exam guide, though it's important to be aware of the technology from a functional perspective. For more information on the document fingerprinting capabilities in Microsoft Purview, see https://learn.microsoft.com/en-us/purview/document-fingerprinting.

This custom sensitive information type is most useful for data stored in forms that your organization uses. Some examples are tax forms, patent forms, health insurance forms, or workplace injury reporting forms.

In this example, you'll use a standard tax reporting form (*Internal Revenue Service W2*) as the basis for a document fingerprint:

1. Navigate to the Microsoft Purview compliance portal (`https://compliance.microsoft.com`), expand **Data classification**, select **Classifiers**, and then select **Sensitive info types**.

2. Click **Create Fingerprint based SIT**.

3. On the **Name** page, enter values for **Name** and **Description**. Click **Next**.

4. On the **Upload file** page, as shown in *Figure 10.10*, click **Upload file** and browse to the location where your source form or document is stored.

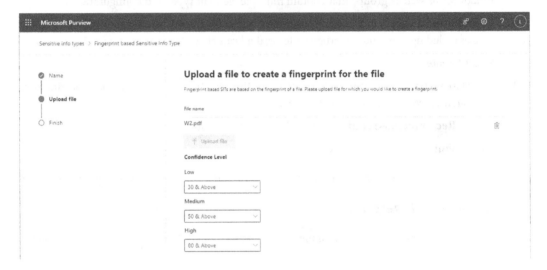

Figure 10.10 – Uploading a form for a document fingerprint

5. Adjust the **Confidence Level** setting. The numbers associated with each confidence level correspond to the percentage of text that must be detected in order to be returned as a match. **Low** confidence matches will contain the fewest false negatives but also the most false positives. **High** confidence matches will contain the fewest false positives, but will have the most false negatives (items that were missed). Click **Next** when finished.

6. On the **Finish** page, click **Create**.

The document fingerprinting sensitive information type can now be used across Exchange, SharePoint, OneDrive, and Teams locations.

> **Additional Information**
>
> You can find the source template form for this at `https://www.irs.gov/pub/irs-pdf/fw2.pdf`.

Using Exact Data Match

Exact Data Match (EDM) is another pattern matching feature that is part of M365 Purview solutions, only instead of matching generic keywords or patterns, Microsoft Purview looks for specific custom data. EDM is a great solution for detecting things such as patient data, client information, and structured organizational intellectual property.

> **Note**
> EDM is not part of the MS-102 exam guide, though it's important to be aware of the technology from a functional perspective.

It takes quite a bit of effort to set up and relies on several components:

- Providing the actual sensitive data that you are trying to protect. Since EDM is being used to detect very specific information, you need to supply the actual information that you're trying to protect, for example, a spreadsheet of patient names and identification numbers.

- Creating an EDM classifier. The EDM classifier is based on a schema (or definition) of how your data is represented.

- A credential that will be used to upload content.

- A dedicated physical or virtual computer that will run the EDM Upload Agent.

In order to ensure that M365 has the most current data, you should develop a process to export the data you want to protect on a regular basis (for example, exporting the table that lists patient names and sensitive information once a day or once a week to the computer running the EDM Upload Agent). After creating the EDM classifier and setting up valid data export credentials, you configure the EDM Upload Agent to upload the data to M365.

> **Further Reading**
> For more information on Exact Data Match, see `https://learn.microsoft.com/en-us/purview/sit-get-started-exact-data-match-based-sits-overview`.

Testing and editing sensitive information types

After you've created a sensitive information type, you can test its effectiveness against sample data and update it to improve its detection capability.

> **Note**
> You can test both built-in and custom sensitive information types, but you cannot edit the built-in types.

To test one of the sensitive information types you've created, you can follow these steps:

1. Create sample data that should be identified by one of the sample SITs that you've created. In one of the examples, we used keywords such as `employee id`, `emplid`, and `employeeid` to create a keyword list-based SIT.

2. Navigate to the Microsoft Purview compliance portal (`https://compliance.microsoft.com`), expand **Data classification**, select **Classifiers**, and then select **Sensitive info types**.

3. Select the custom SIT that you want to test.

4. On the classifier's information page, select **Test**, as shown in *Figure 10.11*:

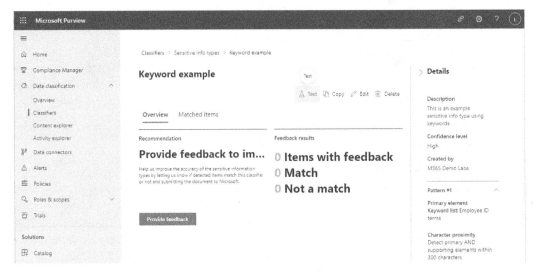

Figure 10.11 – Classifier information page

5. On the **Upload file** flyout, click **Upload file** and browse to your sample data.

Figure 10.12 – Uploading a sample file

6. Click **Test**.

7. Review the output of the **Match results** page.

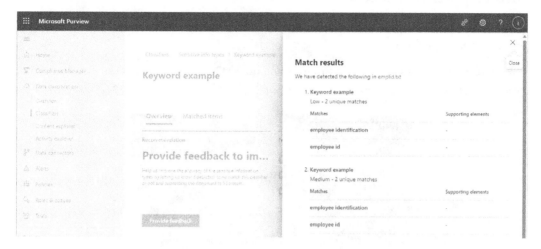

Figure 10.13 – Reviewing the match detections

8. Click **Finish**.

The match results can help you fine-tune the rules around the sensitive information type, including keywords and dictionaries, proximity, and any supporting elements. If you had anticipated the uploaded content to match and it didn't (or didn't with the level of confidence you expected), you can modify the sensitive information type by clicking the **Edit** button on the SIT's information page.

Next, you'll shift to managing labels and policies, and then see how you can use sensitive information types to help manage content.

Implementing retention labels, retention label policies, and retention policies

Retention labels and policies can be used to both retain and remove content based on organizational requirements.

Before we go too far, it's important to understand how M365 handles retention. The diagram in *Figure 10.14* provides a high-level view of Microsoft's principles of retention:

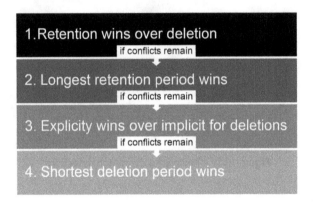

Figure 10.14 – The principles of retention

Here are some examples of the principles of retention in practice:

- If a document has both a retention action and a deletion action applied to it, the retention action always takes precedence. For example, if a document has a retention policy configured to be retained for 3 years but also has a retention policy or label applied to it that says to delete after 1 year, the retain action will be in effect for 3 years. After the retention period has expired, the delete action will take effect.

- If a document has two retention policies or labels that apply to it, whichever one specifies the longest retention period will be the one that governs the minimum amount of time that the document will be preserved.

- If a document inherits a retention policy (for example, from a SharePoint site) with a delete action but also has a manually applied retention label with a delete action, the action associated with the label will take precedence, even if it specifies a longer deletion period than the inherited policy. For example, say a document inherits a retention policy with a delete action after 5 years. If a label is applied to the document that specifies it is to be deleted after 7 years, the document will be deleted after 7 years (not 5 years per the inherited label).

- If a document has multiple deletion policies or labels applied to it, the one with the shortest deletion period wins. Consider a policy that has been configured with only a delete action to take place after 3 years in conjunction with a policy that specifies delete after 5 years. When both policies are applied to a document, the evaluation of the shortest policies ensures that the document will be deleted after 3 years. If another policy is added that forces the item's deletion after 1 year, the 1-year policy will take effect.

In this section, we'll look at how retention labels and policies can be used across the organization.

Implementing retention policies

Retention policies are rule-driven configurations that allow you to manage the lifecycle of data in the organization. Retention policies are created with three core purposes in mind:

- To protect and retain data for a minimum amount of time

- To ensure data doesn't continue to persist after a specific period of time

- To govern the entire data lifecycle—both retaining for a minimum amount of time and ensuring it is disposed of at the end of its lifetime

Depending on the workload, content can be evaluated for retention based on when the content was created or modified. Retention policies are applied at a workload level (think SharePoint Online, Exchange Online, or Teams), with exceptions that can be made for sites, mailboxes, groups, or other container-type items.

To create a retention policy, follow these steps:

1. Navigate to the Microsoft Purview compliance portal (`https://compliance.microsoft.com`), expand **Data lifecycle management**, and select **Microsoft 365**.

2. Select the **Retention policies** tab and then click **New retention policy**, as shown in *Figure 10.15*:

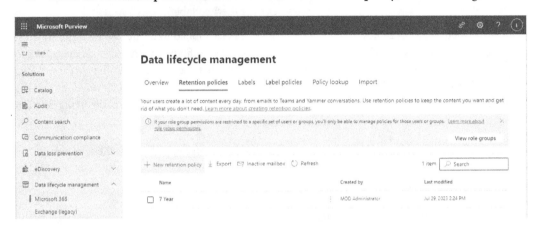

Figure 10.15 – Retention policies tab

3. On the **Name your retention policy** page, enter values for **Name** and **Description** and click **Next**.

4. If you have either M365 E5, **Enterprise Mobility + Security E5 (EMS E5)**, or the Advanced Compliance license, you can choose from the options on the **Policy Scope** page. By default, retention policies apply organization-wide, but with the E5 or Advanced Compliance features, you can choose to restrict the policy to individual admin units. To scope a retention policy to an administrative unit, click **Add or remove units** on the **Policy Scope** page and then select the administrative units from the flyout.

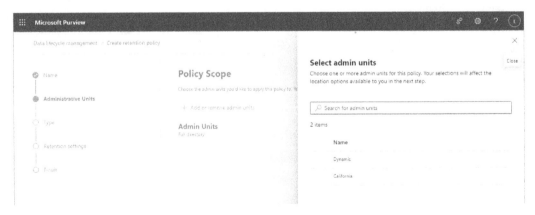

Figure 10.16 – Selecting administrative units

5. Click **Next**.

6. On the **Type** page, select either an **Adaptive** policy (if your tenant has M365 E5, EMS E5, or the Advanced Compliance license) or a **Static** policy. Adaptive scopes are dynamic selection queries that search for attributes of content sources (such as mailboxes for users that have *Marketing* as their department value), while static policies are applied to workloads directly. Click **Next**.

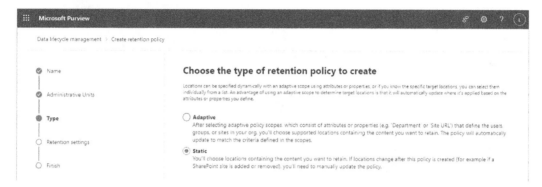

Figure 10.17 – Selecting the policy type

Note

Adaptive scopes can be created while working inside the retention policy wizard or through the **Adaptive Scopes** user interface under the **Roles & scopes** menu. Adaptive scopes can query organization-wide or be limited to administrative units. Adaptive scopes are targeted to **users** (based on Azure AD attributes), **SharePoint sites** (such as the site name, URL, and **refinable strings**), and **Microsoft 365 groups** (based on Azure AD attributes).

7.   On the **Locations** page, select the workloads where the policy is to be applied, as shown in *Figure 10.18*:

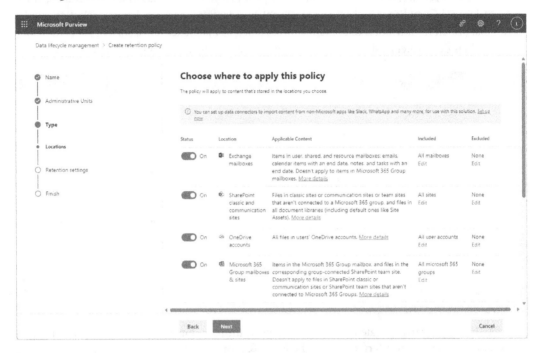

Figure 10.18 – Selecting workloads for policies

There are some caveats on how policies can be crafted:

- A policy that contains **Teams channel messages** or **Teams chats** cannot contain any other workloads. Teams channel messages and Teams chats can be part of the same policy.

- **Teams private channel messages** cannot be included in a policy with any other workloads.

- A policy that contains **Yammer community messages** or **Yammer user messages** cannot contain any other workloads. Yammer community messages and Yammer messages can be part of the same policy.

8.   Further refine the content that the policy applies to by adding entries under either the **Included** or **Excluded** column for the corresponding workload.

There are some caveats that also apply to inclusions and exclusions for static scopes:

- A workload cannot have both inclusions and exclusions in the same policy. For example, you cannot select the **Exchange mailboxes** location, add a mailbox to the **Included** selection, and add a mailbox to the **Excluded** section. You would need to create a second retention policy.

- There are limits to the maximum number of items that can be specified (either included or excluded) per workload, per policy:

- SharePoint and OneDrive for Business sites: 100

- All other workloads (Exchange mailboxes, M365 groups, Teams channel messages, Teams chats, Viva Engage/Yammer community messages, and Viva Engage/Yammer user messages): 1,000

9. Click **Next**.

10. On the **Retention settings** page, specify the retention or deletion settings, as shown in *Figure 10.19*:

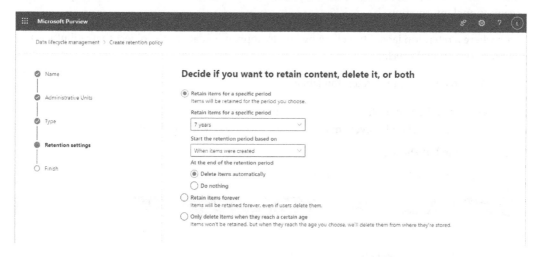

Figure 10.19 – Specifying the retention settings

You can choose to retain for a specified period (options are **5 years**, **7 years**, **10 years**, and **Custom**, with the default being **7 years**) and decide to evaluate items based on when they were created or when they were modified. You can also choose how to handle items at the end of the defined retention period—either leave them alone or delete them as part of a lifecycle governance process. You can choose to retain items forever (which removes the option to select how to deal with content at the end of the retention period as there is no end) or craft a policy whose sole purpose is to delete content based on age.

11. Click **Next**.

12. On the **Finish** page, review the settings. Adjust if necessary and click **Submit**.

Next, you'll look at how **retention labels** can be layered on top of retention policies.

Implementing retention labels

Retention labels are essentially content metadata (like virtual sticky notes) that allows users (or, if using automatic label policies, the M365 platform) to manage the retention of content by exception. The label follows the content wherever it goes.

For example, you may have a retention policy that retains all content for 3 years and then forcibly deletes it. However, the organization's legal department has also stipulated that all documents relating to signed contracts must be retained for 30 years. Since the contract content might be stored in places where content will be deleted after 3 years, it's important to have a mechanism to protect this organizational information.

That's where a retention label fits—allowing you to apply metadata to the object that will ultimately govern its retention lifecycle.

Let's look at creating a sample retention label:

1. Navigate to the Microsoft Purview compliance portal (`https://compliance.microsoft.com`), expand **Data lifecycle management**, and select **Microsoft 365**.

2. Select the **Labels** tab.

3. Select **Create a label**, as shown in *Figure 10.20*:

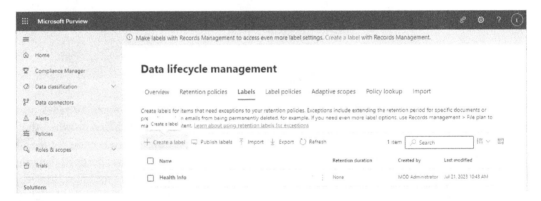

Figure 10.20 – Using the Labels tab

4. On the **Name** page, enter a **Name** value for the label. You can also enter separate **Description for users** and **Description for admins** values. Click **Next**.

5. On the **Label Settings** page, select which type of label settings you want to associate with this label. You can choose **Retain items forever or for a specific period, Enforce actions after a specific period** (depending on your licensing level, this can include relabeling items at the end of the period, triggering a **disposition review**, or running a Power Automate flow), or **Just label items**. If you are going to choose **Just label items**, it would likely be better to choose a **sensitivity label** instead. See *Figure 10.21*:

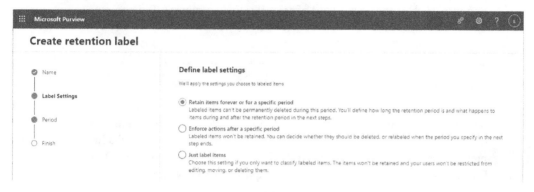

Figure 10.21 – Selecting label settings

6. If you selected either **Retain items forever or for a specific period** or **Enforce actions after a specific period**, you can then define a time period for which this label will protect the data. See *Figure 10.22*:

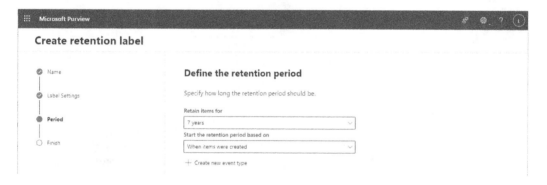

Figure 10.22 – Defining a retention period

Further Reading

If you select the **Retain items forever or for a specified period** option, you also have the option to define events for event-driven or event-based retention policies. Event-driven policies allow you to implement workflows that start the labeling process on a defined business event, such as an employee termination, contract renewal, or other product lifecycle. Event-driven policies require a significant amount of business and records-management planning and effort to configure (such as the assignment of asset IDs to documents). To learn more about the configuration of event-driven labels, see `https://learn.microsoft.com/en-us/purview/event-driven-retention`.

7. Click **Next**.

8. On the **Setting after period** page, choose which type of action to take after the retention period expires. You can choose **Delete items automatically**, **Deactivate retention settings**, or **Change the label** if you have either M365 E3 or E5 subscriptions. However, if you have the M365 E5 subscription (or either the EMS E5 or Advanced Compliance subscription), you also have the **Run a Power Automate flow** and **Start a disposition review** options. See *Figure 10.23*.

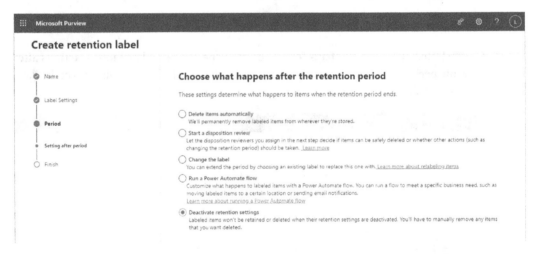

Figure 10.23 – Choosing what happens when the retention period expires

> **Further Reading**
>
> For M365 E5, EMS E5, and Advanced Compliance subscriptions, the additional events that you can take are quite powerful. When you choose to schedule a disposition review, you can create workflows (called **stages**) and assign reviewers to the stages. The idea is for those reviewers to look at the content and decide on an outcome—whether that's to remove the label, delete the content, or assign a new label. You can have up to five review stages, each with its own reviewers. To learn more about the disposition review process, see `https://learn.microsoft.com/en-us/purview/disposition`.
>
> Running a Power Automate flow is a newer option that increases the flexibility of retention even more. By utilizing the **When an item reaches the end of its retention period** trigger in Power Automate, you have the full use of every action available in Power Automate. You could potentially use this feature in the place of event-driven retention as well. For more information on integrating Power Automate with your retention process, see `https://learn.microsoft.com/en-us/purview/retention-label-flow`.

9. Click **Next**.

10. On the **Finish** page, review the configuration and make any adjustments. Click **Create label** to complete the setup.

While the label has been created, it's not yet available for use. Clicking **Create label** now starts the next step in the process—publishing labels. You'll look at the publishing process next.

After creating a label, you're immediately presented with a prompt to do something with the label. The possible choices are shown in *Figure 10.24*:

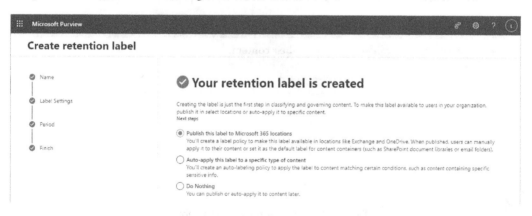

Figure 10.24 – Publishing options

The options allow you to configure label policies:

- **Publish this label to Microsoft 365 locations**: This makes the label available for users to apply in locations such as Exchange mailboxes, as well as OneDrive for Business and SharePoint Online sites.

- **Auto-apply this label to a specific type of content**: This type of policy is used to apply the label to content that matches specific criteria, such as built-in or custom sensitive information types.

- **Do Nothing**: The label is not visible to users.

In this example, let's select **Publish this label to Microsoft 365 locations** to start the wizard to configure a publishing policy. You'll look at that wizard in the next section.

Implementing retention label policies

After you've created a label, it's only visible to administrators of the Microsoft Purview solution—it can't be assigned by users. From here, there are two ways to deploy a label: **publishing** the label so that users can manually apply it to content or **auto-applying** the label based on the given content.

Publishing a label

In this section, you'll pick up where we left off after creating the label and publish it for manual application:

1. On the **Choose labels to publish** page, the label that you created in the previous section is automatically selected, though you can click **Edit** to add additional labels. This is the same wizard that starts when you select **Publish** on the **Labels** page as well. Click **Next**.

Figure 10.25 – Choosing a label to publish

2. On the **Administrative Units** page, you can select which administrative units will receive this label policy. By default, it is scoped to the entire directory. Click **Next**.

3. On the **Scope** page, select which type of policy to create—either **Adaptive** or **Static**. Adaptive-scoped policies cause the label to be available only on certain sites or to certain users whose properties match the connected adaptive scopes. Static-scoped policies apply to all entities in the selected workload.

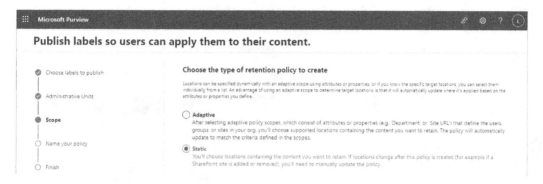

Figure 10.26 – Selecting a scope for the policy

-   If you select **Adaptive** and click **Next**, you'll be presented with the **Adaptive scope** page where you can select the adaptive scopes that you want to use with the policy and specify which locations support this adaptive scope.

-   If you select **Static** and click **Next**, you'll be presented with the **Publish to users and groups** page, where you can select the locations where the label will be published.

4. Click **Next**.

5. On the **Name your policy** page, enter **Name** and **Description** values for the label policy. Click **Next**.

After the publishing policy has been created, the labels will be available for users to apply.

> **Note**
>
> Labels are only published to Exchange Online mailboxes if the mailboxes have more than 10 MB of content.

Next, you'll shift to auto-applying labels.

Auto-applying a label

The challenge with the manual application of labels is that it requires interaction from the end user. If you have an M365 E5, EMS E5, or Advanced Compliance subscription, you can also use auto-application to help ensure your content is labeled.

You can start the auto-application process under the **Data lifecycle management | Label policies** tab in the Microsoft Purview compliance portal.

To create an auto-labeling policy, follow these steps:

1. Navigate to the Microsoft Purview compliance portal (`https://compliance.microsoft.com`). Expand **Data lifecycle management**, and then select **Microsoft 365**.

2. On the **Data lifecycle management** page, select the **Label policies** tab.

3. Click **Auto-apply a label**, as shown in *Figure 10.27*:

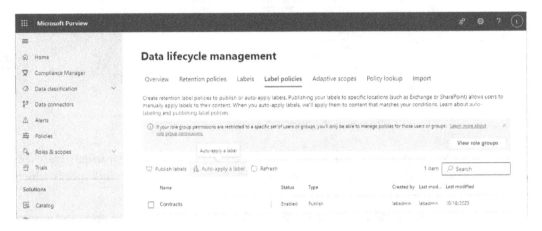

Figure 10.27 – Label policies tab

4. On the **Name** page of the **Create auto-labeling policy** wizard, enter **Name** and **Description** values for the policy. Click **Next**.

5. On the **Info to label** page, select the target of the content. You can choose from the following options:

- **Apply label to content that contains sensitive info**: This option will use either built-in or custom sensitive info types to identify matching content.

- **Apply label to content that contains specific words or phrases, or properties**: With this option, you can create a **KQL** (meaning **Keyword Query Language**, not to be confused with the other KQL acronym referring to the **Kusto Query Language** used with Sentinel and threat hunting) query to identify matching content.

- **Apply label to content that matches a trainable classifier**: This option allows you to select from pre-built or custom trainable classifiers. Trainable classifiers are machine learning-enabled classifiers that have been trained to identify relevant content based on things such as industry-standard terminology, legal agreements, financial forms, and human resources interactions.

- **Apply label to cloud attachments and links shared in Exchange, Teams, and Viva Engage**: This labeling option applies specifically to content that is shared via those mechanisms.

6. Depending on which classification or detection method you use for content, you may have different options presented. When you have finished the selection criteria, click **Next**.

7. On the **Administrative Units** page, specify the scope of the application. By default, the labeling policy is applied organization wide, but can be targeted based on administrative units. Click **Next**.

8. On the **Type** page, select either an **Adaptive** policy (if your tenant has a M365 E5, EMS E5, or Advanced Compliance license) or a **Static** policy. Adaptive scopes are dynamic selection queries that search for the attributes of content sources (such as mailboxes for users that have *Marketing* as their department value), while static policies are applied to workloads directly. Click **Next**.

9. On the **Label** page, select which label to auto-apply. Click **Add label** to choose from the labels configured in your tenant and then click **Add**.

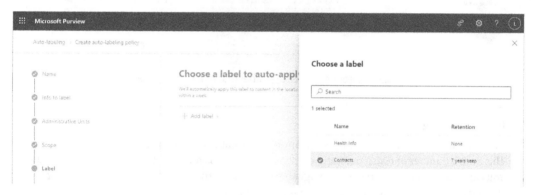

Figure 10.28 – Selecting a label

10. Click **Next**.

11. Depending on the settings configured, you can choose **Test the policy before running** or **Turn on the policy**. Click **Next**.

12. On the **Finish** page, review the settings configured and make any adjustments if necessary. Click **Submit**.

In addition to the label interfaces in the **Data lifecycle management** area, there is another label interface that is available as part of **record management**.

There are advanced record management features, such as associating labels with **file plans** (overall document classification strategy), managing the disposition schedules for content (for customers with M365 E5, EMS E5, or Advanced Compliance licenses), and marking labeled items as **records** (see *Figure 10.29*).

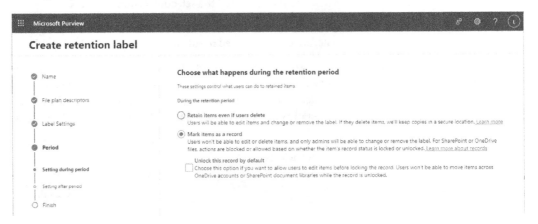

Figure 10.29 – Creating a retention label that marks items as a record

> **Further reading**
>
> Marking an item as a record makes it immutable (unable to be edited, changed, or deleted). There are a number of restrictions and configuration options for records and regulatory records. You can learn more about record management in detail at https://learn.microsoft. com/en-us/purview/records-management.

There are some caveats related to label application that are important to note:

- Content can only have one retention label applied at a time.
- Labels that mark items as regulatory are configured through the **Records management** area.

In previous iterations of the compliance product, it was possible to enable a feature called **Preservation Lock** from the user interface. Preservation Lock is a feature that limits the future updates that can be made to a policy—such as shortening the length of retention. Once content was preserved with a policy that had Preservation Lock enabled, it was impossible to move the content to a less restrictive policy. Modifying this required significant effort through the engagement of a Microsoft support engineer. This feature has been moved to command-line availability only.

The current version of Preservation Lock has the following features for policies:

- The policy cannot be disabled or deleted.

- Locations can be added to the policy (but not removed).

- The retention period can be increased (but not decreased).

- The current version of Preservation Lock has the following features for label policies:

- The label policy cannot be disabled or deleted

- Locations can be added to the policy (but not removed)

- Labels can be added to the policy (but not removed)

To configure Preservation Lock for a policy or retention label, you need to connect to the security & compliance PowerShell endpoint and execute the following command:

```
Set-RetentionCompliancePolicy - Identity <policy> -RestrictiveRetenion
$True
```

The final topic area you'll cover in this chapter is sensitivity labels.

Implementing sensitivity labels and sensitivity label policies

Sensitivity labels, like retention labels, are metadata that helps users and the M365 platform classify content. While retention labels are used to protect and manage the content's data lifecycle (and consequently, its overall existence in the M365 ecosystem), sensitivity labels are used to classify, protect, and manage data from a risk or value perspective.

Sensitivity labels have evolved since their first introduction as part of Azure Information Protection in 2018 as a cloud-based successor to Active Directory Rights Management Services (originally introduced as part of Windows Server 2003) and Azure AD Rights Management Services (originally introduced in 2013).

Modern sensitivity labels have the following protection features and capabilities:

- Content marking (such as markings in headers, footers, or body watermarks)

- Content encryption, allowing it to only be opened by specified recipients

- Apply permissions restricting what others can do with a document (edit, save, comment, print, export/save as, forward, have full control, reply, reply all, view/open/read, copy/extract, view rights, or change rights)

- Allow or prevent offline access

- Assign an expiration date to content

- Content classification

As part of a deployment, you can also force users to apply a label to content they create (a feature called **mandatory labeling**) and organize sensitivity labels in a hierarchical structure (a parent/child relationship sometimes referred to as **sublabels**).

> **Note**
> Once you create a sublabel, the sublabel's parent label can no longer be used to label content.

In the next section, you'll look at configuring sensitivity label prerequisites along with some basic labels.

Implementing sensitivity labels

Sensitivity labels are available to both M365 E3 and E5 subscriptions. Like retention labels, the auto-apply features of sensitivity labels require either the M365 E5, EMS E5, or Advanced Compliance subscription. One additional licensing caveat: applying labels to meetings requires Teams Premium licensing.

Enabling sensitivity labels for Teams, M365 groups, and SharePoint sites

By default, sensitivity labels can't be applied to container objects such as Teams, SharePoint sites, or M365 groups. If you don't go through the prerequisite setup steps, you'll see this warning notification when you create labels or sublabels under the **Information Protection** section:

Figure 10.30 – Notice displayed when creating a sensitivity label

To ensure that you can apply labels to all locations (including container-level objects) inside the M365 environment, follow these steps to enable the feature:

1. Launch an elevated PowerShell window.

2. If not already installed, download and install the Azure AD Preview module:

```
Install-Module AzureADPreview
```

3. Connect to Azure AD using the Preview module:

```
AzureADPreview\Connect-AzureAD
```

4. Configure a directory settings template that enables labels:

```
$grpUnifiedSetting = (Get-AzureADDirectorySetting | where
-Property DisplayName -Value "Group.Unified" -EQ)
$Setting = $grpUnifiedSetting
$grpUnifiedSetting.Values
if ($null -eq $grpUnifiedSetting.Values)
{
      $TemplateId = (Get-AzureADDirectorySettingTemplate | where
{ $_.DisplayName -eq "Group.Unified" }).Id
      $Template = Get-AzureADDirectorySettingTemplate | where
-Property Id -Value $TemplateId -EQ
      $Setting = $Template.CreateDirectorySetting()
      $Setting["EnableMIPLabels"] = "True"
      New-AzureADDirectorySetting -DirectorySetting $Setting
} else
{
      $TemplateId = (Get-AzureADDirectorySettingTemplate | where
{ $_.DisplayName -eq "Group.Unified" }).Id
      $Template = Get-AzureADDirectorySettingTemplate | where
-Property Id -Value $TemplateId -EQ
      $Setting = $Template.CreateDirectorySetting()
      $Setting["EnableMIPLabels"] = "True"
      Set-AzureADDirectorySetting -DirectorySetting $Setting -Id
$grpUnifiedSetting.Id
}
```

5. Connect to the Security & Compliance PowerShell endpoint using the following command:

```
Connect-IPPSSession
```

6. Run the `Execute-AzureAdLabelSync` command to ensure sensitivity labels can be used with Azure AD container objects (such as M365 groups, Teams, and group-connected SharePoint sites):

```
Execute-AzureADLabelSync
```

The cmdlet does not return any data to the screen but should trigger a task that synchronizes labels to Azure AD for use with group container objects.

Enabling co-authoring for files protected with sensitivity labels

Co-authoring (the ability for multiple people to work on a file or document simultaneously) is a powerful feature of the M365 platform. When it comes to encrypted documents, it's important to confirm that the environment meets a particular standard to ensure full compatibility and functionality when editing encrypted documents.

After you have confirmed that all users have the latest M365 apps and that all custom software is using the correct **software development kits (SDKs)** and syntax, you can follow these steps to enable co-authoring on encrypted documents:

1. Navigate to the Microsoft Purview compliance portal (`https://compliance.microsoft.com`) and select **Settings**.

2. Select **Co-authoring for files with sensitivity labels**, as shown in *Figure 10.31*:

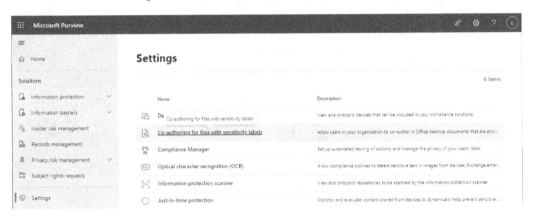

Figure 10.31 – Selecting the Co-authoring for files with sensitivity labels setting

3. Read the information on the page and ensure you fully understand the ramifications of enabling co-authoring. When finished, select the **Turn on co-authoring for files with sensitivity labels** checkbox and click **Apply**. See *Figure 10.32*:

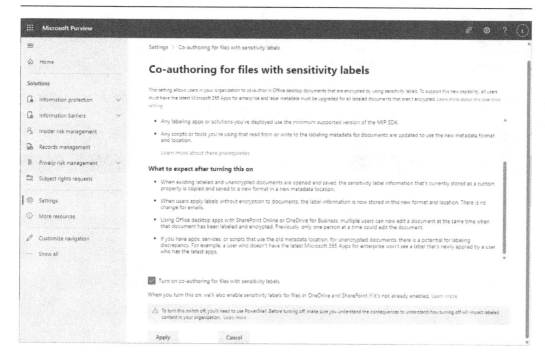

Figure 10.32 – Confirming co-authoring settings

After 24 hours, the feature should be available to use across your tenant.

It's important to note that if you want to roll back co-authoring changes, you cannot do it from the M365 portal. You must do it from PowerShell. There are a number of changes that will be reverted, which may result in the loss of labeling information.

> **Further Reading**
>
> For more information on the potential consequences and limitations of turning off co-authoring after it's been enabled, see https://learn.microsoft.com/en-us/purview/sensitivity-labels-coauthoring#if-you-need-to-disable-this-feature.

Creating a label

Configuring a label is a relatively straightforward process. To create a new label, follow these steps:

1. Navigate to the Microsoft Purview compliance portal (`https://compliance.microsoft.com`), expand **Information protection**, and select **Labels**.

2. Select **Create a label**, as shown in *Figure 10.33*:

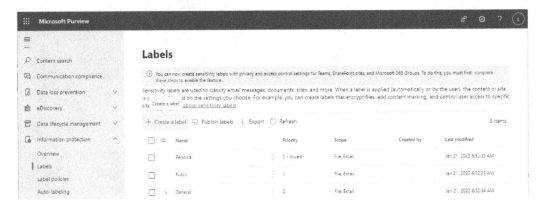

Figure 10.33 – Selecting Create a label from the Labels home page

3. On the **Name and tooltip** page, enter values for **Name** (the value that will be displayed to administrators in the Microsoft Purview compliance portal), **Display name** (the value that will be displayed to users who will be interacting with the label), **Description for users** (the value that will be displayed as a tooltip over content where the label has been applied), and **Description for admins**. See *Figure 10.34*:

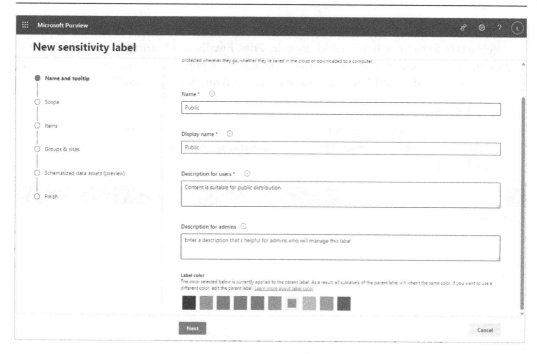

Figure 10.34 – Creating a new sensitivity label

4. Click **Next**.

5. On the **Scope** page, select the options that meet your organization's business requirements for this label.

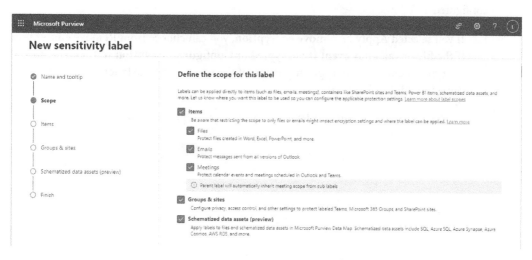

Figure 10.35 – Defining the scope of the label

In this case, the term *scope* determines where the label can be applied. There are settings for leaf objects (referred to as **Items**, which includes **Files**, **Emails**, and **Meetings**) as well as container objects (**Groups & sites**). **Schematized data assets** is a preview feature that includes content visible in the Microsoft Purview Data Map such as Azure SQL, Cosmos DB, or RDS.

6. Click **Next**.

7. If you selected **Items** to be included, you will be presented with some protection settings: **Apply or remove encryption**, **Apply content marking**, or **Protect Teams meetings and chats**. Click **Next**.

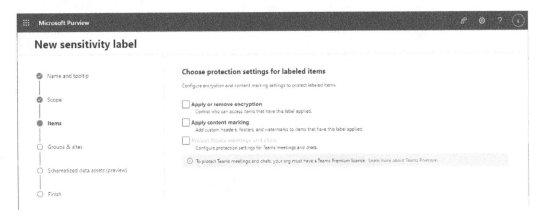

Figure 10.36 – Choosing protection settings

8. For each option you selected in *step 7*, the corresponding protection settings need to be configured as follows:

    I.   If you selected **Apply or remove encryption**, you can choose from **Remove encryption if the file or calendar event is encrypted** or **Configure encryption settings**. Removing encryption ends the encryption portion of the wizard, but the latter configure option presents additional options:

         i.   **Assign permissions now or let users decide** has two options for permissions management:

a. If you select **Assign permissions now** from the dropdown, you are presented with options for content expiration (**User access to content expires**). This option lets you control whether you want users to be able to continue to access content regardless of the date (**Never**), or whether you want to impose time limits on access (**On a specific date** or **A number of days after label is applied**). Assigning permissions now also allows you to choose **Allow offline access** (**Always, Never,** or **Only for a number of days**), controlling how frequently credentials can be used to access content. Under **Assign permissions to specific users and groups**, you have the ability to select which users and groups will be allowed to interact with the content and what permissions or rights are granted (allowing you to choose from built-in options such as **Co-Owner, Co-Author, Reviewer,** or **Viewer**) as well as a **Custom** option where you can configure the exact permissions (**View content, View rights, Edit content, Save, Print, Copy and extract content, Reply, Reply all, Forward, Edit rights, Export content, Allow macros,** and **Full control**). See *Figure 10.37*:

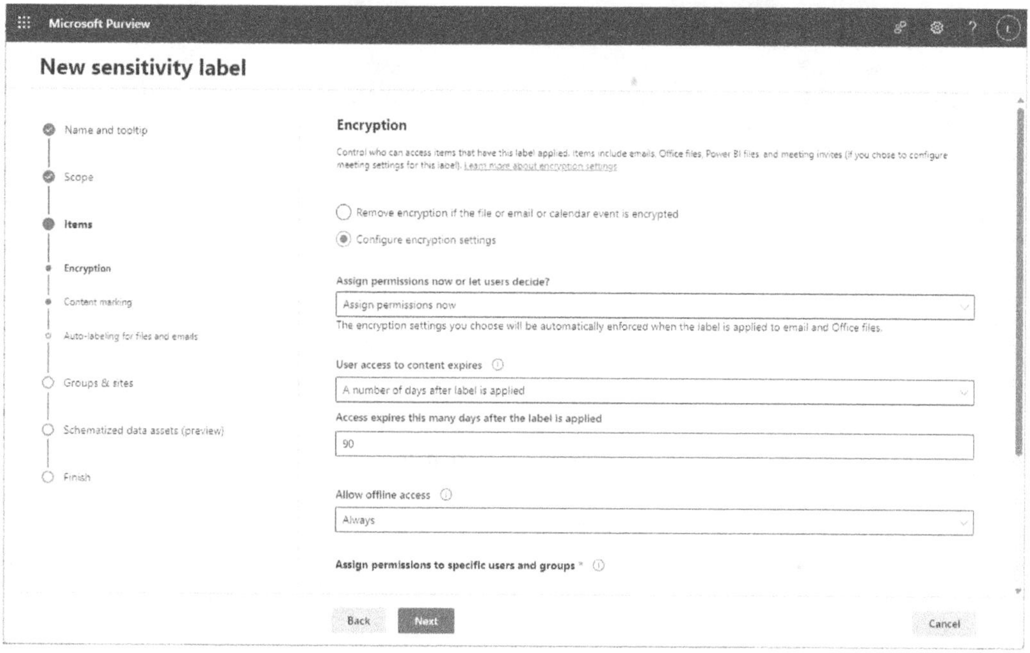

Figure 10.37 – Choosing encryption settings

b. If you choose **Let users assign permissions when they apply the label**, you have a somewhat smaller set of options to configure. You can choose to limit the Outlook actions to **Do Not Forward** or **Encrypt Only** as well as the **In Word, PowerPoint, and Excel, prompt users to specify permissions** option (generating a dialog for choosing users, groups, and permissions).

iii. Finally, you can choose **Use Double-Key Encryption** (requires additional configuration of the double-key encryption service) for content that requires additional protection.

II. If you selected **Apply content marking** you have another set of options. Content marking allows you to place security features such as watermarks in document headers and footers, email messages, and meeting invitations sent via email.

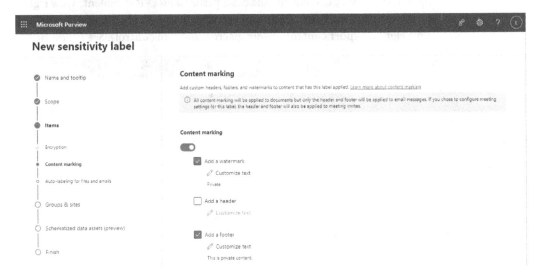

Figure 10.38 – Applying content marking settings

III. Click **Next** to proceed to the next set of pages.

9. If you have selected to apply either content marking or encryption, you are given a final option to enable auto-labeling. See *Figure 10.39*.

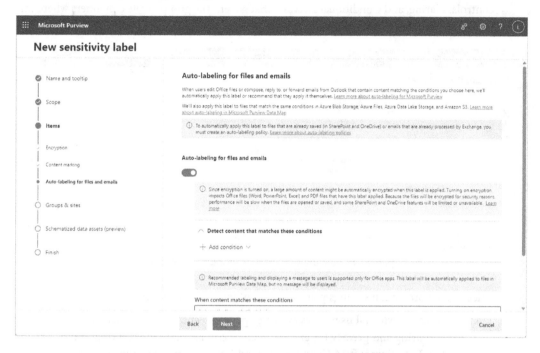

Figure 10.39 – Enabling auto-labeling

Auto-labeling leverages familiar technologies including sensitive information types and conditions to control how content is labeled or marked when it is created. If, however, you want M365 to process content that already exists, you'll need to create a separate policy (which we'll get to in the next section).

10. Click **Next**.

11. If you selected **Groups & sites** as part of the scope at the beginning of the **New sensitivity label** wizard, you'll be able to configure options that manage access and rights—such as privacy controls, sharing, and Conditional Access—that govern the group or site containers where this label is applied. See *Figure 10.40*.

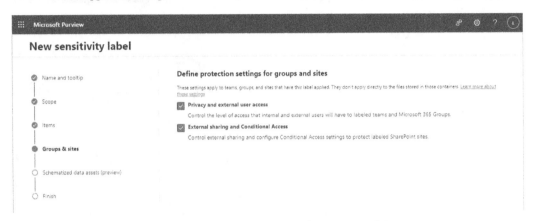

Figure 10.40 – Defining protections for groups and sites

12. Select which protection settings you want to configure and click **Next**.

13. On the **Privacy & external user access settings** page, select the options that you wish to apply to external sharing and privacy for groups, such as configuring the team or group as **Private** and enabling **Let Microsoft 36 Group owners add people outside your organization to the group as guests**. Click **Next**.

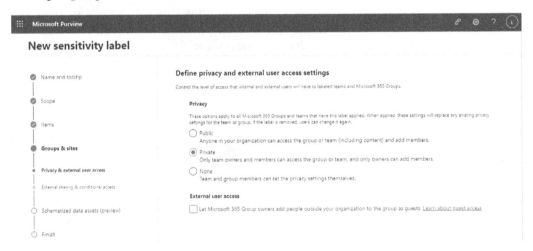

Figure 10.41 – Configuring privacy and external access settings

14. On the **External sharing & conditional access** page, select the options that you want to apply to this group or site. The **Control external sharing from labeled SharePoint sites** option mirrors the SharePoint and OneDrive access slider configured in the SharePoint admin center and, if selected, allows you to choose the scope of users that can be invited to the site. Selecting the **Use Azure AD Conditional Access to protect labeled SharePoint** option allows you to configure access protections through either managed device settings or **authentication contexts**. See *Figure 10.42*.

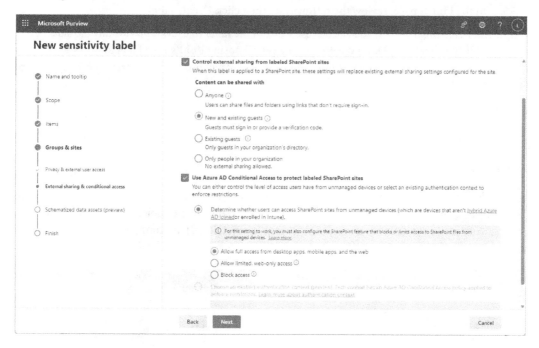

Figure 10.42 – Configuring external sharing and Conditional Access controls

Using an authentication context control

If the authentication context radio control isn't available, it's because you haven't created an authentication context that can be used. An authentication context is essentially a tag that is applied to securable resources that can be used in conjunction with a Conditional Access policy to configure more granular restrictions. For more information on authentication contexts, see https://learn.microsoft.com/en-us/entra/identity/conditional-access/concept-conditional-access-cloud-apps#authentication-context-preview.

15. Click **Next**.

16. If you selected **Schematized data assets** on the **Scope** page of the wizard, you can choose to apply sensitive information types to content stored in SQL, Azure SQL, Azure Synapse, Azure Cosmos, or AWS RDS (as well as other data sources as they are added to the Microsoft Purview Data Map).

17. Click **Next**.

18. On the **Finish** page, review the settings and then click **Create label**.

19. After creating the label, you can choose **Publish the label to users' apps** to start the label policy publishing wizard or **Don't create a policy yet**. Choosing **Publish the label to users' apps** starts a new wizard to apply labels. In this example, you can choose **Don't create a policy yet**, since you will be creating label policies later.

20. Click **Done** when finished.

Next, you'll look at sublabels.

Creating a sublabel

Sublabels function almost exactly like sensitivity labels—you can think of them as higher up the hierarchy to give you more specificity when categorizing data. For example, in *Figure 10.43*, you can see that **Anyone (unrestricted)** and **All Employees (unrestricted)** are configured as sublabels of the **General** label:

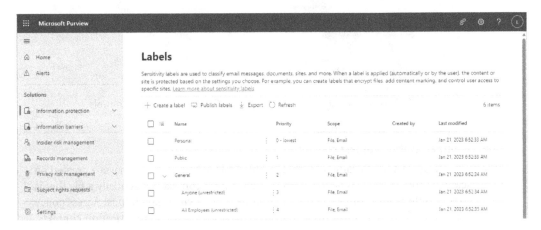

Figure 10.43 – Sublabel example

There may be instances when you have a broad category for labeling content but want to use an additional method or level of classification. This is where sublabels can be helpful.

There are a few important points to consider when using sublabels:

- A sublabel inherits its color settings from its parent.
- When a label has sublabels configured, the parent label can't be used to classify content—only the sublabel can be used.

> **Note**
>
> If a label has sublabels, it's important that the parent label not be used as a default label.

To create a sublabel, follow these steps:

1. In the Microsoft Purview compliance portal (`https://compliance.microsoft.com`), expand **Information protection**, and select **Labels**.
2. Locate the label that will be the parent label and select it.
3. Click **Create sublabel**, as shown in *Figure 10.44*:

Figure 10.44 – Creating a sublabel

4. On the **Name and tooltip** page as shown in *Figure 10.45*, enter values for **Name, Display name**, and **Description for users**. Note that the **Label color** choice is non-selectable. If a label color has already been chosen for the parent, this sublabel will inherit that color.

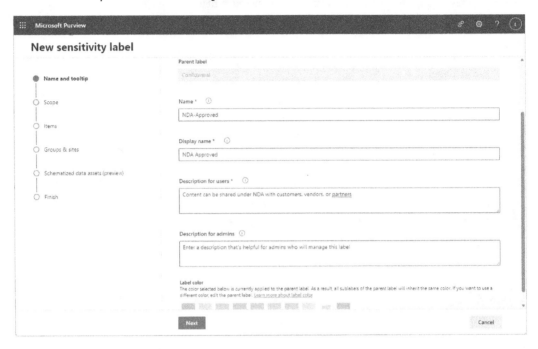

Figure 10.45 – Reviewing name and tooltip settings

5. Click **Next** to continue configuring the label. The remaining steps are the same as configuring a standalone or parent label. Refer to the previous section for details and options.

Now that you've successfully configured labels, let's briefly look at configuring label policies.

Implementing sensitivity label policies

Label policies are the configuration objects that are used to either assign labels to content or make them available for users to apply. Sensitivity labels can be applied in a number of ways:

- Label policies (client-side labeling):

  - Manual labels (with M365 E3, E5, G3, G5, F1, or F3 licensing)

  - Default labels (with M365 E3, E5, G3, G5, F1, or F3 licensing)

  - Recommended labels (with M365 E5 or G5 licensing)

- Auto-labeling (service-side labeling):

  - Available only to M365 E5 or G5 licensing

The automatic label application options can be confusing, since there are two types of label policies that appear at first glance to do the same thing. Let's dig into each of them now.

Label policies

Label policies are on the client side and work inside applications such as Outlook and Word and in the web user interfaces for SharePoint, OneDrive for Business, and Power BI. Label policies can be made available to users via administrative units or to individual users and groups. Additionally, label policies can be made mandatory—that is, users are required to choose from the published labels to apply to content in the Office apps, documents, meetings, and Power BI content.

The wizard to publish label policies can be activated after a label has been created, or separately. In the following example, you'll look at creating a label policy for an existing label:

1. In the Microsoft Purview compliance portal (`https://compliance.microsoft.com`), expand **Information protection** and select **Label policies**.

2. Click **Publish label**, as shown in *Figure 10.46*:

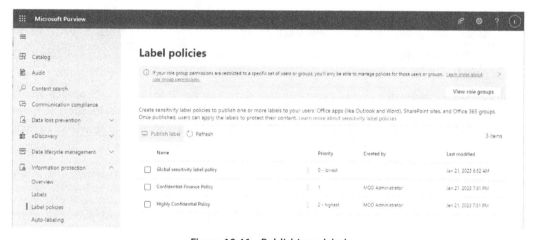

Figure 10.46 – Publishing a label

3. On the **Labels to publish** page, as shown in *Figure 10.47*, click **Choose sensitivity labels to publish** and then select the labels to publish from the list. Click **Add** to add the labels to the list of labels that will be published as part of the policy. Click **Next** to continue.

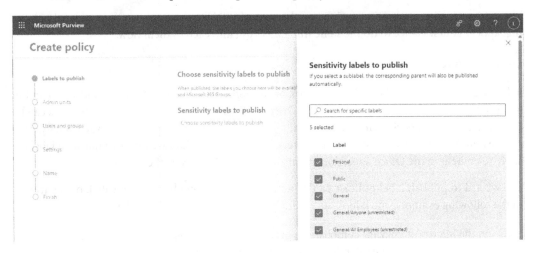

Figure 10.47 – Selecting labels to publish

4. On the **Admin units** page, choose which administrative units to use for scoping the policy. By default, the entire tenant is selected. Click **Next**.

5. On the **Users and groups** page, select which users or groups will receive the label policy. By default, all users and groups are included. Click **Next**.

6. On the **Settings** page, choose the appropriate settings to apply to this policy. You can choose from **Users must provide a justification to remove a label or lower its classification**, **Require users to apply a label to their emails and documents**, **Require users to apply a label to their Power BI content**, and **Provide users with a link to a custom help page**. Click **Next**.

The **Users must provide a justification to remove a label or lower its classification** option has no additional configuration options, but users will have to enter classification text (which will be logged) when changing the label. Lowering a classification corresponds to its priority on the **Label policies** page.

The **Provide users with a link to a custom help page** option has only a single configuration field—a URL—which must be specified on this page.

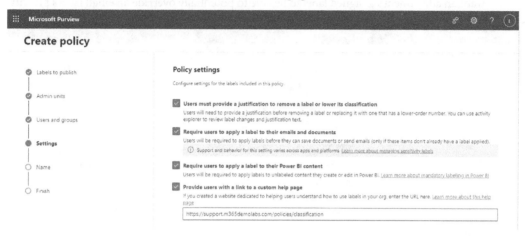

Figure 10.48 – Configuring policy settings

7. On the **Documents** page, if you want to specify a default label, select it from the list of labels. The default label will be applied to the label automatically, though the user can select a different label from their available labels if the sensitivity of the content warrants a change. Click **Next**.

8. On the **Emails** page, select **Default label** (you can choose **Same as document**) to choose the same label as you selected on the **Documents** page or one of the other available labels. It's recommended to choose the **Same as document** label to help users avoid confusion and ensure consistency. If you selected **Require users to apply a label to their emails and documents** on the **Settings** page, you can choose **Require users to apply a label to their emails** on this page. You can also choose the **Email inherits highest priority label from attachments** option if you want an attachment's assigned label to be able to potentially override an email label's priority.

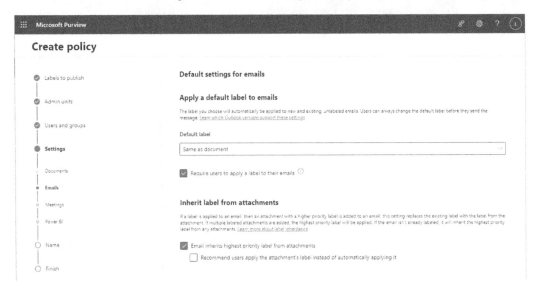

Figure 10.49 – Configuring email settings

9. Click **Next**.

10. If your organization requires labeling of all items (including calendar items), you have options for managing label application on the **Apply a default label to meetings and calendar events** page. You can choose a default label as well as the **Require users to apply a label to their meetings and calendar events** option (if the **Require…** checkbox was selected on the **Settings** page). If you don't have a reason to require labeling of calendar invitations, leave the setting cleared. Click **Next**.

11. On the **Power BI** page, you can choose a default label that will be applied to Power BI content. Organizations that have mandatory classification requirements should configure this option to help ensure compliance. For the exercise, select one of the labels that you have configured and click **Next**.

12. On the **Name** page, enter a **Name** value for the label policy. Click **Next**.

13. On the **Finish** page (depicted in *Figure 10.50*), review the settings and click **Edit** to change them if necessary, or click **Submit** to finish creating the policy.

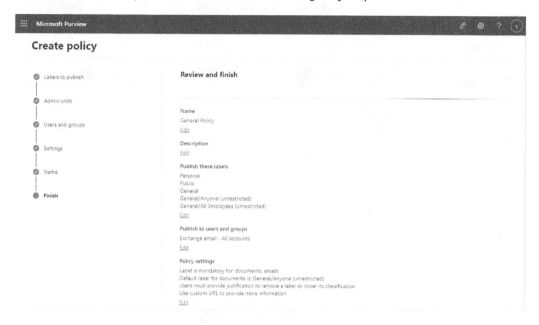

Figure 10.50 – Reviewing the final settings

After you've configured the label publishing policy, the labels will show up for use in application and user interfaces.

Auto-labeling policies

The auto-labeling policies, like other content automation policies in Microsoft Purview, use detection algorithms and processes (such as sensitive information types and trainable classifiers) to apply labels to content in the M365 environment. These are service-side labeling features. After you've laid out a labeling scheme consisting of labels and sublabels and decided how content should be classified, you can use and customize the templates in the auto-labeling wizard to apply labels to content matching your classifiers.

Suppose, for example, you need to identify and classify documents that have sensitive information, such as U.S. taxpayer identification numbers or social security numbers, and have created a label called *Highly Confidential*. You can use an auto-labeling policy with one of the predefined templates to detect taxpayer and social security number patterns and then apply a label to those matching documents.

To create an auto-labeling policy, follow these steps:

1. In the Microsoft Purview compliance portal (`https://compliance.microsoft.com`), expand **Information protection** and select **Auto-labeling**.

2. Click **Create auto-labeling policy**, as shown in *Figure 10.51*.

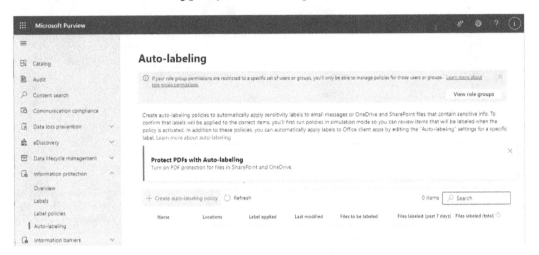

Figure 10.51 – Selecting Create auto-labeling policy

3. On the **Info to label** page, select the template that you want to use to detect sensitive data. You can choose from a variety of sensitive information types including financial, medical, and privacy continuum. You can select **Custom** to create a policy based on your own criteria and sensitive information types. In this example, the **U.S. State Breach Notification Laws Enhanced** template has been selected, which includes detections for a number of personal data elements including financial information, taxpayer data, government identification (such as passports and driver's licenses), and medical terminology.

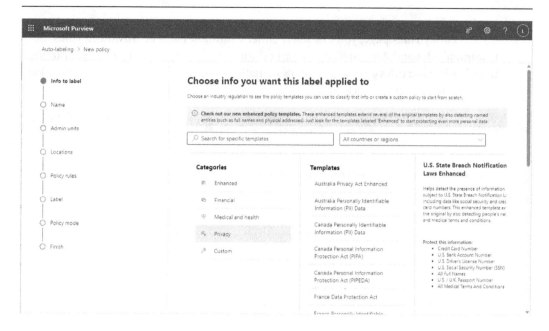

Figure 10.52 – Selecting a category template

4. Click **Next**.

5. Enter a **Name** value for the policy and click **Next**.

6. On the **Admin units** page, choose which administrative units to use for scoping the policy. By default, the entire tenant is selected. Click **Next**.

7. On the **Locations** page, choose where you want this policy to apply labels. By default, all **Exchange email**, **SharePoint sites**, and **OneDrive accounts** are selected as part of the application scope. Click **Next**.

8. On the **Policy rules** page, you can select either **Common rules** or **Advanced rules**. Both **Common rules** and **Advanced rules** start off with a base template that you can customize, though **Advanced rules** gives you more customization ability when it comes to email conditions. Select a rules option and click **Next**.

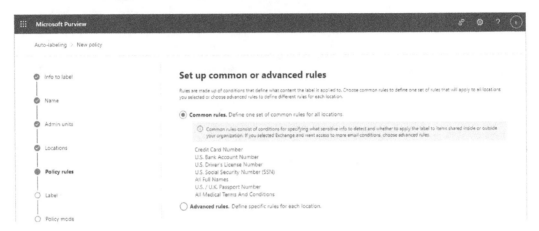

Figure 10.53 – Selecting policy rules

9. Review the rules that are in place, customize if desired, and click **Next** to continue.

10. On the **Label** page, select which label you want to apply to the detected content. Click **Next**.

Figure 10.54 – Selecting the label to apply

11. If you have **Exchange email** selected as a location on the **Locations** page, you have an **Automatically replace existing labels that have the same or lower priority** option. Additionally, if the label you selected has encryption settings, you can choose **Apply encryption to email received from outside of the organization** if required. If you do not choose **Assign a Rights Management owner**, encryption will not be applied to received emails.

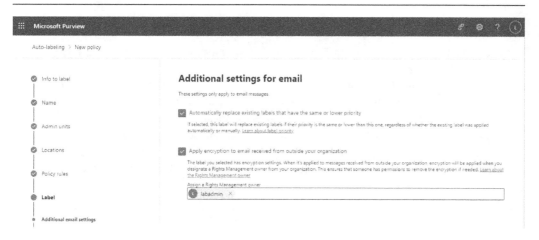

Figure 10.55 – Specifying additional settings for email

12. Click **Next**.

13. On the **Policy mode** page, select how the policy will be implemented. There is no setting to turn the policy on immediately, though you can choose **Run the policy in simulation mode** and then select the **Automatically turn on policy if not modified after 7 days in simulation** option. You can also choose **Leave policy turned off** if you're not ready to move forward with it just yet.

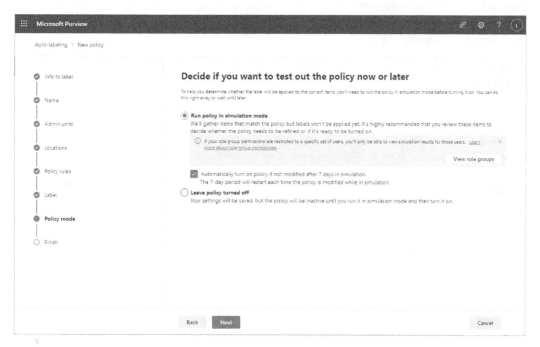

Figure 10.56 – Choosing the policy mode

14. Click **Next**.

15. On the **Finish** page, review the settings and adjust if necessary. Click **Create policy**.

A labeling policy (whether a standard label policy or an auto-label policy) can only apply a single label to content. Additionally, an item may only have one sensitivity label applied to it at a time. If you have multiple labels and sublabels and want to automatically apply multiple labels, you'll need to create a separate policy for each label that you want to apply. Labels also have a concept of priority— where a higher number means it has a higher priority. If a labeling policy identifies content that could potentially match two labels with different priorities, M365 will apply the label with the higher priority to the content.

> **Exam tip**
>
> The core takeaway from the two types of labeling policies is that **label policies** are generally focused on interactive activities (such as navigating a browser interface to apply a label or applying a label while creating and editing a document) while **auto-labeling policies** generally apply to content at rest.

Summary

In this chapter, you learned about some of the important compliance tasks that many organizations face, such as content classification and retention. You learned about the foundational technical concepts around **sensitive information types**. SITs are used to classify content and can be used in the Microsoft Purview solutions including labeling and retention.

In the next chapter, you'll apply the SIT knowledge learned here to another compliance concept: data loss prevention.

Exam Readiness Drill - Chapter Review Questions

Benchmark Score: 75%

Apart from a solid understanding of key concepts, being able to think quickly under time pressure is a skill that will help you ace your certification exam. That's why, working on these skills early on in your learning journey is key.

Chapter review questions are designed to improve your test-taking skills progressively with each chapter you learn and review your understanding of key concepts in the chapter at the same time. You'll find these at the end of each chapter.

> **Before You Proceed**
>
> You need to unlock these resources before you start using them. Unlocking **takes less than 10 minutes, can be done from any device**, and **needs to be done only once**. Head over to the start of *Chapter 7, Managing Security Reports and Alerts by Using the Microsoft 365 Defender Portal* in this book for instructions on how to unlock them.

To open the **Chapter Review Questions** for this chapter, click the following link: `https://packt.link/MS102E1_CH10`. Or, you can scan the following QR code:

Figure 10.57 – QR code that opens Chapter Review Questions for logged-in users

Once you login, you'll see a page similar to what is shown in *Figure 10.58*:

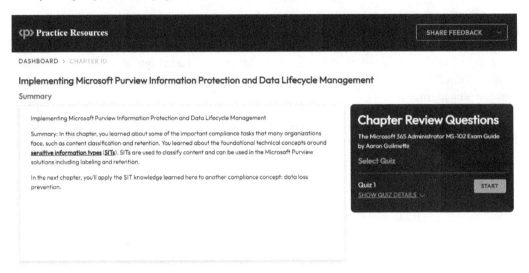

Figure 10.58 – Chapter Review Questions for Chapter 10

Once ready, start the following practice drills, re-attempting the quiz multiple times:

Exam Readiness Drill

For the first 3 attempts, don't worry about the time limit.

ATTEMPT 1

The first time, aim for at least 40%. Look at the answers you got wrong and read the relevant sections in the chapter again to fix your learning gaps.

ATTEMPT 2

The second time, aim for at least 60%. Look at the answers you got wrong and read the relevant sections in the chapter again to fix any remaining learning gaps.

ATTEMPT 3

The third time, aim for at least 75%. Once you score 75% or more, you start working on your timing.

> **Tip**
>
> You may take more than 3 attempts to reach 75%. That's okay. Just review the relevant sections in the chapter till you get there.

Working On Timing

Target: Your aim is to keep the score the same while trying to answer these questions as quickly as possible. Here's an example of how your next attempts should look like:

Attempt	Score	Time Taken
Attempt 5	77%	21 mins 30 seconds
Attempt 6	78%	18 mins 34 seconds
Attempt 7	76%	14 mins 44 seconds

Table 10.2 – Sample timing practice drills on the online platform

> **Note**
>
> The time limits shown in the above table are just examples. Set your own time limits with each attempt based on the time limit of the quiz on the website.

With each new attempt, your score should stay **above 75%** while your time taken to complete should decrease. Repeat as many attempts as you want till you feel confident dealing with the time pressure.

11

Implementing Microsoft Purview data loss prevention (DLP)

In *Chapter 10, Implementing Microsoft Purview Information Protection and Data Lifecycle Management*, you learned how to use and manage **sensitive information types**, **labels**, and **retention policies**.

Data loss prevention (DLP) relies on the same sensitive information types to determine how to handle content from a security perspective. This chapter will build on those labeling and content classification concepts.

This chapter covers the following exam objectives:

- Implementing DLP for workloads
- Implementing endpoint DLP
- Reviewing and responding to DLP alerts

DLP policies allow you to protect sensitive items across workloads, such as Teams, Exchange, SharePoint, OneDrive, and Power BI, as well as on endpoints and within applications such as Word and Excel.

It's the last objective, so let's get going!

Implementing DLP for Workloads

Many workloads and services in the Microsoft 365 platform support DLP capabilities. DLP detects content based on a variety of mechanisms, such as keywords, built-in functions, and secondary matches that are located in proximity to the primary matched content. **Microsoft Purview DLP** can also use document fingerprinting and machine learning algorithms to detect content.

Depending on the workload or application, DLP policies can take the following actions on detected content:

- Display a notification (called a **policy tip**) that warns the users about sensitive content
- Block sharing with or without the ability for the end user to override the block
- Move sensitive items to a quarantine location
- Prevent sensitive content from being displayed in a Teams chat
- Encrypt content

DLP, from the workload perspective, can be applied to data in transit, data at rest, and data in use. In the following sections, you'll review configuring DLP settings for the Exchange Online, SharePoint, OneDrive for Business, Teams, and Power BI workloads, as well as an overview of protecting on-premises file shares with the **Azure Information Protection (AIP)** scanner.

Prerequisites

DLP has license subscription requirements. Depending on the workload to be protected, users need one of the following licenses:

- Microsoft 365 E3/A3/A5/E5/A5/G5
- Microsoft 365 Business Premium
- SharePoint Online Plan 2
- OneDrive for Business Plan 2
- Exchange Online Plan 2
- Microsoft 365 E5/A5/F5/G5 Compliance and F5 Security & Compliance
- Microsoft 365 E5/A5/F5/G5 Information Protection & Governance

In addition, DLP for Microsoft Teams (chat and channel messages, in particular) and on-premises repositories requires one of the following licenses:

- Microsoft 365 E5/A5/G5
- Microsoft 365 E5/A5/F5/G5 Compliance or F5 Security & Compliance
- Microsoft 365 E5/A5/F5/G5 Information Protection & Governance

In order to configure DLP policies, you must be a member of one of these role groups:

- Compliance Administrator

- Compliance Data Administrator

- Information Protection

- Information Protection Admin

- Security Administrator

Organizations with any eligible subscription with DLP features (such as E1, F1, G1, A3, E3, G3, A5, E5, or G5) can create DLP alerts that are triggered on every matching activity.

Organizations with an A5, E5, or G5 subscription or an Office 365 Advanced Threat Protection Plan 2, Microsoft 365 E5 Compliance, or Microsoft 365 eDiscovery and Audit add-on license can configure aggregated alerts—meaning that DLP alerts will only show up based on a certain threshold.

With that being said, let's look at configuring some workload policies!

Configuring Workload Protection

In this section, you'll walk through configuring workload protections at a high level using built-in templates.

Exchange Online, SharePoint Online, OneDrive for Business, and Teams

DLP policies are used in the following contexts for core Microsoft 365 workloads:

- **Exchange Online**: Apply controls or restrictions to messages as they are sent or received by individuals in the organization.

- **SharePoint Online and OneDrive for Business**: Restrict sensitive content as it is added to a sharing invitation.

- **Teams**: Restrict sensitive content as it is entered into a chat or channel message.

- **Devices**: Protect content on endpoint devices. This option requires additional configuration.

- **On-premises file servers**: Protect content in connected on-premises repositories. This option requires additional configuration.

To configure a workload DLP policy, follow these steps:

1. Navigate to the Microsoft Purview compliance portal (`https://compliance.microsoft.com`).

2. Under **Solutions**, expand **Data loss prevention** and then select **Policies**.

3. Click **Create policy**. See *Figure 11.1*:

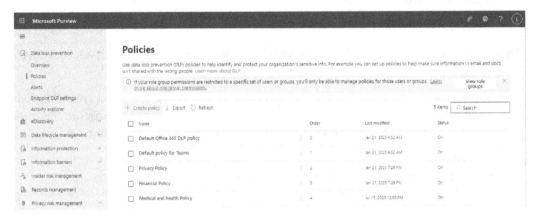

Figure 11.1 – Microsoft Purview compliance policies page

4. Choose whether to use one of the built-in templates or to create a new custom policy.

    Built-in templates are broken into categories such as **Enhanced** (various international legislation, finance, or privacy regulations, which utilize **trainable classifiers** to extend detection capabilities), **Financial** (international financial data types), **Medical and health** (healthcare legislation, terms, and personal information), and **Privacy** (international privacy regulations or legislation). You can only choose one template; if you want to include more than one template data type, you'll need to select **Custom** and add the sensitive information types or other classifiers manually.

5. Click **Next** when the policy type has been selected. See *Figure 11.2*:

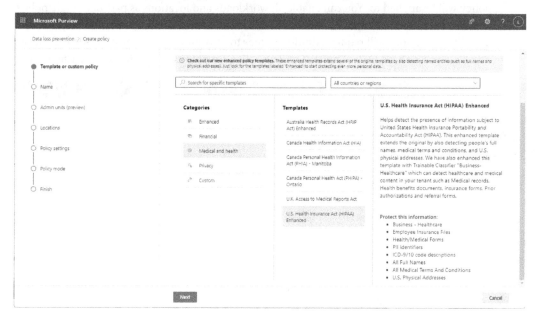

Figure 11.2 – Selecting a template or policy type

6. On the **Name** page, enter a value to identify your policy. Click **Next**.

7. On the **Admin units** page, as shown in *Figure 11.3*, choose whether the DLP policy will apply to the whole organization or only to members of a particular administrative unit.

Figure 11.3 – Assigning an administrative unit

Click **Next** when you're finished.

8. On the **Locations** page, as shown in *Figure 11.4*, choose which workloads and locations the policy will be applied to. You can enable all workloads and locations as part of a single policy, with the exception of Power BI. While you can enable devices and on-premises repositories now, those locations will require additional steps to fully onboard and protect. Also, if you are using a new enhanced DLP template for your policy, on-premises repositories aren't supported.

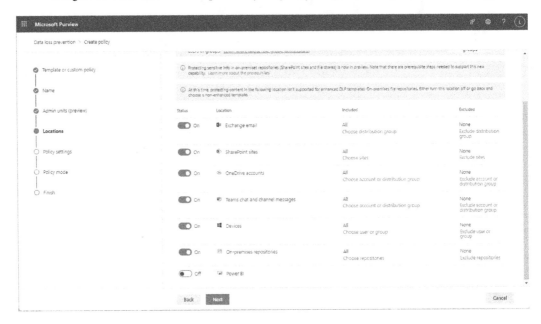

Figure 11.4 – Adding workloads and locations to the policy

For each location, you can apply filters to include or exclude objects (such as users, groups, sites, or devices). When finished, click **Next**.

9. On the **Policy settings** page, determine what DLP rules you want to apply. You could choose from **Review and customize the default settings from the template** or **Create or customize advanced DLP rules**. They both have similar capabilities, though the **Create or customize advanced DLP rules** option has more flexibility in creating conditions with a more complex editing interface. In this example, you'll just choose the **Review and customize the default settings from the template** option, though we'd recommend experimenting with both so you can see the flexibility of the options. Click **Next**.

10. On the **Info to protect** subpage, as shown in *Figure 11.5*, select **Edit** to modify the DLP rule conditions:

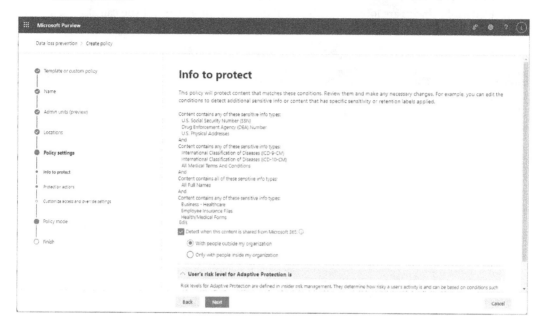

Figure 11.5 – Reviewing the Info to protect page

> **Exam Tip**
>
> If you have selected the **Devices** or **On-premises repositories** location, *you will not see or be able to select* the **Detect when this content is shared from Microsoft 365** option. If you have selected SharePoint or OneDrive locations, you will not be able to see or use the **User's risk level for Adaptive protection is** control. You'll have to evaluate what features you need to use and potentially create separate policies to protect data in different locations with different features.

11. When editing the DLP content matching rules, you can add sensitive information types and trainable classifiers to groups, as well as adjust the confidence and instance count requirements. By default, objects are joined with *OR* conditions (**Any of these**), but you can also set the join criteria to *AND* (**All of these**) to create more stringent requirements for detecting data. See *Figure 11.6*:

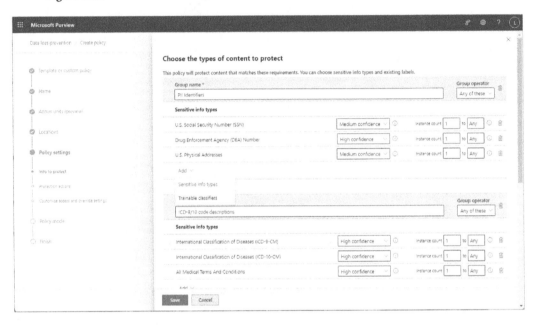

Figure 11.6 – Editing a DLP match rule

12. Additional rule settings that you can modify from this page include alert notifications as well as allowing or prohibiting override conditions. If configuring aggregated alert thresholds, you can select the **Send alert when the volume of matched activities reaches a threshold** radio button and then set numeric values corresponding to the minimum number of instances or detections to trigger an alert and what the monitored time period is.

13. Click **Save** once you've finished editing the rule conditions.

14. On the **Info to protect** subpage, click **Next**.

15. On the **Protection actions** page, as shown in *Figure 11.7*, determine which options to enable.

Exam Tip

If you are customizing a default policy template (as opposed to creating an advanced DLP rule), you will *not* be able to select **Restrict access or encrypt the content in Microsoft 365 locations**. That feature is only configurable inside an advanced DLP rule at this time.

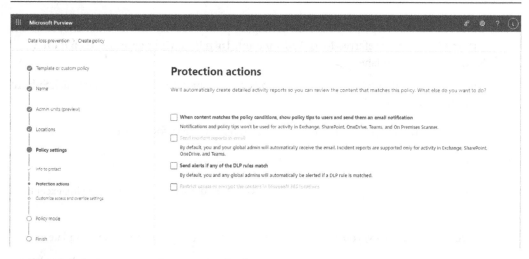

Figure 11.7 – Configuring protection actions

16. For any of the supported options, you can customize the policy tip, email, and alert notifications. When you're finished, click **Next**.

17. On the **Customize access and override settings** subpage, as shown in *Figure 11.8*, edit any options. You may not be able to select options on this page depending on what locations or other options have selected. Auditing or restricting activities on devices, for example, is only available if you have the **Devices** location enabled for the policy.

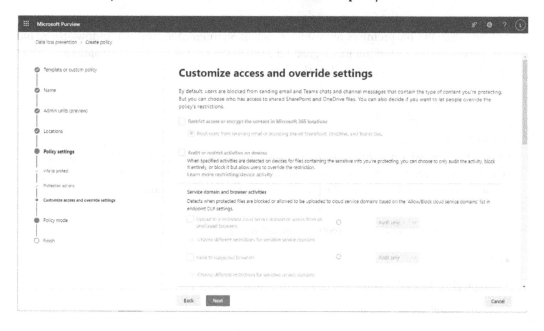

Figure 11.8 – Customize access and override settings

18. On the **Policy mode** page, choose the setting for policy enablement. You can choose **Test it out first** (sometimes referred to as **Audit mode**), **Turn it on right away**, or **Keep it off**. Click **Next** when you're finished.

19. On the **Finish** page, review the policy settings. Edit them if necessary, and then click **Submit** to configure the policy.

After choosing to turn on a policy, it may take up to an hour to be enforced across your tenant.

Power BI

DLP for Power BI includes many of the same features as standard policies, with the following exceptions and caveats:

- When creating a policy, you can only select the **Custom** category and policy template.
- You can only select the Power BI location in the policy. You cannot configure other locations in the same policy.
- DLP actions are only supported in workspaces hosted in Premium capacities.
- You cannot use trainable classifiers to identify data.

All other features and capabilities are supported.

On-Premises File Servers

Despite the high rate of adoption for cloud services and infrastructure, many organizations still have a lot of data stored in on-premises repositories such as SharePoint Server or Windows-based file servers. While cloud-based solutions are great for content stored in the cloud, *what options are there for applying those same protections to data that hasn't been migrated?*

The answer is easy: *Microsoft Purview Data Loss Prevention*!

> **AIP Scanner**
>
> Originally branded as the **Azure Information Protection scanner** in 2018 to help identify sensitive information on-premises, the software has continuously been upgraded with more features. The newest iteration can help support your information protection goals.

Protecting on-premises repositories requires the following tasks to be completed:

- Configuring service accounts
- Deploying the AIP **Unified Labeling** (**UL**) client to an on-premises server
- Configuring the scanner settings

- Creating content scan jobs

- Creating an Azure app registration

- Deploying the AIP scanner to an on-premises server

- Configuring a DLP policy that includes on-premises repositories

As you can see, there are several pieces involved. *Figure 11.9* shows the components in the on-premises DLP deployment:

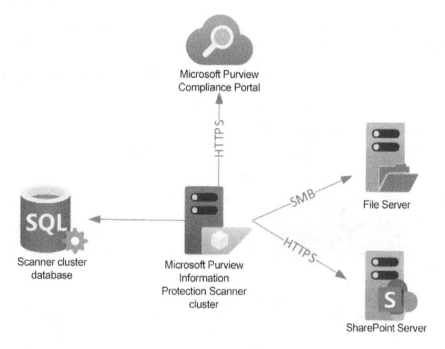

Figure 11.9 – On-premises DLP architecture

The DLP architecture utilizes one or more on-premises servers configured with the **AIP UL client** and the **AIP scanner**. These servers query the DLP policies from the Microsoft Purview compliance portal, store service information in an on-premises SQL database, and are used to discover content in on-premises file shares and SharePoint sites.

> **Note**
>
> For production deployments, Microsoft recommends using a full version of SQL Server. For lab environments, you can use **SQL Express**. To download SQL Express, see https://www.microsoft.com/en-us/Download/details.aspx?id=101064.

Configuring a Service Account

For the scanner deployment, you'll need two accounts—an on-premises account that has access to the file shares and SharePoint document libraries containing content to protect, and either a synchronized or cloud identity that will be used to access the Microsoft 365 service. They can be the same account (this may even make it easier from a deployment perspective). The AIP service does not currently support using a **Managed Service Account (MSA)** or **group Managed Service Account (gMSA)**.

Deploying the AIP UL client

The first step in deploying the Microsoft Purview compliance solution on-premises is to ensure the server(s) you'll be using have the most recent AIP UL client. Follow these steps to deploy the client:

1. On the server(s) where you will configure the **Microsoft Purview Information Protection Scanner** cluster, navigate to `https://aka.ms/aipclient` to download the client. Either the `.msi` or `.exe` download is suitable.

2. Once it has downloaded, launch the installer.

3. Select **I agree** to proceed with the installation. Setup begins, as shown in *Figure 11.10*.

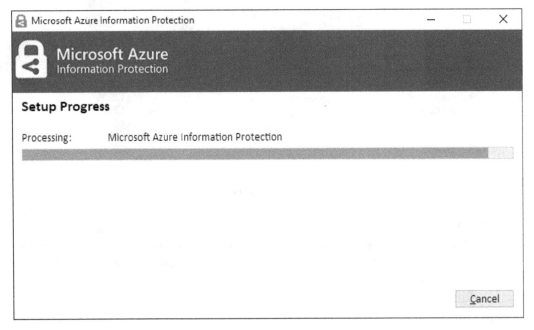

Figure 11.10 – AIP UL client installation

4. Click **Close** to exit the installer.

Next, it's time to move on to the scanner cluster installation.

Configuring Scanner Settings

Before you install the scanner, you need to create a scanner cluster configuration object in the Microsoft Purview compliance portal. This cluster configuration will be used to identify scanner clusters in your organization; for example, an organization with multiple geographic locations may opt to deploy scanner clusters at each site.

To create a scanner cluster, follow these steps:

1. Navigate to the Microsoft Purview compliance portal (`https://compliance.microsoft.com`) and sign in with an identity that is a member of the **Compliance Administrator**, **Compliance Data Administrator**, or **Organization Management** role.

> **Exam Tip**
>
> The product documentation directs you to the Microsoft Purview compliance portal to set up a scanner cluster, though it doesn't actually specify where. The option to configure is only visible after assigning the **Compliance Administrator**, **Compliance Data administrator**, or **Organization Management** role and can take up to two hours to display in the portal console after enablement. The compliance portal settings are located at **Settings | Information protection scanner**. There is also a link at **More resources | Azure Information Protection**, which redirects you to the AIP blade of the Azure portal (`https://portal.azure.com/#blade/Microsoft_Azure_InformationProtection`). The steps are nearly identical in either case.

2. Select **Settings** and then choose **Information protection scanner**.

3. Select the **Clusters** tab. See *Figure 11.11*:

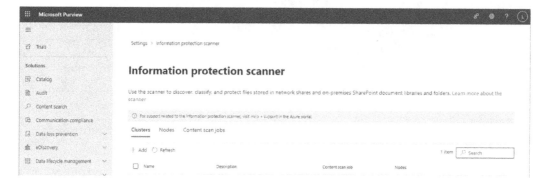

Figure 11.11 – AIP clusters page

4. Click **Add**.

5. On the **New cluster** flyout, enter a name and description. Click **Save**.

Next, you'll create a scan job that will be used to discover content located in your on-premises locations.

Configuring Content Scan Jobs

For this task, you'll need on-premises **Universal Naming Convention** (**UNC**) paths or SharePoint site URLs where the content to protect is stored. Once you have collected file paths, you can follow these steps to configure a content scan job:

1. From the Microsoft Purview compliance portal, select **Settings | Information protection scanner**.

2. Select the **Content scan jobs** tab.

3. Select **Add** to create a new scan job.

4. Enter a content scan job name.

5. From the **Cluster** dropdown, select a configured cluster.

6. Configure a **Schedule** (either **Manual** or **Always**). **Manual** scans will need to be initiated via the `Start-AIPScan` cmdlet on the server or through the portal, while scans set to **Always** will run as background tasks on the assigned cluster.

7. Update the **Info types to be discovered** dropdown to **Policy only** to detect content based on your already-configured DLP policy settings or **All** to detect all sensitive information types available in the tenant (including both default and custom sensitive information types).

8. Scroll the flyout down. Under **DLP policy**, set the **Enable DLP policy rules** slider to **On**.

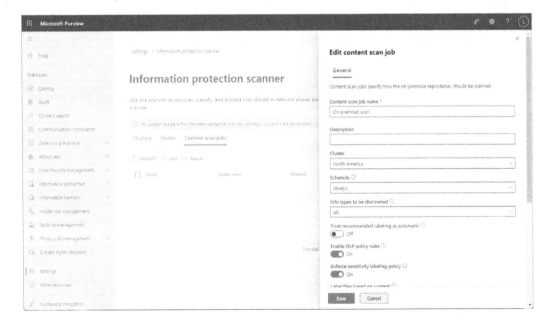

Figure 11.12 – Configuring content scan job settings

9. Click **Save**.

10. Close the content scan job configuration and then re-open it.

11. Select the **Repositories** tab. See *Figure 11.13*:

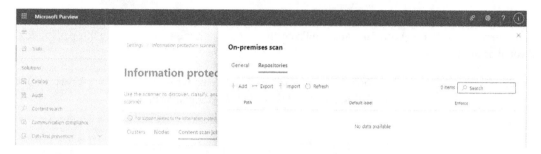

Figure 11.13 – Configuring repositories for the scan

12. Click **Add**.

13. On the **Repository** flyout, add the path and then click **Save**. See *Figure 11.14*:

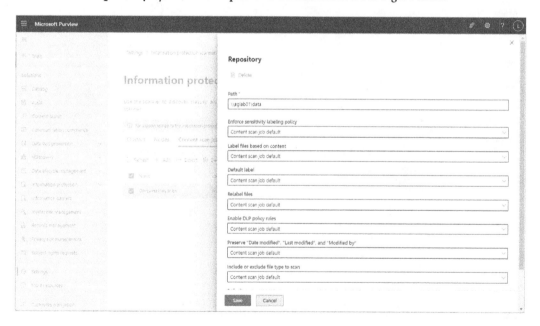

Figure 11.14 – Configuring repository settings

14. Repeat the process for each repository (file share or SharePoint site) that this scanner cluster will be responsible for checking.

After you have finished configuring all of the repositories for this content scan job, it's time to start configuring the necessary app registration.

Configuring an Azure App Registration

The AIP scanner application requires an Azure app registration in order to obtain a token from Azure for interacting with the Azure Information Protection service endpoint. To configure this registration, you'll need to follow these steps:

1. Navigate to the Azure portal (`https://portal.azure.com`). Select **Azure Active Directory** (or **Microsoft Entra ID**) and then click **App registrations**.

2. Select **New registration**.

3. Enter a name, such as `AIPScanner`.

4. Under **Redirect URI**, select the platform as **Web** and enter `http://localhost` in the text box. See *Figure 11.15*:

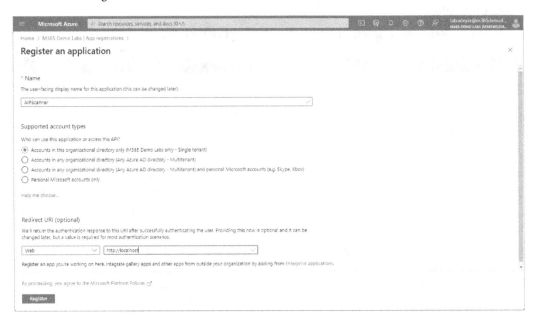

Figure 11.15 – Configuring an app registration

5. On the app's **Overview** page, copy the **Application (client) ID** and **Directory (tenant) ID** values to a temporary storage location.

6. Select **Clients & secrets**.

7. Click **New client secret**.

8. On the **Add a client secret** flyout, add a description and set an **Expires date** value of at least a year. Click **Add**.

9. After the secret has been created, copy the **Secret ID** value to the temporary storage location containing the **App ID** and **Directory ID** values. These values will be used in the next section.

10. On the **API permissions** page, select **Add a permission**.

11. On the **Request API permissions** flyout, select the **Microsoft APIs** tab. Select **Azure Rights Management Services**. See *Figure 11.16*:

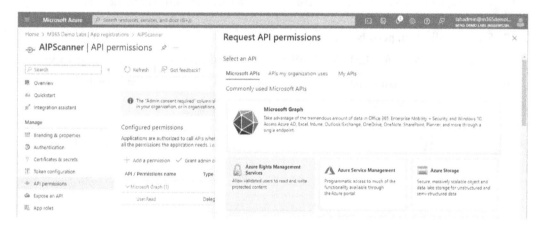

Figure 11.16 – Adding permissions on the Request API permissions flyout

12. Select **Application permissions**.

13. Expand the dropdown for **Content**. Select the **Content.DelegatedReader** and **Content.DelegatedWriter** checkboxes. Click **Add permissions**.

14. Under **Manage**, select **API permissions** and then select **Add a permission**.

15. On the **Request API permissions** flyout, select the **APIs my organization uses** tab.

16. Locate the **Microsoft Information Protection Sync Service** entry and select it. See *Figure 11.17*:

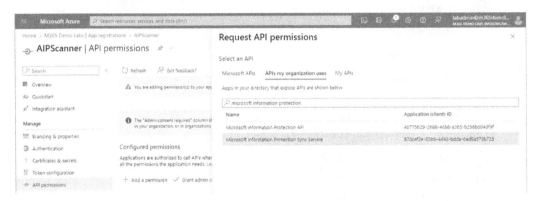

Figure 11.17 – Choosing the Microsoft Information Protection Sync Service API

17. Select **Application permissions**.

18. Select the checkbox for the **UnifiedPolicy.Tenant.Read** permission. Select **Add permissions**.

19. On the **API permissions** page, click **Grant admin consent for <tenant>**. See *Figure 11.18*:

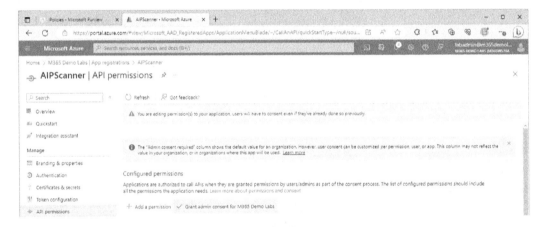

Figure 11.18 – Granting admin consent

20. Click **Yes** to confirm.

With your app registration and client secret details in hand, it's time to install and configure the actual AIP scanner.

Installing and Configuring the Scanner

Once you've got the AIP UL client deployed, the scanner settings configured, and the app registration details, you can begin installing scanner cluster nodes in your on-premises environment. You'll need the name of the scanner cluster that you created in the Microsoft Purview compliance portal to complete this task, as well as a service account that will be used to run the local service.

To install and configure the scanner service, follow these steps:

1. On a server that you wish to use to deploy the scanner, launch an elevated PowerShell session.

2. From the elevated prompt, run the following command:

    ```
    Install-AIPScanner -SQLServerInstanceName <SQLInstanceName>
    -Cluster <AIP Scanner cluster>
    ```

    For example, if you deployed a local SQLExpress database instance and are using a scanner cluster called *North America*, you could enter the following:

    ```
    Install-AIPScanner -SQLServerInstanceName .\SQLExpress -Cluster
    "North America"
    ```

    See *Figure 11.19*:

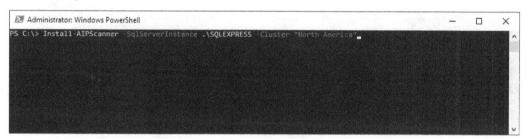

Figure 11.19 – Starting the AIP scanner installation

3. When prompted, enter the service account credential that will be used.

4. Wait for the configuration to be completed.

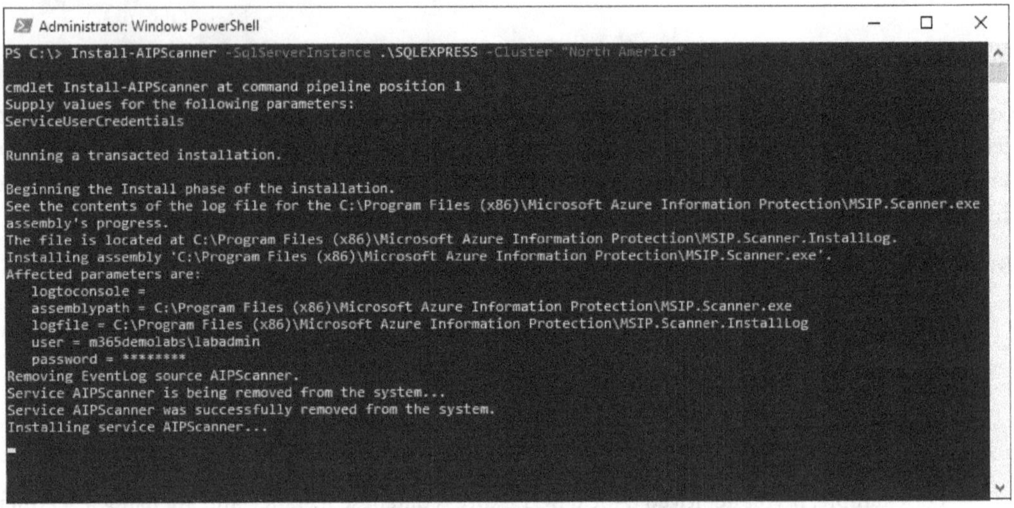

```
Administrator: Windows PowerShell                                              —    □    ×
PS C:\> Install-AIPScanner -SqlServerInstance .\SQLEXPRESS -Cluster "North America"

cmdlet Install-AIPScanner at command pipeline position 1
Supply values for the following parameters:
ServiceUserCredentials

Running a transacted installation.

Beginning the Install phase of the installation.
See the contents of the log file for the C:\Program Files (x86)\Microsoft Azure Information Protection\MSIP.Scanner.exe
assembly's progress.
The file is located at C:\Program Files (x86)\Microsoft Azure Information Protection\MSIP.Scanner.InstallLog.
Installing assembly 'C:\Program Files (x86)\Microsoft Azure Information Protection\MSIP.Scanner.exe'.
Affected parameters are:
   logtoconsole =
   assemblypath = C:\Program Files (x86)\Microsoft Azure Information Protection\MSIP.Scanner.exe
   logfile = C:\Program Files (x86)\Microsoft Azure Information Protection\MSIP.Scanner.InstallLog
   user = m365demolabs\labadmin
   password = ********
Removing EventLog source AIPScanner.
Service AIPScanner is being removed from the system...
Service AIPScanner was successfully removed from the system.
Installing service AIPScanner...
```

Figure 11.20 – Installing the AIP scanner

5. In the elevated PowerShell console on the server where the AIP scanner was installed, run the following command:

```
Set-AIPAuthentication -AppID <app id> -AppSecret <app secret>
-TenantId <Directory ID> -DelegatedUser <scanneraccount@tenant.
com>
```

Once the scanner has been registered with the cluster, the content scan you configured will start. You can then use the on-premises repository location as part of a DLP policy.

Next, you'll shift to managing Endpoint DLP.

Implementing Endpoint DLP

To this point, you've been working with managing DLP capabilities for content that is stored in the Microsoft 365 service or moving across the Microsoft 365 ecosystem—through applications such as Exchange Online and SharePoint Online.

But what if the data is created or stored on an endpoint device? Can organizations use the same types of DLP technology to protect and alert on activities with that data?

Yes! Microsoft's Endpoint DLP can do exactly this!

Some of the features of Endpoint DLP include the following:

- Restricting application access to sensitive data

- Automatically quarantining content being accessed from restricted apps

- Preventing protected files from being transferred via Bluetooth

- Preventing certain browsers from accessing protected content

- Preventing browsers from uploading to restricted domains

- Restricting the transfer of protected content to USB storage devices

- Restricting printing

Many organizations—especially those that deal with confidential information—need to be able to protect data against unauthorized storage and use. Endpoint DLP is a great solution to help achieve that.

> **Further Reading**
>
> For a complete list of monitored activities, see `https://learn.microsoft.com/en-us/microsoft-365/compliance/endpoint-dlp-learn-about?view=o365-worldwide#endpoint-activities-you-can-monitor-and-take-action-on`.

- In addition to preventing certain types of activities, endpoint DLP also monitors activities across a wide variety of files on both Windows and macOS platforms. Out of the box, endpoint DLP monitors documents (`.doc`, `.docx`, etc.), spreadsheets (`.xls`, `.xlsx`, etc.), archive files (`.zip`, `.tr`, etc.), and presentations (`.ppt`, `.pptx`, etc.), regardless of whether a policy is configured to monitor or act on them. Endpoint DLP can even be integrated with Azure **Optical Character Recognition (OCR)** to scan PDF images, JPGs, and other image files.

> **What's in a Name?**
>
> Endpoint DLP supports documents and files based on their **Multipurpose Internet Mail Extension (MIME)** type, so changing a file's extension name won't affect whether Endpoint DLP is able to capture audit log data or enforce a policy against it.

Endpoint DLP has two requirements: a supported operating system and a supported subscription. Endpoint DLP can be enabled for Windows 10, Windows 11, and macOS 10.5 or later devices and requires one of the following subscriptions:

- Microsoft 365 E5/A5/G5

- Microsoft 365 E5/A5/F5/G5 Compliance and F5 Security & Compliance

- Microsoft 365 E5/A5/F5/G5 Information Protection & Governance

With those requirements out of the way, let's go through the onboarding process.

Since endpoint DLP builds on the **Microsoft Defender for Endpoint** (**MDE**) product, it can be onboarded using a variety of methods (Intune, Group Policy, Configuration Manager, and scripts). Microsoft's best practice for organizations using the entire Microsoft 365 suite is to use Intune to deploy and configure policies.

> **Note**
> If using Intune to deploy endpoint DLP, the devices must be Intune enrolled.

If you've already got MDE onboarded, the next step is to onboard the devices into the Microsoft Purview compliance portal. To configure onboarding through Purview, follow these steps:

1. Navigate to the Microsoft Purview compliance portal (`https://compliance.microsoft.com`) and select **Settings** | **Device onboarding**. See *Figure 11.21*:

Figure 11.21 – Device onboarding

2.   In the middle pane, select **Devices** and then select **Turn on device onboarding** in the main window.

Figure 11.22 – Turning on device onboarding

3.   Acknowledge the prompt that existing MDE devices will be automatically onboarded by clicking **OK**.

4.   Click **OK** to acknowledge that device monitoring has been turned on.

That's it! That's all it takes. You can view the status for devices on the **Devices** tab of the **Device onboarding** page, as shown in *Figure 11.23*:

Figure 11.23 – List of onboarded devices

The **Configuration status** column will show that the device has received the updated onboarding configuration. The **Policy sync status** column will show whether DLP policies have been synchronized to the device.

The policy sync status can take up to two hours to show up, so you may need to be patient. You can attempt to trigger the policy application to come down sooner using the **Resync** button in the Intune management portal (**Devices** | **Windows devices** or **macOS devices** | **Overview**) or by restarting the device itself.

After the policy refresh cycle has completed, when you select an onboarded device from the **Settings | Device onboarding | Devices** page, you can see which device DLP policies have been synchronized, as shown in *Figure 11.24*:

Figure 11.24 – Viewing synchronized DLP policies

Next, you'll look at working with DLP alerts.

Reviewing and Responding to DLP Alerts

In *Chapter 10, Implementing Microsoft Purview Information Protection and Data Lifecycle Management*, and so far in this chapter, you've learned how Microsoft's information protection and DLP features can be used to detect sensitive information in your organization and then both classify and protect it. For example, when sending sensitive information through email, a DLP policy applied to Exchange Online can be used to cause Outlook to display a policy tip, as shown in *Figure 11.25*:

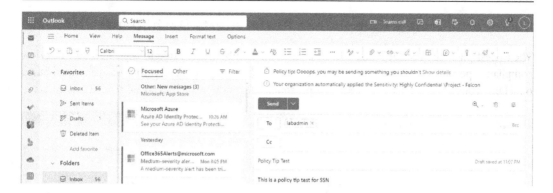

Figure 11.25 – Policy tip test

What happens, though, when users ignore the policy tip warning and send sensitive data anyway? That's dependent on your DLP policy alerting settings.

Organizations with any subscription can create DLP alerts that are triggered on every matching activity. Organizations with A5, E5, or G5 subscriptions or an Office 365 Advanced Threat Protection Plan 2, Microsoft 365 E5 Compliance, or Microsoft 365 eDiscovery and Audit add-on license can configure aggregated alerts—meaning that DLP alerts will only show up based on a certain threshold.

DLP alerts show up in three places:

- **Microsoft Purview compliance portal | Data loss prevention | Alerts**: Only DLP-related events and alerts

- **Microsoft Purview compliance portal | Alerts**: All events and alerts in the compliance portal, including DLP alerts

- **Microsoft 365 Defender portal | Incidents & alerts | Alerts**: All security-related events and alerts, including DLP alerts

In addition to those alert views, the event data is also surfaced in the following ways:

- **Microsoft Purview compliance portal | Data loss prevention | Activity explorer**: All compliance activity, including DLP policy activity

- **Microsoft Purview compliance portal | Data classification | Activity explorer**: All compliance activity, including DLP policy activity

- **Microsoft 365 Defender portal | Incidents & alerts | Incidents**: DLP alerts as exfiltration incidents

- **Microsoft Purview compliance portal | Audit log**: All activity and events in Microsoft 365, including DLP policy activity

In this last section of the book, you'll look at activities you can perform in these areas to both review and respond to DLP events.

Microsoft Purview Compliance Portal Alerts Dashboard

The easiest place to view DLP alerts is on the **Alerts** dashboard, located in the Microsoft Purview compliance portal under **Data loss prevention**. *Figure 11.26* depicts an alert that was generated based on a DLP policy using a template to detect personal information, such as social security numbers:

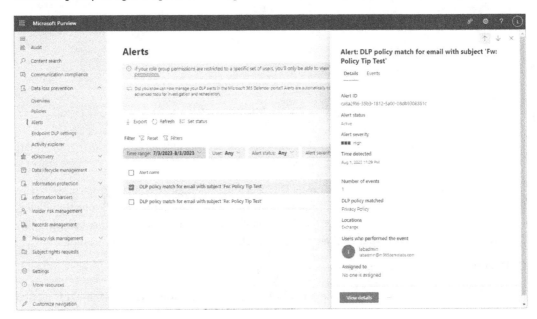

Figure 11.26 – Viewing a DLP alert

You can view more details about the alert by selecting the **View details** button at the bottom of the flyout. The detail view of an alert displays a number of fields on the **Overview** tab, such as a plain-text summary of the event, actor details (who did it), the policy that was matched, and the corresponding rule and sensitive information types inside the rule, basic information about the alert, such as the severity and time detected, as well as other alerts related to the user or actor. See *Figure 11.27*:

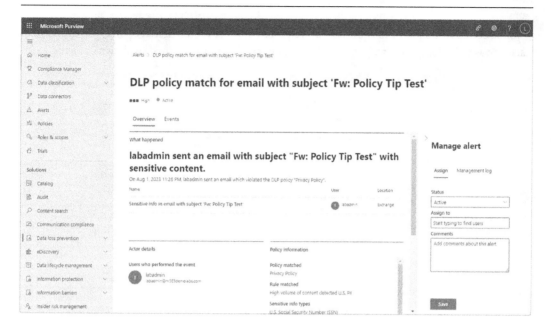

Figure 11.27 – Alert detail page

On the **Manage alert** pane, you can update the status of a particular DLP event. When first detected, the alert is set to **Active**. You can select additional statuses such as **Investigating**, **Dismissed**, or **Resolved**. Updating the status in the **Alerts** dashboard to **Investigating** will set the corresponding event's status to **In Progress** in the Microsoft 365 Defender incident. Updating the alert status to either **Dismissed** or **Resolved** will set the corresponding event's status to **Resolved** in the Microsoft 365 Defender incident.

> **Note**
>
> While setting the alert's status to **Dismissed** or **Resolved** in the compliance portal will update the alert's status to **Resolved** in the Microsoft 365 Defender portal, setting an alert's status to **Dismissed** will also result in the classification in Microsoft 365 Defender being set to **False positive**.

Selecting the **Events** tab on the alert detail page will show much of the same information but arranged in a different order. New data presented, however, includes additional information about actors and intended recipients, classifiers or sensitive info types used to match content, and the context of the data inside the file or message that triggered the alert.

If you've configured a policy to allow user override and the user exercised that option, you can see that data here as well, along with any business justification text that was submitted, as shown in *Figure 11.28*:

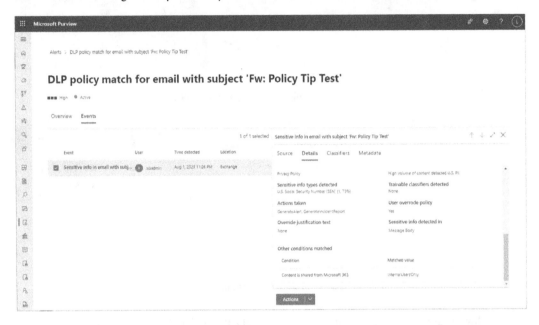

Figure 11.28 – Event detail view of an alert

If you have configured encryption for the items matching the DLP policy, the **Source** tab may display a warning that the content is encrypted, prompting you to download the file or message in order to view it. However, the **Classifiers** tab will show examples of content that matches the policy rules. It's important to only delegate compliance-related roles to individuals your organization trusts to address issues arising from viewing potentially sensitive information. The **Metadata** tab will show the underlying data for the policy match conditions and will also include the matched content values.

On the **Actions** tab for an event, you can choose to download the item or mark it as **Not a match**.

If you select **Not a match**, you have the option of submitting a redacted sample to Microsoft to help improve the accuracy of scan detections. See *Figure 11.29*:

Figure 11.29 – Submitting a redacted false positive sample to Microsoft

While this section specifically covers the DLP view of the **Alerts** dashboard, the broader compliance portal **Alerts** view is the same but also includes compliance events from sources besides DLP. The management tasks, item details, and interfaces are the same.

Microsoft Purview Compliance Portal Activity Explorer

Activity explorer is a dashboard-style interface that displays charts for the various compliance activities in Microsoft 365, including file deletions, archive creations, label applications, DLP rule matches, and content classification.

Figure 11.30 depicts the default view of the dashboard with the **Activity** dropdown selected to show the filter options:

Figure 11.30 – Activity explorer dashboard

You can use the filters to locate and display only the data that matches your criteria. Once you have identified the type of data to display, you can select an individual event to view the details surrounding it, as shown in *Figure 11.31*:

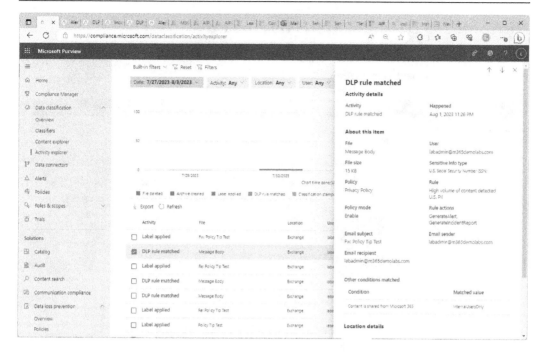

Figure 11.31 – Viewing details of an event in Activity explorer

Activity explorer, whether it is the **Activity explorer** node under **Data classification** or under **Data loss prevention**, shows exactly the same data and events. Some activity details may direct you to individual devices or other items in the Microsoft 365 Defender portal. DLP activities are not typically linked to other pages, however.

Microsoft 365 Defender Alerts Dashboard

The Microsoft 365 Defender **Alerts** dashboard displays security-related alerts generated throughout your Microsoft 365 tenant. See *Figure 11.32*:

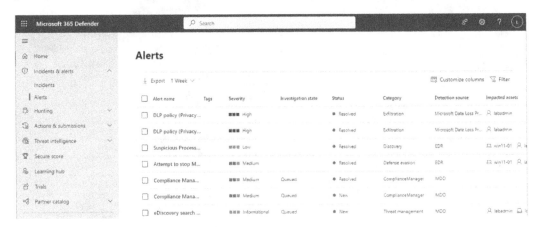

Figure 11.32 – Microsoft 365 Defender Alerts dashboard

The **Alerts** dashboard shows the current status of alerts as well as information about the category of the alert, where the alert originated, its severity, and its impacted assets. In the case of DLP alerts, the detection source is **Microsoft Data Loss Prevention**.

Selecting the row of an event brings up a details flyout, providing information regarding the alert's source and classification. See *Figure 11.33*:

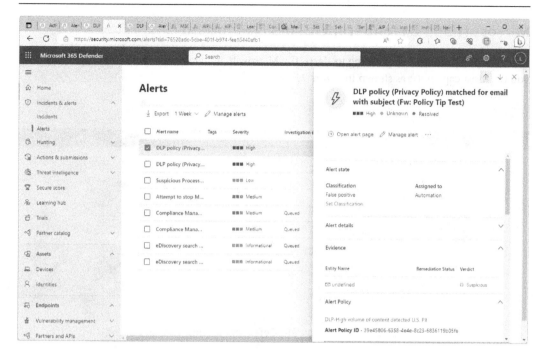

Figure 11.33 – Alert detail flyout

From this flyout, you can select **Open alert page** to view the overall alert and the alert story, **Manage alert** to update its status, or the ellipsis (**…**) for the additional options **Link alert to another incident** and **Ask Defender Experts**.

Like the compliance portal's **Alerts** and **Activity explorer** views, there aren't remediation tasks that can be performed on these pages.

Microsoft 365 Defender Incidents Dashboard

From the perspective of responding to alerts, the Microsoft 365 Defender **Incidents** dashboard gives you the most capability, as shown in *Figure 11.34*:

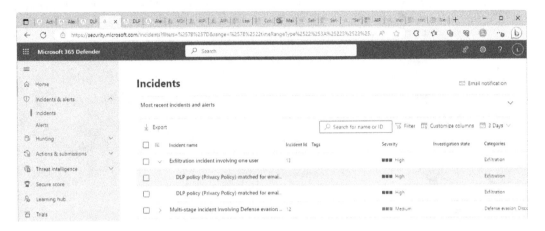

Figure 11.34 – Microsoft 365 Defender Incidents dashboard

While the other dashboards only highlight activity and events, the **Incidents** dashboard allows you to see the most detail and the context of the alert inside the incident's attack story. By selecting an incident, you can review the attack story (chain of related events) as well as the corresponding alerts and assets involved.

In this DLP example, the user sent a file with sensitive information. It could have been accidental or intentional, or it could also have represented a malicious actor who has gained control of the user's account and is attempting to exfiltrate data.

By selecting the **Assets** tab in an incident, for example, you can locate the impacted user and choose to perform activities against that user such as requiring the user to sign in again, suspending the account, or confirming the identity as compromised. See *Figure 11.35*:

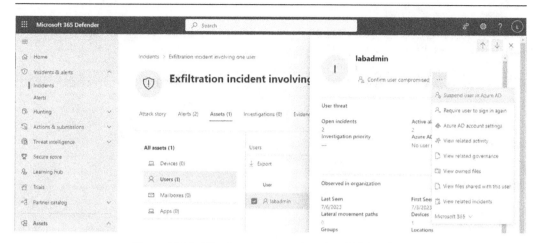

Figure 11.35 – Viewing the user actions in a DLP incident

By selecting the **Evidence** tab of the incident and then selecting an item inside it, you may be presented with the **Go hunt** option. This will create a hunting query targeting this item to help you locate it in the organization. See *Figure 11.36*:

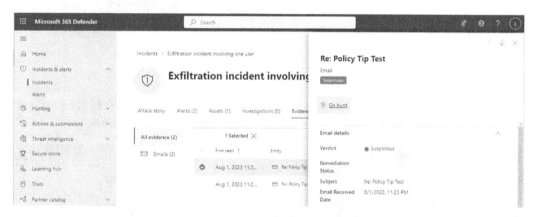

Figure 11.36 – Microsoft 365 Defender incident evidence

Selecting **Run query** on the **Advanced hunting** window will take the pre-loaded query and return corresponding results. See *Figure 11.37*:

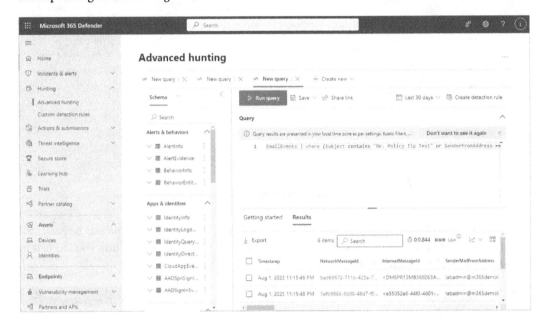

Figure 11.37 – Advanced hunting results

Selecting the hyperlinked value in the **NetworkMessageId** column (shown in *Figure 11.37*) will display details of the actual item (*Figure 11.38*). From there, you can perform remediation tasks.

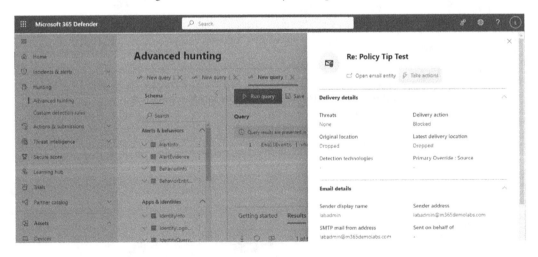

Figure 11.38: Advanced hunting item details

By selecting **Take action**, as shown in *Figure 11.38*, you can initiate a variety of triage and response tasks to help mitigate or resolve the issue. Depending on the data type and risk, you may want to move the item or delete it altogether. You can use the message details to create additional rules for restricting content as well.

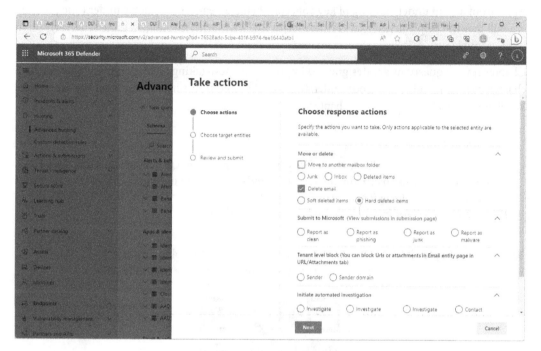

Figure 11.39 – Initiating remediation tasks

Additional remediation options from this page include launching an investigation or contacting the user.

Summary

In this chapter, you learned about the capabilities of Microsoft DLP. Building on the knowledge you previously gained about classifiers such as sensitive information types, DLP policies can be used to detect sensitive information as it moves throughout your organization.

DLP policies can target workloads such as Exchange Online or SharePoint as well as endpoint devices such as on-premises file servers and client computers. Each layer helps provide additional protection against data leakage and compromise.

You also learned about the alerting and troubleshooting tools available in the platform, including the DLP **Alerts** dashboard and the Microsoft 365 Defender **Incidents** dashboard, and the capabilities of incident management to further remediate issues with users and data.

Exam Readiness Drill - Chapter Review Questions

Benchmark Score: 75%

Apart from a solid understanding of key concepts, being able to think quickly under time pressure is a skill that will help you ace your certification exam. That's why, working on these skills early on in your learning journey is key.

Chapter review questions are designed to improve your test-taking skills progressively with each chapter you learn and review your understanding of key concepts in the chapter at the same time. You'll find these at the end of each chapter.

> **Before You Proceed**
>
> You need to unlock these resources before you start using them. Unlocking **takes less than 10 minutes, can be done from any device**, and **needs to be done only once**. Head over to the start of *Chapter 7, Managing Security Reports and Alerts by Using the Microsoft 365 Defender Portal* in this book for instructions on how to unlock them.

To open the **Chapter Review Questions** for this chapter, click the following link: `https://packt.link/MS102E1_CH11`. Or, you can scan the following QR code:

Figure 11.40 – QR code that opens Chapter Review Questions for logged-in users

Once you login, you'll see a page similar to what is shown in *Figure 11.41*:

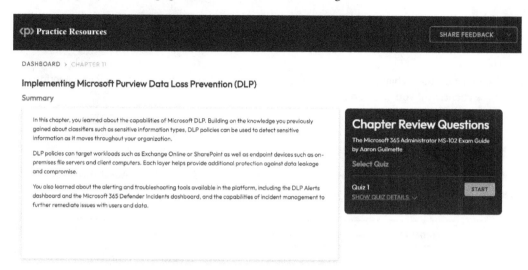

Figure 11.41 – Chapter Review Questions for Chapter 11

Once ready, start the following practice drills, re-attempting the quiz multiple times:

Exam Readiness Drill

For the first 3 attempts, don't worry about the time limit.

ATTEMPT 1

The first time, aim for at least 40%. Look at the answers you got wrong and read the relevant sections in the chapter again to fix your learning gaps.

ATTEMPT 2

The second time, aim for at least 60%. Look at the answers you got wrong and read the relevant sections in the chapter again to fix any remaining learning gaps.

ATTEMPT 3

The third time, aim for at least 75%. Once you score 75% or more, you start working on your timing.

> **Tip**
> You may take more than 3 attempts to reach 75%. That's okay. Just review the relevant sections in the chapter till you get there.

Working On Timing

Target: Your aim is to keep the score the same while trying to answer these questions as quickly as possible. Here's an example of how your next attempts should look like:

Attempt	Score	Time Taken
Attempt 5	77%	21 mins 30 seconds
Attempt 6	78%	18 mins 34 seconds
Attempt 7	76%	14 mins 44 seconds

Table 11.1 – Sample timing practice drills on the online platform

> **Note**
> The time limits shown in the above table are just examples. Set your own time limits with each attempt based on the time limit of the quiz on the website.

With each new attempt, your score should stay **above 75%** while your time taken to complete should decrease. Repeat as many attempts as you want till you feel confident dealing with the time pressure.

Index

www.packtpub.com

Subscribe to our online digital library for full access to over 7,000 books and videos, as well as industry leading tools to help you plan your personal development and advance your career. For more information, please visit our website.

Why subscribe?

- Spend less time learning and more time coding with practical eBooks and Videos from over 4,000 industry professionals

- Improve your learning with Skill Plans built especially for you

- Get a free eBook or video every month

- Fully searchable for easy access to vital information

- Copy and paste, print, and bookmark content

At www.packtpub.com, you can also read a collection of free technical articles, sign up for a range of free newsletters, and receive exclusive discounts and offers on Packt books and eBooks.

Other Books You May Enjoy

If you enjoyed this book, you may be interested in these other books by Packt:

Microsoft 365 Certified Fundamentals MS-900 Exam Guide, Third Edition

Aaron Guilmette, Yura Lee, and Marcos Zanre

ISBN: 978-1-83763-679-2

- Gain insight into the exam objectives and knowledge needed to take the MS-900 exam
- Discover and implement best practices for licensing options available in Microsoft 365
- Understand the different Microsoft 365 Defender services
- Prepare to address the most common types of threats against an environment
- Identify and unblock the most common cloud adoption challenges
- Articulate key productivity, collaboration, security, and compliance selling points of M365
- Explore licensing and payment models available for M365

Microsoft 365 Security, Compliance, and Identity Administration

Peter Rising

ISBN: 978-1-80461-192-0

- Get up to speed with implementing and managing identity and access
- Understand how to employ and manage threat protection
- Manage Microsoft 365's governance and compliance features
- Implement and manage information protection techniques
- Explore best practices for effective configuration and deployment
- Ensure security and compliance at all levels of Microsoft 365

Share Your Thoughts

Now you've finished *Microsoft 365 Administrator MS-102 Exam Guide*, we'd love to hear your thoughts! Scan the QR code below to go straight to the Amazon review page for this book and share your feedback or leave a review on the site that you purchased it from.

https://packt.link/r/183508396X

Your review is important to us and the tech community and will help us make sure we're delivering excellent quality content.

Download a Free PDF Copy of This Book

Thanks for purchasing this book!

Do you like to read on the go but are unable to carry your print books everywhere?

Is your eBook purchase not compatible with the device of your choice?

Don't worry, now with every Packt book you get a DRM-free PDF version of that book at no cost.

Read anywhere, any place, on any device. Search, copy, and paste code from your favorite technical books directly into your application.

The perks don't stop there, you can get exclusive access to discounts, newsletters, and great free content in your inbox daily.

Follow these simple steps to get the benefits:

1. Scan the QR code or visit the link below:

https://packt.link/free-ebook/9781835083963

2. Submit your proof of purchase.
3. That's it! We'll send your free PDF and other benefits to your email directly.